Human Remains

Human Remains

Guide for Museums and Academic Institutions

EDITED BY

VICKI CASSMAN, NANCY ODEGAARD, AND JOSEPH POWELL

ALTAMIRA
PRESS

A Division of

ROWMAN & LITTLEFIELD PUBLISHERS, INC.

Lanham • New York • Toronto • Plymouth, UK

AltaMira Press
A division of Rowman & Littlefield Publishers, Inc.
A wholly owned subsidary of The Rowman & Littlefield Publishing Group, Inc.
4501 Forbes Boulevard, Suite 200
Lanham, MD 20706
www.altamirapress.com

Estover Road
Plymouth PL6 7PY
United Kingdom

British Library Cataloguing in Publication Information Available

Library of Congress Cataloging-in-Publication Data

Human remains : guide for museums and academic institutions / edited by Vicki Cassman, Nancy Odegaard, and Joseph Powell.
     p. cm.
  Includes bibliographical references and index.
  1. Human remains (Archaeology)—Collection and preservation. 2. Human remains (Archaeology)—Conservation and restoration. 3. Human remains (Archaeology)—Repatriation. 4. Museum exhibits—Moral and ethical aspects. 5. Anthropological museums and collections—Moral and ethical aspects. 6. Archaeological museums and collections—Moral and ethical aspects. I. Cassman, Vicki, 1957– II. Odegaard, Nancy. III. Powell, Joseph F. (Joseph Frederick), 1964–

CC79.5.H85H87 2007
930.1—dc22   2006005988

  ISBN-13: 978-0-7591-0954-4 (cloth : alk. paper)
  ISBN-10: 0-7591-0954-0 (cloth : alk. paper)
  ISBN-13: 978-0-7591-0955-1 (pbk. : alk. paper)
  ISBN-10: 0-7591-0955-9 (pbk. : alk. paper)
  eISBN-13: 978-0-7591-1228-5
  eISBN-10: 0-7591-1228-2

Printed in the United States of America

∞™ The paper used in this publication meets the minimum requirements of American National Standard for Information Sciences—Permanence of Paper for Printed Library Materials, ANSI/NISO Z39.48-1992.

To institutionalized human remains wherever they are found.

Contents

Inserts

Acknowledgments

THE EDITORS WOULD LIKE TO THANK ALL THE AUTHORS AND THE STAFF OF ALTAMIRA PRESS FOR THEIR cooperation and willingness to contribute to the volume. Not everyone we contacted was willing to accept the challenge of writing about the often taboo subject of caring for the dead in institutional settings, and we are very grateful to those who felt it in the best interests of responsible scholarship and stewardship to do so. We would especially like to thank Brian Fagan for contributing his foreword and for continuing to support the interconnectedness of conservation and archaeology.

Numerous individuals, organizations, and agencies provided information and resources. Preparation of this manuscript was funded in part by a Foundation of the American Institute for Conservation Samuel H. Kress Conservation Publication Fellowship for Vicki Cassman and the University of Arizona's Provost's Author Support Award for Nancy Odegaard. Individuals deserving special acknowledgment are Bernardo Arriaza, Rodrigo Arriaza, Terry Childs, Melissa Huber, David Hunt, Jannelle Weakly, Linda Gregonis, and Teresa Moreno. The United States Army Corps of Engineers deserves special mention for bringing the editors together as part of the Kennewick Man team, and in particular we want to express our gratitude to Sonny Trimble, Chris Pulliam, Jennifer Richman, Terri Militello, Rhonda Lueck, Cathy Van Arsdale, and Natalie Drew. Others also helped with the Kennewick conservation project, including Madeline Fang, Tom Braun, Marilen Pool, Nichola Langford, Sarah Melching, and the archaeology staff of the Burke Museum of the University of Washington. We are indebted to the following scholars who reviewed or assisted with early drafts or portions of the volume: Bernardo Arriaza, Lane Beck, Reva Dean, Maggie Kipling, Travis Lane, John McClelland, Barnet Pavao-Zuckerman, C. J. Senif, Laura Downey Staneff, Arthur Wolf, Greg Yares, and Werner Zimmt.

Vicki Cassman would like to give special thanks to the museum students at the University of Nevada, Las Vegas; Dean James Frey; as well as colleagues John Swetnam, George Urioste, Daniel Beneyshek, Gary Palmer, and Tony Miranda, because they realize the importance of practical applied science in an academic environment. Nancy Odegaard acknowledges the support of her family, colleagues, and administrators of the Arizona State Museum and the University of Arizona; she is especially grateful for the permission to use institutional policies and laboratory resources. Joseph Powell acknowledges the support of his wife Leah Carson Powell, friends, and the administration at the University of New Mexico.

Many colleagues from various disciplines encouraged and helped us along the way, including conservators, archaeologists, physical anthropologists, collection managers, registrars, tribal cultural preservation officers, museologists, law enforcement officials, and other university scholars. We extend our sincere thanks to them all. Finally, working together as colleague editors on this volume has been a mutually enjoyable experience.

Foreword

BRIAN FAGAN

HUMAN REMAINS HAVE HAD AN ENDURING FASCINATION FOR ARCHAEOLOGISTS AND MUSEUM curators for centuries. Generations of researchers have excavated cemeteries and individual skeletons, writing learned reports on their findings. But few of them have pondered the complex responsibilities of conservation, consultation, and curation that come with such remains. This book is one of the first attempts to discuss these most fundamental problems from diverse and controversial perspectives.

Mention the word *conservation* to most archaeologists and biological anthropologists, and they'll regale you with their minor triumphs in the field—such as lifting a delicate infant burial or piecing together a clay pot. In many scholarly circles, conservation still means conservation of artifacts or of buildings, rock, art, or other tangible remains. This narrow definition stems from the often-specialized nature of conservation work and the complex science that is sometimes involved. Even today, most archaeologists are startlingly unaware that archaeology, biological anthropology, and conservation are closely intertwined. They tend to categorize archaeology into artificial subdivisions: purely academic research, salvaging and protecting the archaeological record, and conservation—the latter being an entirely different activity.

The stereotype of the conservator in archaeology is of someone who mends pots, lifts skeletons in one piece, stabilizes waterlogged artifacts, or achieves miracles of restoration. In fact, conservation encompasses a much broader field than just the care of objects. It has become a multidisciplinary endeavor that encompasses unexcavated sites, excavations, artifacts—and the dead. *Human Remains* presents a new perspective on the ancient dead, in which conservation and respect for the ancient deceased are top priorities whenever fieldwork is planned.

This rising concern with conservation is the culmination of trends that began a quarter century ago. In 1973, the respected southwestern archaeologist William Lipe wrote a now-classic paper in *The Kiva* entitled "A Conservation Model for American Archaeology." The article has become required reading for anyone concerned with conservation of the past. Lipe pointed out that "we are now beginning to realize that all sites are rather immediately threatened, if one takes a time frame of more than a few years." He also distinguished between emergency and "leisurely" salvage, the latter being investigations at sites "when we do not yet know the date at which the site may be lost." Leisurely salvage was the purview of academic archaeologists but, he warned, "if our field is to last for more than a few decades, we need to shift to a resource conservation model as primary." Obviously, archaeologists have to excavate enough to research basic problems and to keep the field intellectually healthy, but their primary responsibility, like that of the biological anthropologists who work with them, should be to ensure that the finite resource base of archaeological sites lasts as long as possible and that human remains are treated with respect.

The Lipe paper appeared in the early days of concern about the destruction of sites, and it grew out of his experiences with a field that had previously been called *salvage archaeology* and that was becoming known as *cultural resource management* (CRM). The new term suggested managing the archaeological record for future generations—a far broader mandate than just the rescue of sites and artifacts from the blade of a bulldozer. This management includes not only survey, excavation, and analysis but also recommendations for long-term management of the resource. CRM was a new type of archaeology, created not by academic questions but by a need to satisfy legal mandates for the management of sites. It has mushroomed since the 1970s and is now the dominant form of field and laboratory archaeology in North America. Under various guises, it dominates archaeology in many other parts of the world as well, among them Australia, Europe, and Japan.

If current trends continue, archaeology and much of biological anthropology, instead of being a purely academic discipline, will become almost entirely a profession focused on managing the past. Most employment opportunities are now in private companies working under tight deadlines and strict legal requirements. CRM projects have serious responsibilities for the past and for human remains, often involving decisions as to which sites are to be excavated, which are to be destroyed, and which are to be saved in their entirety. Often, budgetary issues intervene that weigh archaeological sites against multimillion-dollar construction projects.

In many ways, CRM is a highly sophisticated extension of a nineteenth-century conservation philosophy: dig it up before someone else destroys it. It's an attempt to salvage as much information as possible with the time, money, and methods available. In some respects, it represents the successful implementation of part of Lipe's conservation model.

In his 1973 article, Lipe pointed out that all archaeological excavation, whether CRM based or not, erodes the database; thus, careful research designs, which incorporate conservation as a basic strategy, are essential. All archaeologists, also the biological anthropologists who work with them, are involved with preservation of the resource, in either the long or short term; this means that a conservation ethic must be integral to all archaeological research, especially that on human remains.

The problem is even more acute now than when Lipe wrote his paper. Today there are hundreds, if not thousands, of researchers who are mining sites, often without reference to all the potential stakeholders involved, to answer purely academic—and often very insignificant—questions. This ever-expanding activity (admittedly sometimes carried out as part of a CRM project) is as devastating to the future of archaeology as is industrial activity. Every summer dozens of fieldworkers excavate yet more sites, with little concern for the most pressing problem of all: will there be sites for their grandchildren to investigate? While no one advocates a complete moratorium on excavation, it must be the strategy of last resort, and it should never be total, unless a site is about to vanish forever.

How, then, do we make conservation central to archaeological activity and to the study of human remains? We need major shifts in research priorities, drastic reductions in the number of doctorates in purely academic subjects, and a growth in meaningful graduate programs that meld archaeology and conservation into a seamless whole. We need to start a long-term debate about curriculum within both anthropological and conservation circles. Archaeology and biological anthropology do not need more specialized fieldwork mindlessly culling a diminishing inventory of undisturbed sites. In fact, the basic challenges we face in the future are far more interesting and exciting.

These challenges are best addressed by integrating conservation into the very fabric of all research involving archaeological sites and human remains, as part of the basic design of any project. We should never forget that even the most careful excavation destroys the archaeological record. It is all very well to develop a research proposal for the excavation of an early farming village in Syria or an Andean ceremonial center that promises fresh insights into the origins of agriculture. But in an era when the archaeological record is under threat everywhere, the first concern of any research project should be the maintenance of the site and the stakes of all those concerned with its conservation—be they archaeologists, local landowners, tourist officials, or indigenous peoples.

Some may question this priority, but to challenge it they must answer a simple question: what guarantee do we have that future generations of archaeologists will be able to build on your field research? For example, we can never hope to check the validity of Leonard Woolley's reconstructions of the royal burials at Ur—his records are too incomplete. Nor can we answer many questions about the history and uses of Pueblo Bonito in Chaco Canyon or about the people buried therein—most of the rooms were emptied haphazardly in the early days of gung-ho archaeology. If we are to be responsible stewards of the past, we must make all research subordinate, at least in part, to preservation and conservation. At present, our protective infrastructure and professional training are woefully inadequate to the task.

How can we better integrate conservation into archaeological practice and into the study of human remains?

- First, intensify the present cautious interactions between archaeologists and the conservation community with the objective of fostering specific outcomes. Such outcomes should include a massive revamping of basic anthropological training, which would make conservation strategies central to research. Introduce researchers to such issues as stewardship and stakeholders, as part of their basic academic training.
- Second, foster intensive research into—and development of—nonintrusive archaeological methods to minimize excavation in the future. Important progress has been made in this area, but much more needs to be done.
- Third, require that all doctoral dissertation proposals make conservation the centerpiece of the proposed research. As a corollary, encourage grant-giving agencies, whether government or private, to insist on conservation plans as the first priority in all funding proposals.
- Fourth, require full publication of all fieldwork before future excavation and surveys are funded. The term *publication* would also include specific actions to preserve both the field records and the finds from the excavations.
- Fifth, drastically reduce admissions to academic doctoral programs, but foster and support graduate curricula that make conservation the highest priority.
- Last, decouple archaeology from the publish-or-perish culture, and reward conservation projects as equal partners.

No one suggests that basic research should be abandoned or is unimportant. But we need to look far beyond the immediate gratification of a new discovery or of a peer-reviewed paper published in the pages of *Science*. At present, we are not even debating the ways in which we must integrate a conservation ethic into the core of research into human remains. The sooner we begin, the better—and this book is an instructive start.

As the current managers of the nonrenewable resource, archaeologists, and those who study human remains, bear a heavy ethical responsibility to conserve the past for the future, while maintaining a steady but carefully considered flow of basic research, which gives the discipline its vitality. At present, conservation stands at the margins of the archaeological world. Even faced with crisis, a great deal of archaeology and the study of human remains still proceeds with obscure theoretical debate and with academic specialization that satisfies the publish-or-perish cosmos. Until all studies of human remains and the archaeology that goes with them are grounded firmly in a conservation ethic, archaeology and the study of ancient human remains are doomed to eventual extinction.

Until recently, the treatment of skeletal remains was one of archaeology's dirty little secrets, a scandalous state of affairs that is on a par with the huge backlog of definitive publication, much of it in the hands of senior scholars who should know better. Quite apart from improving curation and scientific standards, the passage of the Native American Graves Protection and Repatriation Act (NAGPRA) in 1990 and the increasingly aggressive posture of indigenous groups, among them Australian Aborigines and Native Americans, have led to a drastic reappraisal of the ways in which archaeologists and biological anthropologists curate, handle, and preserve skeletal remains. There are fundamental and often-ignored ethical issues involved. Who, for example, are the stakeholders in such remains, and how should their voices be heard and their concerns addressed? The Kennewick skeleton from Washington State offers a sobering example of the enormous bureaucratic, ethical, and scientific issues involved in every discovery of human remains.

Until recently, it's only fair to say that both archaeologists and biological anthropologists have been, to put it mildly, cavalier in their treatment of excavated skeletons and skeletal collections. *Human Remains* explores the ethical issues involved in different parts of the world and makes it abundantly clear that the voices of stakeholders are of overwhelming importance when any such discovery is made, whatever the scientific significance of the find. By the same token, science places a heavy responsibility on both stakeholders and scientists to ensure both that information is preserved for posterity and that the ancient dead are treated with the respect they deserve and expected when they died.

This important volume also raises fundamental issues about the treatment and conservation of human skeletons that are often ignored in the literature. There was a time when it was sufficient to lift an entire skeleton in a block of earth or to coat it with glycol and other chemicals before excavating the individual bones so they could be handled in the laboratory and then stored away in a "stabilized" condition. Such careful work, however praiseworthy, misses the fundamental point, which is that any archaeological conservation has to be indefinite, not just for a few years but in perpetuity. This may be an unachievable goal, but that does not excuse us from working toward permanent conservation from the very beginning. The archaeological record is finite: human remains are part of the permanent archive of the past, and they should be treated as such.

It is all very well talking about conservation as something infinite, but the student or curator of human remains comes up against a fundamental conservation issue from the beginning, that of the stakeholders. While the conservation of an Australopithecine, a Neanderthal, or a Bronze Age warrior is purely an archaeological concern, how are scientists to handle human remains that are those of the remote ancestors of living people, or skeletons that come from people with a strong tradition that the revered ancestors return to the land and become its guardians at their death? Anyone who has heard the members of an African village drumming all night to summon the spirit of a dead ancestor will get the point. Under this rubric, one can legitimately argue that the bones of ancestors, however remote, must be returned to the soil. Conserving them means letting them become an integral part of the environment they inhabited, like their ancestors before them. Does science have the right to overrule that which must be considered a permanent form of conservation, albeit an intangible one? The answer must be that we have not as yet worked out this and the many other conundrums that affect the study of ancient human remains.

We live in times when many of archaeology's and biological anthropology's most basic assumptions are being questioned on ethical grounds, when conservation is rapidly assuming center stage in an archaeology that may not exist in the form in which we know it in a century. *Human Remains* is an important first step in a debate that will have many twists and turns in the future as we seek to reconcile the rights of the living, the dead, and scientific knowledge with one another. The chapters that follow bring together an impressive body of experience to bear on the difficulties of conserving the ancient dead, and on one of science's most pressing ethical problems. Maybe it's a cliché, but no student of the past, and especially of skeletal remains, can afford to be without this thought-provoking volume. As the editors point out, in the final analysis, it all comes down to one word: respect.

CHAPTER 1

Introduction

Dealing with the Dead

Vicki Cassman, Nancy Odegaard, and Joseph Powell

HUMAN REMAINS ARE NOT JUST ANOTHER ARTIFACT; THEY HAVE POTENCY. THEY ARE CHARGED WITH political, evidentiary, and emotional meanings but can also be quite mundane, such as classroom anatomical study collections. Where once human remains collections were considered standard materials for museums to curate and the "property" of lone curators and researchers, there are now numerous voices to be heard and considered on the subject. The acts of collecting and studying human remains have become politically and socially more complex, and new unwritten rules of order are slowly developing into standard practice. As editors, we do not pretend to advocate for the permanent maintenance of all currently held human remains collections or for indiscriminate reburial. Instead, we hope to help those charged with daily care, those troubled about their ancestors, or those planning to study collections by providing the first volume on curation issues specifically for human remains.

Human remains collections are surprisingly common, and according to a recent survey, 90 percent of English cultural institutions (132 of 146) possess approximately sixty-one thousand human remains (Working Group on Human Remains 2003: 11). In the United States, no such survey has been carried out, but it is likely that it holds an exponentially greater number of human remains based on the greater number of museums and academic institutions located there. It has been estimated that two hundred thousand Native American remains are held by federally sponsored institutions in the United States. Particularly after the enactment of the Native American Graves Protection and Repatriation Act (NAGPRA), it is vital that descendants, curators, conservators, and physical and forensic anthropologists work together to improve the conditions under which institutionalized human remains currently exist.

Human remains are substantially different from any other type of collection. It is not clear how they should be categorized. Are they artifacts, people, or something different? How we approach the care and management of human remains seems to depend on the degree of distancing or connection that one feels toward them. The use of different vocabularies tends to reveal or impose a level of regard by those that work with the dead. Words that imply the greatest distancing include *artifact, object, specimen, decedent,* and *corpse.* Words that are impartial or objective include *fossil, skeleton, mummy,* and *cadaver.* Words that convey a sense of connection include *individual, person,* and *human remains.* The latter are used throughout this book to reflect greater respect in order to promote improved care and management.

The information provided in this volume aims to help curators improve on their institution's current methods for care and management, as well as help descendents ask better questions and help students know what to expect as present and future researchers. It is not a step-by-step guide, nor is it an indictment of past practices. Instead, through discussions and case studies, we present curation issues that we hope will stimulate improved preservation, management, and attitude. We consider curation to include respectful research, study, collection care, policy, documentation, and education. It is our goal that those working with human remains collections become proactive in practicing and teaching appropriate curation methods.

The volume represents an example of scholarship of integration and application, or the pulling together of research and experiences from multidisciplinary perspectives for the preservation and curation of human remains. There are few sources of information to guide students, stakeholders, and professionals. We have pulled together information from areas including archaeology, bioarchaeology, conservation, forensic anthropology, museology, and physical anthropology. Because the concern for the curation of human remains collections extends beyond the United States, we have invited a diversity of international experts to contribute.

Legislation and policy have directed institutions to become more responsive to the needs of descendants. The impact on professionals working in the United States in federally funded institutions is significant, resulting in a paradigm shift in bioarchaeology and physical anthropology. Human remains collections can no longer be viewed as renewable resources. There must be more public accountability. Multidisciplinary teams promote inclusiveness and are now more common. A broader scope of information is needed in this NAGPRA era, and numerous voices should be considered.

We are deeply committed to a multidisciplinary approach to the curation of institutional human remains collections for a number of reasons. We have been involved in the Kennewick Man case, which has highlighted a number of ethical and practical curation problems. Through this highly publicized example and other similar NAGPRA experiences, we have been struck by the lack of up-to-date information. Conferences such as Human Remains in Colonial Williamsburg in 1999 and Who Owns the Body at the University of California, Berkeley, in 2000 highlight the changing attitudes and need for this type of information.

The motivation behind the current volume is to help those persons assigned with care of institutionalized remains deal with everyday practical decisions to promote preservation. While many individuals will be repatriated and reburied, others will remain institutionalized because of their legal status. We have sought to answer and expand on the types of questions we have been asked to help with and to complement existing information. For example:

- Can associated funerary objects be stored with human remains?
- Is there anything better than adhesives or tape to temporarily hold bone fragments together?
- What are the criteria for evaluating storage for human remains collections?
- Is personal protection needed when handling human remains collections?

This volume covers dry skeletal and mummified remains, which make up the bulk of human remains collections. Unfortunately, this leaves wet specimens in jars, marine, frozen, bog, and fresh remains out of the present discussion. Due to the often very specialized, intensive treatments and manipulations that "wet remains" often receive, we believe they deserve a different handling, one that is beyond the scope of the present volume. However, many aspects of curation presented here do still apply to wet remains (Arnaud et al. 1980; Pearson 1987).

REFERENCES

Arnaud, G., S. Arnaud, A. Ascenzi, E. Bonucci, and G. Graiani
1980 On the Problem of the Preservation of Human Bone in Seawater. *International Journal of Nautical Archaeology and Underwater Exploration* 9(1):53–65.

Pearson, Colin, editor

1987 *Conservation of Marine Archaeological Objects*. Butterworths, London.

Working Group on Human Remains

2003 Report of the Working Group on Human Remains. Department for Culture, Media and Sport, London. Electronic document, http://www.culture.gov.uk/NR/rdonlyres/D3CBB6E0-255D-42F8-A728-067CE53062EA/0/Humanremainsreportsmall.pdf, p. 11, accessed April 22, 2006.

CHAPTER 2

Ethics of Flesh and Bone, or Ethics in the Practice of Paleopathology, Osteology, and Bioarchaeology

MARTA P. ALFONSO AND JOSEPH POWELL

> The dogmas of the quiet past are inadequate to the stormy present. The occasion is piled high with difficulty, and we must rise with the occasion. As our case is new, so we must think anew and act anew.
>
> —Abraham Lincoln

THE STUDY OF HUMAN REMAINS HAS THE POTENTIAL TO EXPLAIN A GREAT DEAL ABOUT THE PREHISTORY of humankind, human evolution, and who we are today (Walker 2000; Ortner and Putschar 1985). Thus, the analysis of human remains is important since it enhances our understanding of histories that have both local and global implications. Because the human body is always embedded and interpreted within various cultural and religious contexts, the pursuit of knowledge alone is insufficient to legitimate the study of human remains (Jones and Harris 1998). Any study of the human body, then, must consider the complexities ingrained within and surrounding the body. Additionally, these studies are obligated to reflect on ethical aspects (Murphy 1995; Rothfield 1995; Csordas 1999; Burton 2001; Morenon 2003), since this type of practice can often be seen as an affront to religious values (Simpson 1996).

The need and legitimacy of scientific studies of the body can be questioned, especially when only Western values are used as validation, because science can in many ways be understood as an expression of Western power. In this light, a code of ethics for the practice of bioarchaeology, paleopathology, and osteology is indispensable. Thus, in this chapter, the term *biological anthropology* will refer, specifically, to these three areas of research.

A strong code of ethics in biological anthropology not only should guide our practice in terms of scientific values but must also consider the understandings we have developed from our experiences—that is, through our individual and collective encounters and "dis-encounters" with other individuals, communities, and colleagues (Jorgensen 1971). This chapter explores the difficulties that biological anthropology faces when it comes to the development of a code of ethics and offers a model for the development of one.

CULTURALLY CHALLENGED: THE ETHICS OF ANTHROPOLOGY

A *code of ethics*, for any profession, is a general set of peer-imposed regulations that provide the guiding standards for practice (Sease 1998; Tugby 1964; Goldstein and Kintigh 1990). Ethical questions, as well as those who ask them, are historically defined and, as such, culturally influenced (Kavanaugh 2001; Goldstein and Kintigh 1990). Since anthropology itself is the incarnation of cultural encounters, the development of a code of ethics in the discipline is a must; its formulation, however, presents a very complex problem because ethical differences between cultural groups need to be taken into consideration.

In general, the need for codes of ethics is rooted in the epistemology of professionalism born in the interwar period. At this time, academic experts promoted attempts to establish public service of the intelligentsia as autonomous from class and political interests (Pels 1999). Codes of ethics that are designed to guarantee the competency and honor of the professional are focused in a Western understanding of science rooted in such Enlightenment values as truth, normative rightness, and universal morality (Pels 1999; Habermas 1987). However, the discussions of ethics in anthropology cannot be exclusively centered on the nature of science, since anthropology has a fundamental commitment to cultural difference, which essentially puts its dual moral obligations at potential odds (Pels 1999).

Anthropology, because it was born as a service rendered to colonial administrations, had a peculiar road to professionalization. It was only after World War II that anthropology began to define and distinguish itself apart from colonialism; thus, it was not until then that academic and applied anthropology separated itself from the colonial project (Pels 1999). The new emphasis on anthropology as an academic project resulted in the belief that anthropology was a "pure objective inquiry with no special ethical or social policy implications" (Fluehr-Lobban 2003:7). According to this definition, anthropology was not influenced by the cultures under study and/or the culture of those conducting the research.

However, during the 1960s, questions about the authority and legitimacy of scientific objectivity, knowledge, and the status of science rendered this "objective inquiry" and "scientific isolation" to be unethical and improbable (Holden 1979; Fluehr-Lobban et al. 2003). As a result, the position of anthropology and anthropologists was transformed. It is not surprising, then, that during this period codes of ethics were voluntarily developed by the members of various professional organizations. For instance, the American Institute for Art Conservation produced and published during the first decade of its existence both a "Standards of Practice and Professional Relationships for Conservators" and a "Code of Ethics for Art Conservators." Although by 1967 the American Association of Anthropology had already established ethics of professional behavior, these statements did not address the proper relationship that anthropologists should create and maintain with the people studied, as well as students, clients, and fellow human beings, even though these problems had, by that time, already been addressed by the Society for Applied Anthropology (Fluehr-Lobban 2003).

Other critical situations, including interventionist political agendas, looting of archaeological sites, theft and trafficking of religious and artistic works, as well as the destruction of buildings and sites that have a special artistic and symbolic significance, have in fact resulted in the development of codes of ethics in cultural anthropology (American Anthropological Association 1998), archaeology (Society for American Archaeology 1996; Fluehr-Lobban 2003; Pels 1999), museum studies, and cultural management (Merryman 1998; Sackler 1998). The norms established in these codes encompass the ethics of cultural property (Merryman 1998), collecting (Sackler 1998), and cultural management (O'Keefe 1998). Problems in these areas, however, are not easily resolved, either, since tensions emerge from the opposition of different private interests (e.g., among nations) and of cultural differences between Western and indigenous cultures (Sackler 1998).

Human bodies hold a special place because they are inscribed with symbolism as well as cultural and political significance. Bodies challenge both the practice of biological anthropology and its purported value-free objectivity, as well as the impartial scientific distance of its practitioners (Berreman 1980). The development of a code of ethics in biological anthropology is, then, imperative because it is the body itself that compels us to act ethically by allowing us to feel both the self and the other, and to embody history and culture (Kavanaugh 2001; Lefort 1990). Thus, by studying the bodies of the living and the dead, anthropologists should be aware, more so than other scientists, of the need for a clear corpus of ethics in the discipline. The absence, therefore, of an explicit code of ethics in biological anthropology is not only paradoxical but also shocking.

WHAT IS A BODY?

Human bodies, when viewed as cultural objects within historical contexts, can be seen from different points of view—scientific, economic, social, political, and religious, among others (Morenon 2003; Murphy 1995; Rothfield 1995). In most cultures human remains are not treated as any other non-human object, but are usually handled with respect and ceremony. Since the body is a source of representation of both the group's unity and the self (Cantwell 1990), dead bodies are necessary for individuals to maintain their conceptions of personhood, and for groups to sustain their own identities (Seale 2001; Shilling 2003).

Mortuary rituals forge, renew, and break social bonds; they also craft social memories and assert the individual's and group's identities (Chesson 2001). Hence, although death can be understood as a "natural fact," it is always also a culturally constructed event (Burton 2001) that may mark the end of the natural life of the body, although its social life may continue beyond the event of death itself. It is not surprising, then, that the bodies of the dead and the places they have been deposited are considered potent memorials and sanctified sites for many generations (Kuijt 1998). In this context, disturbance of the dead is often considered offensive and can be used as a means to demoralize a particular population (Simpson 1996), since the continued well-being and approval of the deceased are, in some groups, considered essential for the well-being of the living. In fact, maintenance of the dead and the places they have been deposited can play a role in the construction or sense of locality and thus in the accessibility to the land and/or other resources (Cannon 2002; Charles and Buikstra 2002; Silverman 2002; Buikstra 1995; Dillehay 1995a).

It is only through the dualistic separation of body and the self, common to the Western philosophical/scientific heritage, and therefore also to medical practice (Deutscher 2001), that it is possible to depersonalize the body and thus objectify it as an object of study or a site of economic production (Sharp 2001). However, the body is a place in which religious and social dimensions can be understood as the individual who experiences the body itself and/or as part of the social body of a group (Shilling 2003; Csordas 1994, 1999).

Although biological anthropologists are aware of the symbolic complexities of the body (see Dillehay 1995b; Vlahos 1979), and in spite of the fact that they should be sensitive to it (Sease 1998), collecting activities, studies, and analyses have usually been conducted without consideration for the relatives or descendants (Simpson 1996). It is here, then, where the contradiction between anthropological practice and theory becomes evident; if as anthropologists we are concerned with people, since that is who and what we study, we then have a moral obligation to listen to them. However, our attitude toward human remains, as sources of data, does not take into account descendants' views, which might consider the remains to be sacred (Grimes 1990). The absence of a code of ethics that considers these complexities emerges as a peculiar paradox in biological anthropology, because it is from within the body, the object of study, that the notions of ethics emerge, as it is the body itself that makes it possible for us to have both an awareness of the self and the other that, in turn, generates an intertwined world of mutual recognition (Madison 1990, 2001; Lefort 1990; Levin 1990).

THE NEED FOR A CODE AND WHERE TO START

The need for a code of ethics in a scientific society is the same as the need for ethical principles in society as a whole; codes of ethics are mutually beneficial as they help to build and maintain satisfying and productive relationships among members of the scientific community, and with the public. According to MacDonald (2000), it is only through the establishment of a code of ethics that we can (1) define acceptable behaviors, (2) promote high standards of practice, (3) provide benchmarks for members to use in self-evaluation, and (4) establish a framework for professional behavior and responsibilities. By subscribing to a code of ethics and acting in accordance with it, scientists are granted the right to perform as such by the public and peers (Tugby 1964).

Only when the particular duties of a group of professionals have been determined can a code of ethics be created (Thomas and Waluchow 1998; O'Keefe 1998). Biological anthropologists have different obligations in accordance to the various roles they fulfill. As scientists, they have obligations toward science, the scientific community, the object of study, and the sponsor. As members of society, they have duties toward the public and the communities directly affected by their practice. As teachers, biological anthropologists have various commitments to their students, the general public, and the institutions in which they work. Finally, as citizens, they have responsibilities toward their own governments. All of these roles must be taken into consideration when creating a code of ethics. Due to the nature of its object of study, biological anthropologists have obligations toward human remains, which should be treated with dignity—not only because of their association with a person but also because of the information they can offer, as this information can illuminate our past as well as influence contemporary political affairs (Shilling 2003; Seale 2001; Walker 2000; Kuijt 1998; Csordas 1994; Cantwell 1990; New South Wales Consolidated Acts 1983; World Medical Assembly 1964).

Ethics in anthropology is a complex subject since this discipline has a moral double role where different obligations may turn out to be antithetical. These obligations include a past that must be saved, people studied who must benefit, and a commitment to truth that should be respected (Pels 1999). The history of biological anthropology has made the development of ethics an even more complex, but necessary, issue. Historically, biological anthropology, with its bond to ethnology, has often been associated with the study of "savages." Traditional discourse in biological anthropology gravitated around ideas of biological determination that served to categorize different populations in hierarchical terms, which also agreed with the image of the "savage" as irrational, inconsequential, and ignorant—in summary, inferior (Stocking 1987). Examples of this can be found in the studies conducted by Samuel Morton, Lest Hooton, and William Seldon in the Americas (Gould 1996; Shipman 1994).

During the 1930s, Darwinian evolution was politicized and demonized by the Nazi Party. Biological anthropologists who rejected the Nazi distortions responded by complying with the antiracist cause, but not by depoliticizing Darwinism (Shipman 1994). Ashley Montagu, Sherwood Washburn, and Theodosius Dobzhansky began combating racist stereotypes, through the use of modern evolutionary biology and its theories (Shipman 1994). Their efforts crystallized when Washburn and Dobzhansky organized the Fifteenth Symposium on Quantitative Biology at Cold Spring Harbor (Shipman 1994; Warren 1951; Dunn 1951; Howells 1951; Washburn 1951). The symposium served to question the concepts and dominance of typology, and it established the basis for the development of a nonessentialist biological anthropology that opened the discipline to the discussion of humans in terms of variation, evolution, and adaptation (Walker 2000; Shipman 1994).

Situated midway between the biological and social sciences, biological anthropology faces unique challenges when it comes to ethics. This discipline, however, shares certain characteristics with other fields of study derived from the application of the scientific method (Gower 1997). The principles of the scientific method include (1) observation; (2) questioning, which generates (3) the formulation of a testable explanation; (4) testing, which must be clearly recorded and reproducible; and (5) reporting of the findings (Gower 1997). These principles translate into a set of rules that constitute the foundation of the scientific practice, which should guarantee the construction of logical propositions and the possibility of duplicating the particular tests and analyses run. Furthermore, researchers must submit the results to peer evaluation so that, to the best of their knowledge, erroneous information will not reach the public. In addition, complete destruction of the sample must be avoided in order to ensure that analyses can be replicated. Behavior that does not conform to these principles must be avoided and prevented, since it could result in negligence and fraud, which are harmful to science. Experiments that cannot be repeated, as well as outside investigations and hearings, waste both time and resources that could have been better allocated to more fruitful research activities (Hammer 1992).

As teachers and researchers, biological anthropologists have educational obligations. The Universal Declaration of Human Rights (United Nations 1948), article 26, states, "Everyone has the right to education, and education shall promote understanding, tolerance and friendship among all nations, racial or religious groups." Thus, biological anthropologists have the obligation to inform the community and educate the public. Because research results are of general interest to all humankind, and because it is usually funded through the state and other types of nonprofit institutions, all findings should be made available to the community, especially to those groups that may have special bonds with the remains. As teachers, biological anthropologists must also provide good education (in both quality and quantity), conscientiously develop competence and effectiveness in the field among students, and encourage the free exchange of ideas among and between themselves and students in order to foster enriching academic experiences (University of Calgary, n.d.).

WHERE TO GO FROM HERE

Considering the contextual complexities that surround and permeate the human body, along with the social and political implications of studying the body, biological anthropology is urged to develop a more specialized code of ethics. Since the effectiveness of a code of ethics will depend in large part on the degree to which those who draft it can agree on particular issues, the constitution of such a code would demand the collaboration between biological anthropologists who have specialized in different areas. This chapter has focused on the ethics of bioarchaeology, paleopathology, and osteology, due to their focus on dead bodies. Dead bodies, however, are not the only object of study in the discipline of biological anthropology as a whole (e.g., primatology, human biology, forensics, genetics, paleoanthropology, etc.); thus, collaboration and contributions from scholars specialized in those areas are indispensable.

The American Association of Physical Anthropology (established in 1930), along with other similar organizations in the United States and other countries, should monitor the application of the code in order for it to be effective. Sections in the code of ethics should specifically address conflict of interest and how to deal with allegations of misconduct. Guidance needs to be provided for both procedure and confidentiality. In case unethical conduct is found, possible actions to be taken should be outlined. In addition, the code, accompanied by discussions about ethics and the consideration of different case scenarios, should be part of the education received by biological anthropologists in their training.

The preparation of the code, then, is only the start of a long process of education and oversight that will provide biological anthropologists with standards of conduct by which to evaluate their practice and that will reassure the public that those who have access to human remains for their study will indeed do their duty.

The constitution of a code of ethics will demand further work, as it will only be effective if it is kept congruent with the multiple developments in the profession. The code and our ethical questions will be limited to the immediate world in which we live, but by questioning the state of affairs in our own discipline, we may be able to liberate ourselves from its fixed history and from an attitude of passive acceptance.

TOWARD A CODE OF ETHICS IN BIOLOGICAL ANTHROPOLOGY

Statement of Purpose
Biological anthropologists should:

1. Strive to maintain objectivity and integrity in the conduct of research and analysis.
2. Adhere to the highest possible technical standards in research, teaching, and publication practices.
3. Report findings without omission of any significant data. To the best of their ability, biological anthropologists must disclose details of their theories, methods, and research designs that might influence the interpretations of research findings.
4. Make every reasonable effort to complete the project on schedule, especially when financial support for a project has been accepted.
5. Establish explicit agreements regarding the division of work, compensation, access to data, rights of authorship, and other rights and responsibilities at the outset of a project when several biological anthropologists, colleagues in other fields, or students are involved.
6. Make their research findings available to other colleagues and the public in a timely fashion.
7. Be aware of the situations that may lead to a misuse of the discoveries and knowledge. This should be conscientiously considered before the information is made available to the public.
8. Be aware of local, state, national, and international laws and regulations that have bearing on professional activities.

Ethical Obligations to the Remains, Science, and the Community
1. Human remains must be treated (and disposed of) with care and dignity, whether for purposes of reburial, handling, storage at an institution, display, and/or analysis.
2. Human remains must be studied or viewed for bona fide research or educational purposes only.
3. Human remains are not to be considered private property.
4. Laws and regulations regarding cultural patrimony or human remains must be respected.
5. Studies and their methodologies must be in adherence to the respect owed to the individuals they represent and the groups to which they are affiliated. Whenever possible, permission authorizing research should be sought if there are, for example, descendants or stakeholders.
6. No human remains may be used for advertising purposes.
7. Commercialization of human remains contributes to their destruction; therefore, biological anthropologists should not traffic, sell, or illegally appropriate any type of human remains. In addition, biological anthropologists must report people who are involved in such activities to the appropriate authorities.
8. Biological anthropologists should refrain from working with or even consulting on material that has been illegally acquired, especially since this work could potentially increase the illicit or commercial value of the remains.
9. All results must be published; ideally they must be submitted, first, to peer evaluation and then made available to the public, via museum exhibit, nonspecialized publications, or other mass media. In cases when the remains are affiliated to a particular group, the group in question should be informed of the results before the rest of the community is. Peer evaluation would help avoid cases of abuse, negligence, and/or fraud.

10. Destructive tests or analyses of any human remains must be considered in light of the type and amount of information they can provide and the possible decomposition and/or reburial of the material.

11. All methodologies must consider the conservation of the remains. Samples must not be completely destroyed. On the contrary, researchers must assure their preservation in order to ensure that duplication of the study is possible.

12. Treatments and invasive actions undertaken for a particular study should not hinder future studies using different techniques. For example, adding a so-called preservation coating to allow for ease in handling could interfere with DNA studies (see chapter 6 on treatment).

13. Because human remains, as the rest of the archaeological record, are partially, and sometimes completely, lost after the excavation, researchers are encouraged to make archival quality copies (see chapter 9, "Associated Artifacts") of the material generated and deposit this information at a corresponding institution. This information includes any type of written record, maps, results of analyses, pictures, drawings, film, and tape recordings.

14. Information about provenience and materials that accompanied the remains is considered part of the record, and they, as well as the human remains, are not a matter of personal possession. These materials and associated documentation should accompany and be deposited with the human material in a responsible institution.

15. Data, analyses, and personal archives, especially involving unpublished research on human remains should not die with a researcher. Efforts should be made to find suitable archives to house such information.

16. Health and safety precautions should be taken to prevent contamination of researchers, students, or stakeholders (see chapter 14).

Publication Process

1. Biological anthropologists must acknowledge all persons who contributed to their research and publications. Claims and ordering of authorship and acknowledgment must accurately reflect the contributions of all main participants in the research and writing process.

2. Data and material taken from another person's published or unpublished written work must be explicitly identified and referenced to its author. Citations of ideas developed in the written work of others should not be omitted.

3. Biological anthropologists must acknowledge and make public the communities, institutions, and/or individuals that supported or funded their research.

4. Images of human remains must not be published without first consulting about appropriate stakeholders' desires. Copyright issues must also be respected.

Teaching and Supervision

Biological anthropologists in teaching roles should be familiar with the content of the code and their own institutional policies and perform their responsibilities within such guidelines. In addition to the particular dispositions of the institution in which they are working:

1. Biological anthropologists should provide students with a fair and honest statement of the scope and perspective of their courses, clear expectations about students' performance, and fair, timely, and easily accessible evaluations of their work.

2. Biological anthropologists should ensure the equal and fair treatment of all students.

3. They should not present the work of students as their own.

4. Biological anthropologists should acknowledge the contributions of students and act on their behalf in setting forth agreements regarding authorship and other recognitions.

5. They also should not coerce personal, sexual, or economic favors, along with any type of professional advantages, from any student or other person, including peers and research assistants.

AMERICAN ASSOCIATION OF MUSEUMS

Position Statement on University Natural History Museums and Collections

The American Association of Museums (AAM) expresses its deep concern that a significant number of America's natural history museums and collections affiliated with universities are currently threatened with severe financial cutbacks, dispersal of collections, and outright closure.

At risk are collections of irreplaceable objects, such as geological, paleontological, zoological and botanical specimens, anthropological and historical artifacts, and archives. These collections are held in trust for the public; they are the priceless heritage of this and future generations; and they constitute critically important resources for new knowledge.

University museums provide unique contributions to the public good through education and research. Their collections are a shared legacy, serving as a constantly growing database to document the diversity and history of life on earth, to develop strategies for the management of natural resources, and to find solutions to some of the world's most pressing problems, from biodiversity conservation to the discovery of new medicines. In addition, exhibits and programs in university museums help to advance broader understanding of the scholarly and scientific enterprise.

AAM urges university administrators, trustees, state legislators, and alumni to do everything in their power to preserve, protect and support their university museums and collections of natural and cultural history. Temporary financial difficulties must not be allowed to interfere with the overriding responsibility of the governing authority to be effective stewards of these collections and to safeguard the public interest by assuring continued access to them.

AAM strongly urges the leadership of universities and their museums to work together to develop creative financial and organizational strategies that will secure their museums and collections for future generations.

AAM also strongly urges universities, museums, governmental agencies, foundations, and other stakeholders to begin a national dialogue with the aim of providing long-term stability for America's university museums of natural history and their irreplaceable collections. A major aim is to strengthen connections to constituencies that can speak in support of these important museums.

6. Biological anthropologists should not allow personal animosities or intellectual differences with other colleagues to prevent the student's access to those colleagues.
7. Students in their turn should acknowledge the time and effort that mentoring involves.
8. Students should strive to achieve a high level of professionalism and academic honesty and assume appropriate responsibility for their own education.

Finally, the code of ethics might include a special section for caretakers or curators to ensure proper curation and security for institutionalized collections. The next chapter on policy provides ideas for formulating an ethics section specifically for human remains collection managers.

Selected Codes of Ethics and Standards of Practice

American Association of Physical Anthropologists
Code of Ethics, approved in April 2003
See http://www.physanth.org/positions/ethics.htm (accessed April 14, 2006).
Borrowed code from the American Association of Anthropology.

American Institute for Conservation of Historic and Artistic Works (AIC)
Code of Ethics and Guidelines for Practice

First approved in 1963, revised in 1994
See http://aic.stanford.edu/pubs/ethics.html (accessed April 14, 2006).
A well-thought-out code with separate commentaries for continuing refinements.

World Archaeological Congress (WAC)
Code of Ethics; return of Indigenous Cultural Property program
See http://www.wac.uct.ac.za/archive/content/ethics.html (accessed April 14, 2006).

World Archaeological Congress
The Vermillion Accord on Human Remains, 1989
Statement on archaeological ethics and treatment of the dead; mutual respect for the beliefs of indigenous peoples as well as the importance of science and education and the need to take into account the wishes of the dead where known or inferred and the wishes of the local community, including issues of repatriation and scientific analysis.
See chapter 7.

Australian Archaeological Association
Code of Ethics, 1991
See http://www.australianarchaeologicalassociation.com.au/codeofethics.php (accessed April 14, 2006).

Society of Museum Archaeologists (SMA)
Standards in Action: Working with Archaeology Guidelines, 2000
Selection, Retention and Dispersal of Archaeological Collections
Guidelines for use in England, Wales, and Northern Ireland, 1993
See http://www.socmusarch.org.uk/publica.htm (accessed April 14, 2006).

Museums Australia Inc.
Previous Possessions, New Obligations: Policies for Museums in Australia and Aboriginal and Torres Strait Islander Peoples, 1993
See http://www.amonline.net.au/pdf/matcon/policy.pdf (accessed April14, 2006).

Museum Ethnographers Group (MEG)
Professional Guidelines Concerning the Storage, Display, Interpretation, and Return of Human Remains in Ethnographical Collections in United Kingdom Museums. *Journal of Museum Ethnography* 6 (1994): 22–24.
See http://www.culture.gov.uk/hr_cons_responses/wg_submission/S20.pdf (accessed April 14, 2006).

UK Museums Association (MA)
Code of Ethics, 1999
See http://www.museumsassociation.org/asset_arena/text/cs/code_of_ethics.pdf (accessed April 14, 2006).

International Council of Museums (ICOM)
Code of Ethics for Museums, 2002; see http://www.icom.org/ethics.html (accessed April 14, 2006).

Code of Ethics of the American Anthropological Association
Approved in June 1998
See http://www.aaanet.org/committees/ethics/ethcode.htm (accessed April 14, 2006).

American Academy of Forensic Sciences Bylaws
Article II. Code of Ethics and Conduct
See http://aafs.org/default.asp?section_id=aafs&page_id=aafs_bylaws#article2 (accessed April 14, 2006).

American Board of Forensic Examiners
n.d. *Code of Ethical Conduct* (American Board of Forensic Examiners, 300 South Jefferson Ave., Suite 411, Springfield, MO 65806); see http://www.abfde.org/downloads/Tab%203-Code% 20of%20Ethics%20(Jan%2004).doc (accessed April14, 2006).

United Kingdom Forensic Science Society
2005 Code of Conduct; see http://www.lib.jjay.cuny.edu/cje/html/codes/codes-forensic/fss-uk.html (accessed April 14, 2006).

Archaeological Institute of America
1991 Code of Ethics. *American Journal of Archaeology* 95: 285.
1994 *Code of Professional Standards* (Archaeological Institute of America, 675 Commonwealth Ave., Boston, MA 02215-1401).
See http://www.archaeological.org/pdfs/AIA_Code_of_Professional_StandardsA5S.pdf (accessed April 14, 2006).

Society for American Archaeology
1996 *Principles of Archaeological Ethics.* (Society for American Archaeology, 900 Second St., N.E., Suite 12, Washington, D.C. 20002-3557).
See http://www.saa.org/Publications/SAAbulletin/14-3/SAA9.html (accessed April 14, 2006).

Society for Applied Anthropology
1983 *Professional and Ethical Responsibilities* (revised 1983)
See http://www.sfaa.net/sfaaethic.html (accessed April 14, 2006).

Register of Professional Archaeologists
Code of Conduct and Standards of Research Performance
See http://www.rpanet.org/ (accessed April 14, 2006).

United Nations
1948 Universal Declaration of Human Rights
1983 United Nations Convention on the Elimination of All Forms of Discrimination against Women
1987 United Nations Convention on the Rights of the Child
Forthcoming United Nations Declaration on Rights of Indigenous Peoples.

REFERENCES

American Anthropological Association
    1998 Code of Ethics of the American Anthropological Association. Electronic document, http://www .aaanet.org/committees/ethics/ethcode.html (accessed June 30, 2003).

Berreman, Gerald D.
    1980 Are Human Rights Merely a Politicized Luxury in the World Today? *Anthropology and Humanism Quarterly* 5(1):2–13.

Buikstra, Jane E.

1995 Tombs for the Living . . . or . . . for the Dead: The Osmore Ancestors. In *Tombs for the Living: Andean Mortuary Practices*, edited by Tom Dillehay, pp. 229–280. Dumbarton Oaks Research Library and Collection, Washington, D.C.

Burton, John W.

2001 *Culture and the Human Body*. Waveland Press, Highland Park, Illinois.

Cannon, Aubrey

2002 Spatial Narrative of Death, Memory, and Transcendence. In *The Space and Place of Death*, edited by Helaine Silverman and David B. Small, pp. 191–199. Papers of the American Anthropological Association, Number 11. American Anthropological Association, Arlington, Virginia.

Cantwell, Anne-Marie

1990 The Choir Invisible: Reflection on the Living and the Dead. *Death Studies* 14:613–628.

Center for the Study of Ethics in the Professions

1994 *International Code of Medical Ethics*. Illinois Institute of Technology, Illinois.

Charles, Douglas K., and Jane E. Buikstra

2002 Siting, Sighting, and Citing the Dead. In *The Space and Place of Death*, edited by Helaine Silverman and David B. Small, pp. 13–25. Papers of the American Anthropological Association, Number 11. American Anthropological Association, Arlington, Virginia.

Chesson, Meredith S.

2001 Social Memory, Identity, and Death: An Introduction. In *Social Memory, Identity and Death: Anthropological Perspectives on Mortuary Rituals*, edited by Meredith S. Chesson, pp. 1–11. Archaeological Papers of the American Anthropological Association, Number 10. American Anthropological Association, Arlington, Virginia.

Csordas, Thomas J.

1994 Introduction: The Body as Representation and as Being in the World. In *Embodiment and Experience*, edited by Thomas J. Csordas, pp. 1–24. Cambridge University Press, Cambridge.

1999 The Body's Career in Anthropology. In *Anthropological Theory Today*, edited by Henrietta L. Moore, pp. 172–205. Polity Press, Cambridge.

Deutscher, Penelope

2001 Three Touches to the Skin: Sartre and Beauvoir on Desire and Embodiment. In *Thinking through the Skin*, edited by Sarah Ahmed and Jackie Stacey. Routledge, New York.

Dillehay, Tom, editor

1995a Mounds of Social Death: Araucanian Funerary Rites and Political Succession. In *Tombs for the Living: Andean Mortuary Practices*, edited by Tom Dillehay, pp. 281–313. Dumbarton Oaks Research Library and Collection, Washington, D.C.

1995b Tombs for the Living: Andean Mortuary Practices. In *Tombs for the Living: Andean Mortuary Practices*, edited by Tom Dillehay, pp. 229–280. Dumbarton Oaks Research Library and Collection, Washington, D.C.

Dillon, Martin C.

1990 Écart: Reply to Claude Lefort's "Flesh and Otherness." In *Ontology and Alterity in Merleau-Ponty*, edited by Galen A. Johnson and Michael B. Smith, pp. 14–34. Northwestern University Press, Evanston, Illinois.

Dunn, Leslie C.
1951 Race Concept and Human Races. In *Origin and Evolution of Man*, Cold Spring Harbor Symposia on Quantitative Biology, Vol. 15, edited by Katherine Brehme Warren, pp. 353–354. Cold Spring Harbor, New York.

Fluehr-Lobban, Carolyn
2003 Ethics in Anthropology 1890–2000: A Review of Issues and Principles. In *Ethics and the Profession of Anthropology: Dialogue for Ethically Conscious Practice*, edited by Carolyn Fluehr-Lobban, pp. 1–28. AltaMira Press, Walnut Creek, California.

Fluehr-Lobban, Carolyn, Paulani Kanaka' Ole Kanehele, and Jennifer Hope Antes
2003 Repatriation of Indigenous Hawaiian Cultural Property by the City of Providence. In *Ethics and the Profession of Anthropology: Dialogue for Ethically Conscious Practice*, edited by Carolyn Fluehr-Lobban, pp. 141–158. AltaMira Press, Walnut Creek, California.

Foucault, Michel
1968 *Las Palabras y las Cosas*. Siglo XXI, Mexico City.

Goldstein, Lynne, and Keith Kintigh
1990 Ethics and the Reburial Controversy. *American Antiquity* 55(3):585–591.

Gould, Stephen J.
1996 *The Mismeasurement of Man*. Norton, New York.

Gower, Barry
1997 *Scientific Method: An Historical and Philosophical Introduction*. Routledge, New York.

Grimes, Ronald
1990 Breaking the Glass Barrier: The Power of Display. *Journal of Ritual Studies* 4(2):239–262.

Habermas, Jürgen
1987 Modernity, an Incomplete Project. In *Interpretive Social Science: A Second Look*, edited by Paul Rabinow and William M. Sullivan, pp. 141–156. University of California Press, Berkeley.

Hammer, Vincent N.
1992 Misconduct in Science: Do Scientists Need a Professional Code of Ethics? Electronic document, http://www.csu.edu.au/learning/eis/www_ethx.html (accessed June 30, 2006).

Holden, Constance
1979 Ethics in Social Science Research. *Science* 206(2):537–538, 540.

Howells, William W.
1951 Origin of the Human Stock: Concluding Remarks of the Chairman. In *Origin and Evolution of Man*, Cold Spring Harbor Symposia on Quantitative Biology, Vol. 15, edited by Katherine Brehme Warren, pp. 79–86. Cold Spring Harbor, New York.

Jones, D. Gareth, and Richard J. Harris
1998 Archaeological Human Remains. *Current Anthropology* 39(2):253–264.

Jorgensen, Joseph G.
1971 On Ethics and Anthropology. *Current Anthropology* 12(3):321–334.

Kavanaugh, John F.
2001 *Who Count as Persons? Human Identity and the Ethics of Killing*. Georgetown University Press, Washington, D.C.

Kuijt, Ian
1998 Place, Death and the Transmission of Social Memory in Early Agricultural Communities of the Near Eastern Pre-Pottery Neolithic. In *Social Memory, Identity, and Death: Anthropological Per-*

spectives on Mortuary Rituals, edited by Meredith S. Chesson, pp. 80–99. Archaeological Papers of the American Anthropological Association, Number 10. Arlington, Virginia.

Lefort, Claude
  1990 Flesh and Otherness. In *Ontology and Alterity in Merleau-Ponty*, edited by Galen A. Johnson and Michael B. Smith, pp. 3–13. Northwestern University Press, Evanston, Illinois.

Levin, David M.
  1990 Justice in the Flesh. In *Ontology and Alterity in Merleau-Ponty*, edited by Galen A. Johnson and Michael B. Smith, pp. 35–44. Northwestern University Press, Evanston, Illinois.

Lock, Margaret
  1993 Cultivating the Body: Anthropology and Epistemologies of Bodily Practice and Knowledge. *Annual Review of Anthropology* 22:133–155.

MacDonald, Chris
  2000 Guidance for Writing a Code of Ethics. Electronic document, http://www.ethicsweb.ca/codes/coe3.htm, accessed April 21, 2006.

Madison, Gary Brent
  1990 Flesh and Otherness. In *Ontology and Alterity in Merleau-Ponty*, edited by Galen A. Johnson and Michael B. Smith, pp. 27–34. Northwestern University Press, Evanston, Illinois.
  2001 The Ethics and Politics of the Flesh. In *Merleau-Ponty's Later Works and Their Practical Implications*, edited by Duane H. Davis, pp. 161–185. Humanity Books, Amherst, New York.

Merleau-Ponty, Maurice
  2001 *The Incarnate Subject: Malebranche, Brian, and Bergson on the Union of Body and Soul.* Humanity Books, Amherst, New York.

Merryman, John Henry
  1998 Cultural Property Ethics. *International Journal of Cultural Property* 7(1):21–31.

Morenon, E. Pierre
  2003 Nagged by NAGPRA: Is There an Archaeological Ethic? In *Ethics and the Profession of Anthropology: Dialogue for Ethically Conscious Practice*, edited by Carolyn Fluehr-Lobban, pp. 107–140. AltaMira Press, Walnut Creek, California.

Murphy, Peter
  1995 The Body Politics. In *Troubled Bodies*, edited by Paul A. Komesaroff, pp. 103–124. Duke University Press, Durham, North Carolina.

New South Wales Consolidated Acts
  1983 Human Tissue Act. Electronic document, http://www.austlii.edu.au/au/legis/nsw/consol_act/hta1983160/ (accessed June 30, 2006).

O'Keefe, Patrick J.
  1998 Code of Ethics: Form and Function in Cultural Management. *International Journal of Cultural Property* 7(1):32–51.

Ortner, Don J., and Walter G. J. Putschar
  1985 *Identification of Pathological Conditions in Human Skeletal Remains.* Smithsonian Institution Press, Washington, D.C.

Pels, Peter
  1999 Professions of Duplexity: A Prehistory of Ethical Codes in Anthropology. *Current Anthropology* 40(2):101–136.

Postal, Susan
  1978 Body Image and Identity: A Comparison of Kwakiutl and Hopi. In *Social Aspects of the Human Body*, edited by Ted Polhemus, pp. 122–130. Penguin Books, New York.

Rothfield, Philipa

    1995 Bodies and Subjects: Medical Ethics and Feminism. In *Troubled Bodies*, edited by Paul A. Komesaroff, pp. 168–201. Duke University Press, Durham, North Carolina.

Sackler, Elizabeth A.

    1998 The Ethics of Collecting. *International Journal of Cultural Property* 7(1):132–140.

Seale, Clive

    2001 The Body and Death. In *Exploring the Body*, edited by Sarah Cunningham-Burley and Kathryn Backett-Milburn, pp. 98–116. Palgrave, New York.

Sease, Catherine

    1998 Code of Ethics for Conservation. *International Journal of Cultural Property* 7(1):98–115.

Sharp, Lesley A.

    2001 The Commodification of the Body and Its Parts. *Annual Review of Anthropology* 30:287–328.

Shilling, Chris

    2003 *The Body and Social Theory*. Sage Publications, Thousand Oaks, California.

Shipman, Pat

    1994 *The Evolution of Racism? Human Differences and the Use and Abuse of Science*. Simon & Schuster, New York.

Silverman, Helaine

    2002 Introduction: The Space and Place of Death. In *The Space and Place of Death*, edited by Helaine Silverman and David B. Small, pp. 1–11. Papers of the American Anthropological Association, Number 11. Arlington, Virginia.

Simpson, Moira G.

    1996 *Making Representations. Museums in the Post-Colonial Era*. Routledge, New York.

Society for American Archaeology

    1996 Principles of Archaeological Ethics. Electronic document, http://www.saa.org/publications/saabulletin/14-3/saa9.html (accessed June 30, 2006).

Spurling, Laurie

    1977 *Phenomenology and the Social World: The Philosophy of Merleau-Ponty and Its Relations to the Social Sciences*. Routledge & Kegan Paul, London.

Stocking, George W.

    1987 *Victorian Anthropology*. Free Press, New York.

Thomas, John E., and Wilfrid J. Waluchow

    1998 *Well and Good: A Case Study Approach to Biomedical Ethics*. Broadview Press, Ontario, Canada.

Tugby, Donald J.

    1964 Toward a Code of Ethics for Applied Anthropology. *Anthropological Forum* 1(2):220–231.

United Nations

    1948 Universal Declaration of Human Rights. Electronic document, http://www.Un.org/Overview/rights.html (accessed June 30, 2006).

University of Calgary

    n.d. University Teachers Code of Ethics. Electronic document, http//:www.ucalgary.ca.

Vlahos, Olivia

    1979 *Body the Ultimate Symbol*. Lippincott, New York.

Walker, Phillip L.

    2000 Bioarchaeological Ethics: A Historical Perspective on the Value of Human Remains. In *Biological Anthropology of the Human Skeleton*, edited by M. Anne Katzenberg and Shelley R. Saunders. Wiley-Liss, New York.

Warren, Katherine Brehme, editor

    1951 *Origin and Evolution of Man*. Cold Spring Harbor Symposium on Quantitative Biology, Vol. 15. Cold Spring Harbor, New York.

Washburn, Sherwood L.

    1951 The New Physical Anthropology. In *Transactions of the New York Academy of Sciences*, Series II (13):298–304.

World Medical Assembly

    1964 Declaration of Helsinki. *British Medical Journal* 7070 (313). Electronic document, http://www.cirp.org/library/ethics/helsinki/ (accessed June 30, 2006).

CHAPTER 3

Policy

VICKI CASSMAN, NANCY ODEGAARD, AND JOSEPH POWELL

A vision without a task is a dream, a task without a vision is drudgery, but a task with vision can change the world.

—Attributed to Black Elk (Oglala Sioux Holy Man)

MISSION AND VISION STATEMENTS, POLICIES, AND PROCEDURES ARE AT THE HEART OF IMPROVING curation standards for institutionalized human remains. While many institutions provide reams of such documents for objects of art, the lack of existing written collection goals, limitations on use, or information about how to handle fragile human osteology collections is remarkable, even shocking. Why has this situation become the norm as opposed to the exception? For museums, one possibility is that human remains seem to fall into a zone between artifact and untouchables, especially for universities, where there appears to be an unspoken myth that the less that is done, the less attention such collections draw. One of the goals of this volume is to encourage those who officially or by default have curation responsibility to err on the side of caution and respect rather than inaction or benign neglect. The latter eventually can lead to losses, resentment, and an openly angry public.

According to the *Merriam-Webster* dictionary, *policy* is

1a: prudence or wisdom in the management of affairs

b: management or procedure based primarily on material interest

2a: a definite course or method of action selected from among alternatives and in light of given conditions to guide and determine present and future decisions

b: a high-level overall plan embracing the general goals and acceptable procedures especially of a governmental body

Guidance from the professional museum associations is minimal in terms of human remains. In its 1994 Code of Ethics, the American Association of Museums states, "The unique and special nature of human remains and funerary and sacred objects is recognized as the basis of all decisions concerning such collections." The International Council of Museums (ICOM) in its 1987 ICOM Code of Ethics states, "Although it is occasionally necessary to use human remains and other sensitive material in interpretive exhibits, this must be done with tact and with respect for the feelings for human dignity held by all peoples." And "where a museum maintains and/or is developing collections of human remains and sacred objects these should be securely housed and carefully maintained as archival collections in scholarly institutions, and should always be available to qualified researchers and educators, but not to the morbidly curious."

The following is a discussion of the various levels of policy that we are advocating for collections of human remains. Policy is the starting point for institutions to improve preservation of human remains collections. Policies should help us proceed with our tasks guided by wisdom and prudence.

MISSION STATEMENTS

A *mission statement* is a short description of institutional goals that guides staff in their work toward common goals; it helps staff and community partners stay on course. Lord and Lord (1999:45) call it the raison d'être that justifies the efforts for establishment and maintenance. Without clearly stated goals, collections are more likely to suffer from misuse or to grow in unexpected and unsupportable ways. According to the American Association of Museums, mission statements are important for the following reasons:

- Museums that use clearly delineated mission statements to guide their activities and decisions are more likely to function effectively.
- A mission statement describes the purpose of a museum, its reason for existence.
- It defines the museum's unique identity and purpose, and provides a distinct focus for the institution.
- A mission statement articulates how the museum understands its role and responsibility to the public and its collections, and reflects the environment in which it exists.
- Every action and activity of the museum should support the purpose set forth in the mission statement.

(http://www.aam-us.org/getinvolved/pr/upload/D9_Acc_MissionExpect-2.pdf, accessed April 11, 2006)

The first and most elemental question is, Do human remains actually fit into the mission of a particular institution? Obviously, universities that teach and carry out physical anthropology research would have need of the "real thing" for both teaching and research. It is harder to imagine how human remains fit into the mission of a history museum unless the institution has a specialized interest in, for example, the history of medicine or Egyptology.

Do human remains belong in art museums? One would not think of human remains as a common collection item in an art institution, yet they are found in these institutions, too. Museum directors worried about waning attendance numbers often suggest dinosaurs or mummies as the surefire answer to draw in the public. Art museums may put on a mummy show and haul out "the mummy and a painted sarcophagus" from the basement to attract new crowds. Is this an appropriate practice? It is debatable but very common.

Hypothetically, human hair, skin, or bone might be included as elements of a particular work of art (see chapter 17 for actual examples). In such a case, the artist must be able to certify where the human remains came from and that they are not compromising laws or disrespecting any particular individual or ethnic group. This scenario is hopefully not terribly common, but there is no debate that death and human bodies fascinate people (see chapter 17 for further discussions).

If human remains are an integral part of an institution's collection, then the mission statement must reflect their presence, especially to give staff guidance. If human remains are outside the institution's mission or inappropriate, then transferring the remains (not selling) to another institution would be an excellent option.

In university collections, mission statements are all too infrequent. Anthropology, biology, and medical departments at most universities maintain human remains collections for teaching and/or research. A mission statement would help such institutions and their staffs define

- the purpose of their collections (e.g., teaching and research)
- the scope of the collections (historic, archaeological, forensic, modern donations)
- types (osteology, mummies, or specimens preserved in jars with formalin [formaldehyde] solutions, etc.)

In this way faculty, part-time teaching staff, adjunct faculty, staff, graduates, outside researchers, and undergraduates would all understand

- what the collections mean to the department or institution
- where they come from (geographic and temporal scope, sources)
- what they are
- their use
- who has access to remains
- what are the responsibilities to remains
- who is responsible

Then there are no misunderstandings or hesitations about what to do, for instance, when the art department calls the anthropology department to ask for a loan of a skeleton, or someone wants to donate a fetus in formaldehyde solution, a skull, or a mummy found in Uncle Ned's attic. Having copies of the mission and collecting statement lets people judge their proposed actions against those stated in the mission of the institution.

Of course, mission statements are not written in stone, and it is hard to imagine all possible future scenarios (changes in laws, etc.), so a mission statement must be revisited at intervals to keep it relevant and useful. A sample mission statement for an anthropology department at a university without an attached museum might look like the sample presented on page 24.

The mission statement in the example gives staff guidance—that the department in question acts as a repository for collections generated from its own fieldwork or those donated by local law enforcement entities. For a number of reasons, an undocumented "Uncle Ned's" skull, fetus, and mummy fall out of the scope of collecting (improper context and not an official department source), and the callers need to know they should instead contact the local coroner or police department. Moreover, if a state law has provisions for human remains found on private property, then these might apply to Uncle Ned's skull (see chapter 15 on law). In this case, too, only collections relating to the western United States or northern Mexico are considered. However, it is important to note, "Mexican cultural property legislation passed in 1972 establishes national ownership of all Pre-Columbian artifacts. Thus, all Pre-Columbian collections or artifacts brought across the U.S.-Mexican border without appropriate permits are subject to the U.S. Stolen Property Act, as interpreted by the McClain case of 1977, which regards cultural property as stolen if there is an unequivocal claim of national ownership" (http://www.utexas.edu/research/tarl/faq/Mexico.html#introduction, accessed April 11, 2006). Therefore, adding new collections from northern Mexico to this collection is unlikely. Additionally, an Egyptian mummy would not fit the mission of this particular institution, either, due to the stated geographic limitations.

Limiting what is accepted (accessions) has very real and practical implications. Instead of a pack rat collecting strategy, you build collections with care and forethought. Storing and caring for human remains and related artifacts is an expensive and time-consuming undertaking; therefore, acquisitions should be planned and well thought out, not haphazard and completely opportunistic. A mission statement acts as a guide and keeps us from constantly reinventing institutional goals with every whim of a new acquisition opportunity. If staff desires more information about collection access and use, then a collection management policy is the next s*

VISION STATEMENTS

Vision statements describe the institutional desires for the future, including plans for new infrastructure or new ways of serving stakeholders and new audiences. They explain why, for whom, and how these new programs or goals are important. These can be institution-wide or broken down by section within an institution. Again, these statements are important to the curator or technician in charge of human remains, because they provide guidance on what goals they should be aiming for.

POLICIES

Though the mission and vision statements set out broad goals and direction for an institution, policies are more in depth and help further define roles and actions for staff. Policies set up the outline for decision making and preferred actions in a specific situation. According to Marie Malaro (1998:11), "A collection management policy is a detailed written statement that explains why a museum is in operation and how it goes about its business, and it articulates the museum's professional standards regarding objects left in its care. The policy serves as a guide for the staff and as a source of information for the public." Policies for human remains collections should include information on

- the purpose of the institution and the collection goals
- acquisition
- accessioning
- deaccessioning and repatriation
- access to collections
- care and handling
- storage requirements
- sampling and destructive analysis
- photography and use of images and research
- exhibition if and when this is allowed

- associated artifact disposition and care
- associated archives and records disposition, access, and care
- mold making for reproductions or castings (e.g., replicas)

Especially for academic collections, written policies are rare. Even many large museums do not have specific policies for human remains; instead, their treatment is no different than for any other museum artifact, or unwritten policies imply minimal touching, for instance. However, human remains deserve a different status and are due greater respect and consideration. A more thorough and devoted collection policy will answer basic questions—for instance, who has access, where, to what, why, how, and under what circumstances. Law enforcement institutions will likely have extremely limited access, with museums having less restricted access especially for descendants, and universities may have relatively liberal access to study collections used for teaching. All of these institutions need to formulate a clearly laid-out policy.

On the one hand, many academic institutions do not even have mission or collection policies since they frequently do not have staff devoted to collection management. On the other hand, it is common for institutional policy to refer vaguely to meeting the federal collections standards in the federal code of regulations, 36 CFR Part 79 or Curation of Federally-Owned and Administered Archaeological Collections. These are excellent recommendations that are elaborated on the website of the National Park Service Archaeology and Ethnology Program. Though this is a very thorough review of general collection management standards, without collection staff or specific human remains collection policy, the standards are difficult to achieve.

At the National Museum of Health and Medicine, in Washington, D.C., the staff has an official collections research policy that repeats goals of the mission that relate to the collections, describes the collection, and covers basic access and research publication requirements (http://www.nlm.nih.gov/hmd/medtour/nmhm.html, accessed April 11, 2006). Other institutions, such as the Cleveland Museum of Natural History, provide additional information on handling (http://www.cmnh.org/collections/research-guidelines.html, accessed April 11, 2006). However, there do not appear to be any institutional examples that cover all the points basic to an overall collections policy as outlined here. Many institutions are starting to develop such comprehensive policies, or they are waiting for good examples to emulate.

Considerations for an Access Policy
A policy with access information needs to discuss first who can have access. For law enforcement, it may be limited to the coroner, judge, and evidence clerk. In museums, curators, collection managers, and accompanied descendants and researchers should have access. The Native American Graves Protection and Repatriation Act (NAGPRA) guarantees affiliated descendants of federally recognized Native American tribes within the United States the right to have access to their ancestors and repatriate them, should they choose. At the National Museum of Health and Medicine in Washington, D.C., descendants and those who have donated a limb—for instance, in a war—have access to that accessioned remain, though few have actually chosen to take advantage of such a visit (Sledzik and Barbian 2001). In any well-thought-out access policy, how much access is permissible?

- Where should access take place?
- Should access take place in a separate room or in the collections area where there are other unrelated human remains?
- Who is responsible for the time and space allocation arrangements?
- What kind of equipment and instruments are allowed?

- How many visitors, students, or researchers can the space safely hold?
- Must visitors wear gloves or other protective clothing?
- Will photography, illustrations, or electronic documentation be permitted?
- Should visitors be able to touch the remains?
- If yes, then how much touching?
- Are ritual services permitted?
- May the remains be symbolically fed offerings in bowls or by sprinkling pollen or corn flour or *chicha* (an alcoholic beverage used in Andean rituals)?
- May the remains be rubbed with red ocher pigment?
- Is burning incense, candles, cedar, tobacco, or sage permitted?

Security and privacy need evaluating. Sometimes the nature of the visit is routine; at other times, extremely serious. Perhaps the well-being of the living community is at stake, and descendants will need a room to compose themselves or to don special clothing before and after their visit. Perhaps the descendants will need to smudge or cleanse themselves ritually and literally. From the institution's perspective, will special ventilation be necessary, especially for important rituals that include incense or burning sage? A policy can help define and provide answers and consistency for many issues. Though answering these questions takes time, it can save time and future energy by providing consistent answers to questions that inevitably will come up.

A log of access is essential, too. It may involve a simple logbook, where everyone, including staff, students, and visitors sign in with day, time, and task. Some formal security systems will monitor which passkeys were used and when access occurred. Such a system has wider applications, such as the ability to account for use of collections for a variety of auditing purposes. If a fancy security system is not available, then a simple logbook will do that has a column for a date, time, names of those accessing the collection, and purpose of the visit.

All human remains, even those that do not fall under NAGPRA, need policies on access. Osteology collections, used by students for learning to identify bones, need to have access policies and handling procedures to help prevent damage and loss of the collection. Students must understand the privilege of working with the real thing and that the bones are those of individuals once living just like them. Without such a policy, students or researchers often unconsciously can become rough and disrespectful. For instance, in a study collection, it is familiar to see a student learning to identify foot bones literally toss aside a fourth metatarsal in search of a third. Researchers or students who are made aware of the respect and care to be afforded a study collection will likely take better care than those that are given no such formal signs of institutional respect. An access policy could require researchers and students to read and sign a copy of care and handling procedures (see "Examination and Analysis," chapter 5). Users would become sensitized and likely be more careful in their handling. Researchers and students might also carry this respect back to their own or other future institutions if given a copy of their signed statement.

PROCEDURES

A third tier of formality that is necessary for human remains collections is that of procedures. These are specific guidelines for specific actions. They provide the method and the details for those specific actions. Procedures allow staff in particular but others as well to know explicit expectations for curation concerns of human remains. Since it is clear that handling causes most damage to remains, we have devoted an entire chapter to a more in-depth discussion (chapter 5). Within the care and handling policy could be procedures for photography and documentation, how to accession, and how to label. (An example of a labeling procedure is given in chapter 8.) Sampling of a collection is an entirely different level of access, and an example of this kind of policy and procedure appears in chapter 5.

CONCLUSION

At a minimum, every collection of human remains should have a mission statement and a collections policy. It would be even better if specific procedures were included as well. When starting out, staff could use the policy list given above to begin to organize tasks. Staff should evaluate which policy and related procedure(s) is most vital for the safe and proper functioning of their collection responsibilities, and set priorities. Ideas for what to include in these policies and procedures are possible to glean throughout this volume since we cover many of the basics in each

---

WEBSITES OF INTEREST WITH SAMPLE POLICIES

Several policies dealing with human remains are available on the Internet. These are diverse in their coverage. The majority of policies cover acquisition, study, and NAGPRA consultation.

- **36 CFR Part 79** or Curation of Federally-Owned and Administered Archaeological Collections; http://www.cr.nps.gov/nagpra/TRAINING/36-CFR-79_Overview.pdf (accessed April 11, 2006)
- **National Park Service 5.3.4** Stewardship of Human Remains and Burials; http://www.nps.gov/policy/mp/chapter5.htm (accessed April 11, 2006)
- **A Code of Practice for the Care of Human Remains in Museums**; http://www.museumsassociation.org/asset_arena/text/de/humanremainscode.pdf (accessed April 11, 2006)
- The **Department for Culture, Media and Sport**, Guidance for the Care of Human Remains in Museums; http://www.culture.gov.uk/NR/rdonlyres/0017476B-3B86-46F3-BAB3-11E5A5F7F0A1/0/GuidanceHumanRemains11Oct.pdf (accessed April 11, 2006)
- The **Natural History Museum, London**, Statement; http://www.nhm.ac.uk/research-curation/science-directorate/science-policies-strategy/assets/3OctMediastatement.FINAL.doc (accessed April 11, 2006)
- The **University of California** Policy and Procedures on Curation and Repatriation of Human Remains and Cultural Items; http://www.ucop.edu/ucophome/coordrev/policy/5-01-01att.pdf (accessed April 11, 2006)
- The **Alutiiq Museum** Collections Policy on Repatriation, Deaccessioning and Exhibit; http://www.alutiiqmuseum.com/pdfs/CollectionsPolicy.pdf (accessed April 11, 2006)
- Archaeological Curation Standards and Guidelines, Office of State Archaeology, Division of Historical Resources, **North Carolina Department of Cultural Resources**; http://www.arch.dcr.state.nc.us/ncarch/resource/curation.htm#3.0 (accessed April 11, 2006)
- **Cleveland Museum of Natural History**; http://www.cmnh.org/collections/research-policies.html (accessed April 11, 2006)
- **Council of Texas Archeologists** Curation Appendix A Curatorial Policy For Human Skeletal Remains; http://www.counciloftexasarcheologists.org/index.php?option=content&task=view&id=41&Itemid=55 (accessed April 11, 2006)
- Preparing Human Osteological Collections for the **Maxwell Museum of Anthropology**; http://filo.unm.edu/~maxwell/pdf_forms/preparing%20archaeological%20collections%20031111.pdf (accessed April 11, 2006)
- The Policy for the Acquisition, Treatment, and Disposition of Human Remains and Funerary Objects of United States Origin by the Department of Anthropology, at the **University of Illinois at Urbana–Champaign**; http://www.itarp.uiuc.edu/loa/policynahr.html (accessed April 11, 2006)

chapter. Once an institution has formally accepted policies, staff must receive and periodically review them so all are familiar and sign on to the responsibilities required of them.

REFERENCES

Lord, Gail, and Barry Lord
  1999 *The Manuel of Museum Planning.* 2nd ed. Professional Museum and Heritage Series. AltaMira Press, Walnut Creek, California.

Malaro, Marie
  1998 Collection Management Policies. In *Collections Management,* edited by Anne Fahy, pp. 11–28. Leicester Readers in Museum Studies. Routledge, London.

Sledzik, Paul, and Lenore Barbian
  2001 From Privates to Presidents: Past and Present Memoirs from the Anatomical Collections of the National Museum of Health and Medicine. In *Human Remains: Conservation, Retrieval and Analysis: Proceedings of a Conference Held in Williamsburg, VA, Nov 7–11th 1999,* edited by Emily Williams, pp. 227–235. BAR International Series 943. Archaeopress, Oxford.

CHAPTER 4

Condition Assessment of Osteological Collections

Vicki Cassman and Nancy Odegaard

Remember friend as you walk by
As you are now so once was I
As I am now you will surely be
Prepare thyself to follow me.

—Anonymous epitaph

IN THE PAST, STANDARD OSTEOLOGICAL DOCUMENTATION HAS INCLUDED CATEGORIES FOR CONDITION that have check boxes for "poor, fair, or good" (Ubelaker 1978:37). But typically there is no common standard, and what means good to one person may mean fair or poor to another or vice versa, because there is no standard point of reference. How can a curator determine whether condition has deteriorated sufficiently to move an individual from a category of good to fair or fair to poor? Without standards and systems for tracking condition, only when an extreme change takes place do conditional judgments and curatorial interventions take place.

The notion of condition assessment is central to our ethical guidelines as stewards of the past. Condition depends largely on guidelines that are found in the codes of ethics for each of the professional disciplines that human remains touch: physical anthropology, anthropology, archaeology, museology, and conservation. Stewardship is not mentioned in the related area of forensic anthropology, which involves the application of science to a court of law, in the code of ethics and conduct for the American Academy of Forensic Sciences. Decent condition matters to all stakeholders, including researchers, caretakers, descendants, politicians, law enforcement officials, and the general public. Though decent condition draws to mind respectful storage conditions (see chapter 8), we are focusing here on the physical state of the remains themselves and the ability to objectively track, record, and react to changes in condition with the specific aim of improving preservation.

This chapter explores the physical properties and deterioration processes of bone, in order to understand deterioration as a conditional change. Next we offer vocabulary that describes most postinstitutionalization conditional processes found in human remains collections. Finally, we will present methods for surveying and monitoring changes in collections as a unit.

THE COMPOSITION OF BONE AND TEETH

Bone

Bones can be viewed simply as rigid but porous calcified connective tissue that makes up the human skeleton (and that of other vertebrates, too). There are 206 bones in the adult human body, counting the three parts of the sternum as one, and these act as our bodies' supports and levers to which ligaments and muscles attach. There are many more individual bones in infants. Bones are "a heterogeneous dynamic system made up of a complex and intimate mixture of organic and mineral components" (Hare 1980:208). Living bone is a complex system that intimately interacts with the other systems of the body. For instance, red and white blood cells are produced in the bone marrow, and these enter into the bloodstream through the porous structure of the bone.

The outer surface of bone, the *periosteum*, is a thin, dense membrane that contains nerves and blood vessels that nourish the bone (see figure 4.1). Beneath this is a thick dense layer of compact bone known as *cortical bone*, and within this are many layers of *trabecular bone*, which is spongy in texture and porous in nature. Cortical bone, which is mostly inorganic, being composed primarily of the mineral apatite, is found primarily in the shaft of long bones and forms the outer shell around trabecular bone at the end of joints and the vertebrae. The spongy, cancellous or trabecular bone is found mostly in the end of long bones, in vertebrae and in flat bones like the pelvis. Trabecular bone is more porous with many blood vessels as compared with the compact cortical bone, but it is still strong (White 1991; Eriksen et al. 1994). In many bones, the trabecular bone protects and supports the center, the bone marrow, which is thick and jelly-like when alive; if it survives, it is delicate, thin, and brittle when dried after death.

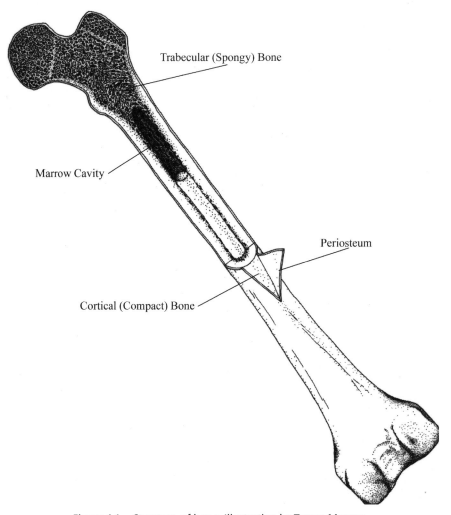

Figure 4.1. Structure of bone. Illustration by Teresa Moreno.

Bones begin as fibrous connective tissues, which through the impregnation of calcium phosphate and calcium carbonate ossify or harden with maturation. Bones in the arms, thighs, hips, and shoulder blade ossify to a greater degree than ribs, the sternum, and the clavicle, which bend more before they break. Bone is generally composed of about 70 percent inorganic lattice structure and 30 percent organic connective tissue that is a protein known as *ossein*. Ossein is chemically collagen. The fibrous bundles of collagen are held together with an amorphous substance made up of minerals and polysaccharides (carbohydrates). The mineral hydroxyapatite, a calcium phosphate compound, is deposited in collagen fibers and the organic matrix; thus, the inorganic and organic matrices are intimately coordinated.

Bones function as a protective storehouse for minerals, and they are constantly being renewed and renovated through mineralization or demineralization. The degree of mineralization within an individual at death varies depending on age, pathology, nutrition, and environment. After death, age and environment are essential factors. During life, while supporting the body, protecting other organs, supplying the bloodstream, and reacting to metabolic, nutritional, and endocrine systems, the skeleton can record a partial life story of the individual, which can be interpreted after death. Diseases, malnutrition, hypernourishment, repetitive labor, and sport are often recorded on the bone as damage, growth stoppage, irregular growth patterns, wear, or thinning (Curry 2002; Larsen 1997).

Teeth

Teeth are considered a most durable material in terms of general preservation, but they are often the most commonly damaged element of a skull. How do we explain this irony? What makes them so vulnerable? First, we must understand that teeth are layered structures. Enamel makes up the outermost layer of a tooth, and this is a hard nonporous layer that does not grow after it has been deposited. Enamel is over 95 percent mineral in composition, mostly hydroxyapatite. Under the enamel layer is *dentin*, a bonelike substance that forms the bulk of a tooth. Dentin provides a base for the enamel and forms the tooth root(s). It is yellow in color, perforated throughout by minute vessels that are continuous from the central area or pulp to its outer surface, and is therefore porous. It is 70 percent inorganic hydroxyapatite, 20 percent organic collagen, and 10 percent water by weight. *Pulp* refers to vascular (vessel) and nervous structures in the central cavity of the tooth, inside the dentin. *Cementum* is the thin layer of calcified tissue covering the dentin of the root. It attaches to the gum tissues, which anchors the tooth to the surrounding bone.

Though enamel is considered the hardest substance found in the human body and is resistant to many chemical attacks, as observed in paleontology with the quantity of fossilized teeth versus bone, teeth do not withstand repeated or sharp mechanical or physical strikes. When the cranium is placed on a hard surface, it is the teeth that absorb the initial impact and easily become chipped (Hillson 1996).

Fossilized and Subfossilized Bone

Curators often make a distinction, especially for faunal collections, between the categories of fossilized, subfossilized, and modern bone, but these categories also are applied to human remains. Collections of modern bone often come from nonarchaeological contexts such as donations, where flesh has been or needs to be purposefully removed in a laboratory setting as opposed to natural decay after burial. Medical "specimens" are examples of such a specially prepared collection of modern bone. Archaeological osteological collections may be categorized as either fossilized or subfossilized depending on the time in the ground and environmental conditions.

In true fossils, the organic component has been completely replaced with apatite (a group of three minerals that have a predominance of fluoride, chloride, or hydroxyl groups) or calcite (calcium carbonate). The voids of trabecular bone are also filled with mineralized substances that especially add weight and solidity. According to Andrew (1996), true fossilized bone or fully mineralized bone breaks smoothly, as opposed to breaks in modern bone, which leave a fibrous surface. In contrast, subfossilized bone has lost some or its entire proteinaceous or organic component, but this loss has not been replaced by mineralization originating from the environment or burial conditions. Subfossilized bone breaks without leaving a fibrous surface, but it is not mineralized to the extent that fossil bone is. It is closer in appearance to recent bone and is associated with the Pleistocene (roughly 1.8 million to 10,000 years ago) and more recent epochs.

But time is not the most important ingredient; environment plays the most vital role in the degree of mineral replacement and loss of collagenous material. Leeching away or loss of the organic component of bone generally results in a general loss of elasticity and strength. This means that contact with acidic or alkaline substances (solids, liquids, or gases) are damaging to modern bone and can cause even more damage to subfossilized bone (Andrew 1996; O'Connor 1987; Shelton and Johnson 1995:60).

DETERIORATION PROCESSES

Despite the claim that bone is a relatively resistant material, institutionalized osteological collections are subject to many forms of deterioration. Though studies of institutional deterioration on collections of human remains are rare, they indicate that bone cannot be regarded as a stable material that can hold its own (Buikstra and Ubelaker 1994:95–106; Caffell et al. 2001; Williams 1999). Caffell et al. (2001) report that common forms of damage include bone element losses, fractures, and surface erosion and that the cumulative amount of handling is the most important factor. Failed repairs are another major source of damage.

Deterioration can be broken into physical or mechanical, chemical, and biological processes. These processes usually do not act in isolation and may interact. Physical or mechanical deterioration processes include handling, erosion, and abrasion in poor, overcrowded storage conditions. It also is influenced by fluctuations in relative humidity and temperature. Organic materials especially change in size and shape through absorption and evaporation, which leads to cracking, splitting, and warping.

Chemical deterioration includes reactions with pollutants or other contaminants that result in fading, bleaching, discoloration, salt migration, and other interactions with applied or associated substances. Increases in either temperature or relative humidity may speed up the reaction. Water is a powerful reagent, and sudden increases in relative humidity can provide enough moisture for reactions to take place.

Biological deterioration is damage caused by living organisms such as insects, bacteria, and mold. Relative humidity and temperature levels determine whether these organisms have a favorable environment for survival.

The deterioration processes are most dramatic during excavation. Table 4.1 illustrates that many forms of deterioration continue even after institutionalization. The causes and types of damage may change between burial, excavation, and museum but decay continues, and as responsible stewards, we must take responsibility for monitoring and improving conditions for institutionalized human remains (Andrew 1996; Shelton and Johnson 1995; Storch 1983). Stewardship is not a onetime event but is the ongoing careful and responsible management of something important.

Table 4.1. Deterioration Processes Divided by Class and Occurrence

	Prior to Institutionalization	*Institutionalization*
Physical (mechanical stress)		
Abrasion	x	x
Cracking	x	x
Breakage	x	x
Trampling	x	
Chewing/gnawing	x	x
Roots	x	
Rapid drying	x	x
Losses	x	x
Chemical		
Extremes and recurrent fluctuations in temperature and relative humidity (e.g., freeze/thaw or RH)	x	x
Ion exchange	x	
Mineral replacement	x	
Salt migration/crystallization	x	x
Alkalinity	x	x
Acidity	x	x
Biological		
Algal growth	x	x
Fungi or mold growth	x	x
Bacteria	x	x
Protozoan	x	x
Insect attack	x	x

Most of the bone in institutional collections is considered to be subfossilized—in other words, bones that have undergone some mineral exchange with their burial environments and have lost some of their collagen content. The following descriptions illustrate the types of stresses that can cause damage on bone in institutional collections. The value of documenting these changes helps clarify the origin and nature of various forms of stress. For example, if there are splits, cracks, warps, discolorations, missing parts, particulates, or stains present, then conditions listed under one or more of the following forms of stress are probably responsible.

Physical (mechanical stress and some visual changes)

- Abrasion from other bones
- Losses that would include misplacing bone elements or mixing up unlabeled bone elements or dropping small bone fragments on the floor that are eventually swept away, for example
- Structural modifications such as cracks, breaks, chips, and losses from handling, impact of bone against bone, or tools against bone
- Stresses from sloppy application or poorly aging adhesives, consolidants, or coatings
- Disfigurements and attacks from insects or rodents
- Warping and cracking due to rapid drying after the presence of water, for example, from aqueous cleaning treatments, housekeeping, or disasters
- Cracking caused by fluctuating relative humidity (teeth are particularly susceptible)

Chemical

- Loss of structural integrity due to repeated expansion and contraction of the bone caused by extremes and recurrent fluctuations in temperature and relative humidity, particularly in basements and attics or sheds without climate control

- Spalling and crumbling brought on by salt migration/crystallization when hygroscopic salts, absorbed by the bone during burial, subsequently migrate due to high humidity and then recrystallize at or near the surface due to a drop in humidity
- Stains from hand oils, packaging, storage materials, or rubber bands
- Residue stains and surface modifications from insects or rodents
- Changes in natural coloring or texture due to high UV light exposures (sunlight, fluorescent tubes)
- Chemical changes due to an alkaline exposure from certain cleaning agents or highly buffered storage products
- Chemical changes due to an acidic exposure from certain cleaning agents, non-acid-free storage materials, or adhesive polymers such as most poly(vinyl acetate) emulsions

Biological

- Algal growth in collections from wet site burials, which causes stains
- Fungi or mold growth that occurs in darkness when relative humidity is high or above 65 percent relative humidity. Mold may induce pathological reactions in humans; it stains and draws insects
- Insect attack, which is most likely if protein or starch sources are available, such as soft tissue, hair, and nails, or if box containers and labels are associated; some insects may consume, while others may just leave acidic defecation specks

CONDITION ASSESSMENTS

For many years, museums have carried out assessments to track the condition of artifacts, but it does not appear to be standard practice for human osteological collections. Curators, researchers, analysts, descendants, and others care about condition as a means to distinguish between pre- and postcollection condition. If damage is postcollection, then changes in handling, examination, or storage may be necessary to approach a solution to the problem. The advantages of tracking condition include the ability to evaluate and promote good handling practices throughout the activities of research, transport, and storage (and display if this is an issue). Without a baseline condition assessment, there is no way to track changes or to know whether damage has occurred.

At this point, the reader may be thinking, "You do not expect me to photograph and describe every bone in the collection, do you?" No, this is not necessary unless there is an extreme problem or a special case. We understand the practical constraints of curating large collections, but we should no longer continue to ignore the consequences of complacency, either. Anyone who has gone back to study or look at older institutionalized osteological collections can tell you that losses and major deterioration are common. To rely on institutional (staff) memory for assessments, or accept laissez-faire care, waiting to react only after disastrous losses have occurred, should no longer suffice as the chief method for curation of human remains collections.

Baseline condition assessments provide a way of distinguishing and recording changes that happen through collection and curation processes as opposed to what happened to the individual prior to collection. Condition assessments are an ongoing responsibility and are useful as a comparative tool. The existence of regular condition assessments tends to promote awareness that the institution is watching the effect of all who come in contact with the collections. This is a critical step in responsible stewardship.

Vocabulary/Terminology

For condition reports to be useful documents, it helps to have a standardized group of terms and generally agreed-on definitions. In our experience, a few terms do cause trouble, because of their

ACCESS AND DOCUMENTATION OF COLLECTIONS IN
LAW ENFORCEMENT AGENCIES: A CASE STUDY

Law enforcement agencies often hold extensive human remains collections in areas referred to as evidence storage lockers, bunkers, or facilities. The need for inventory, policy, and record keeping regarding the access to, use, and condition of these collections is just as important as it is for museums and collections in academic institutions. Loss or damage to human remains collections that are held as evidence can alter the course of a case.

One example of inadequate record keeping within this context occurred in the Kennewick Man case. Since 1996, the remains known as the Kennewick Man have been housed in four different locations (not including the original discovery site).

- First, after the initial deposit of bone fragments and several episodes of additional bone recovery from the site, a basic inventory/study of the remains was conducted at the home of James Chatters. Field notes by Chatters, archived with the Kennewick Collection, curated by the U.S. Army Corps of Engineers, indicated recovery dates and a partial list of major bones.
- Second, after sheriff's officers took possession of the remains at the Chatters home, Chatters and Benton County coroner Floyd Johnson later reported to the *Tri-City Herald* newspaper "all the bones were delivered in a wood box." However, while access to this box was documented, no records indicate that an inventory of each bag inside was made at either end of this transfer.
- Third, after the Corps of Engineers was determined to be the responsible government agency, the remains were transferred to a secure location in the Pacific Northwest National Laboratory in Richland, Washington. A formal inventory was later conducted, and two bone fragments were considered missing. Despite numerous accusations, with tight security and after scrutiny of the collection access log, no indications of theft were evident during housing at this facility.
- Fourth, after determining that a more federally acceptable curation facility was necessary for this collection, the remains were transferred to the Burke Museum at the University of Washington for housing under a curation agreement. An additional inventory and formal rehousing were completed at both ends of this transfer, and it was confirmed that two fragments were missing. The Federal Bureau of Investigation (FBI) was called in to investigate the loss. Formal policies regarding access in addition to detailed inventories and condition assessments have been standard operating procedure during curation at the Burke Museum, and each bone fragment is regularly accounted for.

A lack of record keeping on the part of the law enforcement agency involved made this FBI investigation difficult, and no developments in the case occurred until three years later in 2001 when a reused cardboard packing box containing the missing Kennewick bones was found in an evidence locker in the Benton County Sheriff's Office (see figure 4.2). Apparently the building was undergoing a cleanup in preparation for demolition. The exterior of the box was marked "Columbia Pk II" and addressed to James Chatters from the Vermont Country Store. FBI agents never pursued how or when this box was delivered to the Sheriff's Office. New sheriff Larry Taylor suggested that an older policy that did not mandate that evidence held by the coroner be tagged with a sheriff's department case number might have led to this mix-up. Since this incident, the department has instigated a recording policy of all evidence housed at the facility, and it now carries out a yearly inventory of all holdings, including the coroner's evidence.

(*continued*)

Figure 4.2.   Box in which Kennewick Man's "missing" femur fragments were found. Photo courtesy of U.S. Army Corps of Engineers.

The moral: It is not worth waiting for disaster to strike before initiating record keeping and inventories, in general, and condition assessments, in particular.

varied uses depending on the field of inquiry one comes from. The most notorious misunderstandings come from the following groups of words:

- *Fracture, break, split,* and *crack.* Breaks are all the way through; however, cracks are not all the way through. A split might be used for a crack that does go all the way through at points. For condition assessments, *break* is a more appropriate term since *fracture* often involves degrees of breaks and cracks in living bone.
- *Consolidant, hardener,* and *preservative.* Though these three terms share some similarities (use of an adhesive-type material), they are significantly distinct to merit proper usage. A *consolidant* is applied so that it penetrates and completely binds material; therefore it is *not* a surface coating. A *hardener* is an adhesive or varnish material that is applied as a surface coating. A *preservative* is an additive applied to protect bone from decay, discoloration, or spoilage. Many widely varied products have been used though few actually accomplish their goal. A preservative is usually an ideal rather than a reality since there is no magic spray or coating that does not, in the long run, negatively influence bone preservation. Therefore, merely saying a bone preservative was added is not useful; instead, it is highly recommended that the specific products used are carefully noted with application details and a date. The terms *consolidant, hardener/coating, adhesive,* and *fungicide* are preferred to the term *preservative.*
- *Reconstruction, reassembly, restoration, conservation, bonding,* and *repair.* A process where two broken pieces are reunited is sometimes referred to as *reconstruction* (to construct again), *reassembly* (to assemble again), *restoration* (to bring back to original condition), *mending* (to make repairs), *bonding* (to fasten together), or *repairing* (to fix or mend something damaged). These activities should be distinguished from *conservation,* which includes a range of activities that prevent damage, analyze materials or decay, stabilize fragile materials, compensate for losses, or may even include some degree of restoration. In general, for human bone, it is recommended that reconstruction or reassembly be accomplished with reversible materials.
- *Soiled, dirty, dusty, grimy, smirched,* and *sullied.* These six terms are quite similar; however, *soiled* and *dusty* are the most appropriate for condition assessments for bone.

Suggestions for Efficient Condition Assessments of Dry Osteological Remains
The first order of business is a baseline condition assessment, which is considered routine for most other types of museum collections. A baseline condition assessment allows for evaluation

CONDITION GLOSSARY

Abrasion—mechanical wearing away of the surface caused by scraping, rubbing, grinding, or friction or loss of external surface.

Accretion—the process of growth or enlargement by a gradual buildup; an increase by external addition or accumulation (as by adhesion of external parts or particles). Accretions are not always hard like an incrustation or encrustation.

Articulated—skeletal structure that remains attached at joints or united by means of a joint as in forming or fitting into a systematic whole.

Attachments—extraneous (postcollection) connections of one thing to another, as in an object with tape, rubber bands, ties, metal screws, or sticky notes, for instance.

Break—fracture or split resulting in the separation of parts or pieces. Breaks can be described as spiral, perpendicular, parallel, or diagonal in nature.

Brittle—easily broken, cracked, or snapped. For instance, replacement of calcium phosphate with calcium carbonate in sandy or gravely lime soils leads to light, smooth, chalky and brittle bones.

Chalky—a soft white, gray, or buff powdery texture; chalklike. For instance, the chalky bone surface is soft and easily damaged by scratching or rubbing.

Charred—burned or carbonized; converted to charcoal or carbon usually by heat (as opposed to burning slightly or partly, which is to scorch).

Check—partial split, or a crack usually along and across the grain. Often results in square patterns or tiny cracks. Sometimes it is referred to as an *alligatored* surface. Common especially to burned bone. It is likely a combination of a sudden stoppage of a forward course of a crack and a pattern in squares that resembles a checkerboard.

Chip—a small, usually thin and flat piece cut, struck, or flaked off, leaving a defect in the surface, caused by material that has broken away. Chips are common in tooth enamel.

Coating—covering or spreading the surface with a finishing, protecting, or enclosing layer that is not a natural element of the specimen.

Comminution—reducing to minute particles or pulverize; the fracturing of a bone into many pieces.

Conservation—the profession devoted to the preservation of cultural property for the future. Conservation activities include examination, analysis, documentation, treatment, and preventive care, supported by research and education.

Consolidant—a liquid solution of a resin (normally a synthetic polymer) used to impregnate a fragile object in order to strengthen its structure.

Crack—a *hairline* crack is a tiny fissure; an *open* crack is a larger fissure. Cracking can be directional in nature, and the following terms have been used to describe crack patterns: longitudinal, perpendicular or transverse, parabolic, radial, circumferential, sawtooth (jagged or splintered), depressed, irregular, smooth, stepped (columnar or checked patterns), spiral (radial, oblique, curvilinear), and V shaped.

Crossmended—though this term has been used in the archaeological literature and refers to the part of an object where two or more fragments have been joined back together or to a whole object thus mended, it is a confusing term and should be avoided. *Repaired* would be a better substitute.

Crumbly—to fall into small pieces, disintegrate, or crumble; easily crumbled.

Crush—to squeeze or force by pressure so as to alter or destroy structure. To misshape by pressure, having been squeezed out of shape. With bone this may result in comminution.

Crystalline deposit—compound or residue that is made up of crystals or has crystallized and is deposited on or in the object.

(continued)

CONDITION GLOSSARY (*continued*)

Cut marks—depressions left in a surface from a sharp-edged object or instrument.

Delamination—separation or splitting of layers; common to composite objects such as teeth and bone with layers of varying amounts of organic and inorganic components, or to objects with surface coatings.

Deposits—any sediments that are laid down or placed (e.g., pigments, calcium carbonates or caliche, metal corrosion, insect specks, and salts on the bone surface or in voids).

Desiccated—completely dried up.

Dirt—general term denoting any material that soils, sullies, or smirches; a filthy or soiling substance (as mud, dust, or grime).

Disarticulated—disjointed; skeletal structure that is separated at the joints.

Discoloration—a change of hue or color often unevenly distributed.

Distortion—warping or deformation of the original shape.

Dust—fine particles of matter (as of earth) or loose fine dirt generally distributed on surfaces; it can also be the particles into which something like bone disintegrates.

Efflorescence—the formation or existence of a powdery or crystalline crust on a surface. The change into a powder from loss of water or crystallization leaving a deposit, such as a salt on the artifact. Efflorescence is common to subfossilized bone in the presence of acid vapors in poor storage. It is often a reaction between calcium and the acid.

Embrittlement—decline in the pliability and suppleness of a material to the degree that damage may result in cracks or breaks. An artifact may be crumbling or fragile to the point of easily snapping or breaking.

Encrustation or incrustation—a crust or hard coating that is often thick.

Eroded—surface wear due to chemical or mechanical processes, such as to eat into or away by slow destruction of substance (as by acid, infection, or cancer); to wear away by the action of water, wind, or glacial ice; or to cause to deteriorate or disappear as if by eating or wearing away.

Erosion—an action or process of wearing away, a state of being eroded, or an instance or product of erosive action. *Acid erosion*, for example, is the slow process of destruction of the surface of bone by acid.

Exfoliation—the process of coming off in thin layers, laminae, splinters, or scales. To remove the surface of, in scales or laminae; to split into or give off scales, laminae, or body cells.

Exudation—the process of oozing out; to cause to ooze or spread out in all directions.

Fading—losing brilliance of color or freshness.

Fixative—something that fixes or sets, like a varnish used especially for the protection of surfaces such as loose pigments on a charcoal drawing.

Fluid preservative—liquid (e.g., alcohol, formalin) used as a storage medium for fixed (prepared) or unfixed biological material.

Flake—a thin flattened piece or layer. Often oblong or rectangular in shape and very thin. Common to artifacts with thin surface layers or coatings.

Flaking—lifting and sometimes loss of flat areas of a surface layer. To form or break into flakes or chips. Surface exfoliation or delamination of cortical surface.

Fossilized—condition of an object wherein minerals have replaced the original material of the object, thereby making it a fossil; gradual or partial replacement with inorganic materials.

Fragment completeness—This condition is often given as a percentage of the remaining (e.g., 50 percent of the remaining ulna).

Freeze-drying—a method of freezing a specimen in a partial or high vacuum to remove moisture by sublimation (direct change from ice to water vapor, without melting); also called *lyophilization*.

CONDITION GLOSSARY (*continued*)

Gouge—groove or cavity; a defect in the surface where material has been scooped out.

Grime—soot, smut, or dirt adhering to or embedded in a surface; soil tenaciously held on surfaces (e.g., a smear or a fingerprint are types of local grime).

Grooves—long narrow channels or depressions (e.g., associated with cut marks).

Hardness—the cohesion of the particles on the surface of a mineral as determined by its capacity to scratch another or be itself scratched. The Mohs Hardness Scale, starting with talc at 1 and ending with diamond at 10, is universally used as a way of distinguishing minerals. Apatite ranks 5 on the scale.

Hole—an area of missing material; a void, an opening, a hollow in or through the artifact. An opening through something, often spherical in shape. A perforation or where something is missing, a gap.

Incrustation or encrustation—a crust or hard coating that is often thick.

Infill—material used to replace areas of loss; also called *fill*.

Loss—general term for missing areas; a decrease in amount, magnitude, or degree.

Matrix—the rock or main substance (e.g., soil, sand, or rock) in which something (as a bone, fossil, or crystal) is embedded or material in which something is enclosed or embedded (as for protection or study).

Mold or mildew—a superficial, usually whitish growth produced especially on organic matter or living plants by fungi (as of the families Erysiphaceae and Peronosporaceae). Colored, furry, or weblike surface accretions, sometimes having a musty odor. Especially problematic with waterlogged remains that have not been treated.

Nick—a small notch or groove; a small area in size and depth where material has been scooped out.

Patina—colored, chemically altered surface layer (e.g., corrosion, oxidation, discoloration) caused by chemical reactions between the artifact's surface and the burial environment.

Perforation—a hole or pattern made by or as if by piercing or boring (see *puncture*).

Pest damage—surface loss, tunneling, holes, deposits, fly specks, and frass (coarse particulates or powder made up of insect excrement and food remains that often looks like sawdust) caused by insects or other pests.

Pitting—small irregular, shallow, pinhole-sized, minute depressions on a surface and caused by a chemical reaction such as acid erosion, exfoliation, or spalling.

Pliable—supple enough to bend freely or repeatedly without breaking.

Polish—to make smooth and glossy usually by friction; to burnish.

Polymer application—a category including adhesives, consolidants, and coatings.

Powdery—matter in a finely divided state; fine, particulate matter. This quality is similar to chalky, but without the color restrictions.

Preparation—procedures used in the field or in the institution to process or enhance the utility of an organism, object, or individual for a specified use. The resulting specimen may represent only a portion of the original organism and is altered from its original state. Procedures should be compatible with intended uses and conservation objectives, and they should be documented.

Preparation type—the style of processing and resulting museum specimen (e.g., study skin, fluid-preserved specimen, freeze-dried specimen).

Preparator—an individual who prepares the collection or specimen, by processing it to get it ready for study, display, or documentation; a person who prepares scientific specimens or museum displays.

(*continued*)

CONDITION GLOSSARY (*continued*)

Preservative—a chemical (usually a polymer) added to materials with the hope that it will prolong the life of a collection item.

Puncture—to pierce with a pointed instrument or object (see *perforation*).

Reassemble—to fit together again the parts of an object.

Reconstruct—to construct, establish, or assemble again. *Reconstructed* is a term for an object that has been rebuilt. Reconstructed objects are not restored to their original appearance (using fills, paint or other new materials).

Repair—to put together what is torn or broken; to fix.

Residue—something that remains after a part is taken or separated from the main (e.g., adhesive residue on the edges of a repaired break after failure of the adhesive, or the adhesive that remains on the bone after the tape has fallen off). Residues may come from use and handling, burial environment or treatment.

Restoration—treatment procedures intended to return cultural property to a known or assumed state, often through the addition of nonoriginal material; for instance, missing areas have been filled or replaced with modern replications.

Salts—any of numerous compounds that result from replacement of part or all of the acid hydrogen of an acid by a metal or a group acting like a metal. They often appear as tiny crystals or powdery deposits and may sparkle under bright light or magnification. Common to porous materials.

Sample—a portion of the whole. Depending on the method of selection, the portion may or may not be considered representative of the whole.

Sampling—selecting a portion as a representative of the whole. *Sampling* refers more specifically to the process of removing a portion of a specimen or artifact for analysis. The analysis may be destructive to the sample. It may also be used as in testing.

Scour—to rub hard, especially with a rough material for cleaning.

Scratch—a linear surface loss due to abrasion with a sharp pointed instrument or object; to mark the surface of with something sharp or jagged.

Scuff—to become scratched, chipped; to gouge or wear away the surface of something.

Shred—a long narrow strip cut or torn off.

Shrinkage—distortion that causes a material to become compacted or smaller.

Site number—a unique number identifying the collection site; also may be called *locality* or *provenience number*.

Skin tag—for mammal collections, this is the label made from permanent material and marked with a unique number that is attached to a specimen to ensure continuity of data for the individual specimen. Generally marked with data unique to the specimen, such as collection date, location, and measurements.

Skull tag—label usually for mammal collections, made from permanent material and marked with a unique number that is attached to a skull and/or skeleton to ensure continuity of data for the individual. The number usually is the preparator's number and is cross-referenced in the field catalog.

Soil—to make unclean, especially superficially, dirty (embedded or surface soils); the upper layer or the material on the surface of the ground; earth.

Spalling—often spherical or conical losses of material from a surface due to pressure from salts crystallizing just beneath the surface; to exfoliate or cast off.

Spatter—the result of dried droplets or splashes of foreign liquid material.

Specimen—an individual, item, or part considered typical of a group, class, or whole organism, part of an organism, or a naturally occurring material that has been collected and that may or may not have undergone some preparation treatment. It may exist in its original

CONDITION GLOSSARY (*continued*)

state, in an altered form, or in some combination. A specimen may be composed of one piece or many related pieces. It may be composed of one physical or chemical component or represent a composite of materials.

Splintered—broken or split into thin sharp pieces.

Split—to divide lengthwise usually along a grain or seam or by layers; a rupture running along the grain.

Stabilization—treatment procedures intended to maintain the integrity of cultural property and to minimize deterioration.

Stain (staining)—color change as a result of soiling, adhesives, pest residue, food, oils, and so forth; to discolor.

Stiffness—loss of flexibility and suppleness of fibers, offering resistance to bending; rigidness.

Systematics—the science of classification. Systematics collections are of scientific specimens, collected over a range of locations and time, that can be used to document variation in organisms.

Tear—a break resulting from tension or torsion; to separate parts of or pull apart by force; to rend.

Texture—the visual or tactile surface characteristics and appearance of something (e.g., rough, greasy, dry, brittle, crumbly, or fibrous).

Use wear—polish, striations, battering, breakage, or minor flaking that develops on a tool's edge due to use.

Warping—structural distortion, in which a material is turned, twisted, or bent out of shape.

Wear—surface abrasion or erosion due to repeated handling or friction against another surface; to cause to deteriorate by use; to impair or diminish by use or attrition.

Weathering rind—outer layer of an object produced by chemical reactions between the object's material and certain compounds in the burial environment (common to stone).

Terms and definitions have been gleaned from a variety of sources, but predominantly the following sources were used: LeCompte (1998:15–19), Cato (1998:75–77, 81–83), Buikstra and Ubelaker (1994), Pearson (1987), the American Institute for Conservation website (http://aic.stanford.edu/about/coredocs/defin.html, accessed April 14, 2006), and the online *Merriam-Webster Dictionary*.

of the current state of preservation of a collection by comparison and enables a level of accountability in the event of significant structural or visual change. It takes the guesswork and reliance on institutional memory out of the equation. When condition is tracked, and if negative changes in condition are observed, there is the potential to evaluate the causes of the conditional changes and rectify or slow deterioration. The end goal aids preservation, by helping us evaluate and make collections safer.

It is important not to confuse condition assessments with cataloging or study. Condition assessments serve several purposes, according to Demeroukas (1998:1), including the following:

- To establish the condition of an object at a point in time
- To make future stakeholders aware of potential problems
- To benchmark the type and rate of conditional changes
- To document condition history, providing past evidence for future problems
- To help set priorities for future care and treatment

Some may argue that such an assessment would lead to restricted access. Information about condition should not be used to restrict access but to help guide and improve on current

COMMON VOCABULARY FOR ADDRESSING BODY POSITION OR ORIENTATION

Standard anatomical position—A body should be described as if it is positioned standing with feet forward and hands at the sides with palms forward (Bass 1995:1–4, 321; see also figure 4.3).

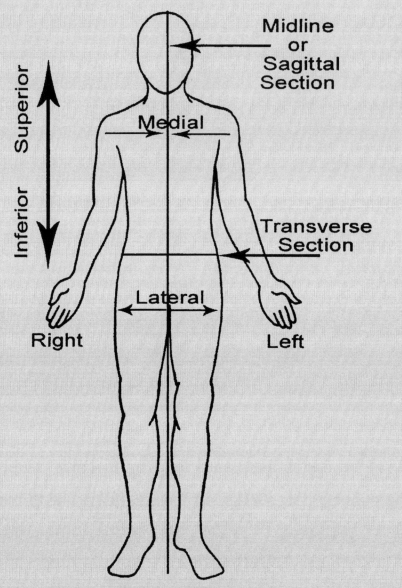

Figure 4.3.   Vocabulary for body position identification.
Illustration by Jennifer Allen and Rodrigo Arriaza.

Axial skeleton—forming the central axis of the body, consists of the skull, the vertebral column, the ribs, and the sternum.

Appendicular skeleton—consists of the upper (anterior) limbs, the pectoral (shoulder) girdle, the lower (posterior) limbs, and the pelvic (hip) girdle.

COMMON VOCABULARY FOR ADDRESSING BODY POSITION OR ORIENTATION (*continued*)

For the axial bones plus pectoral and pelvic girdles:

Superior—upper, situated higher up; cranial end of body
Inferior—lower, situated lower down in the body
Lateral—side, of or relating to the side of the body; away from the midline or sagittal section
Medial—middle, being or occurring in the middle; toward the midline or sagittal section
Anterior—situated before or toward the front (or ventral)
Posterior—situated behind (or dorsal)

For appendicular skeleton or limbs:

Proximal—end of the bone closest to the axial skeleton, located toward the body axis
Distal—end of the bone farther from the axial skeleton, away from the axis of the body

For teeth:

Mesial—surface of a tooth that is closest to the middle of the front of the jaw or where the central incisors are in contact
Distal—surface of a tooth that is farthest from the middle of the front of the jaw or where the central incisors are in contact
Lingual—toward the tongue
Labial—toward the cheek (or buccal)
Occlusal—biting surfaces

practices to make collection access safer. With a baseline assessment in hand, people can periodically assess the collection for changes, taking into account all the handling activities over time since the last assessment. Baseline assessments together with periodic inspections can also serve as verification of inventory.

A baseline condition assessment usually includes photographic and written documentation covering the issues of concern. These can be in the form of a formal written report, sketches with notes, and photocopies of photos with notes and arrows noting areas of concern. It is vital that the notes and language used are specific enough to be clearly interpreted by someone else in the future.

Condition photography must include catalog numbers, scale, and date of the picture within the image. See the section on photography for additional suggestions.

For the written section of the assessment, it is not necessary or prudent to have a form for every individual bone; instead, bones can be grouped by like conditions or similar bone elements. If possible, distinctions should be made between deterioration that occurred prior to becoming a collection (in burial or at excavation) and since becoming institutionalized. For instance, rodent gnaw marks might be assumed to have taken place prior to excavation or recovery, but it should not be automatically assumed that these occurred prior to collecting. Evidence of burial soils or a darkened surface in the gnawed areas would indicate an older condition, whereas clean or light surfaces of gnawing would indicate fresh, even possibly more recent, damage that needs further institutional investigation.

Cleaning is not encouraged as part of the assessment, since no matter how benign the treatment seems, it may damage the bone, the context, or the research potential. However, if cleaning has been performed, it is important to note on the condition report the date of cleaning;

what techniques, materials, or methods were used; who did the cleaning; and what was removed. Instead of cleaning, attached soils should generally be treated as part of the collection—soils are evidence of a different but important context, that of the burial. Soils can be broadly identified as hard and compact (calcium carbonate or caliches), loose and falling (soft clays), or something in between.

When doing a condition assessment, it is useful to set up a standard procedure for observations, for instance, beginning with the top of the body and working down, or describing the potential problem areas first and then noting changes since past assessments (if there are any). Try to be consistent with terms (see the glossary and figure 4.3). When locating damage, use terminology such as *lateral, medial, proximal, distal, anterior,* and *posterior* to avoid confusion. It is convention to refer to the anatomical right, which is the proper right, or the individual's right side, versus the viewer's right, which would be the individual's anatomical left side.

A baseline condition assessment should identify not only past damage but potential problems. This would include cracking, lifting bone, areas of past losses, exposed trabecular bone, delaminating bone, and general weaknesses. Past treatments should also be noted in terms of location and impact, such as

- reconstructions
- adhesives
- consolidants or a "preservative"
- plaster or alginate residues
- plasticine
- wax
- ink
- gum erasers
- rubber bands
- tape

A UV light source might help in distinguishing adhesive residues by their fluorescence. For example, cellulose nitrate (used as a consolidant or adhesive) has a characteristic yellowish green fluorescence, shellac fluoresces orange, while the all-too-often used household white glue fluoresces purple in UV light. In this category of past treatments, cleaning techniques such as scrubbing with a brush, acid washes, or even dry removal of dirt, which often strips the top layer of bone off along with the unwanted dirt clod, should be noted. It must be remembered that recording this is for the purpose of establishing a baseline that helps us understand the present as well as predict future conditions that will ensure preservation.

LeCompte (1998:15) suggests that a written condition assessment include the following categories, which we have adapted for osteological human remains:

Accession and catalog data plus (age, sex, and anomalies)
- Object description—for instance, number of bones present, number of fragments, weight
- Condition/damage/problems including overall condition, surface condition, accretions, areas of weakness or instability, location of losses or damage, and areas that seem vulnerable to future damage
- Previous treatments and evidence of reconstructions including surface coatings, adhesives, labels, use of metal instrumentation, tape, rubber bands, and so forth
- Description of any analyses, date materials, exposures, sampling size, and area (e.g., radiography kV and time)

- Details of the current examination, including whether any special lighting was used during the study for Munsell readings, microscopic magnification, or special photographic techniques
- Details of other documentation such as sketches, tracings, and specialized measuring equipment
- Other suggestions such as needs for upgraded housings or improved handling
- Date of the assessment and name of assessor

Another strategy suggested by LeCompte (1998:13) is to weigh bones to help track changes or losses. Sometimes a measure of the debris remaining in the storage wrapper or box is an excellent way to monitor for losses, especially for collections that are frequently handled.

CONCLUSION

We concentrated our discussion of condition and condition assessment on processes related to postinstitutional status of collections. The majority of human remains in institutional collections has come from burial contexts and has sustained a level of deterioration before entering. Condition assessments are a way of distinguishing changes that happen through collection or curation versus what happened to the individual prior to collection. They should focus on the prevention of further deterioration—that is, improving handling, study, storage, or display. Just as documentation forms and associated records now include more information about who the individuals are and their provenance, the condition report can provide important information about how they are.

Taphonomy is a study that relates to what happened to the individual since death, in the burial and excavation environment. Baseline and subsequent condition assessments take over where taphonomic studies end. Collections need to be reevaluated with time and new events and as new studies or other handling episodes take place. Tracking how things hold up is important. Condition documentation is not undertaken to restrict access, but to identify and respond to the fact that information and the physical state of bone are altered by examination and analysis.

REFERENCES

American Academy of Forensic Sciences
 2004 American Academy of Forensic Science Bylaws. Electronic document, http://www.aafs.org/default.asp?section_id=aafs&page_id=aafs_bylaws#article2, accessed February 7, 2005.

Andrew, Kate J.
 1996 A Summary of the Care and Preventative Conservation of Sub-fossil Bone for the Non-Specialist. *The Biology Curator* 5:24–28.

Bass, William M.
 1995 *Human Osteology: A Laboratory and Field Manual.* 4th ed. Special Publication #2 of the Missouri Archaeological Society, Columbia, Missouri.

Buikstra, Jane, and Douglas Ubelaker, editors
 1994 *Standards for Data Collection from Human Skeletal Remains: Proceedings for a Seminar at the Field Museum of Natural History.* Organized by Jonathan Haas. Arkansas Archeological Survey Research Seminar Series 44. Arkansas Archeological Survey, Fayetteville.

Caffell, Anwen, Charlotte Roberts, Robert Janaway, and Andrew Wilson
 2001 Pressures on Osteological Collections—The Importance of Damage Limitation. In *Human Remains: Conservation, Retrieval and Analysis: Proceedings of a Conference Held in Williamsburg, VA, Nov 7–11th 1999*, edited by E. Williams, pp. 187–197. BAR International Series 934. Archaeopress, Oxford.

Carter, Julian
    1999 Notes of a Talk Given to the Biological Curators Group Meeting at the Natural History Museum in London, March 1999. *The Biology Curator* 16:3–8.

Cato, Paisley S.
    1998 Natural History Specimens. In *Basic Condition Reporting: A Handbook*. 3rd ed., edited by Marie Demeroukas, pp. 73–87. Southeastern Registrars Association, Bartow, Florida.

Curry, John D.
    2002 *Bones: Structure and Mechanics*. Princeton University Press, Princeton, New Jersey.

Demeroukas, Marie
    1998 General Condition Reporting. In *Basic Condition Reporting: A Handbook*. 3rd ed., edited by Marie Demeroukas, pp. 1–8. Southeastern Registrars Association, Bartow, Florida.

Eriksen, Erik Fink, Douglas Axelrod, and Flemming Melsen
    1994 *Bone Histomorphometry*. An official publication of the American Society for Bone and Mineral Research. Raven Press, New York.

Hare, P. Edward
    1980 Organic Geochemistry of Bone and Its Relation to the Survival of Bone in the Natural Environment. In *Fossils in the Making: Vertebrate Taphonomy and Paleoecology*, edited by A. K. Behrensmeye and A. P. Hill, pp. 208–219. University of Chicago Press, Chicago.

Hillson, Simon
    1996 *Dental Anthropology*. Cambridge University Press, Cambridge.

Janaway, Robert, Andrew Wilson, Anwen Caffell, and Charlotte Roberts
    2001 Human Skeletal Collections: The Responsibilities of Product Managers, Physical Anthropologists, Conservators and the Need for Standardized Condition Assessments. In *Human Remains: Conservation, Retrieval and Analysis: Proceedings of a Conference Held in Williamsburg, VA, Nov 7–11th 1999*, edited by Emily Williams, pp. 199–208. BAR International Series 934. Archaeopress, Oxford.

Larsen, Clark Spencer
    1997 *Bioarchaeology: Interpreting Behavior from the Human Skeleton*. Cambridge University Press, Cambridge.

LeCompte, Elise V.
    1998 Archaeological Artifacts. In *Basic Condition Reporting: A Handbook*. 3rd ed., edited by Marie Demeroukas, pp. 9–26. Southeastern Registrars Association, Bartow, Florida.

O'Connor, Terry P.
    1987 On the Structure, Chemistry and Decay of Bones, Antler and Ivory. In *Archaeological Bone, Antler and Ivory*, pp. 6–8. Institute for Conservation, London.

Pearson, Colin, editor
    1987 *Conservation of Marine Archaeological Objects*. Butterworths, London.

Rose, Carolyn L., and Catharine A. Hawks
    1995 A Preventive Conservation Approach to the Storage of Collections. In *Storage of Natural History Collections: A Preventive Conservation Approach*, edited by C. L. Rose, C. A. Hawks, and H. H. Genoways, pp. 1–20. Society for the Preservation of Natural History Collections, New Haven, Connecticut.

Shelton, Sally, and Jessica Johnson
    1995 The Conservation of Sub-fossil Bone. In *The Care and Conservation of Palaeontological Material*, edited by Chris Collins, pp. 59–71. Butterworths, London.

Storch, Paul
 1983 Field and Laboratory Methods for Handling Osseous Materials. *Conservation Notes* 6:1–4.

Sullivan, M. Brigid, and Karl Schram
 1987 Investigation of Exudate Formation of Prehistoric Human Mummified Remains from the American Southwest. *Jubilee Conservation Conference*, pp. 267–272. University of London, Institute of Archeology, London.

Ubelaker, Douglas
 1978 *Human Skeletal Remains: Excavation, Analysis, Interpretation.* Aldine, Chicago.

White, Tim
 1991 *Human Osteology.* Academic Press, New York.

Williams, Stephen
 1991 Investigations of the Causes of Structural Damage to Teeth in Museum Collections. *Collection Forum* 7(1):13–25.
 1992 Methods of Processing Osteological Material for Research Value and Long Term Stability. *Collection Forum* 8(1):15–21.
 1999 Destructive Preservation: A Review of the Effect of Standard Preservation Practices on the Future Use of Natural History Collections. Göteborg Studies in Conservation 6. Dissertation, Acta Universitatis Gothoburgensis. Göteborg, Sweden.

CHAPTER 5

Examination and Analysis

Vicki Cassman and Nancy Odegaard

Humaneness is what it is to be human and its most obvious function is in love for relatives.
Justice means setting things right and its most obvious function is in venerating the good.
The differing levels in loving relatives and venerating the good are expressed through propriety.

—Confucius

PROPRIETY TOWARD THE DEAD

What do we mean by *propriety*? moreover, how does the concept of propriety (decorum, modesty, good manners, decency, correctness, and respectability) translate into curation of human remains in institutional settings? This is the general subject of this chapter. Human remains are entitled to a high level of dignity, and to begin with, curation must include a sense of reverence. Examinations take a variety of forms and are undertaken for a variety of purposes, such as for inventory, condition evaluations, or study and sampling. We begin the chapter with handling and end with analyses.

Handling

MENTAL AND PERSONAL PREPARATIONS. At minimum, human remains should be accorded gentle handling, and handlers must have an awareness of the potency of the remains, the privilege given to handlers, and their responsibilities. Human remains are not specimens; they were people—they are individuals. To begin with, handling should be undertaken only with a specific purpose. One should not browse as if in a library, picking up bones and articulating joints without purpose. Simply put, a mental state of propriety is required of handlers.

Inducing a mental state of propriety is achieved through decorum or having a respectful physical ambience, with guidelines communicated in both written and oral formats, and through example. Ideally, such personal preparations in terms of attitude and protections should be encouraged before entering the physical space where curation of human remains takes place. Perhaps those who are granted access to collections could be asked to sign a statement outlining their responsibilities and asked to re-sign it at regular intervals (annually) so people are reminded of their obligations.

Of course, access to collections should not be casually granted, even for osteology study collections. Anyone interested in examining human remains in museums or academic institutions should be made aware, before their visit, that examination will be entirely nondestructive in nature. In the case of the serious researcher (as opposed to a beginning osteology student), they should also be informed that a copy of the original data forms or notes is to be provided to the

institution to become part of the collection archives, and the institution has the obligation to
protect these for a reasonable period of time until after publication of the researcher's work. A
copy of the final publication, report, dissertation, or thesis should be provided by the researcher
to the institution as well. Likewise, a copy of photographs and radiographs taken at the researcher's expense should be included in the collection archive. Researchers planning on making casts and impressions should consult with appropriate institutional staff (curator,
conservator, and collection manager) beforehand to determine if the process is safe.

Once the researcher arrives, in addition to protecting the remains, it is also important to protect the handlers from undue risks too. Personal protections would include a lab coat or apron,
gloves, and a respirator for dust filtration (see chapter 14, "Working with the Dead: Health Concerns"). Protective clothing needs to be properly and separately laundered or disposed of to
avoid contaminating others.

PHYSICAL SPACE. So what constitutes respectful physical ambience? The meaning varies
from institution to institution depending on the resources available, but there are some gener-
alities. Human remains should be stored on their own or with the funerary objects with which
they were found. They should not be mixed in with other artifacts or in easily accessible or public areas. Instead, they should be stored in a room of their own devoted to their curation and
with limited and controlled access. During consultations, an independent room affords privacy
for the living and respect for the dead. A housekeeping regime should be in place so that authorized personnel attend when cleaning takes place to prevent losses, unauthorized touching,
or contamination. Windows should be blocked to prevent gawking and the entry of damaging
ultraviolet wavelengths from daylight, but the room should have adequate artificial lighting that
is filtered. Though storage is a major aspect of care and handling, it is also a topic in its own right
and will be handled in a separate chapter (see chapter 8).

On the interior, such a room should have a stable table that can serve as a work surface. The
table should be padded with appropriately inert materials (see table 5.1). This is to prevent damage due to rapping together two hard surfaces (i.e., bone on Formica).

If researchers will be studying or taking notes, they will need accommodations for pencil,
pen, or computer so they will not share the same table space with the human remains. This is to
prevent cross contamination, problems with cord entanglements, and leakage of inks. Adequate
space will need to be planned ahead of time. Other instruments, too, should be planned for
ahead of time and kept on a separate surface. These might include pointing tools such as a bamboo skewer, tweezers, measuring instruments, magnifiers, and so forth (table 5.2 describes some
basic tools).

There should be visual aids available such as stereo-zoom binoculars, an Optivisor (figure
5.1), or, at minimum, a magnifying light. In this way, remains do not need to be carried to another room or facility for more detailed examinations.

Table 5.1. Padding and Support Materials

Recommended	Not Recommended
Microfoam	Urethane foams
Ethafoam	Cotton fiber wad
Volara	Toilet paper
Tyvek	Paper towel
Teflon	Newsprint
Mylar (Melinex)	Floral shop foam
Parafilm	Rubber rings
Plexiglas (Perspex)	Rubber bands
Acid-free tissue/paper	Acetate sheet
Polyethylene	Tygon tubing
Polypropylene	Polyurethane foam
Aluminum foil	Polystyrene foam
Inert textiles	Textiles with dyes and finishes
	Polyester batting and filler
	Styrofoam sheets or peanuts
	Wood cork
	Bubblewrap
	Non-acid-free paper and cardboard

Table 5.2. Recommended Basic Tool Usage

Task	Recommended	Not Recommended	Reason
Pointing tool	Bamboo skewer	Metal dental tool or writing implement	Avoids scratching
Writing tool	Pencil	Pen	Prevents ink contamination
Brushing tool	Soft watercolor brush	Toothbrush	Prevents scratching and abrasion
Metal tools	Cover ends with plastic tubing, Parafilm, or Teflon plumbers' tape	Bare metal tools	Prevents scratching and abrasion

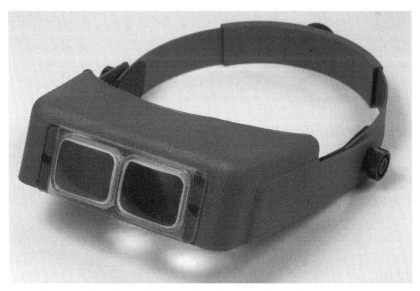

Figure 5.1.   Optivisors are handy magnifying devices that leave hands free. Courtesy of the University of Arizona, Arizona State Museum photographic collections. Photographer: Jannelle Weakly.

MOVING REMAINS IN CONTAINERS. The first rule in moving anything is to clear a space to put the item or container before moving it. The second rule is to use a minimum of two hands. Accidents in handling containers happen because a person is trying to do too much at the same time—for instance, making room for a large box while balancing the box in one arm or against a hip. Other considerations include reducing tipping angles. Instead of taking a heavy box down from a shelf above one's head and tipping the contents in the process, it is better to have a step so you are on level with the box. In addition, some boxes are more awkward than others to lift and carry. Before picking up a box, examine it for potential weaknesses such as failing seams, overall weight, and uneven weight distributions. Acidic cardboard boxes are not meant to last decades, and the adhesive used for seams usually gives out before the cardboard fails. Staples, if used instead of adhesives, can corrode and weaken. Awkwardness within the box can cause handlers to drop or lose their grip. Sometimes, for instance, a skull filled with soils is surprisingly heavy and may make a box extremely unbalanced if the skull is at the far end of a large box. You may not even realize the potential weight until the last moment when the box is lifted off the shelf. Such a sudden change in weight may cause the handler to tip or even drop the box. Though tipping is the lesser of these two evils, tipping is not a good idea because bones tend to shift, causing jumbling, scraping, crushing, and grinding in the process of moving a box. When storage is cramped, as a rule, heavy bones should be placed under the thinner more fragile bones (scapulas and ilium, e.g., should be placed over long bones) to prevent crushing and other forms of pressure damage.

Moving human remains in bags is an especially awkward undertaking. Create a clear and padded destination before you move a bag. It is usually best to find a solid tray, box, or cardboard piece to place under the bag for moving. In addition, the bag must be inspected for holes and failing seams before lifting. Moving bags of remains is even more problematic in terms of grinding, rattling, and jumbling than for boxes. Once the bag is opened and the contents removed, the bag should be turned inside out and carefully inspected for fragments. The static in plastic bags and seams in paper bags make for easy hiding places for small fragments.

DIRECT HANDLING. Directly handling human remains with bare hands is no longer standard practice in museums. Reasons are diverse and range from occupational safety for handlers, and respect for the remains, to prevention of contamination for future analyses (e.g., DNA). Obviously, in study collections in osteology training labs, direct handling can be essential for the learning process. In museums and places where active research is pursued, the concern for contamination prohibits direct contact. Proper gloves should be available. These should not have powders or additives such as lubricants since these, too, can transfer to the remains. When wearing gloves, it is important to avoid touching your face, head, or glasses to prevent the transfer of oils.

Again, the golden rule is use two hands for larger bones and especially for crania. Just as was discussed for moving containers, one must plan ahead for the movement of individual bones and have a padded surface ready to receive a bone. The padded surface should not snag (e.g., Ethafoam or Volara are good choices, while cotton or polyester batting are poor choices). In the case of crania, beanbags or a foam ring should be made ready before moving takes place.

To lift a cranium, it is best to lift it from below and cradle it in both hands. Bass (1995:337) warns never put fingers in the eye sockets (or any other orifice) and lift, since this could easily rupture the thin bone in this area. One should not move the cranium to a surface and then go off to find padding, because in the meantime the cranium might roll off the table. Padding such as an Ethafoam ring or beanbags should be ready to receive the cranium. Padding is especially important since teeth, though considered very strong, do chip, and they often bear the weight and impact when setting skulls down on hard surfaces. It is extremely sad to see a metal shelf

BEANBAGS FOR SUPPORT AND CUSHIONING

Caroline Sakaguchi Kunioka and Vicki Cassman

Beanbags are commonly used for supporting, positioning, cushioning, and spotting bones during examination, photography, and possibly transport. A beanbag is useful when working alone, during photography or examination, to hold a skull in a desired position while providing cushioning and stability. It is part of a physical anthropologist's essential lab equipment, yet how does one make an inert bean bag?

In the past, a variety of fill materials have been used with varying successes and consequences (see table 5.3). For example, none of the traditional bags can be cleaned using water or a detergent.

Table 5.3. Fill Materials

Traditional Fill Materials	Potential Problems
Beans	Water exposure, rendering bag and filling unusable
Rice	Potential vermin attractant
Lentils	Degrades with time and use, releasing dust, odor, or both
Split peas	Subject to mildew and odor
Sand	Salt content unknown and often high
	Salt migration
	Staining from contact with water
	A consistent problem with dust
Lead shot	Lead dust a health hazard and artifact contaminant
	Double-bagging shot in plastic sheet bag and cloth cover, resulting in poor shape and pointed edges
Suggested Fill Material	
Polypropylene pellets	None of the above problems
	Washing possible
	Requires avoiding heat (polypropylene melts above approximately 150°C/300°F)

Marketed under the name "Poly-pellets" by Fairfield Processing, 100 percent polypropylene pellets have only been available a short time but are now easily found in craft supply stores. Inert, uniformly smooth and round, this fill material does not have any of the negative features found with traditional fills. Furthermore, the pellets are washable and heat tolerant to 150°C/300°F (which is particularly good for beanbags used under hot photographic lights). Line drying or no-heat tumble dry (bagged in a closed pillow case or a sock in case of seam failure) is recommended.

Covers for beanbags should be made of a soft cloth. Cotton unbleached muslin is a good choice, and it can be purchased in almost any fabric store. The muslin should be well washed and especially well rinsed (using an additional wash cycle without adding any detergent) to remove finishes, gums, oils, and starches from the manufacturing process. Sometimes for photography a black velvet or velveteen (a pile fabric similar to velvet, made out of cotton, rayon, or silk, but with a significantly lower pile than traditional velvet) is preferred to contrast with the color of bone. Washing of the velvet or velveteen fabric prior to use is also highly recommended to remove unwanted finishes and reduce shedding. Be sure to test the fabric selected for shedding by using a piece of tape on the surface. If there are only a few fibers on the tape, then this material is acceptable, but if many fibers adhere to the tape, then an alternative fabric that sheds less should be found (take tape to the store to test candidate fabrics).

(*continued*)

lined with crania and all the remaining maxillary dentition is chipped or missing, when the damage was preventable with a little padding.

For relatively robust long bones such as arms and legs, it is best to support them by lifting in the area of the shafts. One should examine the bone for cracks especially in the shafts that might be aggravated by lifting without specific support in the area of the crack. The ends (epiphyses) may be more fragile than the shafts since the ends can be easily damaged due to being larger and less dense, and they are easily knocked about. Also, if there is exposed spongy bone from the burial, these areas can be filled with soil deposits, making them surprisingly heavy and awkward. Carefully lift small bones and fragments, avoiding areas of exposed spongy bone or areas that have cracked or lifting surfaces. (See figures 5.2 through 5.8 for illustrations of recommended ways to handle a variety of bones.)

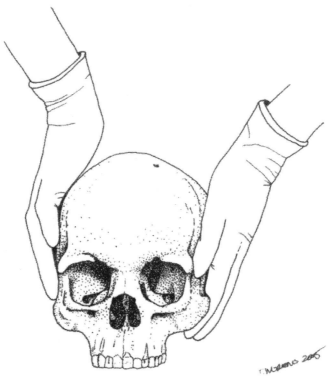

Figure 5.2.   It is vital to handle a cranium with two hands and avoid placing fingers in orifices.
Illustration by Teresa Moreno.

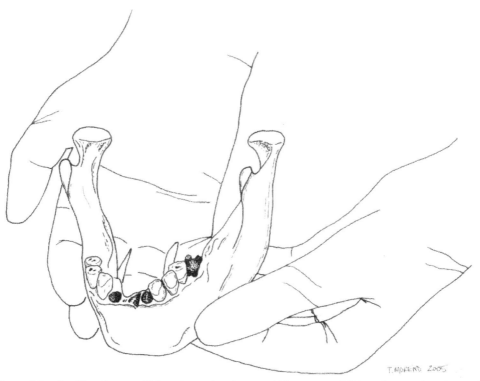

Figure 5.3. Cradling the mandible or lower jaw is a good idea; never pick it up by grasping the teeth since these are often loose. Illustration by Teresa Moreno.

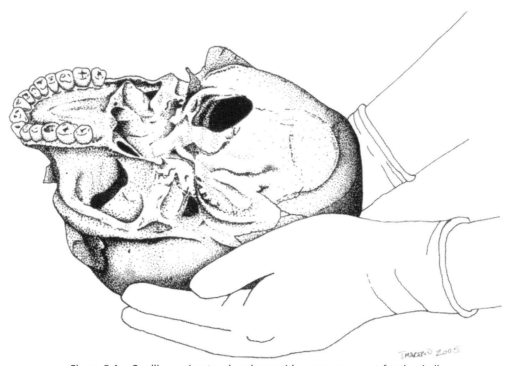

Figure 5.4. Cradling, using two hands, provides proper support for the skull. Illustration by Teresa Moreno.

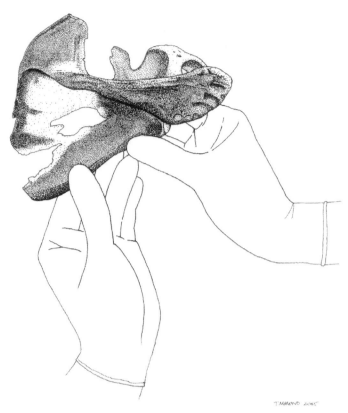

Figure 5.5.   It is important to hold on to and pick up bones by the strongest parts. Avoid touching the thinnest areas. Illustration by Teresa Moreno.

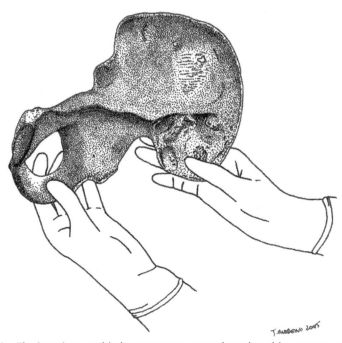

Figure 5.6.   The inominate or hip bone appears very robust, but thin areas are very fragile. Illustration by Teresa Moreno.

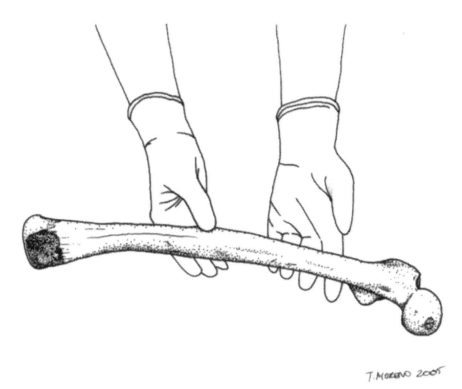

Figure 5.7. It is best to pick up long bones with two hands as shown. Illustration by Teresa Moreno.

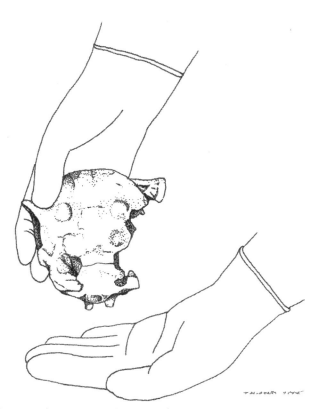

Figure 5.8. When bones or fragments are broken or fragile, delicate, two-handed handling methods are vital to reduce further losses. Illustration by Teresa Moreno.

For extremely delicate or degraded bone, it might be best to slip a sheet of acid-free paper under the bone to move it and avoid direct handling altogether. In this way, the bone can still be pivoted or moved, but one avoids aggravating any ongoing deterioration. Besides paper, a sheet of foam or a tray can facilitate movement, too. Though direct handling is discouraged for delicate bone fragments, gentle fingers are better than metal tweezers since with tweezers the pressure used is not easily regulated. Another reason to limit direct handling may be to avoid loss of soils or accretions.

Articulating bones (to form or fit as in a joint) is a common occurrence when physical anthropologists examine remains, but one must remember that there is no longer any synovial fluid or cartilage that once protected and made such movements smooth. Abrasion damage is common and more intense in dry bone. Also, if there are broken edges, these are extremely vulnerable and easily chipped again. Delicately match the broken edges only when necessary since some loss of surface is inevitable. Be as gentle as possible when articulating joints. Should bone flakes be lost during articulation, pick these up by slipping a sheet of paper under them and placing these losses in a small labeled zip-locking-type bag with a minimum of catalog number, area of loss, and date for documentation purposes. Ideally, record the loss on an overall condition record for the individual (see chapter 4) so that others are forewarned of the brittle nature of the remains or the particular area and can adjust their handling.

Another vital rule is to avoid mixing remains. Separate areas or containers for different individuals must be maintained. When bones of different individuals are to be compared, be sure each bone is labeled before they are brought together. Respect for the individual remains and for the integrity of the curation system is at the heart of this rule.

Associated tissue and artifacts likewise should be afforded the same care as the osteological remains. Associated tissue might include nails, hair, organ, or skin samples. These should be carefully stored in labeled containers within containers (see chapter 8) that allow viewing without touching to keep losses, contamination, and insect activity to a minimum. Associated artifacts should be stored in containers that have been adapted to the special needs of the item (see chapter 9, "Associated Artifacts," for more details).

MEASUREMENT AND DOCUMENTATION TOOLS

Many examinations of human remains by physical anthropologists, bioarchaeologists, and forensic anthropologists involve taking measurements and observations. The uses and ethics of measurements are not debated here. We provide instead a sampling of the most common forms of equipment and their common applications with human remains, so descendants and those responsible for collection care can understand what a researcher is asking for or planning to bring or do for their study visit. We also provide some suggestions for less damaging alternatives for researchers.

Skeletal Measuring Devices
Calipers are commonly used to measure small bones or features of bones, such as nose breadth, teeth size, scars of parturition, or pathology among many other possibilities.

- Sliding—works like an old-fashioned slide rule, with numbers read off a linear ruler (figure 5.9). It measures the space between two points.
- Digital—gives a digital readout of the space between two points (figure 5.10)
- Spreading—is designed specifically for measurements of the cranium (figure 5.11). The device measures the space between two points.
- Coordinate—is a modified sliding caliper that has an attachment to measure the depth or elevation between two points (figure 5.12)

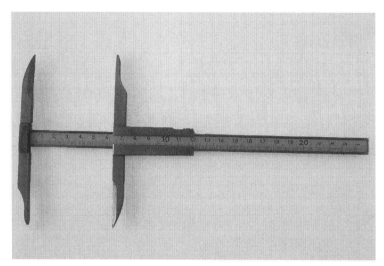

Figure 5.9. Sliding calipers. Photo courtesy of Bernardo and Rodrigo Arriaza.

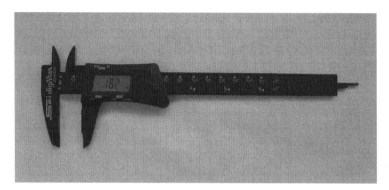

Figure 5.10. Digital sliding calipers. Photo courtesy of Bernardo and Rodrigo Arriaza.

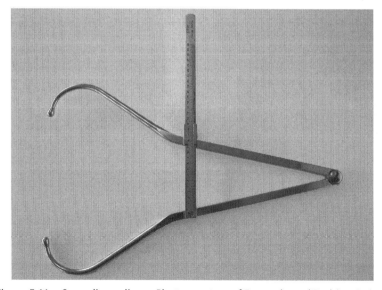

Figure 5.11. Spreading calipers. Photo courtesy of Bernardo and Rodrigo Arriaza.

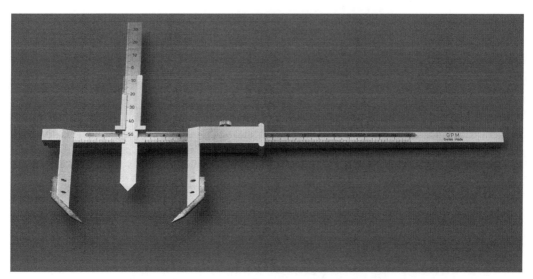

Figure 5.12. Coordinate calipers. Courtesy of the University of Arizona, Arizona State Museum photographic collections. Photographer: Jannelle Weakly.

Osteometric boards are used to measure long bones (figure 5.13).

A *mandibulometer* is a very specific device created to measure the angle of the mandible (figure 5.14). *Goniometers* are more general instruments for measuring angles, and they have many medical applications.

Measuring tapes are generally considered less accurate but are useful when other formal/specific instruments are not available.

- Cloth—made of fabric that has been printed and sometimes receives a coating as well
- Plastic—acceptable as long as they are replaced at regular intervals since the plastic is usually PVC, which becomes brittle as the plasticizer vaporizes
- Metal—though readily available, not recommended since they are rather rigid, with sharp edges, and they can scratch or recoil unexpectedly

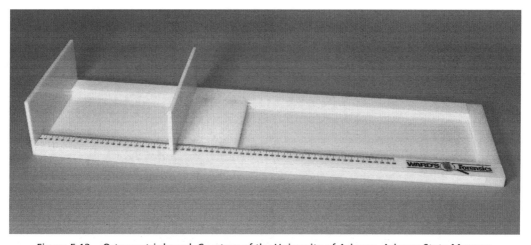

Figure 5.13. Osteometric board. Courtesy of the University of Arizona, Arizona State Museum photographic collections. Photographer: Jannelle Weakly.

Figure 5.14.   Mandibulometer. Photo courtesy of Bernardo and Rodrigo Arriaza.

Special Concerns
Most of these instruments involve bare metal against bone and some of these instruments have sharp points and edges. This means that care is required in placement of the metal against the bone since bone is the weaker of the two materials. Normally, for metal tools, we recommend the points of contact are softened or padded, but padding will interfere with measurements; therefore, calipers are a necessary exception to the padded instrument rule.

Digitizer Measurements
To take measurements, a cranium or mandible is balanced on a stand to provide 360 degree access for touching and recording landmarks with a digital wand. If you use use modeling clay to anchor the bone, cover the clay with Parafilm M to avoid transfering oils.

Endoscopy/Borescope
Endoscopy allows the researcher to examine interior areas that would not otherwise be available. With endoscopic examinations, inspections of the interior of body cavities are possible. This method uses fiber optics and a powerful lens system to provide lighting and visualization of the interior of, for instance, a mummy abdomen or a cranium viewed through the foramen magnum. The portion of the endoscope inserted into the body may be rigid or flexible.

An endoscope uses two fiber optic lines. A light fiber carries light into the body cavity; an image fiber carries the image of the body cavity back to the researcher's viewing lens. There may be a separate port to introduce small folding instruments such as forceps, scissors, brushes, snares, and baskets for tissue excision (removal) or sampling. A record of any examination should become part of the permanent documentation for the individual, and it is imperative that if any sampling takes place, you also photograph the area involved and record this, too. The entry point(s), type of equipment, areas explored, participants, and other observations need to be recorded.

Endoscopes may be used with a camera or video recorder. They typically are used in medicine, while borescopes are used in a wide variety of industrial applications. The diameter of the instrument can vary greatly, with some diameters as small as two millimeters. Endoscopes have been a useful tool in the case of mummy analysis to examine, for instance, the abdominal area. Where once destructive autopsies were the only way to see inside the body, now using already existing entrances to the body, the endoscope tube can be inserted to make observations.

TEMPORARY MARKERS FOR INDICATING BONE LANDMARKS DURING METRIC ANALYSES

Nancy Odegaard and Vicki Cassman

What are metric measurements on bone?

Metric measurements are based on landmarks on the bone. For example, on a cranium or skull terms such as *glabella* (g), *opisthocranion* (op), *gnathion* (gn), *zygion* (zy), or *basion-nasion* may be used to refer to particular landmarks or measurements.

Why are metric measurements done?

Metric measurements are for observing, describing, measuring, collecting, recording, comparing, and contrasting data, or drawing conclusions to determine morphometric relationships and biological affinities. In other words, these are used to get information on limb proportions, skeletal size, robusticity, age, sex, or racial affiliations.

How are metric measurements done?

To measure the distance between landmarks, spreading, sliding, or coordinate metal caliper tips are placed on the designated landmark points, and the distance is noted. These points are often indicated on the bone surface with pen, pencil, gum erasure, masking tape, or even small scratch marks to facilitate relocating the landmark.

What's the problem with marking the landmark points on bone?

Researchers may utilize different landmark points for their measurements. Particular points may be difficult to place the first time and to locate in subsequent measurements. Individual and multiple marks, residues, and scratches compromise the surface condition of the bone and can lead to confusion and disfigurement.

How about a new idea?

Plumber's tape, Teflon ribbon, or narrow rolls of polytetrafluoroethylene (PTFE) film may be used to indicate or mark the metric landmarks. The latter product has already been adapted for use as a nonadhesive barrier or covering with particularly fragile or vulnerable object surfaces, on storage supports, and to cover the tips of metal tools (Odegaard et al. 1997).

Why do we like it?

During the multiple metric studies of the Kennewick Man remains, the use of pen, pencil, gum erasure, masking tape, or even small scratch marks was not permitted. Instead, this film's smooth and pliable characteristics were well suited to protecting fragile surfaces from abrasion and similar mechanical damage. This material has the ability to conform and stay on the surface, while remaining highly visible yet reversible.

How is it used?

Pointed pieces, such as right-angled triangles, can be cut from the plumber's tape roll (half-, three-fourths-, or one-inch sizes are available) with scissors and applied to the surface with tweezers or fingers. The film may be smoothed to the bone surface with a glass rod or other smooth, rounded tool. A triangular point indicates the landmark. These film labels may be removed with tweezers.

Borescopes also have been used to peer into sealed coffins and to take samples of ancient air (see http://www.stmaryscity.org/Lead%20Coffins/project.htm) or to look into medullar cavities for sediment deposition to determine whether an individual was buried formally or ceremonially or whether the body was a "natural" deposition, such as in the case of an accidental burial. Also using a borescope, one can determine the surface of most calcium carbonate concretions, which can tell how the individual was buried and what orientation the individual bones were in during deposition (this can be seen on bone exteriors, too, if they have not been cleaned).

MOLD MAKING AND CASTING

The techniques of casting and molding may be used to restore areas of loss or to replicate. Molds preserve impressions and enable casts or replicas to be formed. Combining sensitivity to the specimen and its condition, with a thorough knowledge of the scientific tools and materials, and the development of an artful touch are important qualities to have prior to casting human remains. Diane France introduces us to the increasingly popular mold-making technique and important considerations before undertaking the process.

PHOTOGRAPHY

Photography is an essential tool for research, curation, and conservation. Despite some objections that it is insensitive to photograph the remains of dead individuals, photography is a necessary step in general professional curation practices. The purposes are for basic and detailed documentation, identification in the case of loss, and assessment of condition and damage. For example, if a photograph is coupled with written descriptions of condition (see chapter 4), then one has an excellent baseline for future preservation assessments or a tool for evaluating any institutional taphonomy (process of decay or preservation for remains). Mead and Meeks (1989) provide a thorough and useful introduction to the technical concepts of film photography for bone, though they do not discuss the care of the objects undergoing photography.

Photographic images may be taken digitally or with photographic film in slide or print formats. Archival standards always include black-and-white film and prints since these are the most permanent media for archival purposes. Digital cameras and microscopes now offer a greater combination of flexibility, speed, and detail. The lighting needs for digital images are much reduced over film cameras, and it is possible to know immediately if the picture has captured what you want. However, independent of what type of camera is used, general considerations apply, including a safe setup and safe lighting.

The setup requires a clean, stable table with padding. Try to position the table out of the path of traffic, vibration, and distracting noises. When a backdrop is used, be sure it is securely fixed and will not fall on the subject of the photograph. If a bone or other object needs to be propped up, do not use materials such as plasticine, wax, wires, or rubber bands. Instead, have wedges (cut from dark colored foam, foam board, or pencil eraser) and small beanbags that can be covered by a photo cloth available for use. Try to work sitting down when photographing small fragments or pieces. Be careful not to bump the photo stand and cause the bones to roll off the prop or, worse, the table. It is advisable to have someone physically spot the setup or have physical buffers to prevent such a disaster. Photographs should always have an identification, date, and measurement guide included in the picture. Many photographers also include a color scale.

Safe lighting refers to the heat and intensity of the bulbs used to create the shot. If photoflood or quartz halogen lights are used, keep them on for as short a period as absolutely necessary to prevent heat buildup and drying out of bone and teeth materials. This is especially true if there is any indication of consolidation, adhesive, or restoration use. Many of the commonly used synthetic polymers are heat sensitive, resulting in possible tackiness of the surface, separation of joins, migration of consolidants, discolorations, and warping, among other things. Also any support materials like foams or temporary construction supports like microcrystalline wax rods (mentioned in chapter 6) will be compromised with excessive heat buildup. The heat buildup could literally cause a meltdown and the assemblage may collapse.

GENERAL CONSIDERATIONS IN CASTING

Diane L. France

Casting has become a popular way to preserve a great deal of information for various kinds of originals. When people think of the kinds of originals typically cast, they usually think of osteological specimens and bone and stone tools. Indeed, the researcher can preserve information using quality replicas that may be very difficult to preserve in other ways, including photography, measurements, and tracings. However, there are some important matters to consider before subjecting a potentially irreplaceable original to the molding process. The questions to be asked depend in part on the general type of material to be replicated, the condition of the original, the need for chemical or DNA tests after the molding process, the time available for molding, and the budget for the process.

Only the molding process will be discussed here because it relates to concerns about preservation of the original. In addition, because this is a volume on human remains, only the concerns surrounding casting bone and soft tissue will be covered in detail. This is not intended as a "how-to" in casting. Rather, it is a guide to be used when considering asking someone to make a replica of your original. If you have not experimented with the molding process, an important original is not the place to start.

> *Mold*—the material (usually a type of rubber) that is brushed or poured over the original to make the negative.
>
> *Cast*—the replica (plaster, plastic, bronze, etc.) made from the mold. This is the positive.

Expect these questions about your original:

- What is the material and condition of your original?
  Note: Porous materials may be darkened by the molding process.
  - Bone
    - Is it exfoliating?
    - Is it fractured, and/or is cancellous bone exposed?
    - Is it oily?
    - Is it wet (water)?
    - Is it infused with embalming fluid?
    - Is it covered with preservative?
    - Are parts of it glued?
    - Is the original expendable?
  - Soft tissue
    - Is it fresh?
    - Is it frozen?
    - Is it infused with embalming fluid?
    - Is it muscle, fat, ligaments, or cartilage?
    - Is the original expendable?
- Do you have to maintain a chain of custody? If you send evidence, ask whether the casting company has a secure site and if the chain of custody can be maintained. Also ask whether the person who will be handling the remains has experience in handling evidence. *Keep in mind that evidence is not often expendable, particularly if the opposing experts have not yet had a chance to study the material.*

My small company (France Casting) has primarily concentrated on making replicas of bone since its start in the mid-1980s (I have been experimenting with the process for over thirty years),

GENERAL CONSIDERATIONS IN CASTING (*continued*)

though we have cast a wide range of other materials including lithics, brains of different animals infused with formaldehyde, panda excrement, and even a living tiger's tongue! Naturally the problems and general considerations in making the molds are different in each of those "originals." For example, it is possible for the molding compound for a dry bone or for lithics to be somewhat toxic and have a relatively long set time, while the material used on the tiger has to be completely safe and fast while still producing great detail (in fact, I tried it out on my own tongue before subjecting the tiger to the process).

I have developed tricks in using various molding materials that enable me to make molds (without damage) to originals that are oily, wet, infused with formaldehyde, dry, brittle, fractured, full of foramina, or even preserved, so it can be done. However, before you hand your original to a company or person who will make the mold, be sure you ask what the potential damage might be. The person who is doing the work should be willing to discuss the possibilities with you. Also, you may be asked whether the original is expendable. The molding materials can be modified (if the mold maker is experienced) to protect the original, but there is sometimes an inverse correlation between the detail captured by the mold and the protection of the material to be molded.

Preservatives and glue added to the original will often interfere with the ability of the molding compound to capture surface detail (and some may be softened by some molding materials). It is important to remember that the molding compound (and therefore all of the casts) "see" the surface texture only and cannot pick up color differences that may enhance (or confuse) the detail as picked up by the eye. If, for example, a clear coat of varnish is applied to the surface, the eye picks up the detail under the surface, while the molding material only picks up the shiny surface of the varnish. This is a sort of "good news, bad news" syndrome, though. The bad news was just stated, while the good news is that many molding compounds will pick up surface texture that the eye cannot distinguish because the eyes (and brain) are interpreting those color differences as part of the entire object. Often detail unseen by the eye is revealed in a cast (I use this fact in forensic cases by molding cuts in bone and cartilage to reveal more detail).

Before you hand over your original, *be sure that you have taken all of the photographs and measurements you need to take, and you have removed any of the chemical or biological materials you wish to remove.* After all, casting can be a somewhat invasive technique, and you should look at these precautions as just a good insurance plan.

Considerations in Molding Different Materials

Whereas casting lithics includes making molds of vastly different sizes and shapes, it almost always involves making a very detailed mold of nonporous materials. Casting bone, however, involves not only different sizes and shapes, but remains that are, to different degrees, fragile *and* porous. The degree of porosity (from fresh, intact cortical bone down the scale to exposed trabecular bone) and the fragility to a large extent determine the methods and materials used on the original. Most of the molding materials discussed here will flow over the surface of the original. If the original is porous, that molding compound will have a tendency to flow into all of the fissures and trabeculae and, when the mold is removed, may tear the original apart. Some mold makers will counteract this by plugging all of the holes with clay, cotton, wax, or some other material, but that approach decreases the amount of detail possible in the mold and cast. Experienced mold makers have tricks to decrease the amount of flow into the subsurface areas without decreasing the detail captured.

Making molds of bone can also be complicated depending upon the complexity of the bone and the number of undercuts (e.g., a humerus vs. a scapula). Expect a mold of a scapula to cost more than the mold of a humerus simply because the mold is more complex to set up.

(*continued*)

Molding soft tissue has become more popular in forensic cases for several reasons. As with bone, a plastic cast is more durable than the original and is more easily given to a jury for study (in addition to addressing the "squeamish" factor of a jury handling human remains), and soft tissue will decay and change shape, while the cast is a permanent record. Also, because many molding compounds flow, it can be introduced into narrow cuts in soft tissue and virtually eliminate the need for further dissection.

A Few Notes on Molding Compounds

Probably hundreds of different kinds of molding compounds are available for creating replicas, each with its own benefits and drawbacks in different situations and on different materials. Four basic material types are described here:

Latex. This naturally occurring substance is one of the earliest used and one of the least expensive. If properly applied and curated, the mold will be usable for years. It is most suitable for casting various types of plaster (there are many different types of plaster as well, each with its own characteristics). The cast detail resulting from a latex mold is usually not as fine as with other molding compounds. If you hand your original to professionals in molding and casting, be suspicious if they say that they are using latex as their molding material—there are many more appropriate materials on the market today.

Alginate. Also derived from a naturally occurring substance, this is the molding compound that many dentists still use to make a mold of your teeth. It is extremely safe to use (it's what I used on the tiger) and has a fast set time, but it is extremely fragile and can usually only be used for one or two casts before it falls apart. Be sure your original can be subjected to water (this is a water-based material) before trying this compound.

Polyurethane-based molding compounds. These give excellent detail to the mold and can be used to cast different kinds of plasters and plastics (if the proper mold release is used). They have a reasonable set time and are relatively easy to use, but they are more toxic than other substances. The molds, if stored properly, can last a few years.

Silicone-based molding compounds. These are probably the most extensively used. They provide excellent detail and can be used for years (depending on what is used as the casting material—plastics are very hard on molds). They are relatively nontoxic but are extremely expensive and can be inhibited by certain chemicals and other materials that may be on your original. Silicone-based compounds will often darken the original somewhat as it leaves a little silicone on the surface as it cures.

Many mold makers will use a release agent on the original so that the molding compound can easily be removed. Unfortunately, this is an additional substance on your original. In most cases, however, experienced mold makers know how to make the molding compound act as its own sealing agent so that a release agent is not required.

How Much Will It Cost?

Keep in mind that the molding compounds can cost as much as about $100 for one gallon, it takes about two hours to set up a cranium for molding (if the cranium is in good condition), four days of intermittent work to finish the cranial mold, and additional time (in hours) to create a finished cast. It is not unreasonable, therefore, to expect to pay about $200 and more for a mold of a cranium and an additional amount (depending on the number of casts needed) for the casts. Other materials (lithics, ceramics, etc.) will vary depending on the setup time needed and the materials costs. At France Casting, we have a program in which you can receive a cast from your original for free if we can offer the casts for sale on our website (if we believe that the casts will sell).

GENERAL CONSIDERATIONS IN CASTING (*continued*)

Questions to Ask the Mold Maker

Before you hand over your original to someone for the molding process, ask these questions:

- How long have you been making molds?
- Do you have references from people who have had molds made in the past?
- Will the process change the original (this includes all changes, including damage)?
- Do you have experience in handling bone and soft tissue?
- Is your work site secured (particularly important with evidence)? Do you have experience in handling evidence?
- What is the time needed for the process?
- How much will it cost?

Finally, if your original is extremely valuable or fragile, consider a casting technique that is not invasive. *Rapid prototyping* is a technique that uses digitized data from computer tomography (CT scan) or magnetic resonance imaging (MRI) from the original. These data are then fed into a rapid prototyping machine that uses that information to build a cast (figure 5.15). This technique can be highly detailed and accurate, but it is expensive (potentially thousands of dollars).

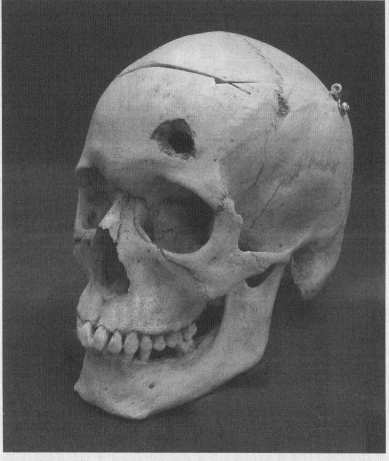

Figure 5.15. Replica of gunshot wound victim. Photo courtesy of France Casting.

Mirrors may be employed to reflect and amplify the available light, thereby enabling the use of less primary light source. Plastic mirrorlike material may be purchased and fixed to pieces of cardboard or foam board. Many artifact curators have used variations of this technique to capture two views in the same photo frame by carefully positioning the mirror behind the artifact. Photographic umbrellas offer a wide angle of light, serve to diffuse light, and create a soft glow for main or fill lights. They can also help to bounce lights and reduce a focused area of heat buildup.

Fabric Softcubes or light boxes provide extremely soft lighting because they fit over the lamp head. Models can be silver lined and double diffused so that minimal shadows and little heat buildup results. The front has a diffusion panel that is translucent white, the sides consist of metal poles attached to an opaque black exterior shell, and the interior is reflective silver. These techniques offer greater protection to bone during photography (see figure 5.16 for a sample photographic setup).

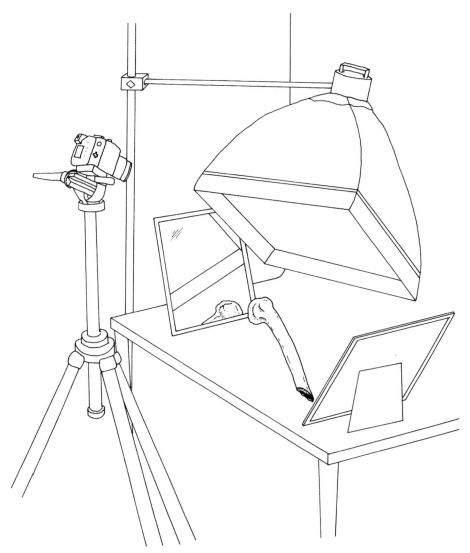

Figure 5.16.   Illustration of a photographic setup inspired by Chip Clark of the Smithsonian Institution. Illustration by Teresa Moreno.

In addition to lamps, photographic lighting can include studio flash units. Mead and Meeks (1989:272) explain two types of studio flash: a self-contained unit and a separate power pack unit. Studio flash units minimize the duration of the light exposure.

There are several forms of scientific photography including reflected infrared, reflected ul-traviolet, and ultraviolet fluorescence techniques that are used to record details otherwise not seen on surfaces in visible light. At best, these techniques can serve as an essentially nonde-structive analytical tool. Reflected infrared photography uses any source of infrared radiation as the light source (incandescent bulbs, sunlight); then, at the camera, an infrared transmission fil-ter over the lens removes all the visible light, and a specially sensitized film then records the re-flected infrared. Details and marks that are just below the surface are sometimes seen. Reflected ultraviolet photography uses ultraviolet radiation as the light source while filtration on the cam-era allows only what is seen with that ultraviolet radiation to reach the film. Ultraviolet fluores-cence also uses ultraviolet radiation as the light source, and the camera records any fluorescence from the object. This type of photography is used to examine and record certain coatings, ad-hesives, and fills (see http://msp.rmit.edu.au/).

Blaker (1976:3) writes, "The purpose of scientifically oriented photography is to inform without prejudice or embellishment." Photography is an important tool, but use of it with hu-man remains requires special levels of respect and protection for the remains. Any techniques and innovations that promote preservation are worth the trouble.

DESTRUCTIVE SAMPLING AND ANALYSIS

Many samples, tests, and techniques have been performed on human remains as a part of their study. Instrumental analysis enables researchers to retrieve information that identifies, sepa-rates, dates, characterizes, or examines the relationship of constituents present in a sample. David Smith provides an introduction to some of the most common forms of instrumentation, the techniques, and how they may be used in applications to human remains. Whether an in-strumental technique will be useful and appropriate depends on the type of questions that are asked of it and how any potential legal, ethical, and ethnic issues pertain to the situation.

Destructive testing requests can be difficult to evaluate at times, and the names of instru-mentation can be bewildering (see the box on "Analytical Instrumentation" for basic guidance). But it is important to understand the basic uses and methods involved with each technique to be able to evaluate the risks and benefits and the utility of the request. In addition, especially in the case of human remains, it is important to know whether any unused sample or residues will come back to the institution and, if so, in what form. Revealing health hazards associated with residues is vital before returning items to the collections.

As the famous physicist Heinz Pagels (1988) said, "Science cannot resolve moral conflicts, but it can help to more accurately frame the debates about those conflicts." Some of the routine concerns that museums and academic institutions may want to consider are outlined on the policy example developed by the Arizona State Museum, which may serve as a guide for others in the process of putting together a similar policy for their own institution. Establishment of sound policy is the first step to achieve propriety toward institutionalized human remains.

INSTRUMENTAL ANALYSIS

David R. Smith

The analysis of human remains using a variety of instrumental methods can provide the researcher with information to assist in answering the many questions that arise during an investigation. Each method provides its own insight into the sample and has its own sample requirements and limitations. In evaluating a request for sample analysis, the researcher and the curator should consider the question being asked and whether the particular method provides the appropriate information to answer that question. The potential impact on the sample and any safety concerns for the sample and the personnel running the analysis both need to be considered for each type of request.

The following discussions of the various techniques found in the literature are a brief introduction to provide the research team with a starting point for discussions. It is suggested that before any analysis is undertaken, the goals of the analysis, sample requirements, and safety issues be discussed as well with the instrument facility. Requirements for the instrumental methods discussed here vary. They range from having no effect on the sample to requiring that a portion of the sample be consumed. In a number of instances, the technique itself is nondestructive, but in order to utilize the method, a sample must be physically removed from the object. In some cases, sample preparation may not have an obvious effect on the sample.

Accelerator Mass Spectroscopy (AMS)

AMS is a specialized mass spectroscopic method for the counting of carbon 14 (C14) nuclei. It is employed as the detection phase of C14 dating because it provides much faster and more accurate counting of the C14 than conventional methods. This requires a sample that contains carbon (i.e., organic material). In bone that would correspond primarily to collagen. A small amount of sample, often about two grams minimum for bone, must be destroyed for the analysis.

Amino Acid Racemization Dating (AAR)

Amino acids occur in two isomeric forms that are mirror images of one another: the L form and the D form. In living tissue, only the L form exists, but the equilibrium condition outside living tissue is a racemic mixture of the two forms where the amounts of D and L forms are equal. After a life form dies, the amino acids slowly convert to form the racemic mixture.

In AAR, the ratio of the forms of the amino acids is analyzed and related to the kinetics of the conversion. This is used to predict the age of the sample. The analysis requires the extraction of amino acids from a sample. The technique requires that a small portion of the sample (milligrams) be removed and extracted; therefore, it is destructive.

The results of this AAR are controversial and dependent on a number of uncontrolled variables that affect the kinetics of the racemization reaction, such as the temperature history of the sample.

Cold Vapor Atomic Absorption (AA)

Atomic absorption spectroscopy is an atomic spectroscopy based on the absorption of light by electronic transitions in atoms. It is particularly suited for the quantitative analysis of metals. The applicability includes elements that are commonly constants of bone such as calcium, strontium, and other Group I and II metals, in addition to the transition metals. AA requires that the analyte (the substance you are analyzing in an experiment) be converted into the free atoms.

Traditional AA has involved conversion of the sample to the atomic form using atomization in either a high-temperature flame or furnace. These atomization methods are applicable to a large number of ions in solution.

Cold vapor AA technique has been developed for the analysis of mercury. Mercury is a unique metal in that it has a substantial vapor pressure at room temperature, which allows for the quantization of mercury. In general, samples for cold vapor AA for mercury are prepared by extraction of the mercury from solid sample into an aqueous solution, reduction of the mercury, and analysis of the vapor. This analysis requires that a small portion of the sample (milligrams to grams, depending on the mercury level) be removed and extracted or digested; this piece of the sample is consumed during the analysis.

Inductively Coupled Plasma Spectroscopy (ICP)

ICP is another type of atomic spectroscopy whose primary application is in the quantitative analysis of metals. It is applicable to the analysis of the constituents of bone, such as calcium, but has the advantage of providing both the major and minor constituent content in one analysis. The technique involves introducing the sample into high-energy argon plasma where the elements in the sample are converted to atomic and ionic species. These species can then be analyzed using a variety of techniques.

The traditional approach analyzes the light emitted by the plasma and quantitatively identifies the elements present based on the emission lines of the elements (this is called either ICP–optical emission spectroscopy [ICP-OES] or ICP–atomic emission spectroscopy [ICP-AES]). A more recent approach to the use of ICP is to introduce the gases from the plasma into a mass spectrometer (ICP-MS) where the elements are analyzed using their atomic masses.

Samples for ICP need to be dissolved or extracted and introduced into the instrument as a solution (usually aqueous). This requires removal and preparation of milligrams to grams of material, depending on the level of the elements of interest, and this is a form of destructive analysis.

Isotope Ratio Mass Spectrometry (IRMS)

Mass spectrometry (MS) is a technique in which a sample of interest is introduced into a vacuum system where it is fragmented and charged by various means (in traditional MS, this is accomplished using an electron beam). The charged particles are then separated by mass and analyzed. The various fragments are used to gain information about the sample. In IRMS, the individual carbon and nitrogen isotope fragments are monitored to determine their ratio. These ratios are related to climate and human diet prior to death.

IRMS requires a small sample (milligrams) to be destroyed and introduced into a mass spectrometer, where the ratios of the carbon and nitrogen masses are measured directly.

Nuclear Magnetic Resonance Spectroscopy (NMR)

NMR measures the magnetic environment of various atomic nuclei. This is accomplished by placing the sample in a magnetic field and measuring the energy needed to change the magnetic state of the nucleus. The results yield information about the molecular structure of the material.

This technique is used in two major ways. Analytically, the technique is used to determine the structure of molecules. NMR is also used as an imaging technique.

The structural identification usually requires destruction of a small sample, while the imaging techniques are nondestructive.

Neutron Activation Analysis (NAA)

NAA is a technique used to identify and quantify the atomic composition of a sample. The sample is irradiated with high-energy neutrons in a nuclear reactor that induces nuclear reactions within the sample. The sample is then removed from the reactor and placed in a spectrometer, which analyzes the decay products from the decomposition of the nuclear products formed in the sample. NAA has found application in geochemistry for the study of the relationships of suites of rocks and soils by monitoring the trace elements that are particularly sensitive in NAA. This same approach can be applied to sourcing in the study of human remains.

(*continued*)

INSTRUMENTAL ANALYSIS (*continued*)

The technique is very sensitive for some elements, and it does not require dissolving or extracting the sample. A portion of the sample must be placed in the reactor. However, the sample does undergo nuclear reactions and may in some cases remain radioactive after the analysis.

Plasma Chemical Extraction (PCE)
PCE is a sample preparation technique that purports to nondestructively remove carbon from a sample for C14 dating analysis.

Raman Spectroscopy
Raman spectroscopy is a molecular spectroscopy technique based on the scattering of light from a surface. A laser is reflected from a surface, and a small portion of the reflected light is shifted by interaction with the molecules in the material.

Raman is used to identify many types of materials. It has broad applicability to both organic and inorganic materials and is useful over a wide range of sample sizes.

It is generally a nondestructive technique, but the sample must fit into the instrument. Some large sampling cabinets exist, but in general no portion of the remains must be removed for analysis. The portions can be microscopic for the microraman technique or macroscopic for standard instruments.

Scanning Electron Microscopy (SEM)
SEM is a microscopy technique that employs electrons instead of light to form an image. A beam of electrons is focused onto the sample through a set of electron optics in a column. The beam produces other electrons at the sample surface that are collected at a detector and used to form an image that is displayed on a monitor.

A wide variety of samples can be examined using SEM. In the conventional instruments, the samples need to be dry and conductive, and they are placed in a vacuum system. This may require that the sample be coated with a very thin layer of metal or graphite in a vacuum sputter chamber.

SEM can be used to examine the surface of human remains samples, either in an unprepared or "as found" condition or as cross sections. In either case, the samples must be small enough to be placed in the chamber of the SEM. Depending on the instrument, this generally requires that the sample be less than ten centimeters in the largest dimension. Very small samples are not a problem for the instrument. The SEM is a relatively nondestructive technique depending on the type of sample analyzed and if a sample can be taken in the first place.

Samples can be examined from five to two hundred thousand times with a maximum resolution of five nanometers. This technique yields both topological and morphological information about the sample.

Environmental Scanning Electron Microscopy (ESEM)
ESEM functions on the same principle as the SEM. The difference between the two techniques revolves around the sample system, which in the ESEM is low vacuum, rather than the high vacuum used in the SEM. This makes the sample requirements for ESEM less stringent. Samples that are "wet" and nonconductive are possible, expanding the applicability to tissue samples. The sample size requirements are approximately the same as for SEM.

X-ray
X-ray radiography employs high-energy electromagnetic radiation (X-rays) to produce an image of the sample. The radiation is passed through the sample and detected with either a photographic film or a detector. The materials in the sample have differing abilities to absorb X-rays depending on their elemental composition, density, and structure, thus producing an image. X-ray radiography is nondestructive.

INSTRUMENTAL ANALYSIS (*continued*)

X-ray Diffraction (XRD)

XRD is a technique that employs an X-ray beam to evaluate the structure of materials. The beam is focused on the surface of a polished sample and is diffracted by the structure of the atoms in the sample. The resulting diffraction pattern is analyzed to determine the crystal structure of the material—for example, a mineral.

The analysis requires a polished flat surface on the sample; therefore, a portion of the remains must be removed and cut to provide the surface.

X-ray Fluorescence (XRF)

XRF is an analytical technique used for the qualitative and quantitative identification of the elemental composition of the surface being analyzed. The principle of operation involves the excitation of the sample using either X-rays or high-energy electrons that causes the ejection of inner shell electrons; as the atoms decay to lower-energy states, characteristic X-rays are emitted, and the energy of these X-rays is indicative of the element excited.

XRF instrumentation has been adapted to a number of applications. Adaptations can enable this technique to analyze for nearly all elements on the periodic table. This technique is used in conjunction with SEM to identify the elemental composition of small areas viewed in the SEM. It also exists as a very powerful laboratory instrument and as handheld instrumentation that can be used for fieldwork. While all types of XRF have limitations, the technique always involves the surface and immediate subsurface of the sample being analyzed.

XRF is a nondestructive technique that can be used directly on the sample surface; however, the sample must be of a size and configuration that allows the instrument to be used. In the case of the SEM-related instruments, the same restrictions that apply to the SEM apply to the XRF. The laboratory instrument generally requires a sample to be removed, although the actual sampling chambers vary in size and type. The handheld instruments are more flexible, but they require clear access to the surface.

Proton Induced X-ray Emission (PIXE)

PIXE employs the same principles as XRF except that the excitation beam is high-energy protons, generally from a linear accelerator. The use of the proton beam increases the sensitivity of the method, making the technique more useful for trace analysis of a wide range of elements.

Samples for PIXE are polished sections; therefore, a portion of the sample must be removed and cross-sectioned for the analysis. It is a destructive technique.

ARIZONA STATE MUSEUM DESTRUCTIVE TESTING POLICY

Arizona State Museum Handbook
Policy No.: 5.1.5 Originally Approved: Draft 11-15-01
Division: Collections Reviewed / Revised:
Subject: Destructive Sampling of Collection Specimens

Policy

The Arizona State Museum supports and promotes research on the collections entrusted to its care in ways consistent with their preservation and protection. The Museum will approve requests for destructive sampling and analysis of objects in its collections when the potential for contribution to knowledge outweighs the loss to the specimen.

In approving requests for destructive sampling, the Museum has a responsibility to ensure that the sampling will cause the least possible damage or loss to the specimen, that the research is likely to yield positive results, and that the results of the sampling and analysis will be fully documented and widely disseminated.

Requests to perform destructive sampling will be guided by the following considerations:

- The potential knowledge to be gained by the proposed analysis.
- The soundness of the proposed methodology.
- The demonstrated competency of the researcher, other involved parties, and, if included, independent laboratories, to carry out and complete the analysis.
- The extent of loss, damage or disfigurement that will be caused to the specimen, weighed against the uniqueness of the specimen.
- Possible cultural sensitivity of the material being requested.

The Museum reserves the right to suspend or stop the sampling process if, in the judgment of the Museum staff, the process is too destructive to the object being sampled or if the object is requested under a NAGPRA claim.

Procedure

The researcher must make a written request to the Curator of Collections, usually by submitting the Museum's Destructive Sampling Request form with attached supporting documentation.

The Curator of Collections, after consultation with the conservator and appropriate curatorial staff, will submit all destructive sampling requests and attachments to the Executive Committee for a final decision.

The Curator of Collections will communicate the decision of the Executive Committee to the researcher in writing, stating the conditions of agreement in the event of approval or the reasons for rejection in the event of denial.

Prior to performing the sampling or receiving the sample, the researcher must agree in writing to:

Cause the least possible damage or disfigurement to the specimen.

Return to the Museum all materials not destroyed, including thin sections or other samples taken. All materials must be accompanied by identification of the specimen of origin.

Provide the Museum a concordance of any new numbers assigned for research purposes with specimen numbers assigned by the Museum.

Provide to the Museum a copy of all raw data resulting from the research.

Acknowledge responsibility and confirm intentions to publish or otherwise disseminate the results of the research.

REFERENCES

Blaker, A. A.
    1976 *Field Photography: Beginning and Advanced Techniques.* W. H. Freeman, San Francisco.

Bass, William M.
    1995 *Human Osteology: A Laboratory and Field Manual.* 4th ed. Special Publication #2 of the Missouri Archaeological Society, Columbia, Missouri.

Mead, Emilee M., and Susan Meeks
    1989 Photography of Archaeological and Paleontological Bone Specimens. In *Bone Modification,* edited by Robson Bonnichen and Marcella Sorg, pp. 267–281. Center for the Study of the First Americans, Institute for Quarternary Studies, University of Maine.

Odegaard, Nancy, Matthew Crawford, and Werner S. Zimmt
    1997 The Use of Polytetrafluoroethylene (PTFE) Film for Storage Supports. *Journal of the American Institute for Conservation* 36(2):249–251.

Pagels, Heinz R.
    1988 *The Dreams of Reason: The Computer and the Rise of the Sciences of Complexity.* Simon and Schuster, New York.

CHAPTER 6

Treatment and Invasive Actions

NANCY ODEGAARD AND VICKI CASSMAN

Never doubt that a small group of thoughtful, committed citizens can change the world. Indeed, it's the only thing that ever has.

—Margaret Mead

A VIGOROUS AND SYMPATHETIC CHANGE IS SLOWLY TAKING PLACE WITHIN MUSEUM WALLS, AND THE transformation is moving into field practices as well. Curators and researchers are incorporating a philosophy reflecting the maintenance of collection integrity. We have learned that museum accessions are not frozen in time when they enter the institution; this is clearly visible from years of accumulated repository experiences and material losses. However, we are still committed to the enormous responsibility of taking on collections on behalf of society. We collect and preserve to be able to utilize the collections for educational and research uses, now and in the future. Unfortunately, we have affected the research integrity of most of our older collections in our enthusiasm to "preserve" and also through neglect. The change that we see beginning and hope to further promote in this chapter and volume, for institutionalized human remains, is a respect for the person and their condition, as well as the present and future research potential of that individual's remains.

In our maturity as a collective of anthropology and museology professionals, we have come to realize that what we do in the name of science can have long-term effects and that science that is destructive or not reproducible is only rarely, if ever, worth doing. Williams (1999:126) describes traditional anthropological and biological attitudes toward collections as a general disregard for specimen and object integrity. Old assumptions about curation developed out of the emphasis on morphological and typological centered research (109). The emphasis on documenting variation and carrying out morphometric analyses led to a concentration on permanent restorations and measurements, especially of crania. Instead of collections or individuals, the spotlight focused on researchers' statistical morphometric databases.

The change that Williams (1999:109) documents and calls "the new assumption" is a significant change that stresses the natural unaltered state of the collection as the preferred condition. Under this new paradigm, use and access is encouraged but with the understanding that collections are not to be permanently altered in the process. In other words, the collections cannot become obsolete for new uses because treatments applied for one purpose preclude others.

INVASIVE ACTIONS

Although it is possible to argue about what should be included in the category of invasive action, we prefer to include any treatment that makes a permanent change. Conservators generally refer to cleaning, consolidation, adhesive repairs, the use of pesticides, and the use of fixed reconstructive materials (screws, wires, fills, pigments) as invasive treatments. Another assumption conservators make is that all treatments must be documented and kept with the individual's records. This type of documentation has not been common practice with human remains in most collections; therefore, it is not uncommon to find bones that have been "repaired" or "preserved" with adhesives or consolidants, with no associated documentation to know what was used or when it was applied. Likewise, fumigations and other pest control treatments have rarely been recorded. When casts have been made, there should be a record of the materials used. In that way one can trace back months or years later to know what is causing problems with, for instance, mold growth or darkening or softening of bone. The documentation and recording of permanent changes must become standard practice for institutions housing human remains (see chapter 2). The ethical obligation of recording all treatments and what materials were used is vital to the ongoing curation or preservation of anything.

CLEANING

One of the most common invasive actions is the intervention of cleaning, which is clearly an irreversible act. Many may think that removing soils is a commonplace routine of processing and that it does not warrant documentation; however, we insist that it does. Processes that have been used in the past with human bone include soaking in warm water, immersing and brushing with soap and water, wiping with cotton dipped in acetone, and using a variety of mechanical techniques involving knitting needles, grapefruit knives, toothbrushes, dental probes, pins, and ultrasonic cleaners. Documentation enables us to understand what was removed and, perhaps more important, what cleaning may have added in the form of residues and surface markings.

Cleaning involves freeing dirt and impurities from something. Understanding the soil environment in which the bone was found allows for some prediction of its condition and type of cleaning and will facilitate further studies. In the past, studies primarily have been based on measurements and visual morphological characteristics. Today, additional analyses enable expanded studies of human biology in the context of human culture and behavior. Unfortunately, the reevaluation of traditional methods of cleaning has not necessarily kept up with these research advances. Cleaning may inadvertently contaminate or inhibit sample analyses.

For example, water may actually remove materials that are important to sample analysis, or it may initiate the efflorescence of soluble mineral salts. Hard water may actually add other dissolved minerals and substances to the bone. Softened water and commercial scale remover additives usually contain acids and sequestering agents that are destructive to bone. Soaps, detergents, chelating agents, bases used to clean soot or grease, or acids for removing calcium carbonate deposits are likely to remain and cause irreversible changes in surface appearance and structure. Mechanical tools used for cleaning may leave additional marks or distortions that can confuse future studies. For example, we have seen remains where investigators used thumb pressure "cleaning" and were unaware that they had also skinned off the top layer of bone. The damage was only later revealed when soil from surrounding areas naturally fell or wore off with time and revealed another higher plane of bone surface in surrounding "uncleaned" areas.

In the decision to clean or not to clean, a balance must always be maintained and evaluated. How much cleaning is acceptable, and how much loss or change is acceptable? Has cleaning been undertaken as part of preparations for accessioning or as a step in a series involving preservation, study, or analysis? By now it should be clear that the use of cleaning treatments should not be routine or taken for granted. It should be a conscious, conscientious, and well-thought-out process and always recorded with information on materials and techniques used.

To summarize, all types of cleaning are a form of intervention by their very nature and application and must be recorded with not only the date but with the methods, materials (e.g., if water was used, what type—deionized, distilled, tap, etc.?), and techniques used. Cleaning may be undertaken as a part of preparations for or as a step in preservation or study, and the goals affect the techniques used. Cleaning should not be routine. There are many alternatives as gleaned from the literature and seen in practice.

Mechanical Cleaning

Cleaning with a tool may remove more than one expects. Moreover, when considering which mechanical cleaning implement is appropriate, it is important to understand that the more vibration bone is subjected to, the less control one has over what is being removed and the more structural damage may be incurred. Any of these techniques listed here have the potential to damage, scratch, or alter the overall physical integrity of the materials to be cleaned. Any scratches that are left behind may be misinterpreted later. Proceed with caution and be observant, remembering that "less is more" in the case of mechanical cleaning.

Mechanical Aids to Cleaning (presented from least to most potential for damage):

- Fine artist brushes are designed to spread paint onto a surface. They can also attract and gently dislodge dirt particles. Natural hair brushes tend to spread out and thus move gently across a surface. Synthetic hair brushes tend to have slightly more rigidity and so can lift and flick particles on the surface. Fan-shaped brushes are used in painting for blending; thus, they have a lightness that can be very effective for removing soils and dust from porous surfaces.
- Bamboo skewers (bamboo is a grass, not a wood) are thin rods that are pointed at the end and are designed for cooking. While they are strong and can be scratched slightly with a fingernail, they offer finer and more rigid mechanical uses than fingers for cleaning in small areas.
- Utility brushes, including toothbrushes, kitchen brushes, laboratory bottle brushes, and small whiskbrooms, can scratch bone surfaces, dislodge soils with bone surface flakes attached, and push dirt and dust into porous surfaces. The type of bristle (metal, plastic, plant), the length of the bristle (long brushes are generally softer), and pattern of bristle layout (rows, spirals, multiple layers) can all affect softer surfaces. Because some soils and accretions are harder than the bone they lie on, the brush needed to dislodge the soil may actually damage the bone.
- Metal probes, dental picks, needles, and pins are commonly used in archaeology to delicately work through soils next to artifacts. Stainless steel knife blades have close to a 5.5 hardness on the Moh's scale. Approximately 70 percent of healthy bone is made up of the inorganic mineral hydroxyapatite, which includes calcium phosphate, calcium carbonate, calcium fluoride, calcium hydroxide, and citrate. The mineral apatite is ranked at only 5 on the Moh's scale. Thus, for most archaeological bone, especially examples that are degraded, the use of metal tools requires extreme caution.
- Specialized vacuum cleaners have been used widely by conservators to gently clean delicate surfaces. Removal of molds and dust may be best accomplished by brushing toward the opening of a small vacuum attachment (the opening must be much smaller than the bone that one is working on!). Vacuums designed for the dental industry can provide variable suction strengths for greater control. The HEPA-filtered vacuums with variable speed control and microtool kit attachments used in many museums can delicately and safely remove particles. However, it is important to remember that vacuum cleaning is nondiscriminatory and will remove anything it can.
- Bulb syringes, canned air dusters, and air brushes use compressed air as a force to dislodge unwanted particles from surfaces. The force is dependent on the air pressure involved. A bulb syringe can direct a gentle puff of air to remove particles from porous materials. Canned air dusters, often used to clean photographic equipment, produce a brief but powerful blast of air. Artist air brushes can be used to direct a stream of air through a nozzle or needle with a varying air source fitting and trigger pad. All of these techniques tend to redistribute dust and soil rather than remove it.

- Electric drills, Foredom flex shafts, Dremel rotary tools, and vibrotools are often mentioned for use in the removal of excess rock around fossil samples and sometimes for use in soil removal on specimens by archaeologists. These tools requires extreme ability and patience in order to use well. Unfortunately, they are noisy and tend to impart a high level of vibration and heat to the sample. They can seem easier to use than they really are. Due to their aggressive nature, they can cause microfractures and pull away bone adjacent to the soil being removed.
- Air-abrasive tools (miniature sand blasters) abrade and clean using a high-velocity air stream and abrasive particles. While these tools produce less heat and vibration, they can easily remove sample surface and introduce abrasive particles that lodge into porous materials. They are normally used on extremely hard materials such as mineral specimens or teeth when changing the surface is desired for appearance or adhesion applications or for the extraction of fossils. The use of a cabinet or specialized venting system is usually required.
- Ultrasonic cleaners and scalers use sound waves (typically at frequencies between 20 and 50 KHz) to dislodge unwanted soil and residue particles from surfaces. While useful in many industrial applications, ultrasonic baths often use heat and are known to generate stress fractures in soft materials like bone (also amber, coral, ivory, and pearl). Ultrasonic scalers, though not recommended here, are mentioned in literature for the cleaning of fossils and sturdy archaeological objects. These tools channel the vibratory nature of the cleaning to a blade and do not involve immersion in liquid.

Aqueous Cleaning

When cleaning is mentioned most people think of liquid cleaning, as opposed to the mechanical cleaning described earlier. There is also a misunderstanding that water is a harmless or weak substance with only mild cleaning power. Washing with water does remove dirt because it is an excellent solvent. However, when porous, degraded, and weakened structures like archaeological bone are cleaned, other reactions may also take place. Water will affect bone in the burial environment through an exchange of minerals and salts from the adjacent soil conditions. If bone is subjected to water cleaning (rinsing, washing, or soaking), it is common that soluble salts are activated that migrate and often collect just below the bone surface during drying. The resulting condition, *spalling* (the loss of bone surface), often occurs. As the bone dries, these salts tend to crystallize and expand, causing pressures that are enough to pop the surface, effloresce, or powder. The rate of the reaction and type of damage will depend on the salt concentration, as well as the bone's porosity and surface condition.

Water is usually not pure. Washing with water may introduce new chemicals to the bone. Waters that contain significant proportions of calcium and magnesium are hard to wash with and termed "hard." Softened waters alter the mineral content by adding salts, acids, and sequestering agents. Washing bone with additive soaps, detergents, and bleaches will certainly add new material. While water filters can be used to remove a range of impurities including small particles, smells, and bacteria, care should be taken to check the specifications as to what is being removed. Reverse osmosis, distillation, and deionization are purification techniques that remove different types of impurities in water using different techniques. These are the most frequently mentioned water sources for artifact cleaning because they have fewer impurities.

An alternative to immersion, or soaking an object in a bath, is spot cleaning. Spot cleaning may involve application of water or alcohol, for instance, to a small area using a fine watercolor brush or swab. In the documentation, a sketch or marked digital image of the spot should be included so the cleaned or affected area is identifiable in the future.

Careful consideration is always required for any aqueous cleaning, but if used, it is critical that bone be supported completely throughout the process. Also, documentation of the materials, methods, locations, and techniques used is essential.

MEXICANS CLEAN BONES TO HONOR THE DEAD

Lisa J. Adams

Antonio Haas pulls a wooden box from a small cement cubicle, brushes a year of dust from the top, and pushes back the lid to reveal a pile of coffee-colored bones and a skull covered with patches of hair.

It's what remains of his father who died five years ago, and with the Day of the Dead approaching, it's time for their annual cleaning.

It may strike outsiders as macabre, but Haas said it's "the most natural thing in the world."

"There is nothing to fear from the dead," he said, tenderly rubbing the skull. "It's the living we should fear."

For this fifty-eight-year-old farmer and dozens of other descendants of Maya Indians in this small village on the Yucatán Peninsula, the last days of October are devoted to cleaning the bones: dusting, polishing, scrubbing, and rearranging the skeletal remains of family members in time for the Day of the Dead, when Mexicans welcome the souls of the dearly departed back to Earth.

Mexicans honor the dead on November 1, when the souls of dead children are believed to arrive, and on November 2, when adults are believed to return.

They celebrate with meals, songs and prayers, both at home and in cemeteries. Tombstones are illuminated by candles, laden with orange marigolds and piled high with the favorite foods of the deceased, including tamales, small skulls made of sugar, and "bread of the dead"—round, sugar-sprinkled loaves topped with strips of crust symbolizing bones and a knob representing the skull.

But Pomuch and a handful of other small Maya communities dotting the Camino Real Alto region of the peninsula go further.

Without blinking an eyelash, Haas pulls one bone after another out of the box, wiping away black grit with an embroidered handkerchief. The handkerchief has served as a bed for his father's remains for the past year.

Bone cleaning is believed to date to pre-Hispanic Maya cultures, and the practice is carried on today "so that when the souls return they will see they haven't been forgotten," said Venancio Tus Chi, forty-two, a cemetery employee who for $2 will clean bones for families who don't have the time.

Modern-day Maya in the Camino Real Alto initially bury their dead in coffins, but after three or four years, they exhume them, dry the bones in the sun, and scrub them with a soft cloth or paintbrushes. The bones are placed in small wooden boxes and laid in cement cubicles, viewable from the outside through wrought-iron doors.

Most Mexicans claim Indian and Spanish ancestry and are at least nominally Catholic, and Christian beliefs suffuse the bone-cleaning tradition. Crosses adorn most of the tombs, and a priest presides over a Mass on November 2—All Souls' Day.

"Some people are afraid of touching the bones," said María de la Luz Canun, fifty-five, who last Sunday cleaned the dismantled skeletons of her son, great-grandmother, and her two in-laws.

"But it's like when you visit your mother: You may help bathe her, dress her, comb her hair. This is the same thing."

Solvent Cleaning

Solvents are used for cleaning because they can remove contaminants. When deciding which solvent might best remove a particular contaminant, it is necessary to consider factors such as chemical type, evaporation rate, solubility parameter, toxicity, and flammability. Because most chemical solvents contain more than one component, purity is also a concern. Solvents used on objects should not include colored or nonvolatile impurities. Thus, it is safe to say that fingernail polish remover should not replace acetone for conservation use. Material Safety Data Sheets (MSDSs) should be checked for solvent composition information and storage recommendations.

Most organic solvents do not swell the substrate and do not dissolve or move soluble salts in the same way that water does. However, it is important to note that because some easily obtainable alcohols contain a percentage of water, one should be aware of the true nature of the solvent to be used before applying it. The adage that "like dissolves like" is also relevant, reminding us that solvent cleaning works best if what you are trying to remove actually is dissolved by the solvent.

Chemists usually classify solvents by the most reactive portion of their molecule. From an operational standpoint, solvents that are miscible with water are considered *polar*, while those that are not are *nonpolar*. Water (or H-O-H) is reactive at the O-H bond and has a polarity index of 9. It generally dissolves soils effectively, while greases and oils are better dissolved by less polar solvents such as hydrocarbons. Some common solvents are listed in table 6.1.

Soap, Detergent, and Bleach Cleaning
When water is used with other substances such as soaps, detergents, or bleaches, it is important to prepare for adequate rinsing or flushing. These additives are not meant to stay in materials to be cleaned, and even careful flushing after the application of a detergent does not guarantee that all of it has been removed. The remaining contaminants could affect obtaining an accurate date, DNA analyses, or a promise to descendants.

Bleaches, though their use is found in the literature, are truly problematic because they are very difficult to flush, have ongoing effects long after application, and may have recrystalization problems. Likewise, acid treatments once commonly used in archaeological field schools to remove unwanted carbonate-based accretions are now discouraged because they are difficult to control and continue to cause degradation years after application.

Note that we are *not* suggesting that liquid cleaning should not be done. Instead, we would hope that cleaning will be undertaken with more understanding, careful consideration, and thorough documentation. For instance, instead of an immersion bath, perhaps particular locations on the bone could be spot cleaned, leaving other areas unclean. A soft watercolor brush (size 0–2) might be used to wet a small area of soil to see whether it might be loosened by means that are more moderate. In all cases, any use of mechanical or chemical cleaning mixtures on human remains should be properly documented as part of their curation.

PESTICIDES
Pesticide treatments are poisonous chemicals used to kill organisms that are considered pests. Pesticides enter an organism's body through the skin (dermal), mouth (oral), or lungs (inhalation). Depending on the type of pesticide chemical and its application mode, the chemical may

Table 6.1. Common Solvents

Solvent Class	Example Solvent	Polarity Index of Solvent[a]
Alcohols	Ethanol	5.2
Ketones	Acetone	5.1
Esters	Ethyl acetate	4.4
Ethers	Diethyl ether	2.8
Aromatic	Xylene	2.5
Halogenated	1,1,1-Trichloroethane	1
Hydrocarbons	Hexane, white spirits	0

[a]See http://www.wcrl.ars.usda.gov/cec/java/solvents.htm.

be considered temporary and require repeated treatments. Others, referred to as *residuals*, remain active, meaning that the applications made many, many years ago are still effective and poisonous today. A *pesticide residue* refers to any chemicals or chemical products that remain on the object after the application process and after any volatile propellants such as water or solvents that were used to distribute them evaporate.

Human remains collections may have been treated by pesticides in the past, though it is less likely than other types of collections. For the researcher or analyst closely examining treated human remains, the danger is usually there without warning because most residues are not easily noticeable. Through NAGPRA, the rights of American Indian tribes to take back human remains from museums, universities, and federal agencies were recognized. If pesticide residues are present, traditional handling practices could be a serious concern to unprotected individuals. The repatriation of remains from museums may affect descendants and practitioners engaged in ritual acts, and, depending on the nature of these processes, there may also be concern for the potential transfer of contamination to air, ground or water sources.

Presently more than ninety chemicals are known to have been used with museum collections (Odegaard and Sadongei 2005). Collecting a history of a museum's pesticide use from records and staff interviews is a first step in determining whether the application included human remains collections or if treatments of other artifacts occurred within the same cabinetry or rooms where they were stored.

General trends may suggest the types of pesticides that could have been used during specific periods of time. Botanical repellents such as cedar wood, creosote, lavender leaves, sage, tobacco, and various seeds were known to be thrown among items, smudged, or constructed into containers to serve as insect repellents. Metal residuals, such as arsenic and mercuric compounds, were applied to various object surfaces throughout the nineteenth century and well into the twentieth century. They were particularly common among taxidermy and herbarium specimens to prevent insect damage. Other metals, including cadmium, chromium, lead, and zinc, were known for their use as pigments; but, like arsenic and mercuric compounds, some of them were also formulated specifically for applications in fungicides and mothproofers.

The use of volatile chemicals to treat all objects within a space became desirable as collections grew and cabinetry became more commonly used. Mothballs or fungicidal crystals, including camphor, naphthalene, paradichlorobenzene (PDB), and thymol, came into use. Nuggets, cakes, flakes, cones, crystals, or balls were sprinkled among material or placed in containers. As the solid chemical turned into a gas and entered the air, insects were killed and effectively repelled because of the chemical absorbed by the cabinetry and objects.

As agricultural pesticide applications developed, a wider range of domestic and museum pesticides became available. Chlorinated hydrocarbons (including recently banned products such as carbon tetrachloride, Chlordane, Lindane, and Dowfume) were used as fumigants to treat large areas. Organic phosphates (including products such as Dichlorvos, Dursban, malathion, and Vapona) were introduced as replacements for many of the banned chlorinated hydrocarbons and have been widely used as fogs, sprays, and in resin-impregnated strips.

Sealed vacuum chambers led to more effective and efficient fumigation treatments. Volatile fumigants, including ethylene oxide, methyl bromide, and sulfuryl fluoride, were used to treat objects. Preventive pesticide treatments were often extended to museum grounds and buildings through the use of "crack and crevice" sprays such as carbamate powders prepared in solution.

Today most museums use pesticides only when nonchemical alternatives prove inadequate. The widely recognized concept of integrated pest management (IPM) is often used to protect collections from pests (see chapter 8). In the early 1980s, conservators adopted the techniques associated with IPM after questioning the widespread use of pesticides in collections. Through the IPM process, they became more knowledgeable of pesticide products, the chemical reactions the pesticide chemicals could have on various collection materials, and the potential human health hazards to museum workers that they might present. Various environmental, occupational, and medical studies have also been done regarding acceptable levels of human exposure to chemicals, leading to the steady removal of many pesticide products from the marketplace.

However, if a chemical pesticide treatment has occurred or is prescribed for human remains collections, it is critical that the following actions be taken:

- Label objects with a warning. Indicate the name of the toxin.
- Put objects into storage containers and envelopes to isolate them and to facilitate handling.
- Place objects in storage cabinets that lock and seal. Post a sign indicating, "Pesticide-contaminated materials are stored here—keep out."
- Use only a HEPA-filtered vacuum cleaner for housekeeping activities in collections work areas that contain contaminated materials. This will prevent toxic particles from passing through the exhaust of a standard vacuum cleaner.
- Contact the Environmental Protection Agency, Office of Poison Programs (http://www.epa.gov/oppfead1/safety/healthcare/handbook/handbook.html), for information on recognition and management of pesticide poisons.

COATINGS, CONSOLIDANTS, AND ADHESIVES

"Preservatives" have a long history of use in the excavation and care of human bone. The use of film-forming polymers enables the same products to serve as coatings, consolidants, and adhesives depending on how they are mixed with a liquid and how they are applied.

Polymers are large molecules that are made from the chainlike formation of smaller identical molecules involving a chemical reaction and they can be natural or synthetic. "Most natural film-forming materials—resins, gums, and waxes—are made up of molecules which are large by comparison with synthetic polymers" (Horie 1990:11) Both forms have been used to impart structural stability to excavated bone but synthetics are more versatile to use and do not deteriorate as quickly.

Coatings

In the past, many sources have recommended covering bones with an adhesive layer as a preventive action even when bones were in stable condition to begin with. Coatings, like the varnish layer on an oil painting, tend to enhance appearance by unifying the surface gloss and texture. While a coating provides some measure of mechanical protection for a delicate surface, it will decay. In the case of an oil painting, the varnish layer may require removal and replacement several times.

However, aging coatings do not protect porous bone. Some coating films become yellow, lose transparency, or become brittle with age. Others may become sticky and attract dust, and some may enhance the destruction by soluble salts that can build up and break apart the bone structure below the intact film layer. The so-called protective coatings are not recommended and should never be standard practice.

Consolidants

These are low concentrations of adhesive polymer in liquid that are sometimes applied to materials that have lost their own cohesive qualities. The low concentration ideally allows for deep and thorough penetration. The use of consolidants in the field is discussed later (see chapter 13), but it is usually best to try to lift without consolidants—for instance, using a block lifting technique since consolidation is difficult in the field and one often gets consolidation of surrounding soils along with the bone. In other cases, descendants' wishes of no added materials need to be honored. A consolidation treatment on inherently fragile material is a decision that cannot be taken lightly since it comes with permanent repercussions. It should not be considered a reversible procedure.

Though several historic references indicate how common the practice has been, the use of consolidants is no longer encouraged for human remains. Perhaps the tradition continues through borrowing from the field of paleontology where the philosophy toward their material is less sensitive. Within paleontology, the term *hardener* is common, and this material is suggested as an important first line of defense against deterioration (http://www.flmnh.ufl.edu/natsci/vertpaleo/resources/prep.htm). This philosophy is not considered propitious or appropriate for human bone.

Adhesives

Adhesives are substances, usually natural or synthetic polymers, used to hold two surfaces together by means of a join. The adhesives used for conservation are generally applied as a liquid, but they may also be activated by heat or pressure. When applying a liquid adhesive, keep in mind three essential requirements for good adhesion:

1. The liquid must cover the surface and have a strong attraction for the surface (i.e., it must wet the surface).
2. The liquid must then set to prevent the relative movement of the objects.
3. A further requirement is that it must be able to adjust to the stresses which develop during and after setting of the adhesive. (Horie 1990:71)

Making recommendations in the favor of particular adhesive products for use on human remains is inappropriate. There are many factors to consider. Manufacturers of adhesive products often change the composition of their products, there may be multiple grades for a product, and some have synonymous names that are used for them in different markets. Adhesive polymers can be made liquid with a variety of solvents and solvent mixtures into a variety of solvent concentrations. "Using the most popular alternative, without a good understanding of various physical factors such as a polymer's working properties, stability, and its effects on later analysis (among other concerns) can lead to failure of the treatment in the short or long term" (Johnson 2001: 99).

A long list of adhesive products has been employed to adhere, consolidate, and coat bone, although many are now considered inappropriate. Such a list is useful for understanding the history of past treatments and current preservation challenges. Products may be grouped based on their chemical structure. Horie (1990) has organized the most common groups of polymers into a single volume and discusses the background, conservation use, and disadvantages of each. The groups cited here are drawn from Horie, but Johnson (2001) and others provide useful discussions on the early use of particular products. The following list is presented to show various categories of products used in the past and should not be taken as endorsement for use (dates reflect earliest uses in the field, not an invention date).

- Acrylic polymers
  ○ Acrylic or methacrylate polymers such as Lucite and Paroloid (consolidant, adhesive, coating, 1955)
  ○ Acrylic monomers including Cyanoacylates such as Alphabond and Krazy Glue (adhesive, 1970s)
  ○ Acrylic emulsions and dispersions such as Plextol, Primal, and Rhoplex (consolidant, 1984)

- Vinyl acetate–derived polymers: polyvinyl acetate (PVAC)
  - Homopolymer resins such as Vinylite or AYAF (adhesive, 1936)
  - Emulsions such as Elmer's Glue-All or Vinamul (consolidant, 1950)
  - Polyvinyl alcohol (PVAL): Gelvatol (adhesive, 1960s; release agent during casting and molding, 1968)
  - Polyvinyl acetal (PVacetal): Alvar (consolidant, adhesive, and coating, 1936)
  - Polyvinyl butryal (PVB): Butvar (replacement for Alvar, 1960s)
- Cellulosic polymers
  - Ethers, including Methocel and Klucel (consolidant, 1981)
  - Esters
    - Cellulose acetate (CA): Eastman CAB (consolidant, 1934)
    - Cellulose nitrate (CN): Zapon, Duco, HMG, and Randolph Cement (coating, 1899; adhesive, 1905)
- Water-soluble polymers
  - Proteins, including hide, bone, and fish glues, and gelatin solutions (consolidant, adhesive, coating, traditional material)
- Natural resins
  - Plant-based resins including dammar, mucilage, and rosin (coatings, traditional material)
  - Insect secretions including shellac and beeswax (coating and adhesive, traditional material)
- Hydrocarbons
  - Polyethylene/vinyl acetate (EVA) copolymers (additive to hot-melt adhesives, 1960s)
  - Paraffin wax (consolidant, 1910)
  - Rubber: natural, cross-linked derivatives, and synthetic polymers (isolators, 1948; molding material, 1930s)
- Synthetic thermoplastics
  - Polyvinyl chloride (PVC): Duracap (consolidant, 1958; molding material, 1968)
  - Polyvinylidene chloride (PVDC): Saran (coating, 1982)
  - Polystyrene (PS; consolidant and adhesive, 1958)
  - Polyethylene glycol (PEG): Carbowax (consolidant, 1982)
  - Soluble nylons: Calaton (consolidant, 1950s)
- Cross-linking polymers
  - Silicone rubber (molding, 1975)
  - Polyester: Akemi (coating, 1950s)
  - Polyurethanes: Excel (isolating varnish, 1980s)
  - Epoxy resin: Devcon (adhesive, 1950s)
  - Formaldehyde resins: Bakelite (consolidant, 1925)

RECONSTRUCTION AND RESTORATION

As mentioned, adhesives are used to hold two surfaces in a join. This process is sometimes referred to as *reconstruction* (constructing again), *restoration* (bringing back to original condition), *mending* (making repairs), or *bonding* (fastening together) (see http://www.alia.org.au/~wsmith/glossary.htm). In contrast, the word *conservation* may include a range of activities that prevent damage, engage a technical study of materials or the study of deterioration processes, treat damaged items by stabilizing them with minimal intervention, or restore damaged items through the addition of new materials that compensate for the losses due to damage. In museums, reconstruction is part of a treatment process that joins together multiple parts that have become separated through breakage.

In science, the role of repeatable and reproducible results is crucial. When beginning an adhesive treatment on bone, reversibility and stability over time should be the first points under technical consideration. Numerous studies have explored the advantages and disadvantages of particular adhesives, so a choice that is based on suitable chemical properties is possible. However, the issue of whether the join itself will be reversible and stable cannot be looked up. Thus, while it may be possible to redissolve a spot of "set" adhesive with solvents, it is rarely possible to completely dissolve and remove adhesive when the adhesive has entered the porous structure of bone or has "fixed" the keys of a break that make up a join. This penetration is impossible to remove even with aggressive treatments. In addition, all film-forming polymers are sticky when liquid and take up space when dry. The alignment of an adhesive join should be considered the result of a permanent subjective process. During alignment and setting, hands are generally used to hold two pieces together in a fashion that "looks about right." Unfortunately, future analysts must forever use this interpretation as the basis for their studies. While specialists from the fields of osteology and physical anthropology have mentioned the process of joining broken parts together, they tend to diminish the role of adhesive selection, stability, and reversibility and refer to the process as "often quick and easy for the competent osteologist" (White 2000:297).

Jeffrey Schwartz describes a situation where a restudy of bone breakage patterns changed the prevailing causal opinion. When so many bone fragments were noted among the Krapina Neanderthals, paleoanthropologists thought it reasonable that they had been cannibalized. Microscopic studies of the broken bones later suggested that the breakage had actually resulted from various factors including: soil compression during burial, rock falls, shoddy excavation techniques, and forced placement in ill-fitting boxes (Schwartz 1998:17). This situation, though it does not involve adhesive reconstruction, is a good reminder that permanent or semipermanent joins can obscure important clues that may reveal a different understanding of a break sometime in the future.

Restorative processes on human remains also have a long history. The use of plasters, waxes, and synthetic putty fillers as well as armatures, wiring, and hardware attachments is well known. Perhaps influenced by the techniques used to restore pottery to aesthetic wholeness, the types of materials, their techniques of application, and their stability over time are similar. Restoration treatments are problematic. The materials used tend to penetrate porous materials and become functionally permanent. They often initiate a chemical reaction with the adjacent bone causing degradation, and these new materials have been shown to contaminate or inhibit future analyses. For future analysts, any information provided by the broken edges will no longer be assessable.

We suggest that the following points be considered prior to any treatment involving adhesives, consolidants, coatings, or restorative fills:

- Any legal or culturally sensitive aspects of the human remains have been considered.
- Any information concerning previous conservation treatment.
- A nonadhesive alternative be considered first (discussed later).
- Any information concerning planned sampling for analysis be identified and considered.
- The individual doing the proposed restoration is able to properly key the fragments together accurately in their original positions.
- No warping or natural expansion during or since the breakage has occurred.
- The adhesive used in the joins will not add measurably to the overall dimensions of the whole.
- The adhesive is resoluble not only in the present but also in the future in an appropriate solvent.
- It is understood that while the join may be reversible, removal of all adhesive residue is not possible, which may affect texture, appearance, and inhibit further analysis.

Finally, if a treatment is undertaken, full documentation should be required. Williams (1999:134) makes an apt point when he states, "An individual can provide superior preservation treatment for a natural history specimen, but if such treatment is performed without appropriate documentation, it is considered nothing more than good craftsmanship."

ALTERNATIVES TO ADHESIVES

Alternatives to the use of adhesives on human bone should always be considered before any adhesives are selected and used. We are at a crossroads in our consideration of human remains collections. We are now able to do many more analyses than in the past, we have more ethical considerations, and we have decades of curation hindsight to build on. It is time to reevaluate what is considered standard practice. After decades of adhesive reconstructions in collections, we are witnessing failures of adhesive products, poor workmanship, and reduced utility of osteological collections in general (Williams 1999). However, many researchers who focus their study on comparative morphometric analysis continue to believe that unless a skeleton is permanently reconstructed and studied as an ongoing single integrated entity or interpretation, the study cannot be convincing.

The problem with this view is that in existing collections, many fragmented skeletal elements have been glued together, several without proper keying, most often anonymously since in the past little in the way of treatment documentation was left behind. This, too, influences or skews the outcome of morphometric analyses, no matter how comparative the data may be from one individual analyst to another. Additionally, reconstructions are subjective. It is difficult to judge quality in an already reconstructed skull, especially by an anonymous adhesive user. A serious analyst would be better off undertaking a temporary reconstruction her- or himself and not rely on the skills (or lack of them) of others!

Permanent reconstructions also preclude a host of other studies and observations that can take advantage of the fragmented nature of the remains—for instance, examination of the medullar cavity of a broken long bone or the interior surfaces of a cranium. One cannot predict what the future researcher will want to study ahead of time; therefore, reversible treatments are most advantageous. A number of techniques (see figures 6.1 through 6.6) that facilitate preservation of bone may also enable a nonpermanent reconstruction for morphometric analyses or a host of other research purposes:

- Immobilizing bone and bone fragments may be done using a study/storage box. Custom-made boxes constructed of acid-free cardboard and chemically inert plastic foams and sheets enable fragile pieces to be held safely in proper position, thus eliminating excess movement and chatter between fragmentary pieces, minimizing handling due to searches for particular pieces, and preserving a reassembled order or "dry fit" for the next analyst.
- The keyed position of broken bone pieces can be secured with Parafilm M. Parafilm enables fragments or pieces of bone that fit together to be held in position without adhesives. The joined state facilitates handling and measuring, while enabling analysts to remove the film and view the broken edges or realign the join. Parafilm is a waxy-like material that is self-sealing, moldable, and flexible. It has a thickness of 0.005 inch (127 µm), stretches up to 200 percent, and clings to itself around irregular shapes and surfaces. Parafilm M is used primarily as a laboratory film and is quite inert. The manufacturer expects the materials to last three years without deterioration under normal environmental conditions. This material works particularly well for long bones and ribs (see http://www.2spi.com/catalog/supp/supp4b.shtml).
- Microcrystalline wax sticks can buttress joins for temporary reassembly of multiple joins when Parafilm M cannot be used—for example, in the reconstruction of crania. Bone fragments are positioned, and then the wax is placed on either or both surfaces (front and back), spanning the break. Wax may be placed mostly on the inside so that it does not interfere with measurements or image processing. The wax should not remain on the bones but be removed as soon as the objective for the reconstruction has been achieved. Products such as Plasticine, soft waxes, kneaded erasers, and mold-making dough have oils and additives that readily transfer to porous materials, causing visual discoloration and contamination or inhibition of certain analyses. Photographic

lights, for example, can generate heat that will accelerate the transfer of contaminants from Plasticine-like materials to bone; they should be avoided altogether.

• New scanning technology allows for individual fragments to be scanned, and then, with the aid of a computer, the fragments can be reconstructed into a complete skull for instance digitally. This, too, would increase the ability to share data with those that are not physically able to see the remains and has the potential to reduce handling enormously. Documentation on the original scanning method should be made available, too, since this technique is in its infancy and it is likely to improve with time.

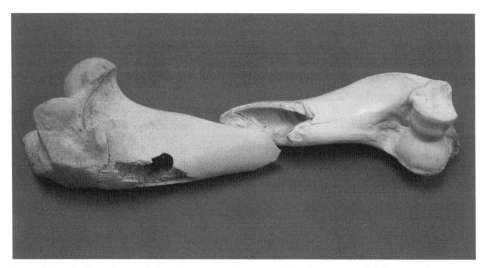

Figure 6.1. Broken *Sus scrofa* (pig) humerus. Courtesy of the University of Arizona, Arizona State Museum photographic collections. Photographer: Jannelle Weakly.

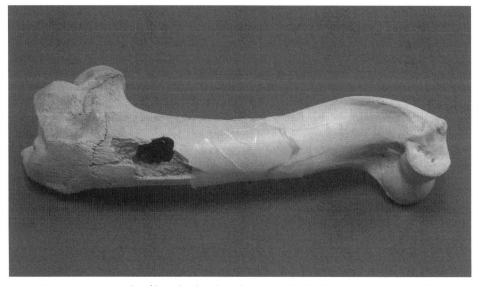

Figure 6.2. Example of how broken long bones can be held together with Parafilm. The break is still visible and a well-aligned and keyed fit is possible with this method. Courtesy of the University of Arizona, Arizona State Museum photographic collections. Photographer: Jannelle Weakly.

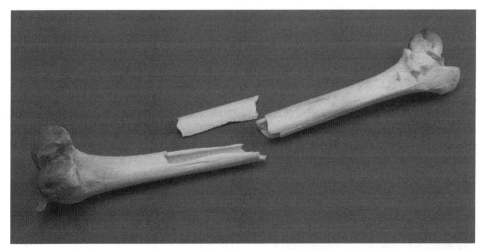

Figure 6.3.   Broken animal bone. Courtesy of the University of Arizona, Arizona State Museum photographic collections. Photographer: Jannelle Weakly.

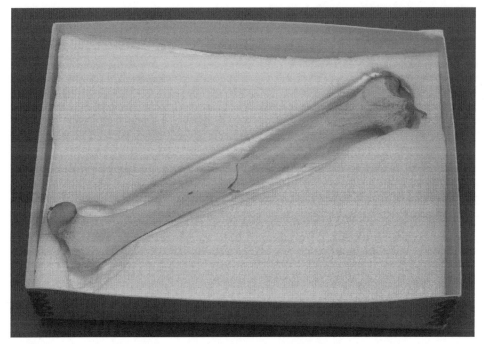

Figure 6.4.   Same broken bone held together with a passive cavity cut support tray, with layers of polyethylene foam and Tyvek cloth in an acid-free tray. Courtesy of the University of Arizona, Arizona State Museum photographic collections. Photographer: Jannelle Weakly.

The advantages of these four suggestions over adhesive use are multiple. Admittedly, they are not as "quick and easy" as using adhesives, and they will increase handling in some cases, but the results are far superior for the following reasons:

• These methods do not add a substrate between the bones to be joined. Adhesives add bulk or volume by the very nature of where they are placed (i.e., in the join). This means that reconstructions and measurements can be more accurate without the use of adhesives.

- If multiple breaks are to be reconstructed, the multiple applications in the joins can add up to a substantial difference in some fine measurements.
- The other great advantage of using microcrystalline wax sticks is found in the ability to make adjustments to fit as one continues to build up, for instance, a cranium from many fragments. With adhesives, once the first piece has set, it is difficult to soften most adhesives to correct a misalignment. With wax sticks, there is nothing between the joins, and if joins are found to be slightly off, they can be easily adjusted at any point in the reconstruction.

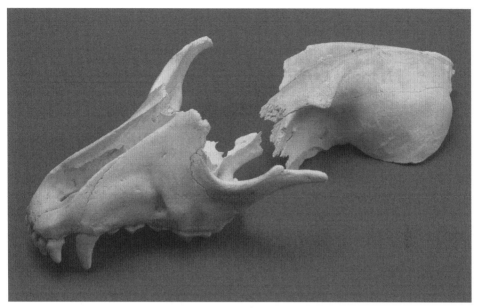

Figure 6.5.   Broken skull of *Canis familiaris* (domestic dog). Courtesy of the University of Arizona, Arizona State Museum photographic collections. Photographer: Jannelle Weakly.

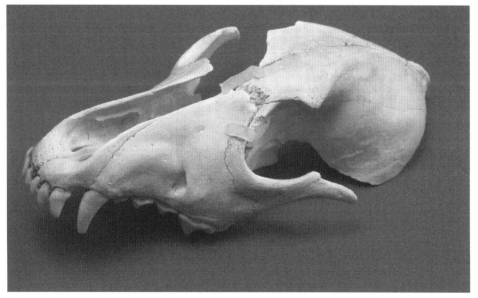

Figure 6.6.   Bones that cannot be held together with Parafilm can be fitted and held temporarily with microcrystalline wax sticks, which can be easily removed. Courtesy of the University of Arizona, Arizona State Museum photographic collections. Photographer: Jannelle Weakly.

In the end, better fit and better reconstructions are produced. When the tasks for which the physical reconstruction was produced are complete (e.g., measuring, photography, radiography, etc.), the reconstruction can be easily taken apart by removing the wax sticks. Some wax residue may remain after removal, but this is a small price to pay for higher accuracy, substantially greater reversibility, and the potential for a wider range of current and future analyses and observations.

CONCLUSION

The paradigm switch to maintenance of integrity includes not only the individual but the entire context, including field notes, treatment histories, and other related accumulated archives. In this chapter, we have covered a variety of treatments that have, in the past, been sanctioned as standard fare without sufficient scrutiny. Now with hindsight and experience from watching institutional collections age, we are turning to less invasive treatments.

Many challenges lie ahead, and it will take a team of professionals working together on the same goals to come up with new and more sympathetic methods for maintaining collection integrity and efficient access to collections. Williams (1999:110) is adamant about the need to view long-term preservation at the molecular level. In other words, we must try to preserve collections as unaltered as possible to provide for unforeseen possible future research opportunities or other uses. He also points out the ugly consequences if we do not change our ways: in short, we will be caring for vast collections with limited usefulness.

THE IMPACT OF PRESERVATION TREATMENTS ON DNA

Annick Vuissoz and M. Thomas P. Gilbert

The DNA analysis of archaeological curated and conserved specimens can be a powerful technique, providing novel and often otherwise unachievable insights into many issues, including kinship between specimens, genetic background and phylogenetic position, sex, and the history of past populations. However, the retrieval of DNA from such specimens is not straightforward and often involves at least partial sample destruction in order to retrieve tissue for the analysis. Furthermore, scientists who seek to make paleontological or anthropological interpretations based on ancient DNA often require access to the most pristine and/or well-preserved samples. Therefore, the decision to proceed with ancient DNA analysis requires careful consideration from both curators and the would-be analysts. In particular, strict criteria for the sampling procedure, transport, and handling are warranted (Hofreiter et al. 2001), and those involved must be aware of three serious problems that are often encountered during such analyses: contamination of the endogenous DNA, degradation of the endogenous (i.e., that originally derived from the tissue) DNA, and inhibition of the subsequent analytical tests.

Sample contamination in this perspective refers to the incorporation of exogenous sources of human DNA into the sample (i.e., DNA derived from outside the specimen), which can confuse the subsequent genetic analyses, often resulting in the generation of misleading results. Although many early studies paid scant attention to this issue, recent research has demonstrated that DNA contamination of the sample is important (e.g., Richards et al. 1995; Kolman and Tuross 2000; Hofreiter et al. 2001; Gilbert et al. 2005), particularly in those that are porous to liquid uptake (Gilbert et al. 2005). In the archaeological and curatorial context, serious risks are therefore represented by unprotected handling or washing (i.e., without the use of impermeable gloves), whereby modern human DNA is likely to be inadvertently introduced in the sample.

Additionally, preservation treatments may also offer a route for contamination to enter specimens. For example, bone glues, a natural adhesive derived from animal tissues that have been

THE IMPACT OF PRESERVATION TREATMENTS ON DNA (*continued*)

widely used as an adhesive or consolidant on paleontological material, have recently been demonstrated as an effective source of contaminant DNA, at least with regard to nonhuman samples (Nicholson et al. 2002). Although not directly related to human samples, the implication of this finding is clear: any treatment that might similarly convey human DNA onto or into a sample represents a problem.

Finally, recent studies have demonstrated that there are currently no good, effective methods available for decontaminating previously contaminated porous materials, such as bone and teeth. (Kolman and Tuross 2000; Hofreiter et al. 2001; Gilbert et al. 2005).

An additional problem facing DNA analyses that target old specimens is degradation of the DNA itself. As with many other molecules, DNA degrades in dead tissue as a function of temperature and time (Lindahl 1993). Therefore, the older samples are, and the warmer the environment they have been stored in over their entire history, the less likely it is that analyzable DNA will remain within a sample. To deal with this issue, various methods have been proposed that enable researchers to prescreen the sample using a range of methods, in order to gauge DNA survival (Hofreiter et al. 2001). Furthermore, not all DNA degradation is due to natural causes—chemical treatments also play an important role in DNA survival. That most commonly studied is the effect of tissue fixation in formaldehyde or Bouin's solution, both of which lead to severely damaged DNA (Vachot and Monnerot 1996). Intuitively, though, any treatments that involve extended periods of heat or chemicals that are known to interact adversely with DNA may represent a problem for future DNA analyses.

The third problem facing DNA analyses on old materials is inhibition of the most commonly used technique for genetic analyses, the polymerase chain reaction (PCR), by the presence of various chemicals in the DNA extract that are often coextracted with the DNA itself. Until recently, very little attention has been given to whether the preservatives used in the past, or the conservation treatments used today, are a problem in this respect. Recently however, one study has started to address these issues by looking at the effects of common conservation treatments on the retrieval of amplifiable DNA from samples of both old and recent cow leather (Vuissoz 2004). In brief, samples were treated with a range of common conservation products, including solvents, detergents and antideposition agents, diluted acids and complexants, lubricants, and various adhesives and consolidants (see the list later in this box). Subsequently, DNA extractions were performed and the extracts were subject to PCR to determine whether amplifiable DNA could be retrieved. While overall the results were promising—DNA could be retrieved from all treated samples—in many cases the DNA extract required dilution up to a hundredfold, prior to amplification success. Therefore, the data from this study strongly indicate that although the treatments tested on the new cow leather did not contaminate or degrade the DNA, in many cases they acted as PCR inhibitors and needed to be diluted to a sufficiently low concentration before DNA could be amplified. Although this solution appears simple, one associated problem is that should the DNA concentration in the original extract be sufficiently low, it may be lost during the dilution.

Conclusion

Current knowledge indicates that samples best suited for DNA analyses are those that originate from places that are cold and dry and that have been protected from potential sources of contamination and inhibition. Therefore, prior to the removal and/or destruction of any sample, we suggest that those involved seriously consider whether there is likely to be any amplifiable, uncontaminated DNA left in the sample and whether any PCR inhibitors might be present. Naturally those involved should further consider the effect of sampling on the specimen (e.g., further damage and/or contamination) and whether the resulting destruction is justified by the potential gain.

(*continued*)

Finally, those involved should ensure that if sampled, specimens be taken in a controlled manner and kept in such a way that further contamination, damage or inhibition is not likely. Examples include the use of sterile techniques and packaging, as well as storage at subzero temperatures until the time of the genetic analysis.

List of Conservation Products Used for the Study

Solvents: acetone; ethanol; toluene; Stoddards solvent

Detergents: carboxymethlycellulose; Orvus WA paste; Vulpex; Triton X-100

Dilute acids and complexants: Calgon sodium hexametaphophate; hydrogen peroxide; EDTA—ethylenediamine tetra-acetic acid (synthetic amino acid); citric acid; oxalic acid

Lubricants: lanoline; ceresin leather dressing; TSL-Technical Library Service Leather Protector; Bavon ASAK-ABP Leather Preservative

Adhesives and consolidants: Poly(vinyl alcohol); UHU poly(vinyl acetate) resin, Bookbinders poly(vinyl acetate) emulsion, Lineco Neutral-pH poly(vinyl acetate) emulsion; Paraloid B-72 acrylic resin, Rhoplex AC-33, AC-234 and N-580 acrylic emulsions, Primal AC-33 and WS24, Acrysol ASE-60 acrylic dispersion; methylecellulose, Klucel G and Cellugel hydroxypropycellulose ethers; HXTAL NYL-1 epoxy resin; rabbit skin protein glue; shellac (insect secretion in ethanol), wheat starch paste

REFERENCES

Appelbaum, Barbara
    1987 Criteria for Treatment: Reversibility. *Journal of the American Institute for Conservation* 26(2): 65–67.

Gilbert, M. Thomas P., Lars Rudbeck, Eske Willerslev, Anders J. Hansen, Colin Smith, Kirsty E. H. Penkman, Kurt Prangenberg, Christina M. Nielsen-Marsh, Miranda E. Jans, Paul Arthur, Niels Lynnerup, Gordon Turner-Walker, Martin Biddle, Birthe Kjølbye-Biddle, and Matthew J. Collins
    2005 Biochemical and Physical Correlates of DNA Contamination in Archaeological Human Bones and Teeth Excavated at Matera, Italy. *Journal of Archaeological Science* 32:785–793.

Hofreiter, Michael, David Serre, Hendrick N. Poinar, Melanie Kuch, and Svante Pääbo
    2001 Ancient DNA. *Nature Reviews Genetics* 2:353–358.

Horie, Charles V.
    1990 *Materials for Conservation: Organic Consolidants, Adhesives and Coatings*. Butterworths, London.

Johnson, Jessica S.
    2001 A Long-Term Look at Polymers Used to Preserve Bones. In *Human Remains: Conservation, Retrieval and Analysis: Proceedings of a Conference Held in Williamsburg, VA, Nov 7–11th 1999*, edited by Emily Williams, pp. 99–102. BAR International Series 934. Archaeopress, Oxford.

Kolman, Connie J., and Noreen Tuross
    2000 Ancient DNA Analysis of Human Populations. *American Journal of Physical Anthropology* 111:5–23.

Lindahl, Thomas
    1993 Instability and Decay of the Primary Structure of DNA. *Nature* 362:709–715.

Nicholson, Graeme J., Jürgen Tomiuk, Alfred Czarnetzki, Lutz Bachmann, and Carsten M. Pusch
    2002 Detection of Bone Glue Treatment as a Major Source of Contamination in Ancient DNA Analyses. *American Journal of Physical Anthropology* 118:117–120.

Odegaard, Nancy, and Alyce Sadongei

    2005 *Old Poisons, New Problems: A Museum Resource for Managing Contaminated Cultural Materials.* AltaMira Press, Walnut Creek, California.

Richards, Martin, Bryan Sykes, and Robert Hedges

    1995 Authenticating DNA Extracted from Ancient Skeletal Remains. *Journal of Archeological Science* 22:291–299.

Schwartz, Jeffrey

    1998 *What Bones Tell Us.* University of Arizona Press, Tucson.

Vachot, Anne-Marie, and Monique Monnerot

    1996 Extraction, Amplification and Sequencing of DNA from Formalin-Fixed Specimens. *Ancient Biomolecules* 1:3–16.

Vuissoz, Annick

    2004 The Impact of Conservation Treatments on DNA Retrievals from Leather. Master's thesis, Haute Ecole d'Arts Appliqués, University of Applied Sciences of Western Switzerland, Neuchâtel (in French).

White, Tim

    2000 *Human Osteology.* Second Edition. Academic Press, New York.

Williams, Stephen

    1999 Destructive Preservation: A Review of the Effect of Standard Preservation Practices on the Future Use of Natural History Collections. Göteborg Studies in Conservation 6. Dissertation, Acta Universitatis Gothoburgensis, Göteborg, Sweden.

Williams, Stephen, and Catherine A. Hawks

    1987 History of Preparation Materials Used for Recent Mammal Specimens. In *Mammal Collection Management,* edited by H. H. Genoways, D. Jones, and O. L. Rossolimo, pp. 21–49. Texas Tech University, Lubbock.

CHAPTER 7

Indigenous Value Orientations in the Care of Human Remains

ALYCE SADONGEI AND PHILLIP CASH CASH

An old man's son was killed far away in the Staked Plains. When the old man heard of it he went there and gathered up the bones. Thereafter, wherever the old man ventured, he led a dark hunting horse which bore the bones of his son on its back. And the old man said to whomever he saw: You see how it is that now my son consists in his bones, that his bones are polished and so gleam like glass in the light of the sun and moon, that he is very beautiful.

—N. Scott Momaday (Kiowa), excerpt from "The Colors of Night"

THE INHERENT ETHICAL DIMENSIONS IN THE TREATMENT OF HUMAN REMAINS HAVE AN EVER-INCREASING practical relevance to science practitioners, conservators, and indigenous rights advocates when such treatment fulfills the mandates of repatriation legislation, such as NAGPRA, or when such treatment involves long-term preservation. While the ethical dimensions regarding the treatment of human remains are universally acknowledged, conventional and appropriate ethical behaviors in the academe or museum institution do not always exist cross-culturally. As a consequence, indigenous communities tend to be greatly affected by institutionalized practices that, in their eyes, lack the appropriate ethical behaviors in the care and treatment of human remains with whom they are potentially affiliated. Indigenous communities who have implemented NAGPRA by claiming and repatriating ancestral human remains to their homelands can readily attest to the unequal status that exists both for remains and descendant populations. The general observation is that the origins of ethical differences in treatment of human remains are institutional as much as they are cultural.

Our inquiry into this problem calls for renewed interests in the development of ethical norms that take into account the aspirations and rights of affected descendant populations. The goal of this chapter is to identify a minimal set of ethical treatment protocols that incorporates the concerns of affected populations in the treatment and conservation of indigenous human remains from the Americas. Our hope and concern is that our brief review will not only open a dialogue that informs current scientific and museum practice but will enable practices that ensure greater cultural sensitivity to affected indigenous populations.

BACKGROUND

The development of ethical treatments emanating from Western notions of claim, control, and property over indigenous human remains as scientific objects of study have largely relegated the aspirations and rights of descendant populations to the periphery. As a consequence, affected indigenous populations have had very little involvement in how ethical treatment protocols can and should be developed. In fact, the interests of indigenous peoples have been and often continue to be viewed as a barrier to research. So long as this perception exists, the claim and control over indigenous human remains by Western institutions have been reason enough to resist any development of ethical standards or treatments that overcome cultural barriers and provide for basic civil rights concerning treatment of the dead.

The passage of human rights legislation, such as NAGPRA of 1990 and the National Museum of the American Indian Act (NMAIA) of 1989, is an attempt to rectify this situation by granting federally recognized tribes the right of disposition over ancestral human remains with whom they are culturally affiliated. However, in the post-NAGPRA era, the call for the ethical treatment of ancestral human remains by indigenous peoples continues to be misunderstood or trivialized because they express values that are, in many ways, diametrically opposed to entrenched Western science standards. In fact, some would claim that a renewed call for ethics debates in light of NAGPRA is unwarranted because the application of the law is itself a sufficient fulfillment of NAGPRA's moral mandate.

Our position is simple. The ethics surrounding the treatment of indigenous human remains are not simply concomitant measures defined through legal frameworks; rather, we feel that ethics should emerge naturally from a universal commitment to our global humanity.

VALUE ORIENTATIONS IN THE TREATMENT OF HUMAN REMAINS

At the most basic level, our shared value orientations, as science practitioners, conservators, and indigenous rights advocates, are formed in part from the physical material remains of deceased persons as represented by the body and their associated units of information (see figure 7.1).

Value orientations thus obtain their coherence from systems of meaning that arise through the interaction with one's environment. That is, each value orientation treats the material remains of deceased persons as a set of heuristic symbols, as in the case of the indigenous value orientation, or as a set of heuristic objects, as in the case of the Western value orientation. Our claim is that the human significance attributed to the material remains of deceased persons is universal. However, our cultural diversity is such that the way we treat and care for human remains varies across its local and global environments. Thus, to view ancestral human remains as heuristic symbols is to imply that there is a global dimension to the generation and persistence of meaning. Likewise, to view human remains as heuristic objects is to imply that there is a strictly local dimension to generation and persistence of meaning. Despite these generalizations, it is fairly predictable that inequalities and conflict can and do arise when there is an insistence on the validity of one system of meaning to the exclusion of the other.

We can begin to discern how the values regarding the material remains of deceased persons (i.e., the body) guide human behavior in important ways. For example, it is common for descendant indigenous populations to claim an affinity to ancestral human remains based upon a set of value orientations that are informed by beliefs and attitudes arising from the natural, so-

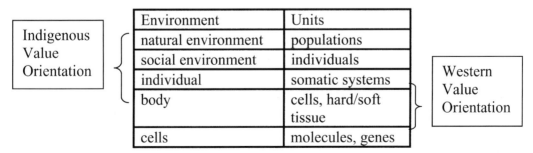

Figure 7.1.   Shared value orientations (adapted from Dow 1986).

cial and individual sphere. Understandably, the accretion of these value orientations, diverse as they may be, provides the basis for past and current cultural practices regarding the care, treatment, and reinterment of human remains. In our experience as indigenous scholars and as community members who have participated in the repatriation process, a particularly important but little-known fact often goes unstated when a claimant community comes face-to-face with the remains of their dead ancestors in a museum. That is, the act and experience of repatriation bears witness to the history of indiscriminant removal of thousands of ancestral remains from Indian lands, which is inextricably tied to the experience of colonization and past injustices. For many indigenous communities, the removal of an ancestor from his or her final resting place is an unnatural and desecratory act that belies human comprehension. Preserving human remains in a museum is contrary to the most fundamental aspirations of indigenous culture and society. Ultimately, however, many view the act of repatriation as a life affirming, healing process. It is also transformative, thus enabling indigenous communities to intervene where Western science has benefited disproportionately from the study and curation of indigenous human remains.

The compelling issue indigenous communities are most often confronted with is the problem of "how" to repatriate an ancestor. It involves two interrelated but crucial dilemmas. The first is how to naturalize the desecrated dead from their unnatural state. The second is how to apply care and treatment protocols to a curated ancestral remain with the greatest human dignity possible and with the least "risk" to both the dead and the living. While reburial is often the ultimate solution, interim solutions are hard to come by due to the diversity of indigenous mortuary traditions and to the complexity of each curatorial context. Therefore, the challenge of applying ethically informed care and treatment protocols in a postmortem context is unprecedented because the risks and consequences of treating the material remains of deceased persons *outside the life world of their community* are largely unknown. Thus, we claim that the repatriation process is largely reconstitutive whereby indigenous communities are *reconstituting a potential life world* for ancestral human remains, one that may include but not be limited to reburial, interim storage and curation (with appropriate care and treatment protocols), or even permanent curation in a museum repository.

Our human complexity will always be at issue in clarifying ethical behavior; however, we believe that we can arrive at an ethics of integrity in the treatment of the material remains of deceased persons. The ethics of integrity suggest that science practitioners and conservators are in a key position to broaden the notion of care in the treatment of curated human remains that helps minimize some of the potential risks and consequences to indigenous communities. Thus, it is of vital necessity to expect institutions not just to consult but to initiate meaningful cross-cultural dialogue with indigenous communities to mutually determine what minimum thresholds of care may apply toward any particular collection of concern. Likewise, indigenous communities should look on scientists and conservators not as adversaries but as key players who can assist indigenous communities in caretaking relations within institutions where indigenous remains are housed. Nevertheless, the common denominator for the mutual development of ethical behaviors in this context is a fundamental desire to maintain and preserve the integrity in the material remains of deceased persons in their former, present, and future state, whether it is for purposes of repatriation, long-term preservation, or scientific study.

MINIMAL GUIDELINES FOR TREATMENT OF INSTITUTIONALIZED INDIGENOUS HUMAN REMAINS

The proposed guidelines are intended to support the foundation of indigenous value orientations that are so often neglected. They affirm a central theme in the goal of repatriation—that under the impact of death, the human body retains at least some degree of autonomy to self-synthesize with the universe at large whether it is through the process of decay or otherwise.

Completeness in the Integrity of Persons
- All of the intact physical human remains must be stored together in terms of their individual completeness; this includes bone dust, crematory ash, bone fragments, and any other type of residues originating from the original burial context.
- All the intact physical human remains must be stored together with any associated funerary objects obtained from the original burial context.
- Research activities that employ deconstructive analyses and potentially endanger the physical integrity of the human remains minimally require consultation with affected descendant populations to obtain informed consent.
- Researchers should ensure that their activities do not unnecessarily cause the accidental shedding of their own individual hairs, skin, and/or the transfer of bodily oils while in contact with the institutionalized human remains. Such contact is perceived as violating the integrity of persons.

Artificial Reconstructions
- Physical human remains that have been disfigured by the application of ink, artificially reconstructed or stabilized by means of adhesives, wiring, plaster fills, or any other device should be removed at the request of the affected descendant populations, using techniques and materials that do not endanger the physical integrity of the human remains. Any future reconstructions should be with consent and employ temporary systems that will be completely removed after the task is completed, without harming the remains.

Isolation
- Physical human remains and any associated funerary objects should be isolated from other non-mortuary collections, except associated funerary goods. The isolation of mortuary collections will help reduce the risk of casual contact by affected descendant populations. Such isolation can be the actual physical separation or the use of aesthetic or psychological devices to intentionally distinguish these types of collections for purposes of overall care and respect.

These basic guidelines address those areas that have been identified as being important by indigenous communities through consultation and public dialogue.

CONCLUSION

Our inquiry sought to address a gap in knowledge regarding indigenous values and ethics concerning the care and treatment of human remains and their potential to inform current institutional practices. We identified and contrasted two value orientations that inform ethical consciousness not as an end in itself but as a conceptual tool for rethinking our understanding of the cultural status of indigenous human remains in museum repositories. Based on this summary, we have proposed that an ethics of integrity must minimally recognize the aspirations and rights of affected indigenous populations by incorporating what we believe to be culturally appropriate guidelines in the care and treatment of ancestral human remains.

We are confident that the ethical practices rooted in the social sciences are resilient enough to accommodate the value systems of indigenous communities. Certainly, part of this change is incumbent on a critical self-reflection and a greater awareness by scientists, conservators, and museum curators as to how their ethical practices can and do affect the indigenous community. Open communication, collaboration, and the application of real-world knowledge are all dynamic elements that open the doors and minds of all involved.

THE VERMILLION ACCORD ON HUMAN REMAINS

The Vermillion Accord was adopted in 1989 at the South Dakota WAC (World Archaeological Congress) Inter-Congress. The World Archaeological Congress is a nonprofit organization dedicated to promoting interest in the past, encouraging regional histories, and fostering international academic interaction. The Vermillion Accord helped pave the way for inclusion of indigenous interests in the archaeological and museum fields' professional codes of ethics.

1. Respect for the mortal remains of the dead shall be accorded to all, irrespective of origin, race, religion, nationality, custom and tradition.
2. Respect for the wishes of the dead concerning disposition shall be accorded whenever possible, reasonable and lawful, when they are known or can be reasonably inferred.
3. Respect for the wishes of the local community and of relatives or guardians of the dead shall be accorded whenever possible, reasonable and lawful.
4. Respect for the scientific research value of skeletal, mummified and other human remains (including fossil hominids) shall be accorded when such value is demonstrated to exist.
5. Agreement on the disposition of fossil, skeletal, mummified and other remains shall be reached by negotiation on the basis of mutual respect for the legitimate concerns of science and education.
6. The express recognition that the concerns of various ethnic groups, as well as those of science are legitimate and to be respected, will permit acceptable agreements to be reached and honored.

REFERENCES

Dow, J.
   1986 Universal Aspects of Symbolic Healing: A Theoretical Synthesis. *American Anthropologist* 88:56–69.

Joseph, Chief
   1879 An Indian's View of Indian Affairs. *North American Review* 128:412–433.

Momaday, N. S.
   1976 *The Gourd Dancer*. Harper & Row, New York.

CHAPTER 8

Storage and Transport

VICKI CASSMAN AND NANCY ODEGAARD

> Ay, but to die and go we know not where;
> To lie in cold obstruction and to rot;
> This sensible warm motion to become
> A kneaded clod; and the delighted spirit
> To bathe in fiery floods or to reside
> In thrilling regions of thick-ribbed ice;
> To be imprison'd in the viewless winds,
> And blown with restless violence round about
> The pendant world.
>
> —William Shakespeare in *Measure for Measure*

FEW WOULD SUSPECT THEY WOULD END UP CONTAINED IN AN INSTITUTION, INSTEAD OF, AS SHAKESPEARE describes, blown by restless viewless winds. Lack of individual consent (not to mention lack of title) is problematic for human remains collections, and for this very reason, holdings in museums and universities are becoming more heavily scrutinized. The ethical debates about the position of institutional remains aside, all parties are interested to some degree in preservation and protective access of remains. Preservation, protection, and respect are the baselines for consideration in the development of storage recommendations for human remains. As was discussed in chapter 4 on condition, there are several handling and environmental concerns where storage plays a vital role. Well-designed storage provides short- and long-term benefits.

Unfortunately, there are no publicly available housing standards, nor has there been any unspoken minimum agreed on by the diverse communities that have a stake in the issues surrounding human remains. Published information regarding the care and storage of human remains has been infrequent (Bowron 2003; Rose and Hawks 1995; Trimble et al. 2001), and it rarely covers the long-term housing of large collections of human remains. Assessment of appropriate housing for human remains is compounded by a lack of communication within institutions and descendants, if any still exist or can be identified.

Storage is a topic that covers a lot of ground in terms of curation and preservation concerns. Proper storage is one of the most direct ways of contributing to preventive care. Most frequently the focus is on storage immediately surrounding a set of remains, but in this chapter, we will look at the bigger picture of the environmental envelope provided by the building, too. We prefer to approach the topic of storage as "packages within packages," hence the analogy of the Matryushka dolls. These packages include building structure, room, cabinetry, and various levels of containers and materials around the individual.

Figure 8.1
Matryushka or Matryoshka Dolls

Building   Room   Cabinet   Box   Tray   Bag

THE BUILDING AND ROOM SELECTION

A building plays many roles as the outermost package, or the largest or exterior Matryushka doll. The building and its mechanical air-handling system determine the ambient environmental conditions and security on which the preservation of human remains depends. The importance of a building may seem obvious; however, a few institutions still use outdoor storage for archaeological human remains because they are overwhelmed by volume and are without an adequate operating budget. Buildings with humid conditions due to leaky roofs or faulty overhead plumbing offer only slightly more protection than outdoor storage. The role of a building is to defend collections from the elements and extremes of climate and seasonal changes, as well as pests and theft.

Preventing deterioration or damage is the number one goal for storage. Years ago, during a presentation to an audience of international conservators, mention was made of thousands of archaeological human remains stored in small, humid buildings in southern Europe. The conservator had taken hundreds of badly deteriorating human remains and consolidated them with an acrylic polymer to save what remained of the rapidly disintegrating bones. It was a very impressive system the conservator developed, but at the end of the talk, someone asked whether the consolidated bones would have a new home. The unhappy reply was the remains will go back to the same storage that caused the initial problems due to the politics of the situation. At that point, it was clear that efforts would have been better spent improving or finding a better storage location for all the bones rather than treating the worst cases. Even though this conservator advanced the field in terms of creating new techniques for working with deteriorated bone, the conservator's efforts at changing the building conditions had been futile, and in hindsight the collection as a whole may not have been optimally served by the intervention of treatment.

Since the early 1980s, preventive conservation has been a dictum for conservators. The American Institute for Conservation (AIC) defines this concept as "the mitigation of deterioration and damage to cultural property through the formulation and implementation of policies and procedures for the following: appropriate environmental conditions; handling and maintenance procedures for storage, exhibition, packing, transport, and use; integrated pest management; emergency preparedness and response; and reformatting/duplication" (AIC 2005:47).

It is rare to find an institution where the design and layout of the building have considered the storage needs of the collection. Instead, we find collection storage often in the least desirable areas. Typically the design and appearance of the building receive more attention than the functions the building will hold. Collections are typically placed in the leftover closets, awkwardly shaped rooms, attics, basements, off-site warehouses, or even outdoor sheds. These locations are not adequate in terms of preservation and protection. As in the analogy of the Matryushka dolls, the innermost doll is the most protected. Her larger sisters provide ever-increasing levels of protection from changes in humidity, temperature, pollutants, light damage, pests, theft, and vandalism. In the same way, the interior of a building usually provides the most stable environment for collections, because outer rooms, basements, and attics (or top stories) buffer or cushion environmental effects. Rarely is such prime real estate given to collections, especially human remains. However, with the concepts of buffering in mind, one can weigh the risks and benefits of any location within a building to determine the best-fit or most beneficial environment to house a collection. It means determining which room has the fewest outside walls, which walls have the most insulation, or which room has the fewest overhead pipes that pose potential humidity or leakage problems. Collections that are the most vulnerable to environmental conditions and most sensitive to policies of restricted access should have their storage location carefully considered.

When new facilities are designed or changes are considered to existing structures, risks and benefits need to be assessed. Conservators refer to the nine or ten pathways of deterioration in their assessments. In this way, they can weigh risks and benefits and make decisions based on the best fit for each circumstance. Rarely are ideal conditions found in any institution, especially in older or retrofitted buildings; therefore, with an institutional survey in hand, staff can consider the implications and make informed decisions. Once optimum collection areas have been identified, limited resources can be allocated to provide the greatest benefits.

In the conservation field, we refer to nine agents of deterioration (Michalski 1990; Waller 1994):

1. *Direct physical damage.* Collapsing structures during an earthquake, mishandling including dropping, or inappropriate support are examples of modes of deterioration that fall under this agent.
2. *Radiation (light).* Exposure to daylight and artificial light causes not only fading or bleaching but weakening of the materials. The effects of radiation are cumulative.
3. *Thieves, vandals, and displacers.* Robbery is usually planned or a spontaneous willful act of malintent; however, a great deal of damage to collections is done by displacers. *Displacers* are people who misplace items or separate materials from their contexts or, through sloppiness, end up losing items. Removing labels and forgetting to replace them is one example.
4. *Fire.* Damage may be directly from fire or collaterally from fire retardants or water damage during fire extinguishing.
5. *Water.* Damage can result from leaking pipes, fire repression or sprinklers in a false alarm, and flooding from bathrooms or leaky roofs.
6. *Pests.* Within a museum context, this risk usually refers to insect and rodent activity in and around the collections, but it might also include mold.
7. *Contaminants.* These agents include pollution, off-gassing from building materials, nicotine deposits, pesticide usage, or something as seemingly innocent as direct handling that could interfere with DNA studies.
8. *Incorrect temperature.* Extremes of temperature and rapid, repetitive fluctuations are most problematic. Comfortable temperature for the living is likewise recommended for human remains.
9. *Incorrect humidity.* Too high or too low or rapid and repetitive fluctuating humidity are all highly problematic for human remains.

The tenth agent of deterioration is curatorial neglect, which may include any or all of the other nine agents. When collections are completely ignored for long periods, any of the agents of deterioration can take an enormous toll on collections. More than any other container, the building and the room can provide the greatest protection from the majority of these agents.

CABINETRY SELECTION

With a room selected for maximum buffering from the most likely risks, attention to preservation-quality cabinetry would be next in a plan to improve storage conditions for human remains. The basic function of cabinetry, besides organization, is to further assist in protection from the nine agents of deterioration.

Cabinetry and closed shelving provide another protective layer from all nine agents of deterioration and should be a goal for human remains collections. Cabinetry offers a sealed secure enclosure with drawers or shelves. Flexibility in arrangement, smooth glides for the drawers, and inert gasketing are among the conservation standards for museum cabinetry. Cabinetry can be freestanding, stacking, or part of a mobile compacting assembly. Steel with a powder coating, anodized aluminum, and heavy-gauge chrome-plated steel wires are good materials for storage. Closed shelving is a storage unit that is enclosed on all sides. A lockable unit provides even greater protection. Providing sturdy, wide platform ladders is recommended to facilitate access to higher shelves. Keeping collection areas clean is yet another challenge for collections managers. It is essential to have storage containers that are made of easy-to-clean materials. Dust tends to collect even in the best of environments, so it is good to have the boxes and shelves made of a material that can quickly and easily be cleaned.

Open shelving does allow for quick assessments of inventory, but there are other more protective means to survey collections without the total exposure of open shelving. If one has open shelving for human remains but no immediate budget for upgrades, the National Park Service (see http://www.cr.nps.gov/museum/publications/conserveogram/04-02.pdf, accessed April 16, 2006) offers instructions for quick and inexpensive dust covers for metal shelves that can act as a stopgap measure. In several collections nationally and internationally, open shelving is used for crania. Though this setup does provide researchers with an at-a-glance preview of such things as cranial deformation, malnutrition, or interpersonal violence (broken noses), it provides no protection from any of the agents of deterioration. This is especially risky in seismically active areas of the world. In such cases, a stopgap measure to reduce damage to remains for, at least, low-level earthquakes would be to pad shelves and use fishing line or rope suspended between the uprights to provide a restraint and prevent crania rolling off and smashing onto the floor. However, the most common upgrade to open shelving is the use of closed boxes, and this is certainly better than exposed remains (see the insert on page 110).

CABINETRY BASIC REQUIREMENTS

Many of the following suggestions were adapted from the National Archives of Australia's website (http://www.naa.gov.au/recordkeeping/rkpubs/advices/advice1.html#equip, accessed April 16, 2006).

- Wooden shelving should be avoided since it is highly acidic, gives off harmful vapors, is a fire danger, and can attract and house insects.
- Powder-coated metal shelves or cabinets are recommended because they do not emit corrosive volatiles, do not rust, and are durable.
- Light-colored cabinets (and floors) are preferred to allow for quick monitoring for pests.
- Shelves should start *at least* ten centimeters (four inches) off the floor in case of a flood and to prevent direct access by insects.
- It is often recommended to have at least twenty centimeters' distance from walls to permit air circulation, inhibit mold, and prevent insect access.

- Stability is vital especially for high or stacked units. There should be no risk of toppling from placement of heavy items at the top or front of the unit. Anchoring to the wall or between units is an important consideration, especially in seismic areas.
- Shelves should be designed to bear at least the maximum weight of the heaviest box in a collection.
- Aisles between shelving should allow easy and adequate access to and removal of remains. Rolling ladders are required to match the required shelf height with a calculated width at the base for safety.
- Tables should be located next to the storage cabinets to comfortably and safely check or retrieve the contents of boxes and/or drawers.
- Cabinets, shelves, drawers, and boxes should all be clearly labeled with their contents so retrieval can be accomplished with minimal handling (see the Bones Version 1.0 software found on the AltaMira website associated with this volume).
- Cabinets with moving parts, such as for compact storage, or cabinets with drawers or doors should operate smoothly, have lips at the front to prevent items from falling onto the floor and one at the back to prevent them from falling behind the cabinet, and, in the case of drawers, have stops to prevent them from being pulled completely out.
- When estimating spacing for shelving, leave enough room to allow for hands to fit around containers. And be sure to leave enough aisle space to easily maneuver containers, drawers, and cabinet doors.

Airing and Checking New Cabinetry

With the arrival of new storage equipment, it is vital that it be allowed to air for several days before putting collections into the units. Doing so allows any of the last vapors from curing, packing, and manufacturing to be released. Sometimes museum staff have noticed an odor that they may describe as "chemical" or "like a solvent" even beyond the initial airing. There are most likely two sources for such a smell that could emanate from the interior of the cabinetry itself. The paint may not have cured well; the "baked enamel" may have been heated enamel paint, which is continuing to give off vapors from the paint application. Or the gasketing material may be the source of the odor and chemical off-gassing. When problems with the gasketing in storage cabinetry are suspected, the manufacturer should be contacted, or replacements can be made with food-grade, postcured silicone rubber gasketing.

DESIGNING FOR NEW STORAGE: COMPACT STORAGE?

Many decisions are involved in the initial design or selection of storage cabinetry. The most obvious considerations are the special needs and size of the collections to be stored and the space and funds available. If the collection is relatively uniform in size and needs, then modular systems are an excellent choice. Standard-size cabinets can be ordered and this reduces costs greatly. Manufacturers have developed such systems for use in museums, and these are often well tested and of archival quality (see, e.g., the National Park Service's article on modular "Museum Storage Cabinets": http://www.cr.nps.gov/museum/publications/conserveogram/04-01.pdf, accessed May 22, 2006).

However, if one does not have sufficient floor space to accommodate the collection comfortably in the area available, then a substantially more expensive option is to look at compact or mobile storage. Here the aisle spaces are utilized to provide more space for storage, and the shelf units move on a track to provide an aisle only where needed. Compact/mobile storage versus static storage can hold twice as much in the same space (see International Council on Archives, http://www.ica.org/biblio/FAQ1E.pdf, accessed May 22, 2006).

Besides the increased cost of compactor or mobile units, other considerations arise as well. For example, will the building support the weight of the compactor system, and will the floor allow for the tracks that must be anchored or embedded in a level floor? Also, it is vital that a system with very low vibrational coefficients be used since the inherent movement of the system could actually increase deterioration of collections and act as an accelerated aging system if they vibrate too much. Most manufacturers that deal with museums regularly are aware of this factor, and their systems are wonderfully smooth while moving and especially well gasketed and buffered for the impact at closing. Options are also available for inclusive lighting, end panels for inventory/catalog information, and security/safety features to be considered during planning.

Skeletalized adult human remains are relatively uniform depending on age, unless the collection has individuals who have suffered (during life) from arthritis that has left them with fused bones or those with some or all of their soft tissue remaining. In the case of nonuniform collections, such as mummy bundles (or large faunal remains), or individuals with many associated artifacts, customized systems may be required. This will increase the costs substantially, and the manufacturers will need to have clear specifications in order to safely accommodate and carry out the special order. In the end, it is a balance among the needs of the collection, the space available, potential future needs and growth of the collection, and the funds available.

CONTAINERS

Containers are the curator's most common line of defense in care and preservation. Good preservation-quality materials are needed since the containers are in the most intimate contact with the individuals of concern. Preservation-quality housing at the most basic level starts with a storage box made from inert and acid-free materials. Materials that are inert do not off-gas or give off vapors or plasticizers. The box must also be durable and able to support the weight of larger individuals. Common materials are acid-free cardboard, acid-free mat board, and polypropylene or polyethylene corrugated board.

Good design provides the greatest defense from one of the most destructive of the museum forces curators must deal with—human handling. Well-designed containers reduce direct handling, because they provide for clear labels, indicating contents and any special information. Often a diagram, digital image, or photocopy of a photograph is an excellent addition to the outside of the box because it prevents unnecessary movements or openings of the box. Good containers always start with good labels. For individual human remains, download Bones software at the AltaMira website (www.altamira.com) to produce diagrams or visual inventories suitable for the outside of boxes.

Collection managers' and conservators' main concern is conservation (Williams 1999: 20–23). They make selection decisions about box materials, size, durability, organization, cataloging, and registration based on long-term preservation strategies. Because collective experience has shown that handling causes the most damage to institutionalized human osteological remains, it is vital to create a box that allows controlled access but reduces the damage caused by excessive or inappropriate handling (Bowron 2003; Caffell et al. 2001; Ganiaris 2001). Proper storage must allow for minor tilting—for example, when removing a box from a high shelf. During tilting, the contents of boxes should not be allowed to roll around and become damaged.

Organizing collections in numerical order by catalog number greatly reduces the amount of time spent locating individuals. It is preferable to organize individuals numerically by catalog number rather than by age, sex, race, or some other variable because catalog numbers represent a clear and understandable system that does not make presumptions about a researcher's interests or specific questions. However, often it is very desirable to have individuals from the same site or culture housed together. These decisions should be made with the help of consultations with descendants or other stakeholders. Having a sortable electronic database containing a biological (i.e., age, sex, and ethnic information) and provenience profile (see chapter 10) as well as a bone inventory (see the Bones software) is recommended to reduce initial handling.

In addition to proper organization, it is essential that the storage container be of adequate size. Researchers often find it frustrating to waste valuable time trying to fit an individual back into a box that is clearly too small. A box that is too small is also the cause of a great deal of wear caused by bone rubbing against bone. It is also helpful to have bones grouped together within a box. For instance, keeping the hand bones together and sorted by right and left sides, keeping the ribs together, and keeping the vertebrae together reduces the amount of time a researcher spends looking for and placing specific bones. Grouping also reduces the amount of handling a skeleton is subjected to and reduces damage to the bones.

Descendants, researchers, or conservators may raise other concerns. It is important to consult with descendants when considering specific housing and ritual needs. Some consultations have revealed that, in general, it is important for human remains to resemble a human form in storage. The bones should not be randomly scattered throughout the box, nor should different parts of an individual be stored in separate areas of a room or building or in different containers. For example, crania are sometimes housed separately from the post-cranial skeleton, and this is often offensive to descendants. In addition, Sadongei and Cash Cash suggest in chapter 7 that burial goods or associated funerary objects be kept with the individual. It is preferable that the body be presented in a manner that is close to its position prior to excavation, keeping in mind that a box for a fully extended adult is too large and awkward to be safely handled. Some descendants may prefer that remains are in contact with inert organic materials, such as cotton muslin cloth or paper as opposed to plastic. Accommodations may need to be available for ritual offerings or feedings, and these should be discussed with all parties involved.

For researchers such as physical anthropologists, time constraints and accessibility are two prominent concerns. Researchers often have a limited amount of time in which to study a given collection. Constraints related to the cost of conducting research may limit the amount of time a researcher can spend with a given collection. Accessibility influences the amount of time a researcher spends with collections. The operating schedule of a repository, the time constraints of museum personnel, permission restrictions imposed by stakeholders, and the needs of other researchers may also restrict time. A well-organized storage system will aid researchers.

Housing of human remains is a basic issue that has not been standardized or actively discussed. Despite the indispensable function of a box, the issue of how to best create satisfactory housing has been sorely neglected. Two new osteological boxes have been designed with preservation in mind. Bowron (2003) has a very elaborate system of boxes and trays within a box that is being tested at the University of Durham, United Kingdom. Another box that was recently designed (Cassman et al. 2001) is commercially available from Hollinger Corporation in Fredericksburg, Virginia.

BAGS AND INDIVIDUAL WRAPPINGS

Bags seem like an easy issue, but the variety of bags found in collections is surprising. For instance, muslin bags are used frequently for small bones such as those of the hands or feet, and during excavations, paper bags, zip-locking bags, twist-tie bags, and Tyvek envelope bags are common. Sometimes even larger black plastic storage bags are used.

THE OSTEOLOGY BOX

Vicki Cassman

Several years ago, with the prospect of new storage areas, graduate students and I began to explore how to improve conditions for the institutionalized human remains housed in the Department of Anthropology at the University of Nevada, Las Vegas. Our storage boxes were clearly inadequate; the bone dust was accumulating at an alarming rate, though staff had upgraded the storage boxes only ten years earlier with what was considered the standard at many museums at the time of purchase. Skeletal remains, especially for complete adults, suffered from crowding and crushing, and the boxes were made from acidic cardboard. The crowded conditions also meant increased handling because individual bones were difficult to find.

Since nothing on the market at the time was adequate, and since we did not find a model storage system at any other institution, we decided to create a box to suit the apparent need. A team was formed with physical anthropologists, archaeologists, and museologists. First, we listed various perceived needs:

- Made of inert sturdy materials
- Sized to avoid bones crushing each other but small enough to be handled by one person and fit through a door easily
- Allow for anatomically logical placements
- Reduces need to handle bones
- Flexibility for various-size individuals

With these qualities in mind, we created several prototypes and tested them. Some of the goals were easier to achieve than others. For instance, we were able to create a system that reduces handling substantially. On the other hand, we had hoped to have an anatomically correct distribution, but the needs for balancing the weight distributions within the box took precedence to increase ease and safety in handling. In the resulting box, the skull is protected at one end, the spine has a tray the length of the box that lifts out, and the long bones are together in a tray that also lifts out. The long bone tray prevents a heavy femur head from crushing other bones, which we found to be a frequent event. Also, the main tray of the box includes slots to add dividers if other bones need special care (e.g., a pathologically articulated pelvis) or if several partial or subadult individuals need to be accommodated in the same box. A muslin-covered Ethafoam pad can be added for greater cushioning and traction, and the cotton provides a natural plant material in association with the remains, which is a NAGPRA-consistent courtesy.

The final version of the box was sent to Hollinger Corporation, an archival products company, which further improved on the technical aspects of the design, and the box is now manufactured and available (see http://www.genealogicalstorageproducts.com/hurebox.html, accessed April 16, 2006). This box, combined with a custom homunculus diagram on the end of it, allows for quick visual inventories, saves much unnecessary handling, and greatly improves preservation (figures 8.2 and 8.3). A homunculus diagram can easily be generated by the Bones Version 1.0 software available for free from the AltaMira website.

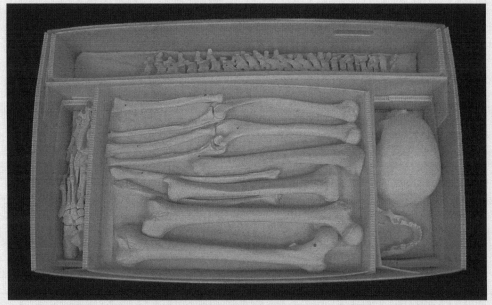

Figure 8.2.   Osteology box specially designed for storing an adult human skeleton using inert and sympathetic materials. A plastic model was used in this image. Photo courtesy of Rebecca Lockwood.

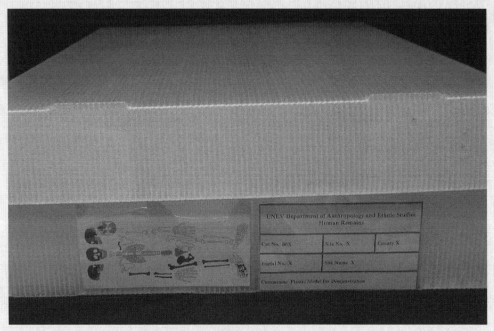

Figure 8.3.   Exterior of osteology box with labels that help with inventory and recognition and significantly reduce the need for handling the remains. The homunculus was created with the free Bones 1.0 software available at this book's webpage at http://www.altamirapress.com. Photo courtesy of Rebecca Lockwood.

What Is the Best Solution?

First, we need to ask what the purpose of bags in museum storage is. Usually they serve to hold smaller or fragmentary items and to prevent loss. The next question is, Should bags unite or isolate items? From a conservation point of view, bags should have the capacity to do both. They should unite similar items or those that relate to each other in some way, but they should also isolate the individual parts to prevent one from damaging another. For instance, a small fragment of a larger bone should not be placed in the same bag if there is danger that the larger bone will crush, abrade, or chip the smaller one.

Experience suggests that it is best to find a bag that fits the individual object snugly (though not tightly), rather than use a bag that allows the object to move freely. Some references suggest the use of a large bag that folds over. In our experience, this type of system is less than desirable. We call this "mummy wrapping," and with this approach, you exponentially increase the amount of handling and movement the bone receives. Tissue paper wraps are even more problematic since it is not possible to see ahead of time where the bone is or in what state it is until it has already received a substantial amount of handling or fallen onto the tabletop. Likewise, cotton fiber batting clings to bone surfaces and fragments when applied, can unnecessarily draw moisture to or from the bone during storage, and pull away fragile surfaces or edge material when unwrapped.

The advantages of housing fragments in zip-locking bags are many. Handling is greatly reduced. Because these bags are clearly visible from all angles, researchers can inspect bones, and managers can complete inventory and condition checks without removing them from the bag. When individual bones are snugly contained, they do not roll around or slip over labels; therefore, minimal dislodging of soil or bone flakes results. Individual bags of bones can be placed in boxes or with other bags if needed to maintain unity.

In the case of the Kennewick Man, where the safe transport of many small bone fragments was a worry, we came up with a bagging system that worked extremely well during the move from eastern Washington to the Burke Museum in Seattle (see the box on moving the Kennewick Man). We obtained a variety of preservation-quality zip-locking bags in different sizes and made use of a bag sealer (e.g., a Seal-a-Meal apparatus with no vacuum air extractor; see figure 8.4). This allowed us to customize the size of each bag by heat-melting the bags, before the bones were placed inside, to fit individual bones and fragments. Compartments could be made to separate various fragments of a single bone from each other while containing them within a single bag. Labels could be added to one end of the bag, followed by a heat seal. The remaining portion of the bag could hold the bone below the zip-locking closure.

LABELING

Labels or the assignment of a number may seem disrespectful at first glance; however, without an identifier, the often more than 206 bones of an individual could get lost, misplaced, or confused with someone else's. Labeling is essential for keeping individuals intact and being accountable for them. All collections must have individual identifiers for tracking, and if the name of the individual is not known, then it makes sense for efficiency to use an institution's preexisting numbering system. If one is starting out, in the case of a collection that has never been cataloged, short numbers are recommended. The museum registrar's preferred method of year, plus the sequential accession number for that year, might be an adequate system to adopt (e.g., year.accession, or, e.g., 2007.2 for the second accession in 2007). To distinguish individual fragments or bones, a third number can be added (year.accession.sequential fragment number, or 2007.2.1-206). For example, a cranium that is the third accession of the year 2007 would receive

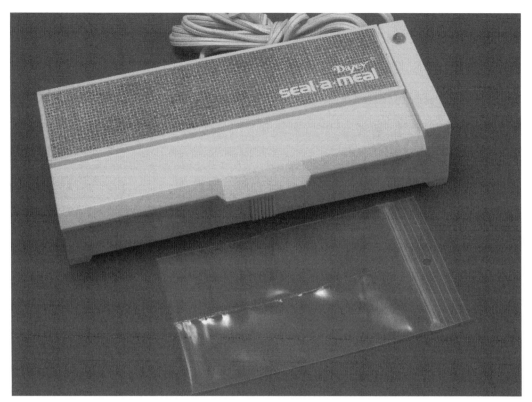

Figure 8.4. Seal-a-Meal device for customizing polypropylene plastic bags. Courtesy of the University of Arizona, Arizona State Museum photographic collections. Photographer: Jannelle Weakly.

a number such as 2007.3. If, however, there is a desire to distinguish the skull and the mandible of this individual, then the skull might be 2007.3.1, while the mandible would be 2007.3.2

Once staff has defined how the numbering or labeling system works, the next step is to define how that number will be used. Can the number for our imaginary cranium be shortened further to 7.3.1? Or perhaps using two numbers separated by a period (07.03.01) would be a better convention so the number will always be a consistent length. Should the year be four digits or two? All these decisions should be carefully considered and addressed in a formal labeling procedure for uniformity.

The most frequently asked question concerns how to place or attach a number to bones. Many haphazard methods have been used in the past, with varying success. One of the most common was to directly apply India ink to the bone. This provided a permanent number, but it was often too permanent. The porous nature of bone means that the number is absorbed into the bone, which compromises many aspects of curation, especially those of respect, readability, and research potential. Labels, like treatments, should theoretically be reversible, and India ink applied directly to bone is not. Some have sought to mitigate the permanence of the ink by placing a barrier layer on the bone first such as Whiteout, Elmer's Glue All, or fingernail polish. These materials, due to their poor preservation properties, are not recommended as a substrate for labeling human remains. Paraloid B-72, an acrylic polymer known to be inert and have a long preservation record, is a better choice. However, one must consider that handwriting can be difficult to interpret, especially after one has written the number perhaps several hundred times, one for each bone fragment, or if one has various student workers with varying handwriting

LABELING PROCEDURES FROM THE ARIZONA STATE MUSEUM

Items with firm surfaces can have a laser-generated label attached to their surface. The Century Gothic (12345679) or Arial (123456789) type fonts work well for this purpose. Depending on the font, anywhere from a 3-point to 11-point size can be used (in Microsoft Word, using fonts below 8 is possible by typing the number in the selected type font, then block highlighting it, then changing the Font Size in the Tool Bar by blocking and replacing with the lower font size number, then hit the enter key to complete the change). Legibility of a number may be enhanced by expanding the character spacing by .3 or .4 (this option is found on the Format menu, under Font and then under Character Spacing).

Determine the size of lettering required for the label. The lettering size depends upon the size of the item and the surface available for label placement. As a general rule, use the largest point size on big items and the smallest point size on small items. The numbers also will be clearer if the Font **Bold** feature is used. Some guidelines:

a. Century Gothic point size 11 (9 7 – 8 6 – 5 4 3) for large items.

b. Century Gothic point size 8 (9 7 – 8 6 – 5 4 3) for medium items.

c. Century Gothic point size 6 (9 7 – 8 6 – 5 4 3) for small items.

d. Century Gothic point size 4 (9 7 – 8 6 – 5 4 3) for tiny items.

When labeling many items, it is most efficient to create a consecutive, columnar, single-spaced list of numbers. Create numbers and sizes in the appropriate word processing package, load the laser printer with laser-quality, acid-free paper, and send the print job. Do not use labels printed on daisy, dot matrix, or ink jet printers. These types of printers do not use a stable ink fusion process. Laser printers, in contrast, use the same xerographic process as modern photocopiers. The laser toner is composed of carbon-based ink with a stable thermoplastic polymer (polystyrene, acrylics, or polyesters) that is thermally fused to the paper.

To separate the numbers, cut the paper with scissors as close as possible along one vertical side of the numbers. Cut horizontally between each of the single-spaced numbers, and then cut the paper along the second vertical side allowing the numbers to drop on the table. If possible, cut the labels with rounded, rather than square, corners. It is generally not feasible to round the corners of the smaller letter point sizes.

Attach the label using an undercoat of undiluted Rhoplex B60-A and a fine artist's brush. A second application of Rhoplex might be required to create a sufficient, protective top coat. Rhoplex B60-A or Primal B60-A (the name used outside the United States) is a low-viscosity, water-based acrylic emulsion manufactured by the Rohm and Hass Company that is available from Conservation Resources Int'l, LLC, 8000-H Forbes Place, Springfield, Virginia 22151, 800/634-6932.

Allow the label to completely dry and lose its tack. Before the Rhoplex sets up, it is soluble in water. For this reason, keep a vial of water and paper towel nearby to clean the fine paintbrush. After Rhoplex has set, it may be softened with water or is soluble in acetone.

If it is necessary to remove the label at a later date, moisten the paper label with water on a fine artist's brush to soften the Rhoplex, and carefully use tweezers to gently peel back the label. Alternately, acetone applied by fine artist's brush to the paper can be used to dissolve the Rhoplex. For a complete removal of the label adhesive, gently roll acetone dampened on a cotton swab tip over the surface until the remaining Rhoplex residue has been removed.

MATERIALS USED FOR STORAGE SUPPORTS

Nancy Odegaard

Boards

Polypropylene board (Coroplast, Corex)—a lightweight, rigid corrugated sheet used in supports and boxes.

Acid-free cardboard—a corrugated sheet with single or double ply used for boxes, supports.

Foam board (Foam-Core, Gatorboard, ArtCore)—a sandwich of extruded polystyrene backed with paper or plastic sheet. Ask for acid-free paper. A rigid, lightweight material used for supports and boxes.

Acid-free mat board—a noncorrugated rigid sheet used in framing and for boxes and supports with lightweight items. Ask for rag, acid-free.

Blue/gray boxboard—a sandwich sheet of lignin-based paper inside with smooth acid-free paper exterior used for boxes.

Acid-free blotter—a porous absorbent paper used for barriers between materials.

Film/Sheets

Polytetrafluorethylene (Teflon)—a smooth film with low static charge used as a wrap or barrier between materials.

Polyethylene sheet—a smooth, flexible clear film used as sheet or in bags. Recycled polyethylene contains harmful plasticizers that may become sticky and yellow with age. Ask for virgin material, and watch out for condensation.

Polyester (Mylar)—a clear, inert, semirigid film used to encapsulate or create barriers between materials.

Acid-free tissue, unbuffered—a lightweight, smooth cellulose paper of about pH 7 used for interleaving, covering, wrapping, or padding objects.

Polyester tissue (Reemay)—a nonwoven sheer material used for interleaving, covering, wrapping objects.

Polyester tissue (Hollytex)—a fine nonwoven sheer material used for interleaving or wrapping objects.

Polyolefin (Tyvek)—a tough nonwoven, spun-bonded polyethylene olefin used for wrapping and lining.

Polyethylene/metal (Marvelseal)—a heat-sealable aluminized polyethylene and nylon barrier film used in packing and passive humidity control.

Foams and Padding

Polyethylene (Ethafoam)—a stable, open-cell foam in a variety of densities and thicknesses including planks. Used for lining, cavities, trays, and packing. A standard conservation material.

Polypropylene (Microfoam)—a stable, open-cell foam used for lining, trays, and packing.

Polyethylene (Volara)—a soft, flexible, stable, closed-cell foam used for lining, wrapping, and packing. Good for close contacts with objects. Different densities and thicknesses available. Can be used with a heat gun.

Polyethylene rod (backer rod)—an extruded closed-cell polyethylene foam rod material in several sizes used for supports.

Polyester batting—a 100 percent polyester, needle-punched material with no resin bonding or flame retardant additives is preferred. Used to line containers, stuff pillows, and pad packing products.

Stockinette—a smooth, soft, seamless tubular knit fabric used to cover supports and create cushions and supports.

(continued)

MATERIALS USED FOR STORAGE SUPPORTS (*continued*)

Cotton fabric (muslin)—an unbleached cotton used to cover or create a barrier between objects and rough support materials. Always wash before use to remove finishes and sizing.

Cotton tie—a soft, strong woven cotton tape used to secure objects in packing.

Polyester fabric—a smooth, soft, strong fabric used to create a barrier between objects and support materials. Avoid colors.

Unsuitable

Bubble pack—an air-filled polyethylene cushion material used for wrapping. Should only be used for temporary packing. Polyvinyl chloride or nylon may be used in the bubbles. Product can etch metals, damage waxed or varnished surfaces, and cause impressions.

Cotton batting—a 100 percent lignin-free material used to line containers, stuff pillows, and provide ballast in packaging.

Ester urethane foam—a slightly open-cell (often somewhat shiny) foam that is used to cushion and mitigate shock at low static shock levels. They are unsafe for long-term conditions as they undergo photo thermal degradation (a problem for cellulosics, resins, and paints), they give off volatile fumes, and they dust. Also, watch out for fire-retardant and antistatic additives. Ester urethanes are said to provide better cushioning and have better rebound energy than ether urethane foams. Gray is common because it hides the discoloration from UV degradation.

Ether urethane foam—a smooth, soft foam that is used to cushion and mitigate shock at low static shock levels. They are unsafe for long-term conditions as they undergo photo thermal degradation (a problem for cellulosics, resins, and paints), they give off volatile fumes, and they dust. Also, watch out for fire-retardant and antistatic additives. Ether urethanes are considered inferior to ester urethanes for packing.

Organic (starch) peanuts—a water-soluble extruded material used for floating objects in packing. Should only be used with a barrier between them and the object.

Polystyrene peanuts—an extruded polystyrene product used for floating objects in packing. They may dust, so they should only be used with a barrier between them and the object. Better for insulation and shock than cushion.

Polyvinylidene chloride (PVDC, Saran)—a smooth, flexible plastic used in sleeves, containers, tubing, and films

---

styles. Some people make 4s and 9s in a similar fashion. Similarly 1s and 7s, and *b*s and 6s can be easily confused. Anyone who has worked with older collections can testify to the numerous times when you wonder about the number on a handwritten label, and this is especially true when the fragments are small and the numbers must be scaled down to fit.

A better solution to labeling human remains involves printing numbers on acid-free paper using a laser printer in various font sizes for varying size fragments. This method provides labels that are standardized, legible, and reversible. This label is cut out with scissors and applied using an adhesive (see the labeling procedures box).

Once a label system is chosen, where should one put the number? There are several competing concerns. First, the number should be in an area where it is easily seen, to avoid unnecessary handling. One should not have to pick up the bone to find the label. On the other hand, the number should not be so large and awkward that it disfigures, hides features, or draws unnecessary attention.

A label or number is intended to be there for a long time—it functions as a permanent feature; therefore it might be necessary to think not only about respect and minimizing handling but also about potential researchers' needs. For instance, one should not cover an essential marker used for making measurements or an area used for the diagnosis of pathology.

OTHER ENVIRONMENTAL ISSUES

Light (Radiation)

Daylight is considered the most damaging agent, especially to organic materials, and should not be used for illuminating storage areas. Daylight contains not only visible light but large components of infrared (IR) and ultraviolet (UV) light as well. IR produces heat that is damaging at high exposures and long duration. Exposure to high-intensity examination lights or photoflood lights should be minimized. UV light (wavelengths from 100 to 400 nanometers) is more damaging than visible light (electromagnetic radiation with wavelengths between 380 and 700 nanometers). Daylight has up to one thousand times more intensity than indoor lighting. Every light source produces some UV, but natural daylight has much more than artificial lighting. Blocking daylight is a vital preventive measure that can be achieved by painting or, better, blocking and filling in window depressions.

As far as interior lighting is concerned, compact fluorescent lights produce more UV wavelengths than incandescents (ordinary lightbulbs) do. Damaging UV components of interior illumination can be reduced with diffusers or UV filters placed directly over existing fluorescent lightbulbs. The filters are not expensive, slip on over fluorescent bulbs, are hardly noticeable, and significantly reduce the UV component without taking away from efficiency for viewing (the visible spectrum).

Human soft tissue and hair, which have higher organic material components than bone, can be more easily damaged by exposure to light, but all light sources have a cumulative effect on artifacts. All lights within storage areas should be kept dark when not in use and any natural daylight blocked.

Pests or Integrated Pest Management

For the last thirty years, conservators have promoted prevention as opposed to treating pest invasions. Once infested, a collection becomes an immediate problem and one that must be treated without delay. Treatment is time-consuming, problematic, and potentially dangerous for staff, and it can leave collections contaminated or altered. Instead, it is best to act before an attack. Such preventive measures are known as integrated pest management (IPM) systems. IPM emphasizes the prevention of pest damage by combining monitoring and eradication methods with the least possible hazard to people, property, and the environment. Monitoring collection areas with sticky traps and nonchemical techniques such as freezing, heating, and anoxic environments have become popular examples of nonchemical alternatives to the use of pesticides. Preventive measures start with identifying entry points and then blocking these entries. This may mean caulking or sealing areas around windows or pipes, weather stripping around doors, and keeping doors and windows shut. Also, require staff and visitors to leave coats and other exterior wear outside the storage area. Of course, food and plants, which easily attract or harbor insects, should not be allowed in or near storage areas at any time.

Collections of purely osteological materials are not as vulnerable as those that have soft tissue, nails, or hair. Preventive pest control or IPM is vital for collections of mummified remains. Skin and other organics are choice foods for protein-consuming pests, such as a variety of clothes moths, carpet or furniture beetles, and even at times cockroaches, crickets, and flies. Other common collection pests such as silverfish are known to graze surfaces and information off labels when left undisturbed for long periods. They are attracted to cellulose and particularly cardboard, coatings, and some pen inks on paper. Pests are especially attracted to areas that are undisturbed for long periods.

Regular inspections are required for a successful IPM program because the stepwise approach requires (1) an initial assessment of insect activity, (2) control of insect entry points, (3) a procedure of eradication, and (4) evaluation of the plan (Odegaard 2004).

It is important to be able to find and deal with any pest invasions early and swiftly. In the past, chemical sprays, fogs, dusts, and fumigants were applied too liberally to control pests. The application of a pesticide requires serious consideration as most products pose a risk to the collections and can present ongoing human health hazards long after application. When evidence of pests is found, such as live insects, insect carcasses, or insect deposits or frass, then the collection involved should be isolated in a plastic bag and removed to another area. Any debris should be documented and then removed. The potentially infected collection should be monitored carefully for several weeks to see if the attack is active or old/inactive. If no activity is noted, then returning it to storage is appropriate as long as staff continue to regularly monitor the area with traps and visually inspect the objects for the next few months.

If there is an active infestation (live insects or larvae found) or fresh activity (more frass) in the isolated collections, then decisions must be made on treatment. Anoxic environments, freezing, and solar bagging are three nonchemical options that are common alternatives. None of these pose toxic threats to staff.

Anoxia, or the removal of oxygen, suffocates the pests, and is a good choice, though relatively expensive requiring a pump, a tank of inert gas (e.g., nitrogen, helium, argon, or carbon dioxide), an oxygen scavenger (e.g., Ageless), and specially coated plastic sheeting that does not allow any outside penetration of oxygen (Burke 1996).

Freezing requires items to be placed within plastic bags in a freezer. A domestic chest freezer may be used if it can achieve and maintain −20°C for several days (Florian 1990; Raphael 1994; Odegaard 2004). Special considerations are necessary when freezing skin and tissue (Williams et al. 1995).

Solar bagging is still experimental, but in an environment with limited resources, this approach may be a cheap alternative. It kills with heat generated from solar energy (Baskin 2001). After treatment, the exposed collection must be monitored for reoccurring problems, usually for several weeks, before returning to the main collections.

Prevention is the key to integrated pest management. If a problem arises, then regular inspections are needed to quickly identify the problem before it spreads into a collection-wide issue, followed by quick isolation and treatment with monitoring. Simply put, prevention and blocking access to pests is much more important and effective than chemical treatment.

STEPS FOR AN INSECT MONITORING PROGRAM

Nancy Odegaard

Setting up an insect monitoring program using traps should include the following steps.

1. Obtain a floor plan of the museum, and identify all doors, windows, drains, air vents and returns, food sources, and plants.
2. Mark on the floor plan the places where traps should be put. Initially, traps should be placed at various heights, including on the floor, on shelves, and in false ceilings. Other critical locations include near doors, in collection work areas, around perimeter walls,

under furniture, inside storage cabinets, and near heat and water sources. In areas where infestation is suspected, more traps should be placed. Traps should not be placed on, or directly adjacent to, museum objects—the sticky adhesive may be damaging and difficult to remove. With good placement, it will be possible to determine where the pests are entering and why they are surviving.

3. Choose the traps to use for monitoring. The size of the area to be monitored, the budget and the types of insects expected will factor in choosing the trap style. However, many conservators find the "pup tent" style that hooks at the top to be the easiest to set, handle and examine. It is often suggested that a monitoring program should stay with the same brand of trap because many variations can make your data more difficult to interpret.

4. Before placement, each trap should be labeled with a placement date and a location number keyed with the floor plan. If room numbers are already assigned to the building, it may be most useful to utilize that system in labeling the traps. For example, "5/1" might be used to indicate room 5, location 1. If several buildings are being monitored, a building number or abbreviation could precede the room and location numbers.

5. Establish a regular schedule for inspecting and collecting the traps. All traps should be in place for the same length of time so that comparisons between trap catches can be made. An initial check should be made 48 hours after the traps are set. The check is a simple visual inspection of the types and numbers of insects present in the trap—a head count. The same trap can be replaced and a final count may be taken during the scheduled pick-up and trap change. The traps should be checked every week for the first three months. After that, four to six times a year probably will be adequate. Record in a logbook the quantity, life stage, and type of insect found in each trap. Also note the trap number, trap location, date inspected and date the trap was set. Without documentation, the monitoring program is of little use. By checking traps 48 hours after the initial placement, it will be possible to locate the heart of the infestation because the trap nearest this spot should contain the most insects. Routine inspection of the traps will provide important information about the insect types present. A trap with many insects caught on one side and few on the other will indicate the direction of the infestation. The distribution, population, and type of insects found in traps will indicate whether a severe problem exists or merely that a harmless insect was lost in the museum. The stage of development of the trapped insects also can tell something about the duration of the infestation. A mixture of adult males and females and various sized nymphs means that the infestation has been around for months, while a collection of mostly medium sized nymphs means that the infestation is fairly new. A comparison of traps before IPM and after IPM will provide information about the success of such a program.

6. Over time, an insect monitoring program will require refinements based on the information gained about types of insects present, seasonal changes, building structure and housekeeping methods. Traps should be replaced every two or three months because they tend to lose their stickiness. Also, the dead insects within become bait for other insects and allow new insects to enter without crossing over the sticky surface. Trapping will result in insect reduction for some insect species but should not be considered the primary control measure for an infestation.

7. Sticky traps do not replace the need for regular housekeeping and inspection of objects in storage or exhibit. These activities should be done monthly or at least two times per year.

Note: This text is part of an article that appeared in "Insect Monitoring in Museums," *WAAC Newsletter* 13(1):19–20.

MOVING THE KENNEWICK MAN

Vicki Cassman and Nancy Odegaard

Our role as consultants for the preservation of the human remains known as the Kennewick Man began in 1998. The nine-thousand-year-old remains have been the focus of a court battle challenging the concept of cultural affiliation for ancient remains under NAGPRA (see chapter 9 for an introduction to the case). Plaintiffs in the case have also alleged that the government has not been able to properly care for the remains.

In November 1998, we were asked to assist with the condition assessment for the remains following the formal examination and inventory by plaintiffs and curation team members from the U.S. Army Corps of Engineers representing the government of the United States. Notes and Polaroid photos were permitted to document the inventory. We were also asked to prepare and package the remains for transfer from eastern Washington to the Burke Museum of Natural History and Culture at the University of Washington in Seattle.

With only twelve hours until departure, it became obvious that traditional museum-style condition reports could not possibly be completed before transport for each of the 340 fragments. A more practical and streamlined method had to be developed quickly, or the conservators would become a hindrance. We adjusted our response to this assigned task to specifically inspect and record the individual bones for (1) adhering soils, and noting whether these soils were stable or likely to fall with simple movement or handling; (2) obvious signs of weakness in the bone itself, such as presence of lifting, delaminating, cracking, and areas of exposed trabecular (spongy) bone that is inherently weak; and (3) isolating and containing individual fragments in sealable plastic storage bags or to create individual compartments by modifying bags to suit the bone fragments involved. Labels accompanied each fragment to facilitate inventory as each fragment was packed and later unpacked.

The bagged fragments, depending on anatomical position, size, and condition, were placed inside polyethylene plastic food-grade containers with resealable lids. Closed- and open-celled polyethylene foam sheeting provided cushion between the layers of bagged fragments and filled any headspace within the container. These containers were then placed inside plastic Rubbermaid Action Packer (heavy-duty cargo boxes with lids often used for carrying heavy gear or tools) containers with padding throughout. This system for packing is illustrated in figure 8.5.

After a private Native American religious ceremony in the parking lot and a public sunrise ceremony by the Asatru Folk Assembly (coplaintiffs), a caravan of officials, Native American representatives, Corps of Engineers staff, security, and press left for the five-hour drive from Richland to Seattle. The condition assessment method proved to be highly successful in many ways, and we were able to document and make snug-fitting sealable bags for most of the fragments using a domestic plastic bag–sealing apparatus (see figure 8.4).

Upon arrival at the Burke Museum, the unpacking and arrival inventory took place. A condition assessment accompanied the inventory. Each bag was observed for dislodged soils or bone fragments through the sealed storage bag, without disturbing the microclimates inside, and the Polaroid photos and written documentation were consulted. Damage was found in the form of small amounts of dislodged soil that were loose in the bags. It was noted that the bags with dislodged soil were not the custom-fit bags but larger bags that allowed movement of the fragment within. This kind of minor change in condition was felt to be acceptable and even inevitable considering the intense physical manipulations that the fragments had received by the physical anthropologists and curators in the hours preceding the arrival to the Burke Museum and the handling required during packing, unpacking, and inventory.

The one item that suffered more than dislodged soils was a tooth. In this situation, the molar was bagged, like all other bones, and labeled with an acid-free card identification number. But,

MOVING THE KENNEWICK MAN (*continued*)

since the tooth was much smaller than the piece of card, the bag had been fitted to the dimensions of the card rather than the tooth; this allowed too much movement of the molar within the bag, and a pinhead-sized piece of accretion was dislodged from the base of the tooth. Despite this unfortunate loss, only the most minimal of damage occurred to the remains, and the packaging/transport was judged to be a success.

Our first reporting of condition in this case was specific to the move, but we have continued to adapt and use this system of evaluating the amount of soil and bone shed by the remains. We have noted that very little conditional change over time has occurred if the remains are not handled; many more changes result when there are handling and especially sampling episodes. This methodology has allowed us to measure the degree of deterioration and the sources of the deterioration over an extended period. Informed recommendations regarding storage, handling, and study are now possible.

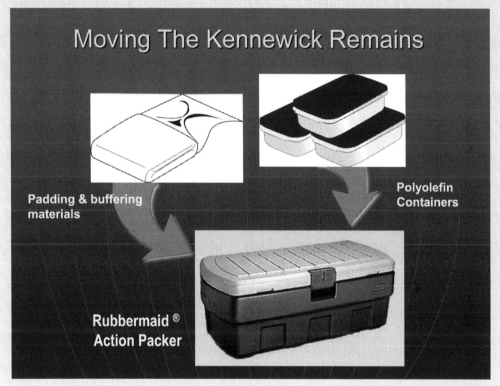

Figure 8.5.   Courtesy of the U.S. Army Corps of Engineers.

REHOUSING THE KENNEWICK REMAINS

In 1999, after the remains had acclimatized to the environmental conditions in the Burke Museum, rehousing of the collection was needed. The remains were rehoused in custom-made cavity-cut boxes that act as both housing and support trays. The materials used in the construction of these boxes were carefully selected and the design was crafted to facilitate the inventory, condition assessment, and study activities. For five intense days, a team of curators and conservators worked to provide supportive acid-free padded boxes for the fragments. The fragments were placed into twenty-five different boxes by bone type. A physical anthropologist was most essential to the team since she identified, sided, and positioned the fragments anatomically in the boxes. Boxes were constructed from acid-free cardboard; added to this were, in order from bottom to top, polyester needled padding, Tyvek fabric isolating liner, and Volara closed-cell polyethylene foam cushion. The Volara was custom cut to position the fragments safely within cavities. Tyvek pillows with polyester filler were placed over the cushioned fragments to fill the headspace between the fragments and prevent vertical shifting while boxes were handled and moved. The boxes also allow for quick inventories and display in anatomical relationships, which greatly reduces need for handling individual fragments (see figure 8.6).

Once the containers were made, item labeling could take place. Each fragment had been given its own unique number by the Corps of Engineers' curators, and for inventory and security purposes, the team requested that these numbers be physically attached to the fragments. The conservators sought a labeling system that would withstand repeated handling and yet be easily reversible. The method used involved the efficient application of a small laser-printed, acid-free paper label using a very thin layer of Rhoplex AC-33 (acrylic emulsion) adhesive (see the labeling section in this chapter). These small labels are firmly fixed to the bone surface but can be mechanically removed if needed.

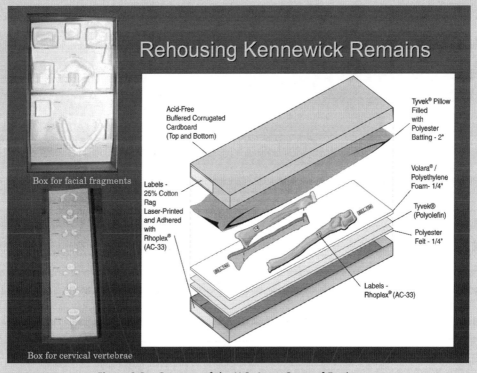

Figure 8.6.   Courtesy of the U.S. Army Corps of Engineers.

PACKING ROYALTY

Ronald S. Harvey and Renée A. Stein

Acquisition

When the Michael C. Carlos Museum at Emory University acquired a collection of ancient Egyptian funerary objects, coffins, and mummies in 1999, the museum and its employees were faced with the challenge of transporting the collection to Atlanta, Georgia, conserving the objects and the remains, as well as displaying and storing the new collection. The Carlos collection has included human remains since the 1920s, when the museum was established as a repository for objects brought back by theology professors traveling to the biblical lands of the Middle East. The recent acquisition included ten coffins and ten mummies (not necessarily paired), as well as more than one hundred funerary and daily life objects made from textile, stone, bronze, wood, ceramic, glass, and faience. This collection was purchased from the Niagara Falls Museum and Dare Devil Hall of Fame when the privately owned and operated Canadian museum closed and sold its diverse collections. Most of the Egyptian collection had been amassed by the museum's founder, who sent his son to Egypt in the mid-1800s to buy antiquities. It is likely that additional items were purchased in the succeeding decades of the nineteenth century. The collection was moved several times and eventually housed in an old shirtwaist factory on the main road leading to the falls.

Identification

A team of conservators, curators, preparators, and packers stabilized and crated the collection for its overland journey by truck. As soon as the collection arrived in Atlanta, conservation and research efforts began in tandem. Scholars immediately studied the hieroglyphs in order to reassociate coffins with remains and most importantly identify a name for the human remains. Since the remembrance of the name was a central theme of the Egyptian quest for a continued presence or afterlife, recognizing the name of a mummified individual offered some measure of respect. When no name could be determined, the profession such as scribe or priest recorded on the coffin was used as an identifier, providing a reminder of life before the remains became synonymous with an inventory number.

Scholarly inquiry in the 1980s had proposed that one mummy in the Niagara Falls collection was that of a pharaoh, most likely Ramses I. A respected and high-ranking military officer, Paramessu became pharaoh around 3242 B.P. and took the name Ramses. He ruled only two years until his death, but he established the nineteenth dynasty and was the first of eleven rulers by the name Ramses. The mummy bears striking physical resemblance to identified remains of Seti I and Ramses the Great (Ramses I's son and grandson, respectively), both preserved in Cairo. The mummy of Ramses I was not recovered from the royal tombs excavated at Deir el-Bahri by the Egyptian Antiquities Service in 1881. The tombs had been previously raided, and many items were sold through a dealer before the authorities seized the tomb contents. The Niagara Museum is known to have purchased from that same dealer, contributing circumstantial evidence to the identification of the mummy as Ramses I.

Noninvasive examination of the mummy including X-ray radiography and CT imaging further revealed the thorough and elaborate mummification as well as the exceptional state of preservation, as compared with the other mummies in the collection (Lacovara et al. 2001). Without more sophisticated testing techniques such as genetic analysis, the identity of the mummy will remain somewhat speculative. Many scholars do, however, accept the attribution, and Egypt's Supreme Council of Antiquities agrees that it is a royal mummy. Research relating to the attribution of the Ramses I mummy was organized into a temporary exhibit and an educational website still linked to the museum's home page (www.carlos.emory.edu/RAMESSES).

(*continued*)

PACKING ROYALTY (*continued*)

Offer of Return

Even before the historical and medical research was compiled, the Carlos Museum made the offer to return Ramses to Egypt, believing that the remains of a pharaoh belong in the possession of the Cairo Museum. Ramses was deaccessioned and shipped to Egypt in the fall of 2003. This gesture of goodwill and collaboration received worldwide attention. All planning with regard to the handling, packing, crating, and shipping of the mummy attempted to balance the numerous requirements imposed by the overseas transport of fragile human remains with the unique circumstances of an international event with significant government and media involvement.

Packing Requirements

The need to eliminate or minimize damage from handling, vibration, and impact applies to the movement of all antiquities. However, transporting human remains involves the added consideration of respect, not simply for physical integrity but also for the fact that the remains were once a living being with human needs (physical, emotional, social, spiritual, etc.) not unlike our own. Whether from an excavation or a museum storeroom, identified or unknown, intact or damaged, the remains are still connected to a life. Although abstract and far removed from a collection context, the concept of their humanity cannot and should not be ignored. This shift in perception fosters an intellectual and emotional leap that should be incorporated into any project involving human remains. This ideological premise must guide the practical approach to handling, packing, crating, and transporting human remains.

Ramses' remains had been completely unwrapped long before the Carlos's acquisition and perhaps even before the mummy left Egypt in the mid-nineteenth century. The mummy's fragile surface was therefore completely exposed. Although the body is intact and complete, the remains are desiccated, brittle, and incapable of supporting additional weight. The packing system required the even distribution of weight, providing uniform support without localized pressure or abrasion, while also protecting especially delicate areas such as the ears, wrists, and toes. The crating was designed to minimize vibration and cushion impact. Since the crate would be transported by plane with an international transfer, the dimensions had to conform to cargo bay capacities and the structure had to withstand the pressures of two takeoffs and two landings. Because the remains would be publicly received at a press event, the crate had to be designed for easy unpacking and possible use for immediate display.

Packing Support

Ramses was placed on a rigid support board prepared with stable inert materials that could be used for long-term storage or display if desired, thus avoiding the need to repeatedly lift and move the fragile remains. Birch plywood was used to make the support board and reinforcing struts were glued to its underside. The wood was covered with the multilayer laminate film Marvelseal to restrict off-gassing. The top surface was lined with the closed-cell, cross-linked polyolefin foam Volara, and carved blocks of polyethylene foam were added to support the contours of the body. The padded board was then wrapped with prewashed, undyed, unbleached linen.

Crate System

The mummy was covered with a layer of the nylon sheeting Dartek to prevent abrasion and was essentially encased in blocks of polyester foam carved to fit the contours of the body. This foam was not intended as long-term housing but provided support and cushioning during transport. The multilayered mummy, board, and foam package was surrounded with a wall of archival cardboard and covered with nylon sheeting. This cardboard enclosure contained the layers as a single unit that could be easily removed from the crate without stressing the foam that was in direct contact with the body. The unit consisting of the support board, mummy, foam layers, nylon sheeting, and card-

PACKING ROYALTY (*continued*)

board was then placed inside a wooden crate. This crate was constructed of birch plywood with reinforcing battens, a removable top, and sidewall. The interior of the crate was covered with laminate barrier film, gasketed with polyolefin foam, and lined with more than four inches of polyester open-cell foam (without fire retardants). Sealing and gasketing the crate limited air exchange and therefore minimized changes in temperature and relative humidity within the crate for a minimum of forty-eight hours. Vinyl cutouts of the cartouche of Ramses I and the flag of modern Egypt were applied to the exterior of the inner crate.

This inner crate was placed inside a larger wood crate of similar construction with removable top and sidewall, both gasketed with polyolefin foam. Extruded polyethylene foam blocks (2.2-pound density) held the inner crate in position, centered within the outer crate. The outer crate and its foam blocks were intended to absorb shock from impact and offer additional protection to the crated mummy. The foam blocks in the outer crate were wrapped in Tyvek to aid in sliding the heavy inner crate into and out of the outer crate. Once bolted closed, the removable sides of the outer crate were sealed with aluminum tape. Step-by-step unpacking instructions were sent with the crate (including the corresponding socket wrench and drill bits). These instructions were illustrated with photographs of each component and layer of the packing system. A detailed condition report describing the mummy was also provided, with numerous digital images on CD-ROM.

Return Shipment

Before assembled media, Carlos Museum director Bonnie Speed presented the crated mummy of Ramses to Zahi Hawass, secretary-general of Egypt's Supreme Council of Antiquities. The crate was wheeled from the museum and then ceremonially draped with the Egyptian flag. The crate was raised by hydraulic lift into a fine arts moving truck and taken to the airport, where a press conference was held, officially transferring ownership of the mummy. The crated mummy was to travel in the cargo bay of a passenger jet, making a transfer en route. The crate system had been designed to fit into a cargo container that could be transferred between the two flights without unloading the crate, thereby offering an additional measure of protection. On the day of the flight, a jet with a different cargo bay configuration was assigned, and the crate had to be secured to an open palette and wrapped with plastic. This palette was then strapped between the cargo containers in the bay of the plane. The crate arrived safely in Egypt and was transported to the Cairo Museum, where it was immediately unpacked for a public unveiling the following morning.

Conclusion

While the handling, packing, crating, and shipping of any fragile collection is a complex task involving many factors, the delicate balance is further complicated when dealing with human remains. Whether in a high-profile example such as the return of a royal mummy to Egypt or in the more routine movement of human remains, a sense of respect and reverence must guide the project's planning and execution. The specific requirements or circumstances of any particular scenario should not overshadow an awareness of the fact that the remains were once a living individual.

REFERENCES

American Institute for Conservation
> 2005 *Directory of the American Institute for Conservation of Historic and Artistic Works.* American Institute for Conservation, Washington, D.C.

Andrew, Kate J.
> 1996 A Summary of the Care and Preventative Conservation of Sub-fossil Bone for the Non-specialist. *The Biology Curator* 5:24–28.

Baskin, Bonnie

    2001 Solar Bagging: Putting Sunlight to Work to Eliminate Insect Infestations in Mere Hours. *WAAC Newsletter* 23(2):20–21.

Bowron, Emma L.

    2003 A New Approach to the Storage of Human Skeletal Remains. *The Conservator* 27:95–106.

Burke, John

    1996 *Anoxic Microenvironments: A Simple Guide.* Leaflet #1, Vol. 1(1), Spring 1996. Society for the Preservation of Natural History Collections, Washington, D.C. Electronic document, http://www.spnhc.org/documents/leaflet1.pdf, accessed April 16, 2006.

Caffell, Anwen C., Charlotte A. Roberts, Robert C. Janaway, and Andrew S. Wilson

    2001 Pressures on Osteological Collections: The Importance of Damage Limitation. In *Human Remains: Conservation, Retrieval and Analysis: Proceedings of a Conference Held in Williamsburg, VA, Nov 7–11th 1999*, edited by Emily Williams, pp. 187–197. BAR International Series 934. Archaeopress, Oxford.

Campbell, Mei Wan

    2002 Recessed Support for Fragile Specimens. In *Storage of Natural History Collections: Ideas and Practical Solutions, Volume II,* edited by Carolyn L. Rose and Amparo R. de Torres, pp. 31–32. Society for the Preservation of Natural History Collections, New Haven, Connecticut.

Campbell, Mei Wan, and Eileen Johnson

    2002 Housing Units for Skeletal Material. In *Storage of Natural History Collections: Ideas and Practical Solutions Volume II*, edited by Carolyn L. Rose and Amparo R. de Torres, pp. 21–22. Society for the Preservation of Natural History Collections, New Haven, Connecticut.

Cassman, Vicki, Kristen Martine, Jennifer Riddle, and Sali Underwood

    2001 Neglect of an Obvious Issue—The Storage of Human Remains. Conservation and Archaeology: Case Studies in Collaboration. *Cultural Resource Management* 24(6):11–13.

Costain, Charles

    1994 Framework for Preservation of Museum Collections. *Canadian Conservation Institute Newsletter* 14:1–4.

Cumberland, Donald R., Jr.

    1993 Dust Covers for Open Steel Shelving. *Conserve O Gram* 4(2). National Park Service. Electronic document, http://www.cr.nps.gov/museum/publications/conserveogram/04-02.pdf.

Florian, Mary-Lou

    1990 Freezing for Museum Insect Pest Eradication. *Collection Forum.* Vol. 6. Society for the Preservation of Natural History Collections, Washington, D.C.

Ganiaris, Helen

    2001 London Bodies: An Exhibition at the Museum of London. In *Human Remains: Conservation, Retrieval and Analysis: Proceedings of a Conference Held in Williamsburg, VA, Nov 7–11th 1999*, edited by Emily Williams, pp. 267–274. BAR International Series 934. Archaeopress, Oxford.

Hawks, Catherine A.

    2002 Cushion and Subdivider for Mid-Sized Skulls in Storage Boxes or Trays. In *Storage of Natural History Collections: Ideas and Practical Solutions, Volume II*, edited by Carolyn L. Rose and Amparo R. de Torres, p. 195. Society for the Preservation of Natural History Collections, New Haven, Connecticut.

Holst, Malin, and Charlotte A. Roberts
  2003 *Field Archaeology Specialist: Skeleton Boxes*. British Association of Biological Anthropology and Osteoarchaeology, Bournemouth.

Kautz, Robert R.
  2000 Archaeological Artifact Attrition: Time's Arrow and Collection Depletion. *Collection Forum* 14(1–2):33–41.

Lacovara, Peter, Sue D'Auria, and Thérèse O'Gorman
  2001 New Life for the Dead. *Archaeology* 54(5): 22–27.

Michalski, Stefan
  1990 An Overall Framework for Preventive Conservation and Remedial Conservation. In *9th Triennial Meeting, Dresden, German Democratic Republic, 26–31 August 1990: Preprints*, pp. 589–591. ICOM Committee for Conservation, Los Angeles.
  1994 A Systematic Approach to Conservation: Description and Integration with Other Museum Activities. In *Preventive Conservation, Practice, Theory and Research: Preprints of the Contributions to the Ottawa Congress, 12–16 September 1994*, edited by A. Roy and P. Smith, pp. 8–11. International Institute for Conservation of Historic and Artistic Works, London.

Odegaard, Nancy
  1991 *A Guide to Handling Anthropological Museum Collections.* Los Angeles: Western Association of Art Conservators.
  2004 General Procedures for Freezing Museum Collections to Eliminate Insect Pests. In *Caring for American Indian Objects: A Practical and Cultural Guide*, edited by Sherelyn Ogden, pp. 228–229. Minnesota Historical Society Press, St. Paul.

Raphael, Toby
  1994 An Insect Pest Control Procedure: The Freezing Process. *Conserve O Gram* 3(6). National Park Service. Electronic document, http://www.cr.nps.gov/museum/publications/conserveogram/03-06.pdf.

Rose, Carolyn L., and Catharine A. Hawks.
  1995 A Preventive Conservation Approach to the Storage of Collections. In *Storage of Natural History Collections: A Preventive Conservation Approach*, edited by C. L. Rose, C. A. Hawks, and H. H. Genoways, pp. 1–20. Society for the Preservation of Natural History Collections, New Haven, Connecticut.

Rose, Mark
  2003 Mystery Mummy. *Archaeology* 56(2): 18–25.

Sullivan, Brigid
  2002 Clamshell Box for Skulls and Other Irregularly Shaped, Three-Dimensional Objects. In *Storage of Natural History Collections: Ideas and Practical Solutions, Volume II* edited by Carolyn L. Rose and Amparo R. de Torres, pp. 169–170. Society for the Preservation of Natural History Collections, New Haven, Connecticut.

Strang, Thomas
  1994 Educción del Riesgo Producido por Plagas en las Colecciones de Patrimonio Cultura. *Apoyo* 5(2):3–4.

Trimble, Michael K., Nancy Odegaard, Vicki Cassman, and Teresa Militello
  2001 The Conservation and Rehousing of the Kennewick Remains. In *Human Remains: Conservation, Retrieval and Analysis: Proceedings of a Conference Held in Williamsburg, VA, Nov 7–11th 1999*, edited by E. Williams, pp. 237–247. BAR International Series 934. Archaeopress, Oxford.

Valentín, Nieves

    1994 Tratamientos No Tóxicos Desinsectacion con Gases Inertes. *Apoyo* 5(2):5–6.

Waller, Robert

    1994 Conservation Risk Assessment: A Strategy for Managing Resources for Preventive Conservation. In *Preventive Conservation, Practice, Theory and Research: Preprints of the Contributions to the Ottawa Congress, 12–16 September 1994,* edited by A. Roy and P. Smith, pp. 12–16. International Institute for Conservation of Historic and Artistic Works, London.

    1995 Risk Management Applied to Preventive Conservation. In *Storage of Natural History Collections: A Preventive Conservation Approach,* edited by C. L. Rose, C. A. Hawks, and H. H. Genoways, pp. 21–27. Society for the Preservation of Natural History Collections, New Haven, Connecticut.

Williams, Stephen

    1999 Destructive Preservation: A Review of the Effect of Standard Preservation Practices on the Future Use of Natural History Collections. Göteborg Studies in Conservation 6. Dissertation, Acta Universitatis Gothoburgensis. Göteborg, Sweden.

Williams, Stephen L., Sarah R. Beyer, and Samina Khan

    1995 Effect Of "Freezing" Treatments on the Hydrothermal Stability of Collagen. *Journal of the American Institute for Conservation* 34(2):107–112.

CHAPTER 9

Associated Artifacts

ANN H. PETERS, VICKI CASSMAN, AND MONICA GUSTAFSSON

> We cannot live only for ourselves. A thousand fibers connect us with our fellow men; and among those fibers, as sympathetic threads, our actions run as courses, and they come back to us as effects.
>
> —Herman Melville

AS MICHAEL SCHIFFER (1999) HAS NOTED, FOR MILLENNIA HUMAN BEINGS HAVE MEDIATED AND expressed their social relationships through the creation and manipulation of material objects. Funerary practices are no exception, and deceased members of the community have been mourned and appeased through grave offerings at the least since Neanderthal burials of the middle Paleolithic. In the analysis of human remains, separation of artifacts from the bodies is almost standard practice, and there is great potential for a resultant loss of context—both for the bodies and for the artifacts. Here we illustrate the wealth of information that may be recovered by careful attention to all components of a burial context, through three examples from the Andean region of South America.

Presented with a mass of caked earth and textiles encrusted over dried tissue, many researchers may long for the relative simplicity of bone. Human remains that have been preserved through natural or artificial mummification present a wealth of potential information, continued and complemented by information provided by the artifacts that surround the body. While the human body itself can only be directly observed by some degree of unwrapping, it is vital that interest in study of the corporeal evidence of a human biography does not lead to destruction of the surrounding cultural evidence.

The ancient peoples of Andean South America honored their deceased by preserving their bodies in ways that facilitated bringing out the dead to participate in ceremonies or, at the least, ensured their continuing presence in tombs that could be visited or reopened on future occasions. Even today, in some Andean communities, an ancestral skull may occupy a niche in the home or place of worship, and preserved human remains or a person's tomb may be visited to seek a miracle or honor a promise. Burials in stone tombs, caves, and dry desert hillsides have been preserved that provide not only a wealth of information about past populations but also information about individual and community identities and practices. Our three examples of the study of funerary contexts in the Andes are drawn from different kinds of Andean societies in different historic periods and environmental contexts. They demonstrate the importance of the information that can be drawn from the details of dress and wrappings and the vital need to preserve the unity of the funerary context, both body and associated artifacts.

These case studies represent more than what is often thought of as associated artifacts, such as the ceramic vessel next to the body or the lithic point. What is presented here are the extremely personal effects that represent an extension of the body. They are not just "dirty old clothing." Clothing, textiles and personal adornment act as extensions of the body and give us further clues to who the person was, what the person did in daily and ritual lives, and how he or she lived. We learn this from the types of materials, the forms of the garments, the age of the garments, the technology, and use wear. Even the wrinkles and creases have a story to tell. We are accustomed to hearing what can be learned from the bones and the more common grave goods. However, we present these not so familiar detailed case studies by Ann Peters to argue that textiles should be given the same respect and documentation as other finds. Mortuary textiles not only carry messages about how the clothing was made and worn but how the environment was utilized. Each line of evidence, body, common grave goods, and personal adornment, including textiles, are vital on their own, but together they give powerful insight into the past that is only possible through attention to preservation of the artifacts, as well as detailed descriptions and documentation that are then preserved and accessible to future researchers and stakeholders through publications and archives.

CHINCHORRO AND ARCHAIC BURIALS OF NORTHERN CHILE

On the desert coast of the Central Andes, hunting and gathering societies of the Archaic period regularly occupied sites with fresh water sources and abundant ocean resources for thousands of years before the development of agricultural practices. In the case of the Chinchorro burial complex, the cultural practices associated with complex mummification blur the line between the study of the human remains and the study of associated artifacts. In the postmortem treatment of deceased individuals, wood splints, reed cordage, sculpted mud or ash paste, animal skin, and mineral pigments may be used to reconstruct the body interior and body surface (Arriaza 1995). At the same time, other artifacts made from the same materials typically surround and adorn the body of both artificially and naturally mummified individuals.

Arriaza (1995) draws on detailed study of twentieth-century research on Chinchorro for his synthesis of the burial patterns characteristic of northern Chilean sites between 8950 and 2950 B.P. While postmortem treatments of the body include a diversity of styles and procedures, all burials are in a dorsal extended position. Reed mats constructed with spaced twining of reed cordage appear in some burials in every period, wrapped around either artificially or naturally mummified individuals. Cordage wrapped around the hips is the most common article of dress present. In the classic Chinchorro black mummies, camelid fiber is reported in cordage used to construct an apronlike female garment. In transitional Chinchorro, leather breech clouts for men and grass skirts for women are reported. Headbands begin to appear in this period, while annular head modification, together with headbands, become more common in late Chinchorro burials characterized by only natural mummification. Tools included in the burial wrappings include a variety of coastal fishing, hunting, and gathering implements such as fishhooks and line, spear throwers and harpoons, stone points and scrapers, and looped and knotted nets and bags. Pelican-skin pelts, as well as the reed-twined mats, could have been used as wraps and bedding for chilly nights prior to their inclusion in burials. Squash and native cotton, as well as the reeds and other plants used in cordage, mats, and baskets, were gathered and perhaps propagated.

Despite the emphasis on a coastal subsistence base evident in tools and organic remains associated with the Chinchorro sites, materials in the burials and middens also demonstrate access to resources of inland areas. Camelid skins or hair used in cordage included the guanaco, a wild ancestor of the llama, present in valley oases and highland slopes. Other skins and hair from the wild vicuña, together with skins of the ostrichlike rhea, came from high pastures and lakes above 3,800 meters above sea level. The presence of feathers of tropical birds demonstrates some contact with forests of the eastern slopes of the Andes (Arriaza 1995:47). In a few better-preserved contexts, skeins of yarn appear wound around the head and in a crisscross pattern bind the matting around the body. In later burials, the spaced twining on reed mats may be carried out with camelid fiber yarns, and in one case bits of color embroidery adorn a twined body wrap. Consideration of diverse components of burial wrappings, even the small samples of those elements that are rarely recovered, offer information on social practices such as long-distance travel and exchange relationships, not at all evident based on consideration of the bodies alone.

It is important to point out that the Chinchorro did not leave behind monumental architecture; the twined reed mummy bundles are what remain of this culture. Though very little attention has been paid to the twined mats, they are the most enduring Chinchorro characteristic. Twined mats were used like casings, enshrouding the bodies like a postmortem amniotic sack made from vegetal fibers. The twined reed cloth carried the individuals to the other world protected in the belly of the earth, and some have protected their charges for ten thousand years.

Special treatment of the head is important throughout Andean history and appears even in these early burials. In some cases, head and body are swathed in fine layers of bird feathers and vegetable fiber. Shell ornaments, bone pins, and fishing implements may be inserted in the wrappings. Complex cordage wound around the head may have embodied aspects of personal identity, as well as magical and religious practices that formed part of the person's life, the practices that surrounded their death, or postmortem treatments that transformed the social person into a deceased, ancestral, and supernatural figure.

Toward the end of the Archaic period, contemporary with evidence for cultivation of a wider range of plants and the appearance of hair and pelts from domesticated varieties of camelids, head treatments in burials become more elaborate and achieve effects of great beauty. Certain patterns of head treatment characterize certain clusters or burials, or a particular pattern may recur exactly in burials found in different places—indications that head adornment was consistently employed to symbolize shared social meanings. For instance, along with gender and age symbolism, head treatments might symbolize kin group affiliation or specialized social roles achieved by particular individuals. The structure of head-wrapping styles of burials of natural mummies of the late Archaic and Formative periods in northern Chile has been studied by Carolina Agüero (1994), who has proposed a typology of head-wrapping procedures. A few examples from the transition between the late Archaic gatherers and hunters and early Formative agricultural societies serve to demonstrate the wealth of information present in funerary head adornment.

Early researchers engaged in salvage operations in shoreline sites south of the Azapa valley typically worked to recover naturally mummified human remains that had been previously disturbed. Often only the head and selected artifacts were removed to the museum for conservation and further study. Operating without institutional support or transportation or storage facilities, and faced with substantial numbers of disturbed burials, they usually combined reburial with selective collection. As a result, neither individual bodies nor tomb lots can be reconstructed. Interest in study of cranial modification and more elaborate artifacts also has led to a skewed sample of both human remains and artifacts. Information on sex, age, occupational stress, and pathology is limited, and the reconstruction of funerary wrappings and artifact associations in these cases also stops at the neck.

As many burials were disturbed prior to study by archaeologists, the precise arrangement of funerary wrappings is seldom preserved. At the museum laboratory, some heads were later dissected to facilitate study of cranial modifications and pathologies. In cases where scalp and headdress were separated from the cranium, the associations have been preserved but the original form cannot be fully reconstructed. Where the cultural information provided by hair arrangements and head wrappings has been prioritized, the headdress is in situ. However, the headdresses as seen today are frequently the result of attempts to reconstruct possible headdress arrangements prior to disturbance. Subsequent handling within the museum also may lead to some slight rearrangement of headdress elements or loss of associations or contextual information. In the case of heads whose headdress arrangements have been best preserved, information on cranial modification, and evidence of sexual dimorphism and pathology, may be limited to that available in X-ray studies.

The Archaic period Quiani 7 burials are later than most at a site also known for earlier Chinchorro-style burials. Dated to approximately 3450–3750 B.P., they are among the earliest of the elaborate yarn head wrappings and among the most beautiful (see the Quiani 7 headdress pictured in figure 9.1). Excavated and reported by Percy Dauelsberg (1974), this head is the only human remain conserved from seven burials exposed by road construction to a fishmeal processing plant on the coast south of Arica. Identified as a male, this person's hair is pulled to above the forehead, where it is coiled into a knot. The complex wrapping over the hair and around the topknot is composed of four different types of cordage. The attention to detail in this headdress suggests that it reflects an aesthetic and social identity that included adornment both

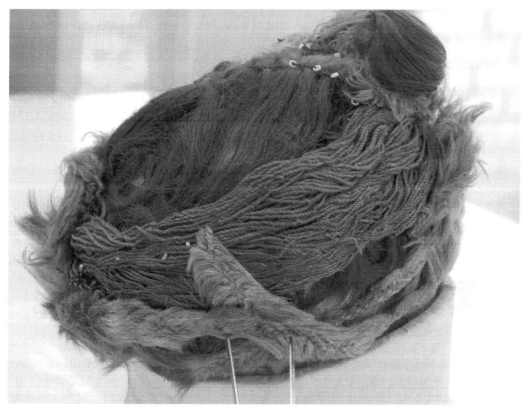

Figure 9.1.   Quiani 7 Formative period headdress from Arica, Chile, Collection of the Museo de San Miguel, Universidad de Tarapacá. Photo courtesy of Ann Peters.

in life and in funerary regalia. This combination of materials not only is strikingly beautiful but also embodies the long-distance movement among the high-altitude humid pastures of the vicuña, highland valley slopes, pockets of canyon bottom vegetation, and desert shores abounding with shellfish.

Dauelsberg's tomb description makes no mention of the position or condition of the body. Other burials in the group are in a lateral flexed position, lying on the left side, their backs to the sea, with arms and legs doubled. A photograph appears to show this burial in a similar position. A large coiled basket was placed over the head, and other associations include a small disk-shaped basket with linear decoration, a loincloth constructed of a camelid hair fringe doubled over a set of cords and secured by rows of spaced twining, and a spear thrower fragment. A fragmented body wrap of bird skins was not recovered. A fragment of bone spatula resembles those associated with the taking of hallucinogenic snuff, a practice associated with ritual and long-distance political relationships in the later history of this region. Two stones stained with red pigment are considered by the excavator to be tomb markers (Dauelsberg 1974).

In other burials of this group, two have similar stones, one of which is considered to have been used to grind the pigment. Similar baskets appear in other burials, as well as body wraps of bird skins or camelid skin. Some have loincloths of plant fiber fringe. Two have thick mantles constructed of a heavy camelid hair warp secured by weft twining and ending in a fringe. There are fragments of shell bead necklaces, cordage adorned with bone pendants, and bags made from complex looping in camelid hair and plant fiber. Also present are more fragments of bone spatulas and a cord of human hair plied with cut reddish hairs (identified as fox) inserted to create a chenille-like effect. There is cordage of strips of sea lion skin, braided reeds, and spun and plied cotton, as well as cactus spine fish hooks and wood or bone harpoons tipped with bone or cactus spine hooks. A fragment of twined reed matting, a container made from a dried squash rind, two seashells, remains of food, and flaked stone tools were recovered in association with the burials (Dauelsberg 1974). In short, associated tools are specifically related to shoreline fishing activities, while containers and elements of dress embody hunting, gathering, and incipient horticulture in diverse environments ranging from coastal oases to high mountain pastures, as well as ritual activity.

Continuing research on social identity expressed in head and headdress in the Andes is made possible by the decision of our colleagues in physical anthropology in northern Chile who have been careful to conserve head and headdress in a form as close as possible to their arrangement when recovered. The Arica collection represents the best information on complex social identities expressed in the head and headdress in Archaic period societies in the Andes, and one of the best for that period in the world. Removal of headdress elements to facilitate the study of the head might provide some interesting information. However, those who study burial practices and social identities in societies from five to ten thousand years ago in other parts of the world can surely appreciate the importance of the elaborate and differentiated late Archaic and early Formative headdresses of northern Chile.

THE PARACAS NECRÓPOLIS

The elaborate embroidered textiles buried between 2100 B.P. and 1700 B.P. in the Paracas Necrópolis site are among the most famous artifacts from Andean South America. These brilliantly colored representations of human figures, animals, and supernatural beings often adorn the covers of books on the Andes, as well as tourist brochures and posters promoting travel to Peru. The cemeteries on the Paracas Peninsula were archaeologically excavated in the 1920s by a team from the National Museum led by Julio C. Tello, the father of Peruvian archaeology.

CONSERVATION CONVERSATION I: GREAT FIND—NOW WHAT?

Consider the following rescue mission phone conversation—fictional but based on past experiences:

Archaeologist: Conservator Amparo, we are seeking your advice. We have rescued a Quiani individual from the beach and have just brought it back to the museum. How should we proceed? We want to be able to study it. What should we do to preserve it?

Conservator: First, it is necessary to understand the context and environmental conditions and the state of the mummy bundle. What are the conditions at the museum now? Is the bundle damp to the touch or dry, and is it in stable condition or fragile?

Archaeologist: It is a typical foggy morning in northern Chile, but the sun will likely break through in the afternoon, and it should be a warm, sunny day, about 22°C. The Quiani bundle is a natural mummy from a coastal site, and it is damp but not wet to the touch, but it is drying out fast in some areas. There is a deteriorating leather cord that is very damp, and apparently it was used to loosely wrap the bundle. We have the bundle sitting in the semishaded courtyard of the museum for now as we make room for it in the museum.

Conservator: Is it a typical Quiani bundle with a reed textile surrounding an animal skin or fur mat with a flexed natural mummy inside?

Archaeologist: Yes, it is, but the exterior leather tie is different.

Conservator: Has the bundle been opened?

Archaeologist: Yes, on site the construction workers who found the bundle yesterday opened the bundle, and then they closed it up and reburied it and called the museum. This morning we went to excavate it, and we brought it back to the museum as soon as we had finished checking the site for more burials, which we did not find. The mummy itself appears only slightly damp and well preserved inside its bundle.

Conservator: Good. Do keep the bundle intact—this will continue to buffer the individual inside—but I would suggest that you move the bundle indoors to a cool interior room of the museum, and drape it with a clean canvas or muslin cloth and then a sheet of polyethylene plastic to slow the rate of evaporation and allow the bundle to acclimatize in a less dramatically different environment than it had underground. It is best to avoid direct sun or daylight on a bundle, especially one that is at least two to three thousand years old! With the changes in ambient temperature, rapid evaporation can lead to concentration of salts, near the drying surfaces, that were likely absorbed from the coastal burial environment. The salts at the least cause stiffening of the reed bundle exterior and eventually losses with time. Can you describe the condition of the exterior reed and the cord?

Archaeologist: The reed is intact except for where it was cut by the workers, and it is pliable and in relatively good condition. However, the cord appears wet and even sticky to the touch.

Conservator: It sounds like the cord requires some immediate action. Is it still in its original position or context, or was it removed when the mummy was opened?

Archaeologist: According to the workers, the cord was in perfect condition when it was exposed and lay loosely around the head. They slipped it off and replaced it after they had looked at the mummy. They said that the cord began to become gooey within a few hours, and this scared them into reburying the mummy and calling us at the museum. As we speak it, actually looks as if it is becoming more sticky and shrinking.

Conservator: The workers did the right thing by reburying the bundle. I would recommend that you immediately move the mummy indoors. It sounds like the cord is saturated with salts, and it is reacting with the humidity in the air. Once the bundle is inside, you should immediately take documentation photos of the exterior of the bundle (and use a flash since hot floodlights will aggravate the situation), and someone else should sketch the position and knotting and context of the cord in relation to the bundle. I have been told by early archaeologists that animal skin cords can literally be transformed within hours to a gelatinous mass after excavation. This is most likely due to salt saturation and structural degradation, and it sounds like what you have now. You will need to act very quickly, decisively, and rationally. It will be important to archive this photo and sketch with a note that the context was disturbed on site, but according to nonexpert witnesses, it was replaced as it was found upon discovery. This documentation may be the only evidence of this object that will remain in a few years. When you have accomplished this, call or e-mail me again.

The next day:

Archaeologist: The bundle was covered with tarp material and plastic after documentation with photography and drawings. The cord's degradation has slowed dramatically, but it is still mushy. What is going on, and why is the cord in such bad shape when the condition of the mummy and bundle are good? And can we reverse the damage to the cord?

Conservator: It is difficult to judge condition without examining it in person, but the cord is likely in poor condition precisely because it was outside the bundle. The reed, fibers, and textiles have protected the mummy from salts and helped wick initial moisture away from the body during desiccation after burial. The mummy was shielded in burial from environmental changes by the layers of textiles, but the cord was completely exposed. The cord apparently was made from animal skin, which is a protein, and it had obviously reached an equilibrium status with the surrounding soils if the construction workers said it was in perfect condition upon its discovery. Unfortunately, it is impossible to reverse this type of decay, but we can try to prevent it from completely self-destructing into a mass of gelatinous goop.

Archaeologist: Now that we have dealt with the immediate needs of the outer context of the cord and the bundle, and we have moved the bundle into the most environmentally stable area of the interior of our museum and slowed the environmental shock, what do we do to prevent the cord from oozing onto the reed bundle, since it may continue to self-destruct? Isn't there a spray or consolidant to use?

Conservator: First, you should realize that you are dealing with an extreme situation; the cord has been degrading at an alarming rate since exposure from excavation. This is a potential problem for skin of ancient mummies or of other animals from burials that are exposed to heavy salt concentrations. Under the right conditions, these react with or possibly aid in breaking down the proteins in the skin. This is not an area that has been studied in detail, but here are two references to start with: Sullivan 1987 and Horie 1987.

Despite this emergency situation, you should not jump into your decision on how to treat this skin cord; you must first weigh the consequences. First, adhesives or consolidants are not recommended. To spray it with a consolidant or to dip it in some kind of "preservative" will not resolve the degradation problem. It might even exacerbate it. In addition, the research value of the cord would be lost since the "preservative" would interfere with many future analyses. To treat this object with an adhesive, consolidant, or "preservative" is not appropriate without understanding first the condition and the materials involved, and even then it is unlikely to be a good idea.

(*continued*)

Second, you can slip a polyethylene plastic or polyester sheet, such as Mylar, between the cord and the reed textile to prevent transfer and staining, and continue to monitor the cord for changes and hope that it equilibrates with its new environment soon. It is essential that you glean as much information from this artifact now before it self-destructs any further. Is there someone locally who can identify the type of skin that was used to make this cord?

Finally, if degradation continues and is too rapid, you could remove the cord by slipping it off the bundle and carefully placing it on a Tyvek, Mylar, or polyethylene sheet, and place under it a stiff acid-free inert museum board for support. This can then be placed in a large zip-lock bag, sealed, and put in a freezer to stop the process temporarily until professional help can be brought in.

Archaeologist: OK, I will observe the cord for the next day or two, and in the meantime, I will look into appropriate freezer space if necessary. We have a special mummy expert visiting who would like to investigate this mummy. How would you suggest that we proceed?

Conservator: If at all possible, keep the context of the mummy and artifacts together. The expert should not assume that the mummy will or should be disrobed or unwrapped as has been traditional in the past. Since the body has already been exposed twice without complete disrobing, you should suggest that the body is observed by the expert in a similar fashion, and if more details are needed, suggest they bring portable X-ray and CT equipment instead of completely unwrapping the bundle. Good luck.

Nonetheless, the provenience information that would link the famous textiles to 429 individual burials is in most cases difficult at best to reconstruct.

The Necrópolis was uncovered near the end of the field season of 1927. An emergency excavation was organized to avoid leaving the massed burials to the *huaqueros*, or semiprofessional looters of the region. One group was removed in late November and early December 1927. Systematic sampling uncovered a second group, removed in April 1928. Offerings outside the funerary bundles—such as ceramics, baskets, and bundles holding foodstuffs, "signal" staffs, and other staffs—were cataloged, and most funerary bundles were removed intact, sewn into jute sacking, and transported to Lima. Transport by truck over rough roads led to changes in bundle shape and, in many cases, some disarticulation of the human remains within. Many of the funerary bundles were opened over the next few years in controlled conditions at the National Museum.

In the studies of the most elaborate burials, spatial relations among associated artifacts were carefully recorded in drawings and photographs. Whole artifacts and fragments were cataloged. However, repeated movement of the materials in subsequent years led to the separation of some objects from their catalog numbers. Some textiles were washed and mounted. Carbonized masses of deteriorated textiles were separated from decorative fragments in better condition. Some of the best-preserved, most beautiful pieces were placed on mannequins for exhibit. Finally, the separation of objects housed in different departments of the National Museum has made it difficult to study the textiles in relation to associated ceramics, tools, or organic materials and particularly difficult to reconstruct their associations with the bodies they once enveloped in the tomb. For many years, the original archives, including field notes and catalogs, were unavailable to researchers.

Prior to Tello's excavation, there had been looting in the Cabezas Largas sector of the Paracas cemeteries. In the early 1930s, looters gained access to the Paracas site on at least four occasions, extracting many burials whose contents were shipped overseas from the port of Pisco (Daggett 1991). A theft at the museum led to loss of a few objects. A few funerary bundles and well-preserved objects were sent to provincial museums, museums abroad, and international expositions. By these means, components of a large number of grave lots either looted or properly excavated at the Paracas site had found their way into museums in Europe and the United States. Studies of elaborate woven and embroidered textiles from private collections (e.g., d'Harcourt 1962 [1934]; Stafford 1941) suffer from a scarcity of contextual data. They were able to describe details of technique, patterns of design, or make general statements about the nature of the imagery, but they lacked information that would contribute to an understanding of the social meanings of these extraordinary funerary wrappings.

Prior to his death in 1947, Tello had only published preliminary discussions of the Paracas materials. The most well-known report (Tello 1929) was based on initial field observations and the experience of opening the first bundles. It presented invaluable summaries and photographs documenting the structure of the most elaborate funerary bundles. Although Tello was educated as a physician and trained in physical anthropology and archaeology at Harvard's Peabody Museum, his initial conclusions that bodies had been artificially mummified, extensively prepared, and smoked prior to burial at special facilities near the cemetery were not supported by subsequent examination of the human remains and funerary wrappings (Tello and Mejía 1979). Conditions of preservation of the bodies varied. All bodies have clearly been manipulated in several early postmortem processes in which they were undressed, bound into a seating position, packed with cotton fiber and items of clothing, and had sheet gold ornaments inserted into the mouth or placed over the eyes. While the presence of necrophagic insects provides further evidence that bodies were exposed and dried to some degree prior to wrapping, the presence of dried body fluids caking textiles at the base of most bundles provides sure evidence for decomposition subsequent to the initial layers of wrappings. This key information has only been preserved thanks to the detailed documentation of the unwrapping of the first bundles studied by the National Museum team.

Tello's principal field assistant, Toribio Mejía Xesspe, assembled his two posthumous publications on this site. The first (Tello 1959) presented a series of essays and extensive color and black-and-white lithographs illustrating materials from the excavations, particularly some features and artifacts of three elaborate funerary bundles that had been unwrapped and studied in detail. The second publication (Tello and Mejía 1979) presents extensive excerpts from original field notes and Tello's unpublished writings, as well as summaries of Mejía's later work on analysis of the Necrópolis bundles. Unfortunately, in the later work, the illustrations are scarce and so poorly printed that many images are indecipherable. Without the complementary information provided by the cataloged artifacts, the field notes are of limited value.

Tello worked with a number of Peruvian and international researchers, many of whom wrote studies based on data from the team research at Paracas (Carrión Cachot 1931; Yacovleff 1932, 1933; Weiss 1958, 1961) as well as from independent fieldwork (Yacovleff and Muelle 1934). Eugenio Yacovleff and Jorge C. Muelle (1934) published a detailed description and catalog of the contents of funerary bundle 217, which remains the best-published account considering all types of objects included among the funerary wrappings.

An Illustrative Funerary Bundle
A brief summary of the contents of funerary bundle 217 illustrates how context can give greater meaning to a particular human body and to the few extraordinary artifacts that later may appear in isolation in a photograph or museum display. Yacovleff and Muelle describe at the core

of the bundle the cadaver of an elderly man in a sitting position with knees pressed to the front of his face and arms folded tightly at his sides. The position is secured with a three-strand braided cord of human hair. The partially preserved, headless body of a dog is pressed at his side. A tiny sheet gold disk has been placed in his mouth, a custom typical of the Paracas Necrópolis funerary complex. The lower half of his face is covered by a large gourd bowl (*Lagenaria sicer-aria*), which is also a recurrent feature in the Necrópolis burials. Above the bowl, his face is covered by a fragment of netting and a plain cotton cloth.

Over his elongated cranium (modified by annular binding in early childhood), the man's hair is in many fine braids that gather in a knot over his forehead. A hammock-shaped head wrap of fine knotted netting made with gray-green cotton yarns is bound with a maguey fiber sling. Over the sling, a polychrome headband of dyed camelid hair yarns in slit tapestry (*kelim*) follows the path of lifelong annular binding and is knotted over the knob of coiled hair to create a tasseled effect. Woven in dark blue, gray-blue, yellow-gold, brown-gold, bright yellow, dark green, red, and black, it carries woven images of a rayed human head, a warrior carrying spears, a feline, and several types of bird figures.

Among the folded limbs are tucked a loincloth, a tiny looped bag holding a small stone and piece of animal tissue wrapped in cotton yarns, and a sea snail shell (*Thais chocolata*) packed with cotton. Two cotton bags constructed of knotted netting with skeins and balls of colored cotton and unidentified yarns, a wooden sewing needle, a maguey fiber sling, a maguey fiber headband, and more net headdresses. *Spondylus* shell beads are encrusted in the wrists of the cadaver, though the cords that joined them into bracelets have disappeared. There is no mention of red yarns twined around the fingers, a recurrent feature in burials of the period. The body was wrapped in a fine, plain-weave, cream white cotton shroud. Necrophagic insects (*Demestes* sp.) and fly larvae capsules were identified among these wrappings closest to the body. A simple cotton tunic made of a single warp-striped fabric woven to size was placed over the body as worn in life.

The body below the chin is wrapped in a large knotted net of white cotton and placed in a large basket constructed of *totora* or cattail reeds (*Typha* sp.) in a diagonal interlaced twill structure. The spaces around the body are padded with raw cotton impregnated with a white alkaline powder and a large cotton cloth, constructed of two plain-weave panels sewn together, is wrapped around the body, gathered at the top, and sewn to the shroud below, forming the first layer of the funerary bundle. A set of miniature garments and a cloth bundle are packed into the basket. The miniatures consist of sixteen cloths between sixteen and thirty centimeters in length, some with slit openings, borders, and embroidery in the shape of mantles and tunics. At least two "sets" are indicated by a miniature tunic and mantle stitched together. It is hard to tell the exact order of elements at the base, due to rotting and carbonization of the wrappings in this region. A number of types of foodstuffs also are found inside the funerary wrappings, including eight corncobs (*Zea mays*), one fragment of yuca or manioc root (*Manihot esculenta*), eight shelled peanuts (*Arachis hypogaea*), six black beans (*Phaseolus vulgaris*), and ten *jíquima* roots (*Pachyrrhizus* sp.).

A large cloth constructed of two plain-weave cotton panels sewn together and then dyed a gray-blue color wraps the entire bundle, two corners tied up in a double knot. Over this cloth, a series of articles of embroidered clothing are bound tightly around the apex of the bundle, forming a restricted "neck" that turns the cloth above it into a "false head." The base cloth of these pieces was found deteriorated, but their forms can be identified from their embroidered borders.

One is a kiltlike cream white cotton cloth with camelid hair embroidery, designed to wrap around the waist and be secured with long diagonal-interlaced ties ending in embroidered squares that match the L-shaped embroidered border. The polychrome block-color figures depict a splayed winged creature with insectlike features. A second kiltlike yellow-gold cotton garment has a similar structure. The block-color embroidered figures on the purple-blue border depict human-headed bird figures holding a tasseled spear and small human head. A third garment is a small open-sided tunic (*esclavina*) worn over the shoulders with an attached panel at the back. Rectangles of dark blue cotton, plain-weave fabric are embroidered with polychrome camelid hair borders in stepped sections, each with a block-color human figure in a horizontal or "flying" position, carrying a fan and two staffs. The fourth garment is a fine cream-colored cotton headcloth. Its narrow, red embroidered borders carry polychrome figures of double-headed serpents, in an embroidery style specific to the Necrópolis headcloths.

A large, dark green cotton mantle with red embroidered camelid hair borders and a narrow strip of cross-knit looped embroidery down the middle is draped as if over the "shoulders" of the bundle. The borders carry polychrome figures of a splayed catlike being with a bird at its mouth in an early block-color style. A small fan of yellow macaw feathers (*Ara ararauna*) bound on a *totora* reed handle is set in place.

The whole is then wrapped in a well-preserved, yellowish, white cotton cloth constructed of two plain-weave panels sewn together, stitched in place. Above this is wrapped another cotton cloth, found in a deteriorated "carbonized" state. Above it, a well-preserved, large, white cotton cloth made of two plain-weave panels sewn together wraps the whole bundle and is stitched up the sides to form a large rectangular sack. This is bound at the top with a cotton cord to form another false head, above the actual head of the cadaver within. On this new symbolic body, a yellow-gold cotton mantle with separate purple-blue camelid hair embroidered borders and a block-color design of standing human figures is draped, decorated side facing in. The figures each carry a knife or spear point and small human head, and they wear a long headcloth and a distinctive two-layer tunic. Two sets of deerskin panels of a form similar to that tunic, identified as hides of the small Andean deer or *taruka* (*Hippocamelus antisensis*) are placed like an open-sided poncho falling on either side of the false head.

On this outermost level, the false head is adorned with a fox skin (*Canis azarae*), opened along the ventral side, slit down the back and decorated with yellow macaw feathers. A polychrome headband constructed of red, yellow, green, and black (carbonized, original color uncertain) camelid hair yarns constructed by complex diagonal interlacing and a maguey fiber sling are wrapped around this "head." A long wooden pin with a brown-gray tassel of *yanahuico* or puna ibis feathers (*Plegadis ridgewayi*) topped with long yellow macaw feathers is adjacent. A dark blue camelid hair mantle with red-based linear style embroidery is placed as if around the shoulders. Its borders and checkerboard-like squares carry figures of a human with a flowing headdress carrying multiple spears. A fan of condor feathers (*Vultur gryphus*) bound onto a *totora* reed (*Typha* sp.) handle is placed on top of this mantle.

Before burial, this outer layer is wrapped in a large beige cotton wrap constructed of two plain-weave panels sewn together. The new bundle is placed in the ground, closely packed among other bundles, and sits on a fragment of reed matting. Adjacent to this bundle is a wooden club, a wooden staff bound with rings of sinew or skin binding, a basket, two low ceramic bowls, and two ceramic jars. So it was found hundreds of years later in 1927 by the excavation team led by Julio C. Tello and Toribio Mejía Xesspe, and described by Eugenio Yacovleff and Jorge C. Muelle (1934).

The specific figures woven or embroidered on each decorated textile in bundle 217 connect it to other funerary bundles in the Necrópolis cemetery that include one or more textiles with the same figure, usually in a slightly different style. The nontextile objects in this bundle are typical of a set of objects associated with most high-status burials. Yacovleff's analysis of the raw materials employed in constructing the regalia in this funerary bundle leads him to point out the presence of animals and birds from a cross section of diverse Andean environments including the shores and oases of the coastal desert, the pastures and lakes of the high Andes, and the rain forests of the eastern slopes. He also notes similarities with elements of dress associated with ritual occasions and high status in the Inka period, as described in early colonial accounts (Yacovleff 1933; Yacovleff and Muelle 1934).

Other Necrópolis Textile Artifacts

Due to the physical separation of materials in the National Museum and other museum collections into categories such as ceramics, textiles, metals, botanical, and zoological specimens, combined with the loss of access to original catalog information, this kind of portrait is extremely difficult to reconstruct for the hundreds of other Necrópolis burials. Although they were originally carefully documented and conserved, much of the wealth of information from this cemetery has been lost with the death of each member of the original research team.

A series of outside researchers began to work in the 1970s with National Museum staff on the cataloging and conservation of textiles from this extraordinary site. In the process, they began the painstaking task of trying to recontextualize the objects. Jane Dwyer developed a style seriation of textile designs and used that technique to propose a sequence of burials associated with those textiles (Dwyer 1971). Anne Paul created a photo archive of textiles and began to carefully reassemble the catalog of textiles associated with each of the most elaborate funerary bundles (Paul 1990, 1991). Despite these efforts, since the 1950s no one has been able to conduct a detailed analysis of an elaborate Paracas Necrópolis grave lot. Nor is it possible to compare the abundant evidence of the social importance of these buried individuals with the nature of their life and death as reflected in their physical remains.

The lack of systematic documentation of correlations among age, gender, artifacts, and indications of social status in the entire cemetery population has impeded understanding of the nature of the society that created the Paracas Necrópolis. Tello and the National Museum team inventoried and documented the more elaborate funerary bundles as they were unwrapped, but they have only published inventory and descriptions of artifacts associated with four large and four medium-sized bundles. Some smaller bundles in poor condition were examined during the excavation process. Others were unwrapped later, but only twelve brief descriptions have been published. Based on 118 bundles unwrapped by the National Museum team, the high-status burials are identified as males of advanced age, while simpler burials are said to include a diverse group of men, women, and children and a greater diversity in the style and function of associated artifacts (Tello and Mejía 1979).

Analysis of artifact associations in the high-status burials and comparison with the depiction of human and supernatural figures in associated textile images highlights a set of artifacts consistently associated with social and ritual leadership (Peters 2000). These include a set of feathered objects comprising headdress ornaments, feather-adorned cotton cloth and camelid or deerskin tunic, feathered bands to ornament wrists or ankles, and a sinew-banded staff often adorned with feathers. In most cases, the feather-adorned fox skin headdress is also present. The packet containing sets of miniature garments is also a recurrent feature. The most elaborate burials also contain a cloth bundle holding mineral pigments, yarns, and needles that could be used to create the painted and embroidered imagery, as well as the large quantities of elaborately decorated textiles found in these same high-status funerary bundles.

Other typical associations include artifacts that are also found in less elaborate burials, including weapons such as spear throwers and cane spears, usually without their wooden tips set with obsidian points, which may appear as separate artifacts. Ground stone mace heads mounted on stout wooden handles are found in some elaborate and some simple burials, and they appear to have caused head injuries like those identified in high-status burial 49 (Tello and Mejía 1979). Maguey fiber slings are also broadly distributed in elaborate and simple burials. While embroidery tools and materials are always present in elaborate burials, spinning and weaving tools found in some simpler burials are markedly absent.

In short, the burials marked as high status by the labor invested in the funerary wrappings are those of elder males associated with implements of hunting and warfare and labor-intensive artifacts that both embody and depict the products of horticulture, gathering, mining, herding, and hunting in diverse environments. Symbolic associations with high-status burial are fashioned with the material products of long-distance travel or exchange relationships. Evidence of ritual leadership includes both the imagery of the elaborate textiles and headdress adornments and the tools involved in designing and producing that imagery. Apparently the implements of hunting and warfare are shared with lower-status male burials, while the implements of weaving are unique to lower-status burials. Association of weaving tools with female burials is common in Andean societies, but the loss of contextual associations in the Necrópolis samples is an impediment to development of a model of social roles and patterns of correlation among gender, age, and social status.

Future Directions

Research on the Paracas Necrópolis is at a point where study of the human remains in the context of their grave lot associations is essential. Further understanding of social roles and status differences in this society require a restudy of gender and age attributions and a careful examination of physical features and artifact associations that may provide information on social roles in production, warfare and ritual. If it is possible to recontextualize the human remains, a study of genetic distance could make a vital contribution to our understanding of the nature of this society.

The Tello Archive, housed in the National University of San Marcos, has been officially opened for researchers, and National Museum staff is seeking to improve access for researchers. However, until we are able to reconstruct the grave lot associations so carefully recorded initially by the excavators of the Necrópolis site, the meaning of Paracas for today's Andean societies and the rest of the world cannot move far beyond the travel poster.

HIGH-ALTITUDE SACRIFICES OF THE INKA EMPIRE

Many researchers may be familiar with Johan Reinhard's work in high-altitude sanctuaries in the Andes. The sacrificed adolescent girl known as "Juana" from Cerro Ampato in southern Peru achieved international fame in *National Geographic* (Reinhard 1996, 1997) and created international conflict when her remains were taken to Washington, D.C., to be exhibited and studied. Other high-altitude Inka sacrifices from the volcanoes and neighboring peaks of the southern Andes have been studied and preserved in Peru, Argentina, and Chile.

The child sacrifices found to date in frozen mountaintop tombs of the south central Andes, both to the north and south of Lake Titicaca, are linked to rituals specific to the Inka state. The largest numbers of preserved sacrificial burials located to date are from the snow-capped peaks that form the frontier between Chile and Argentina. Chronicles of the early colonial period

CONSERVATION CONVERSATION II: CURATION CRISIS

Archaeologist: We are a small archaeological museum with a collection of mortuary bundles that were opened years ago. At that time, we were advised to separate the bundle contents by type (i.e., mummy, textiles, ceramics, wooden tools, lithics, foodstuffs, and basketry) to better preserve them. However, we realize that some of the contexts are beginning to get lost or forgotten, especially when labels have been removed for long-term exhibitions or the labels have been lost. Also, we realize how time-consuming it is to try to locate all the grave goods for an investigator or descendant. It used to be that researchers were interested in mummies, ceramics, or lithics. But now researchers and descendants are interested in seeing entire bundle contents, and this makes retrieval difficult and time-consuming because the bits are often found in different buildings and warehouses. So we are reconsidering our collections policies and think that it might be better to house a bundle as a unit, instead of dividing all the pieces up by type. What do you think?

Conservator: Remodeling storage sounds like a wise plan of action under the circumstances. Your wish to comply with descendants' wishes is admirable; after all, the entire tomb with body and grave goods was most likely considered a package or a unified whole at the time of burial. Also your observation of the investigators' changing needs does nicely reflect the current research paradigm changes in archaeology, and this, too, is a legitimate reason for making a policy change of this magnitude, especially since you are primarily a research organization.

Of course, the original reasoning for storage by type was to be able to efficiently deal with preservation problems for each material. For instance, if all the corn cobs/kernels, jicama roots, black beans, quinoa, and squash seeds from various bundles were packaged individually and stored in the same area, then they could be more easily monitored for insect attack than if they were spread out among many different bundles in many different storage areas. They could also be quickly treated by more frequent monitoring and freezing, if an attack was discovered. It was also helpful to have standard storage containers and spaces to use existing space more efficiently. However, if this is not working for descendants, staff, or investigators, the contexts of the bundles are suffering, and you have storage space, then it *is* time for change.

Archaeologist: If the contents of bundles are to be stored as a unit, how would we need to change our storage systems? We will need to apply for grant money to do this since we would likely need new infrastructure. How do you suggest we start?

Conservator: In planning for improved storage, I like to plan for the ideal and, just in case, work on a fall-back plan if funding is denied or reduced. In either case, you need to begin by analyzing your collections and needs. Though the parts of the bundle will be stored together, you will still need separate storage containers for the mummy, the textiles, the foodstuffs, and so forth. The idea is not to re-create the original bundle but to, as respectfully as possible, unite the now disparate parts of the mummy bundle so they are in close proximity. You might start by answering the following questions:

- Are there higher-priority collections? Start by analyzing the needs of these collections first.
- Perhaps you house unique collections that only your institution has?
- Are there very old collections that might also be more vulnerable than less ancient ones?
- Are there bundles that are more frequently visited or analyzed?
- Are there exceptionally fragile bundles? If so, what are their particular needs?
- Are there great differences in bundle type and size? If so, can you test and measure how much space is needed on average by selecting and measuring the space required of representative bundles?

describe the Inka practices of sacrificing children and adolescents in times of crisis—a supreme sacrifice denominated the *qhapac hucha* (Guaman Poma de Ayala 1980 [1608]). As the chroniclers describe, children were contributed by different local polities under the aegis of Inka institutions that established expectations that pure and unblemished youths and maidens would be chosen for ritual service in a variety of roles and contexts. In times of crisis, human sacrifice was expected. Both the children chosen for sacrifice and the artifacts that accompany them may have come from a nearby region or a distant part of the empire. The sacrificial process involved a long journey and culminated with a climb of several days in extreme conditions to altitudes of over five thousand meters and several days of ceremony that included the wrapping and burial of each child after death.

A number of the sacrificed children have been found due to glacial melting and avalanches that disturbed the burials and left human remains displaced and partially exposed. In these cases, the contextual evidence is limited to those funerary wrappings still around the body. The earliest published study of a mountaintop sacrifice was that of a young boy of Cerro El Plomo in northern Chile (Mostny 1957). However, earlier finds are known, including a child sacrifice from Cerro Chuscha in Argentina. In the 1960s, on Cerro El Toro, an Argentine team led by Juan Schobinger recovered a well-wrapped bundle containing the body of a young boy. Another well-wrapped young boy was found by climbers on Cerro Aconcagua in 1987 and recovered by an Argentine team directed by Schobinger. In the 1980s, Reinhard had worked on Inka sanctuaries among the volcanoes that line the border between northern Chile and Argentina, and in 1999 he returned with Maria Constanza Ceruti to study sacrifices conducted on Cerro Llullaillaco (Reinhard 1999). While the southern Peruvian sacrificial sites are best known internationally, the Argentine cases have been published in greater detail.

Schobinger (2001) produced a detailed study of the high-altitude sanctuary on Aconcagua, including study of the child sacrifice in the context of other offerings, structures, and evidence of ritual process. Together with previous publications by the team, it provides some fine examples of the potential information provided by contextual data. The sacrifice is presented in the context of early postconquest Spanish accounts of the *qhapaq hucha*, or supreme sacrifice, of the Inkas.

The Argentine team provides detailed description of the evidence provided by organic remains and artifacts associated with the body of the child. As in all the child sacrifices, Inka-style artifacts associated with ritual hospitality are present, such as an aryballoid vessel, jar, and duck-handled flat serving plate. Groups of miniature male or female figures worked in gold, silver, and *Spondylus* shell are dressed in gender-specific clothing and feather headdresses and accompanied by figures of camelids, all specifically Inka in style. The children themselves also may be associated with Inka-style textiles. However, the Aconcagua boy is wrapped in textiles of styles known from the central coast of Peru, far from his resting place in the southern Andes (Abal 2001). His body and clothes are covered, and his stomach and colon are filled with a reddish material identified as annatto or *achiote* (*Bixa orellana*), a seed pulp used as a red body paint, yellow dye, or medicine (Bárcena 2001). Documentation of the exact placement of funerary wrappings and associated organic materials, in combination with study of the child's body, is vital for interpretation of his origins and identity, as well as reconstruction of the rite of sacrifice.

Reinhard and Ceruti (2000) describe the three burials found in 1999 in a ceremonial platform on the peak of Cerro Llullaillaco. One adolescent girl, one preadolescent girl, and one preadolescent boy had been sacrificed and carefully wrapped and buried with accompanying offerings. The report contains a description of the fieldwork and conservation procedures. It includes only preliminary results of the analyses of artifacts and physical remains, but the contextual descriptions are invaluable. The preservation of the bodies of the children and contextual information are the best to date, due to the stable high-altitude conditions and the fact that they were recovered intact in their original tombs. For this reason, the offerings, ceremonial dress, and processes of ceremony, sacrifice, and burial are also best preserved in this case. As in the previous cases, the children may have come from non-Inka communities, but some principal elements of their dress, as well as the offerings left by the ceremonial process, correspond to Inka practice, design, and imagery. Due to the preservation of contextual information, these burials provide unprecedented information on the ceremonial feathered headdresses or sheet metal headdress ornaments used to adorn the sacrificed children, as well as parallels between the dress of each child and that of the groups of statuettes that accompany him or her. They also demonstrate details of their final days and treatment after death, such as coca leaves placed at their mouth, and the offerings sent to support their journey in this world or the next, such as slings and extra sandals (Reinhard 1999; Reinhard and Ceruti 2000).

For many researchers, the contextual evidence provided by the objects surrounding the body has revolutionized understanding of Inka material culture and associated practices. Each piece of information has wide-ranging repercussions. The context of the statuettes that accompany the sacrifices, their recurrence in groupings of gold, silver, and *Spondylus*, and their miniature garments and adornments provide new understanding of the possible lost contexts of many figurines that stand alone and naked in museum exhibits in the Andean nations and around the world. Details of the dress and wrapping of the children, such as *Spondylus* shell necklaces and feather headdresses, demonstrate surprising parallels with funerary practices of a very different society at Paracas some fifteen hundred years earlier. The arrangement of items of their clothing provides information on the use in life of hundreds of textiles previously know only as flattened rectangles or in a fragmentary state. As the sample size becomes large enough to demonstrate significant regularities, researchers approach new finds with greater information on the types of physical and contextual observations they should look for in the next case.

We have a new appreciation of the degree of accuracy of the early colonial documents, as well as their limitations. We understand the contribution in valued human lives made by subject peoples to the Inka state rituals, and something more about the relationship between regional

CONSERVATION CONVERSATION III: ONCE A FROZEN MUMMY, ALWAYS A FROZEN MUMMY

Dear Conservator Amparo:

We are a very small museum with a very small operating budget. We have heard that there are freeze-drying techniques for wet archaeological remains, and we were wondering if this is an option for the treatment of an ice mummy in our care. Also, we have two natural dry mummies that a group of visiting paleopathologists would like to examine. They want to remove the textiles for this exam and perform what they call minimally invasive autopsies. How would we help them remove the clothing? And is this really an acceptable practice?

Dear Archaeologist Alvaro:

Your questions are not easy to answer, but I will attempt to tackle them. First, there have been experiments and attempts at freeze drying bog bodies in the past, but the results have not been found to be entirely encouraging. Freeze drying occurs when a body is frozen and moisture is removed by sublimation, which transforms frozen water directly into vapor without passing through the liquid phase. This process is accelerated by a partial vacuum. A very substantial amount of shrinkage is to be expected even when there are bulking agents used. In addition, the bulking agents used (e.g., polyethylene glycol, or PEGs,—a relative of what is put in your car radiator) will most likely interfere with many future analyses. The visual characteristics change dramatically as well, the most noticeable being a shiny dark surface. Textiles that the individual is wearing would not likely fare well in the process, and these would have to be removed beforehand. And removing frozen textiles from a body that froze in a huddled position, protecting itself against the cold, is no easy task! In the case of the Ice Man, he was found in an extended position, with much of his clothing already missing from his back. These losses and his position made clothing removal by comparison relatively easy. Though the Ice Man was not freeze dried, the analysts wanted to be able to closely examine his body. To remove his remaining textiles, the work proceeded at a snail's pace while staff worked for a few minutes at a time before returning him to the freezer to prevent defrosting and decay of the body (Dickson et al. 2003).

No, I would not recommend freeze drying, because the mummy is already in a sense naturally freeze dried, but further manipulation would involve drastically altering its visual character and research potential. If you are having trouble with the expenses of maintaining a special freezer to house the frozen mummy, perhaps consider transferring the mummy to a larger institution or invent a unique community or international fund-raiser to support the preservation efforts.

The second question on disrobing or unwrapping a mummy bundle is not so easy to answer without seeing the mummy in question, but I will try to provide general guidelines. Disrobing and undressing dry desiccated mummies was a common practice decades ago in the Andes. The problem was that contexts after removal were lost, and the disrobing was often done by the people who were examining only the body. Record keeping was minimal if notes or photos were taken at all. The textiles in those days, if they were not visually beautiful, were a nuisance, almost expendable. Though crude, it was common to tear or cut the clothing off the bodies. *None of these practices are acceptable today!*

Most mummy bundles are kept intact if there are no problems with the individual inside (decay or collapse). If opening is determined necessary by a multidisciplinary team, then all layers of the bundle must be well documented with photos, drawings, and careful notes by subject matter experts so that the contexts of how the textiles and all other objects of personal adornment (clothing, jewelry, hairstyles, tattoos, bags, etc.) were used can be easily pieced together by later investigators, caretakers, and other stakeholders. The individual artifacts need to be carefully labeled and

(*continued*)

associated with their position in the bundle. The most difficult and awkward issue surrounds items of clothing that are difficult to remove because they are pinned by flexed limbs or cemented to the body during periods of active desiccation or decay. No general rules can be given here. It will require a team approach to make the blow-by-blow ethical decisions of whether the risk and potential benefits merit the destruction. In these cases, decisions often weigh destruction of the artifact or damage to or manipulation of the body.

The outer layer is frequently the easiest to remove, involving untying knots and loosening or unfolding the outer cloth in order to lift it off. Of course, this is done after very exacting documentation of the original state. Doing this on a humid day or in a humid atmosphere often helps. However, if it was sewn closed, you should carefully record the sewing technique used (notes, drawings, and close-up photography) and save the thread or yarn used for the sewing. Then remove as little as possible to open and safely remove the cloth from the bundle. Be sure to be ready to support anything loose below this outer cloth, such as loose beads, shoes, sandals, hair, or bones. Have padded acid-free trays of various sizes ready to receive these artifacts, and be sure to record their positions, too.

In regard to the inner layers or personal adornment, unfortunately, disrobing a mummy from this point on (or even earlier) is not usually so easy because the body may be flexed, and the clothing is often pinned under or between limbs. In addition, body fluids may have done a great deal of damage to textiles, including turning them into stiff but brittle crackerlike brown materials or carbonized black powder. Usually the textiles most affected by body fluids are those where gravity has played a role. These correspond to the posterior or lower side depending on whether the individual was lying on the back, side, or in a sitting position. Sometimes different layers of textiles in these areas will appear glued together in a stiff mass or even adhered to the body. If there are too many complications at this point, reevaluate the plan and see if relevant areas of clothing can be loosened enough to allow the pathologists to use an endoscope [see chapter 5] to examine the body without further disrobing. If disrobing must proceed, and the clothing is not in a cementlike clump, then loosen folds and evaluate how to remove clothing with the least amount of damage. In the past when full autopsies were undertaken, dislocated limbs allowed for removal of shirts, for instance, but full autopsies are no longer standard practice. Do not allow anxious researchers to rush you into decisions you will regret. Be sure the team has carefully discussed possible scenarios and does not make rash decisions.

diversity and centralized power, as symbolized and in actual practice. While sacrificial statuettes have long been identified as typical Inka artifacts, for the first time we know that they were dressed like specific individuals and employed in specific rituals. We can see how the textiles, ceramics, and other artifacts made in the official Inka styles were employed in the acts of supreme sacrifice unique to the Inka state. Specific spatial arrangements and object associations demonstrate details of the last days and final hours of the life of each sacrificed person. This new information is not only due to the extraordinary preservation of the human remains and other organic materials; it is also due to the details of context preserved in these relatively inaccessible sites. Despite the difficulties faced by archaeologists working under extreme conditions of altitude and weather, such details demonstrate the importance of carefully documenting contextual associations.

CONCLUSION

The three examples discussed in this chapter represent the value and diversity of the information that may be drawn from careful study of the contextual relationships among objects

ASSOCIATED FUNERARY OBJECTS: RELIGIOUS VOTIVES
Teresa Moreno

The veneration of relics, tombs, images, and icons associated with saints, martyrs, and other significant holy persons by the offering of votives is a long-held tradition among Roman Catholics and Orthodox Christians. The handling and treatment of objects of such spiritual importance and association present challenges that are similar to those encountered when caring for collections of human remains and funerary objects. In referring to the care of human remains and associated sacred objects, Elke Beck (2001:21) writes, "Their treatment will always be a delicate bridge between aesthetic, historical, physical, and conceptual integrity."

Religious votives are the tangible offerings that accompany a prayer to a deity or saint by pious and devout believers. Originating from the Latin word *votum*, meaning "vow, prayer, wish, desire, or offering," the terms *votives* and *ex-votos* (from a vow) have been used historically in the Christian world to refer to any variety of offerings ranging from flowers, candles, devotional paintings such as icons or *retablos*, or any image made of wax, metal, wood, ceramic, or bone. The offering of votives is believed to encourage saints or beatified persons to intercede on behalf of the believer. Votives are offered to invoke healing from illness and disease, the survival of babies and farm animals, and improve virility and fertility. They also are gifts of thanks after a prayer is answered or a miracle is performed. While various types of votives continue to be produced and offered, the parameters of religious sensitivity that determine their ritual value tend to vary. The following examples contrast the roles of respect in the care of votives through time.

A rare collection of fragments of hollow-cast wax *ex-votos* discovered in 1943 in the Cathedral Church of St. Peter in Exeter is evidence of the veneration of holy remains in medieval England (Moreno 2001). The fifteenth-century votive images were found hidden behind a screen high above the tomb of Bishop Edmund Lacey who in the later years of his life became infirm and lame. After his death in 1455, Lacey was venerated unofficially as a saint for his thaumaturgic (i.e., miracle-working) powers, and his tomb became a site of religious pilgrimage for the sick and infirm. Written accounts from the sixteenth and even as late as the early seventeenth century recall miracles of healing at this tomb. The wax images found there were probably among hundreds, even thousands, that had been placed around the tomb by religious pilgrims either as a request for a miracle or as thanks for one already performed.

The sixteenth century, however, was a period of great change in the Catholic Church throughout Europe. This period of Enlightenment in northern Europe emphasized the word of the Lord rather than symbolic imagery. A significant element of the Protestant Reformation was the rejection of the very concept of saints and the veneration of their relics. As a result, much of the Catholic ornament and furnishings were pulled down and destroyed. The tomb of Bishop Lacey was defaced, all its adornments were destroyed, and pilgrims were no longer openly able to pay reverence to the bishop. Though there was much fluctuation in thoughts and beliefs during the sixteenth and seventeenth centuries, by the eighteenth century, the veneration of relics began to seem backward, disgusting, and embarrassing even to many European Catholics (Beck 2001:19).

Ethical questions that arose when determining an approach to the handling and treatment of the Exeter *ex-votos* included these:

- Were the fragments of votive images considered to hold any religious significance since the conversion of the church from Catholicism to Protestantism?
- Were they now regarded as merely historic artifacts?
- How should they be treated?

(*continued*)

preserved as funerary wrappings, as well as the practical conservation issues faced when we seek to preserve this information and achieve effective preservation and study of human remains. Whether we are dealing with fragmentary burials or intact funerary contexts, all contextual information is vital. Certain types of studies may be prioritized at the time of an excavation or rescue intervention, while other types of questions and forms of analysis may be prioritized by future stakeholders. Whether we are working with human remains from Archaic hunting and gathering societies, early agricultural communities, chiefdoms, states, or empires, the analysis of funerary contexts in their entirety plays a key role in building understanding of social roles, cultural practices, and relationships of power. Surely, it took a family, team, or community effort to properly bury these individuals; likewise, today it takes a multidisciplinary team effort to preserve them as unified entities that include individuals, associated artifacts, and resulting excavation/rescue and research archives.

REFERENCES

Abal de Russo, Clara
   2001 Cerro Aconcagua: Descripción y Estudio del Material Textil. In *El Santuario Incaico del Cerro Aconcagua*, edited by J. Schobinger, pp. 117–170. Editorial de la Universidad National de Cuyo, Mendoza.

Agüero, Carolina
   1994 Madejas, Turbantes y Pelos: Los Turbantes del Formativo Temprano en Arica, Norte de Chile. Thesis for the professional degree in archaeology, Universidad de Chile.

Arriaza, Bernardo T.
   1995 *Beyond Death: The Chinchorro Mummies of Ancient Chile.* Smithsonian, Washington, D.C.

Bárcena, Roberto
   2001 Pigmentos en el Ritual Funerário de la Momia del Cerro Aconcagua. In *El Santuario Incaico del Cerro Aconcagua*, edited by J. Schobinger, pp. 117–170. Editorial de la Universidad National de Cuyo, Mendoza.

Beck, Elke
　2001 "Es Ist Alles Tot Ding?"!? Considerations in Dealing with Relics. In *Human Remains: Conservation, Retrieval and Analysis: Proceedings of a Conference Held in Williamsburg, VA, Nov 7–11th 1999*, edited by Emily Williams. BAR International Series 934. Archaeopress, Oxford.

Carrión Cachot, Rebeca
　1931 La Indumentaria en la Antigua Cultura de Paracas. *Wira Kocha: Revista Peruana de Estudios Antropológicos* 1(1):37–86.

Daggett, Richard E.
　1991 Paracas: Discovery and Controversy. In *Paracas Art and Architecture*, edited by A. Paul, pp. 35–60. University of Iowa Press, Iowa City.

Dauelsberg, Percy
　1974 Excavaciones Arqueológicas en Quiani (Provincia de Tarapacá, Dept. Arica). *Chungará* 4:7–38.

d'Harcourt, Raoul
　1962 [1934] *Textiles of Ancient Peru and Their Techniques*. Edited by Grace G. Denny and Carolyn M. Osborne, translated by Sadie Brown. University of Washington Press, Seattle.

Dickson, James H., Klaus Oeggl, and Linda L. Handley
　2003 The Iceman Reconsidered. *Scientific American* 288(5):60–69.

Dwyer, Jane Powell
　1971 Chronology and Iconography of Late Paracas and Early Nasca Textile Designs. Ph.D. dissertation, University of California, Berkeley.

Foccacci, Guillermo
　1973 Excavaciones en el Cementerio Playa Miller 7, Arica (Chile). *Chungara* 3:23–74.

Guaman Poma de Ayala, Felipe
　1980 [1608] *Nueva Corónica y Buen Gobierno*. Critical edition by John Murra and Rolena Adorno; translation and textual analysis by Jorge L. Urioste. Siglo Veintiuno, Mexico City.

Horie, C. V.
　1987 *Materials for Conservation: Organic Consolidants, Adhesives and Coatings*. Butterworths, London.

Maunder, Michelle
　2000 The Conservation of Sacred Objects. In *Godly Things: Museums, Objects and Religion*, edited by C. Paine. Leicester University Press, London.

Moreno, Teresa K.
　2001 *A Collection of 15th Century Wax Votive Images: Identification, Analysis, and Conservation*. Unpublished master's thesis, Durham University, Durham.

Mostny, Grete
　1957 La Momia del Cerro El Plomo. *Boletín del Museo Nacional de Historia Natural* 27(1).

Oktavec, Eileen
　1995 *Answered Prayers: Miracles and Milagros along the Border*. University of Arizona Press, Tucson.

Paul, Anne
　1990 *Paracas Ritual Attire: Symbols of Authority in Ancient Peru*. University of Oklahoma Press, Norman.
　1991 Paracas Necrópolis Bundle 89: A Description and Discussion of Its Contents. In *Paracas Art and Architecture*, edited by A. Paul, pp. 172–221. University of Iowa Press, Iowa City.

Peters, Ann H.
　2000 Funerary Regalia and Institutions of Leadership in Paracas and Topará. *Chungara* 32(2): 245–252.

Reinhard, Johan

1996   Peru's Ice Maidens: Unwrapping the Secrets. *National Geographic* 189(6):62–81.

1997   Sharp Eyes of Science Probe Peru's Mummies. *National Geographic* 191(1):36–43.

1999   Frozen in Time. *National Geographic* 196(5) (November):36–55.

Reinhard, Johan, and Maria Constanza Ceruti

2000   *Investigaciones Arqueológicas en Cerro Llullaillaco.* Ediciones Universidad Católica de Salta, Salta.

Schiffer, Michael Brian

1999   *The Material Life of Human Beings: Artifacts, Behavior and Communication.* Routledge, London.

Schobinger, Juan

2001   *El Santuario Incaico del Cerro Aconcagua.* Editorial de la Universidad National de Cuyo, Mendoza.

Stafford, Cora E.

1941   *Paracas Embroideries: A Study of Repeating Patterns.* Augustin, New York.

Sullivan, M. Brigid, and Karl Schram

1987   Investigation of Exudate Formation of Prehistoric Human Mummified Remains from the American Southwest. In *Jubilee Conservation Conference,* pp. 267–272. University of London, Institute of Archeology, London.

Tello, Julio C.

1929   *Antiguo Perú: Primera Epoca.* Comisión Organizadora del Segundo Congreso Sudamericano de Turismo, Lima.

1959   *Paracas: Primera Parte.* Institute of Andean Research, Lima.

Tello, Julio C., and Toribio Mejía Xesspe

1979   *Paracas: Segunda Parte.* Universidad Nacional Mayor de San Marcos e Institute of Andean Research, Lima.

Ulloa Torres, Liliana

1982   Evolución de la Industria Textil Prehispánica en la Zona de Arica. *Chungara* 8:97–108.

Weiss, Pedro

1958   *Osteología Cultural: Prácticas Cefálicas, 1a parte: Cabeza trofeo—Trepanaciones—Cauterizaciones.* Librería Juan Mejía Baca, Lima.

1961   *Osteología Cultural: Prácticas Cefálicas, 2a parte: Tipología de la Deformaciones Cefálicas y de Algunas Enfermedades seas.* Librería Juan Mejía Baca, Lima.

Yacovleff, Eugenio

1932   La Deidad Primitiva de los Nasca. *Revista del Museo Nacional* 1(2):103–160.

1933   Arte Plumaria entre los Antiguos Peruanos. *Revista del Museo Nacional* 2(1):137–158.

Yacovleff, Eugenio, and Jorge C. Muelle

1934   Una Fardo Funerario de Paracas. *Revista del Museo Nacional* 3(1–2):63–153.

CHAPTER 10

Documentation

History and the Sources of Skeletons in Collections

ALAN G. MORRIS

IN HIS 1983 BOOK *THE NAME OF THE ROSE*, UMBERTO ECO TELLS US A STORY OF A CLASH OF TRUTHS AND cultures. While the papal emissaries argue the nature of angels, the apprentice monk dabbles in witchcraft, and the abbot and his monastic brothers live lives separate from the reality of the starvation in the countryside. The monk-detective is the personification of science, and the chief librarian is the guardian of secrets known only to the initiated. The story is a murder mystery set in mid-fourteenth-century Italy, but despite being fiction, the tale is not far from the truth of our own museum stories at the start of the twenty-first century. The demands for reburial, but most especially the demand to make museums more relevant to the communities in which they are situated, are embodiments of Eco's tale. Instead of witchcraft and imaginary angels, we have mainstream versus traditional belief systems. Instead of isolated monasteries, we have "ivory tower" institutions; and instead of monk-detectives and chief librarians, we have archaeologists, forensic specialists, physical anthropologists, and museum curators.

At the heart of our modern clash of truths and cultures lies the assembly of skeletons and associated material in museum collections. As scientists we feel we are above the hurly-burly of the debate on the "spirituality" of the bones, yet in reality, simply by keeping the skeletons in the collections, we invite debate on the nature of science and the role of scientists in society. Part of the debate centers on the reasons why we have collected the skeletons at all. There is no question in my mind that the collections have been of immense value in building our knowledge of the past. Yet such knowledge has often not been passed down to the descendants of the very people whose bones reside in the storerooms. Sadly, science often has been only interested in itself rather than the communities it should be serving.

The dynamic between science and descendant communities often surfaces in the debate about the identity of the skeletons. The reason for the argument is that "identity" is not a simple factor and is seen differently by different people. Identity can change with time. It is also possible for a single skeleton to have many identities depending on whether biology, ethnicity, or history is used as an identifier. From the museum perspective, the documentation of the skeletal material is key to this debate. Although the records may seem neutral, they need to be examined and interpreted in the light of their context.

SKELETONS IN COLLECTIONS: WHERE DO THEY COME FROM?

Modern museum collections of skeletons tend to have three different sources for skeletal material. The first source is primarily from forensic investigations or from cadaveric dissections, but it may also include teaching skeletons purchased from supply houses. A second major group of skeletons is from culturally affiliated or ethnically identified contexts. Included here are a wide range of archaeological skeletons excavated primarily in the twentieth century as well as the problematic typological skeletons collected by racial science in the eighteenth and nineteenth centuries. Lastly are the skeletons with no known cultural affiliation but of clearly archaeological origin. Often these are from rescue operations or are old museum skeletons for which context has been poorly recorded or entirely lost. Each of these needs to be considered in a different manner because of their origins and because of public interest in the skeletons themselves.

Forensic and Cadaveric Remains

Forensic and cadaver skeletons are probably the least problematic. Anatomy acts in various forms around the world give registered repositories permission to hold such skeletons. In the case of forensic material, the usual request from authorities is that the remains are clearly labeled and that should identification be made at a later date, then the material should be deaccessioned and returned to the family of the deceased. Cadaveric material, on the other hand, has been donated for the purposes of scientific research and is therefore available for a wide range of investigations. Problems can still occur in making use of the documentation even for cadaver skeletons. Research that explores ranges of variation in age, health, or morphology in cadavers often ignores the source of the skeletons (Morris 2003). Self-donated bodies are drawn from a completely different social pool, usually well educated and of high social class, than pauper acquisitions. Paupers are often drawn from prisons or from communities too poor to afford the relatively high cost of inhumation. This means that observations that reflect different lifestyles will differ dramatically between samples no matter what the biological origin of the groups. Researchers often also refer to such skeletons in "ethnic" terms despite the classification being based often on racial assessments loaded by current national political contexts.

Real human skeletons used to be a common item purchased from scientific supply houses. Until the early 1980s, there was a trade in human skeletons from India for purchase by medical schools, but the advance payment of the living poor for their bodies on their death has now been banned by the Indian government and that particular source has dried up. The availability of high-quality casts of human skeletons has also dampened the trade, and virtually none of the legitimate supply houses still stock human material. Despite this, museums should still be aware that donations of bones from retired medical doctors or dentists may very well originate from this source.

Culturally Affiliated or Ethnically Identified Skeletons

Ethnically identified skeletons are often the central focus both of repatriation requests and demands for reburial. Some individuals were actually known in life, and linkage with living descendants is often possible, but more often these skeletons have simply been labeled with specific ethnic names (often down to the level of tribe). Their identity therefore rests with the ability of the museum curator to interpret the historical information that is associated with the specimen.

Most of the great collections of human skeletons in Europe and North America had their origins in the nineteenth century. Specimens of eighteenth-century origin were predominantly of anatomical "abnormalities," but by the nineteenth century, the focus had switched to racial origin and racial types. Nearly all of the museum collections were purely Linnaean in the sense that the bones were solely there to illustrate human typological variation. Typical of these were Blumenbach's collection in Göttingen and Morton's collection in Philadelphia (Gould 1978, 1981). The collections were not extensive but were constructed to try to represent a wide range of hu-

A CASE STUDY: COLONIALISM AND THE RETURN
OF SARAH BAARTMAN

The nineteenth-century typological collections were not acquired through any systematic means. Although some of these institutions did solicit skeletons of specific population groups, the majority of skeletons were assembled by a wide range of nonprofessional collectors and donated to the institution of their choice. These collectors included missionaries, soldiers, colonial administrators, doctors, traders, and scientists of various sorts. The curators of the collections actively solicited these collectors in order to collect as wide a range of skeletons as possible. The curators looked "outward," with the underlying assumption that subject matter in the museum collections was "other" people, not their own.

The late nineteenth and early twentieth centuries were a murky time for anthropological science. The questions posed were invariably ensnared in the issues of race and ethnogenesis. The prime interest of the collectors was race science and the collections were considered a form of national archive. Therefore, the collections in the vault were intended to represent the purity of national biological heritage, usually with the object of demonstrating superiority of the colonial power over the colonized.

The activities of the eighteenth- and nineteenth-century collectors resulted in the remains of people being kept in places that were far from their original homes, and this has resulted in claims not just for reburial but also for repatriation. A classic example of this has been the return of Sarah Baartman from France to South Africa (Tobias 2002). Baartman had been taken to England in 1810 and died in France in 1815. Her skeleton, pudenda, and brain were kept in the Musée de l'Homme. Baartman's precise ethnicity is unknown, although it is accepted that she was of Khoisan genetic ancestry. No direct descendants have been identified, but Baartman's body parts were claimed by the Griqua of South Africa, a historic group of partial Khoisan descent (Morris 1997). The Griqua identified themselves as a descendant group defined by ethnic relationship and used this relationship to claim her remains. The remains of Sarah Baartman were returned to South Africa and buried with Christian rites in August 2002.

Although the Griqua and other Khoisan people were given a central role in her return and burial, her return was very much a national issue rather than an ethnic one. The burial party included not only a range of ethnic claimants but also several cabinet ministers and Thabo Mbeki, the state president himself. In his funeral oration, Mbeki (2002) emphasized the "monstrosity" of the European race scientists and how Baartman had been used as an example of African "inferiority" through her transportation to Europe and her dissection and display subsequent to her death. A similar national response to repatriation took place in Botswana the same year with the return of "El Negro," an unknown individual returned to southern Africa from Barcelona in Spain (Davies 2003).

man types. Although archaeology as a subject was forming in the same period, collections of archaeological material remained rare until well into the twentieth century.

By the mid-nineteenth century, the pressure to document colonial possessions became the overwhelming drive for collection. Collections in London, Paris, Brussels, Berlin, and Vienna began to swell with skeletons from the colonial periphery. Although still colonies of Britain themselves, South Africa and Australia began to develop their own museum collections on the European model. The museum curators began the task of documenting groups they felt would soon cease to exist as European settlement disrupted native populations and forced them to transform or disappear (Tobias 1985; Morris and Tobias 1997). This included the collection of skeletons.

LINNAEUS AND THE ORIGINS OF TYPOLOGY

Carl Linnaeus (1707–1778) is the undisputed father of taxonomy. The Linnaean classification system is both logical and based on observation, yet it has been constructed entirely outside the framework of evolutionary theory and genetics. Linnaeus's sole objective was to name and describe all of God's creation. In this, he relied on the Aristotelean concept of "The Great Chain of Being." Each link of the chain was represented by a separate species, and the arrangement of the species on the chain represented the plan of God (Lindroth 1983). Linnaeus labored to discover the key to God's plan as revealed in the anatomy of fauna and flora. Hence, he referred to his system as a "natural" order.

The lynchpin of the Linnaean system was the species. Without a concept of fixed and precisely defined species Linnaeus was helpless, because the plan of the Creator would be hidden. For Linnaeus, the invariability of species was the condition for order in nature and each living creature was a copy of the first parents (Lindroth 1983:24). Despite the fact that in his later years Linnaeus began to accept the fact that new varieties could and did appear, he downplayed their importance. He felt these deviations were at odds with nature, and in particular with the "nature" of the species (Eriksson 1983). In his first edition of *Systema Naturae*, Linnaeus cataloged human races as full species in their own right, yet by the tenth edition, he had transformed the races of humanity into varieties. But these races did not fit his standard approach to varieties. Each was provided with a brief description of its essence and its own binomen in Latin as if it were still regarded as a separate species. Linnaeus clearly intended these human variants to be considered fundamental units in the order of nature.

The Linnaean vision of fixed species, and by extension fixed varieties, was an outgrowth of the philosophy of Plato. The Platonic view considered that each species had an "essence" that reflected the eternal ideal. Linnaeus adapted this to his concept of a species in which he "considered that the archetype was the most important measure of a species, and that variations were only shadows of the archetype" (Magner 1979:353). To describe a species was to describe its archetype. By the nineteenth century, this concept had become firmly rooted in the young field of anthropology. The technique of racial description that developed in this era became known as *typology*.

The fixity and therefore "natural" delineation of races were inherent in typological classification. The "type" was defined as an ideal individual who possessed all of the important characteristics of the race. The focus was thus only on those features that could differentiate between races. Features that indicated the unity of races were ignored. A corollary of the type was the concept of "purity." A "pure race" was one that had not intermixed with other races and whose component individuals were still exactly like the original type. The place of the individual was well defined in typology. Since the type was an ideal standard, the individual could be compared to the type and his or her purity assessed. Variations were impurities but the characteristics of the type could be dissected out through careful observation (Stepan 1982).

Genetics researchers working in the first three decades of the twentieth century did provide a genetic rather than typological foundation for human variation, but typology remained the technique of choice for most anthropologists right until the 1950s. Why was this so? Stepan (1982) has proposed that because "race history" was still the major focus of anthropological research, scientists did not want to leave the easily understandable shores of typology. Racial classification was for most anthropologists the whole point of their measurements. It was to take the horrors of the Nazi race policy to force a change of view.

The United States developed a holistic view of anthropology especially to deal with the anticipated demise of its own native "colonial" people. The American concept of anthropology encompassed the four fields of archaeology, linguistics, social anthropology, and physical anthropology. This gave the American anthropologists the opportunity to study all aspects of a community that they believed was sliding into ethnological oblivion (Hultkrantz 1980).

The typological approach ensured that each museum vied to assemble an appropriate range of "types." Numbers were less important than ensuring all of the various racially "pure" types could be found in the collection. The context of the skeletons was almost totally ignored, and all that was considered significant was an ethnic identity, one usually established by European ethnologists. The documentation was usually colored by the biases of the collector and ethnologist who confirmed the identity.

Archaeological skeletons usually have better documentation, but often they are seen as contested assets specifically because of the debate about how archaeological cultures relate to one another and to living descendant communities. The American NAGPRA legislation has used ethnic identity as the main factor for linkage between living and archaeological communities. Because of this, American law sees proof of cultural continuity over time as the primary authority in claiming the past. The debate about identity is muddied by the confusion over the definitions of ethnicity, race, and community and how these can be linked to past archaeological occurrences. For many modern marginalized native populations, substantiating their archaeological linkage with past populations also is a way of obtaining both land ownership and negotiation rights with current political powers. The most precise way to demonstrate long-term tenancy is to link oneself with the presence of ancestral graves.

Skeletons with No Known Cultural Affiliation

Not all archaeological skeletons have good associated documentation. Rescue excavations are often too late to preserve crucial archaeological information from a site destroyed by erosion or vandalism. Older museum specimens may have become disassociated from the original documentation or were never accompanied by records at all. Often these skeletons are used as teaching material, but since their origin is not through the usual route of cadaveric donation, certainly some discomfort arises over the moral and ethical issues.

Rather than using cultural identity for the identification of such skeletons, some researchers have attempted to use biological identity to demonstrate a linkage to one or another modern group. The ethnic identity (based on physical features) is determined by the application of complex statistical techniques. The unknown cranium is measured; the numbers are run through a computer; and the skull is assigned to the nearest group average in the database. Since biology and culture overlap but are not codependent (note the lessons of apartheid), such statistical wizardry is really no better than nineteenth-century craniology.

The whole issue is confounded by the fact that both ethnicity and biology change over time. How far back in time can ethnicity be identified and when does a morphological difference indicate a different group origin? Ancient DNA research may have a role here, but given the current expense involved in these analyses and the high risk of failure due to contamination in the lab, we are far from near a point where ancient DNA would become a standard technique applied to unknown individuals. Also the ethical implications of destructive analysis need to be sorted out before such analyses become routine.

Despite this confusion, it may be perfectly reasonable to accept a skeleton as that of an aboriginal person if the archaeological context is consistent with a pre-European contact situation in various parts of the world. In the United States, such skeletons are known as "unaffiliated" and are defined as being Native American but not associated with a particular past or present tribe. It seems likely that new NAGPRA legislation will include such individuals as well, so it may very well be imperative that some way be found to link unknown skeletons to specific archaeological assemblages or modern descendant communities. Osteological features that demonstrate behavioral characteristics may be extremely useful in this context. Dental mutilation, cranial deformation, patterns of dental wear, squatting facets, or even specific pathologies may give clues to ethnic origin. Such features do not guarantee identity but at least point in a direction that may be useful given the specific context.

From the practical perspective, curators of collections must recognize that how they deal with skeletons in their collections will depend on the original source of the bones. Many of these will be problematic and will involve them in public debate. This is neither rare nor bad. The recent survey of museum collections in Great Britain noted human remains in 132 of 146 institutions (Working Group on Human Remains 2004). Material from archaeological contexts will probably provide the greatest challenges for all museums, especially when contextual information is minimal.

DOCUMENTATION AND DATA STORAGE

The bottom line for documentation of any collection is to be as thorough as possible. Description and measurement of the material are critical, but the associated historical and archaeological data are just as critical. In the case of archaeological material, my personal response is to entirely avoid ethnicity! Skeletons should be cataloged in terms of precise geographic location (map grid), time (C14 date), and archaeological association (Morris 1992). No attempt should ever be made to assign ethnicity to skeletal material based on morphology.

For those of us who curate collections of human skeletons, we need to ask ourselves very clearly at the outset, "What are we holding the bones for, anyway?" Are we no better than the chief librarian in Umberto Eco's tale? If not, then for whom are we keeping the bones? One hundred years ago the answer to the question would have been simple. The skeletons were racial archives for scientific study, but today we must recognize that we are also stewards for the descendant communities, holding the remains for repatriation, reburial, or further study. They, and we, must note that the current context of scientific study is very different from the racial analyses of the nineteenth century (Sealy 2003) and that the questions posed of the skeletons are as much to do with osteobiography as they are about origins. As a once living body system, the skeleton records a wide range of information about an individual. Growth, pathology, biological stress, lifestyle, posture, and behavior all leave marks on bone. In a sense, "reading the bones" for a scientist is actually reading the biography of the individual.

A useful assumption is that all skeletons will eventually be reburied. Although this is hopefully not the case, it does demand the creation of an observation bank so that the scientific knowledge can be stored even if the actual bones are lost. The advent of the NAGPRA legislation has generated several possible checklists for observations.

The best one is probably the guide by Buikstra and Ubelaker (1994), but there are other options. For example, which measurement bank is the best one to use? Most American researchers have been using the measurement set defined by Howells (1973, 1989), but European workers have tended to use either the Biometric school (Fawcett and Lee 1902; Morant 1923) or the German school (Martin and Saller 1957; Knussmann 1988). Techniques for the identification of age and sex of skeletons can be found in a wide range of texts, but again there tend to be different but overlapping standards for American and European studies. Krogman and İşcan (1986) provide a comprehensive list of the American standards, while the European standards are described in Ferembach et al. (1980), recently summarized in Maat et al. (2002). No matter which standards are used, the recorded documentation must clearly indicate which were used and what features were used to establish age and sex. Remember, age and sex identities from skeletons are diagnoses, not certainties.

DOCUMENTATION SYSTEMS IN HUMAN OSTEOLOGY

Lane Anderson Beck

Since institutions began accumulating collections in natural history, it has been critical that they have a method for keeping track of what they have and where it is. Such catalog systems have undergone a series of changes reflecting both the increase in the technology of record keeping and the increase in precision of observations in human osteology.

During the nineteenth century, institutional collections were often cataloged in ledger books. At the Smithsonian Institution, human remains were curated within the Division of Mammals. The ledger catalog included brief information only primarily reporting species, location collected, and donor information. The catalog ledger system used at the Peabody Museum of Archaeology and Ethnology at Harvard University began with a similar system. Supplemental information on the human remains themselves was not included in the catalog itself but kept either in the director's correspondence files or in a collection of records pertaining to the accession.

Around the turn of the twentieth century, these ledger-based catalog systems had become unwieldy. Flipping through pages in a bound book was not an efficient way to locate a particular collection or the remains from a specific location. Many museums at this time switched from the ledger system to a card file format. Often multiple copies of each catalog card were made with a primary set filed numerically and a secondary set cross filed by provenience, pathology, or other criteria. The content of these catalog cards varied widely. For some institutions, the information was limited to that of the old ledgers. At other institutions, the cards included a more detailed inventory of the human remains and basic observations on age, sex, and pathology.

These varied formats for documentation of human remains in museum collections were often based on the particular interests of the curator charged with oversight of the collection. They also reflect the academic lineage of the different curators. For example, the analysis forms used by Larry Angel at the Smithsonian Institution were a modified version of those used by Ernest Hooton, Angel's adviser at Harvard University. Similarly, Bob Blakely's skeletal observation forms at Georgia State University were taken from those used by his graduate adviser, Georg Neumann at Indiana University.

Often the catalog record and the research observations were separate records. For example, the card catalog at the Peabody Museum of Archaeology and Ethnology did include a bone by bone inventory and some summary data on demography and pathology. The research files, which were maintained by the individual scholar rather than as part of the collection record, included much more detailed observations (e.g., cranial and postcranial metric data).

In the late 1980s, with NAGPRA looming in Congress, osteologists recognized an urgent need to create a standard for skeletal inventories and observations. With the potential that major collections might not be available for reanalysis in the future, it became critical to have a consistent suite of data that allowed scholars to compare collections they had not personally observed. This led to Buikstra and Ubelaker's (1994) book, *Standards for Data Collection from Human Skeletal Remains*. Although variation remains in how these standards are used, most researchers now rely on this reference for a basic foundation on which their documentation is built.

At the Arizona State Museum, we utilize a dual documentation system. One level is represented in our computerized database catalog of the collection and the other is represented by more detailed paper records of our observations. The computer catalog does include a bone by bone inventory as well as summary data on demography and pathology. It includes two primary data screens, one for geocultural provenience and legal history of the collection and one for the biological inventory data. The paper archives ideally include the field records for the individual burial and up to thirty-five to forty pages of detailed osteological documentation. Our documentation is based on Buikstra and Ubelaker for the major inventory, metric, and nonmetric data but diverges in the area of pathology. For pathology, we focus on detailed description and, as needed, standardized sketches of each bone

(continued)

DOCUMENTATION SYSTEMS IN HUMAN OSTEOLOGY (*continued*)

or area of the skeleton, which can be annotated to describe anomalies, pathology, or taphonomic features. (This expansion is in line with that of most researchers in terms of recognition that medical data require more extensive information rather than stopping at the level of a checklist.)

One of the key changes in museum catalog records for human remains has been driven by NAGPRA. For more than a century, catalogs recorded collections with the archaeological site as the critical provenience unit. Today the site and its general location no longer suffice. The legal status of the land ownership at the time a site was excavated has become a critical unit of information. Although in practice museums that held collections were authorized to oversee daily care and access, legal authority was always determined by the land ownership of the archaeological site at the time of excavation. For example, an archaeological site located on tribal lands is under the legal control of the Bureau of Indian Affairs. A museum may serve as a repository for collections from that site but the authority for repatriation is vested in the federal agency and not in the repository.

A second change in museum records since NAGPRA pertains to the temporal and cultural identification of archaeological sites. In the past, museums relied on the individual researcher to know which sites they wished to examine. Specific date and archaeological culture were not necessarily recorded in the catalog. For NAGPRA, cultural affiliation is critical in determining which Native American nations an institution should notify about specific collections. Data fields recording affiliation data are now part of most catalog systems.

A final change in osteological catalog records since NAGPRA has been the need to link catalog records for human remains with the archaeological artifacts associated with them. Although most catalog systems have long included a feature or burial number as the intrasite provenience, the actual catalogs for human remains and artifacts were usually separate card files or database tables. Neither computer systems nor card files provided a ready mechanism to connect these different record systems. Although the same information was originally used to record intrasite provenience, there was no guarantee that the archaeology cataloger and the osteology cataloger had transcribed the information in an identical format. Although smaller collections could be reintegrated by hand, this level of matching was not practical for larger institutions. Our solution at the Arizona State Museum has involved creating a bridge across multiple databases.

The human remains database exists in Microsoft Access on a computer that is not connected to the Internet and is located in a restricted location. This means those data are protected against unauthorized access. Each set of remains has been assigned an arbitrary record number. The artifact database is maintained on a central computer system. It includes a data field for burial record number. Even if the specific intrasite provenience is entered differently in the two databases, the burial record number allows all artifact data to be linked to the burial record. Artifact records also contain a flag field that is checked if the artifact is believed to come from a burial context. An ASCII file of artifact data can be created from the central database and transferred to the human remains database. By using a master/detail join (one to many relationships), we can readily create the listing of artifacts by burial.

We also have instituted a double-check procedure to identify potential problems. Using the field burial forms, a memo field in the human remains database includes a listing of all grave goods reported during excavation. By comparing the memo field to the artifact database, we are able to trouble shoot both sides of the catalog. This allows us a method to double-check ourselves for identifications as well as typographic errors.

Although catalog systems have changed dramatically over the past century, there is no reason to feel that they now incorporate a professional standard that will be stable for the long term. Human osteology continues to be a dynamic field of research, and additional methods and standards are developed each year. While many of these additional data sets will be maintained in supplemental archives, others are likely to become core observational standards in the future. Just as in the past, catalog documentation systems today incorporate basic data on the human remains they record. As such, they form a history of scholarship as well as a record of collections.

BONES VERSION 1.0 SOFTWARE

Jennifer Riddle and Vicki Cassman

Included on the AltaMira website (http://www.altamirapress.com) with information on this volume is Bones Version 1.0, a free downloadable software program designed to catalog human osteological collections, inventory records, and, most important, create inventory diagrams for storage boxes based on data entered by the user. The idea for Bones grew out of the frustration of witnessing the damage from handling osteological collections for informal, spontaneous, or planned inventories and studies within both academic and museum settings.

Bones was created to streamline the skeletal inventory process, making it computerized, fairly easy, and as efficient as possible. In the past, laboratory managers have had to inventory skeletons, fill in data sheets for a catalog, create a catalog, and then finally fill in, by hand, inventory diagrams used on the outside of boxes or for reports. All of these steps are time-consuming and, by necessity, somewhat redundant. Bones seeks to correct this by offering the user the ability to accomplish all of these mentioned steps at one time. It allows the user to click check boxes indicating the status of every bone in the human body, fill in fields for catalog numbers, site numbers, and observer, and then create editable files for each skeleton. The program's skeletal element checklist includes options for absent, complete, and partial. All elements are listed in a logical order that follows Bass's groupings and can be checked off individually or as a group.

When the inventory is complete, the program will generate an Access database containing all of the skeletal information. Once the user is ready for a storage box diagram, he or she needs only choose the size and color and the program will print the image. If at some point information in the catalog needs to be changed, users can open the Record Editor within Bones and make the updates. Bones will automatically update the database and the diagram. Conversely, any changes made in the database will carry over to the main Bones Record Editor, which will also update the diagram. (For those who are not familiar with Access, the information can also be opened as an Excel spreadsheet, which is often easier to manage.)

We find that the diagrams, when placed inside polyester sleeves and adhered to the outside of a box, cut back dramatically on wear and tear of collections. The analyst, student of osteology, collection manager, visitor, and researcher can without even opening the box survey the collections by reviewing the diagrams. Before we used Bones diagrams, it was common to see boxes opened and bones pushed aside to find out whether the individual in question had, for instance, a third metacarpal or not. This type of handling inevitably causes a great deal of damage that is recognized by bone dust, soils, and fragments that accumulate in the bottom of the boxes. You may say well why don't they use the catalogs first? In practice, catalogs are rarely consulted first, and the diagrams produced using Bones for placement on boxes or in reports are easily accessible and immediate. It is our hope that Bones will aid in the preservation of your collections as well.

Beyond a measurement bank and age and sex identity, there is little that can be standardized in terms of observation. Buikstra and Ubelaker (1994) have presented a list of paleopathology observations, but it is not exhaustive. Ultimately, the thoroughness of any set of observations will depend on the skill and experience of the observer.

Scientists will primarily be interested in the data recorded for each skeleton, but they will also need to be certain as to how the cultural/ethnic identity of the skeleton was made. Unfortunately, if these data were not documented by the original donor, then there is virtually no way in which the identity can be retrieved or confirmed. Multivariate assessment of ethnic identity from morphology can be done, but its reliability is suspect because ethnic identity is based on culture, not biology. In the case of archaeological skeletons, cultural identity can be determined from the archaeological context, but this can only be transformed into an ethnic identity if there is a clear cultural continuity between the archaeological and the descendant historical or modern culture.

Perhaps just as important as maintaining a measurement and observation bank is a thorough description of the nature of the collection itself. Each institution needs to evaluate the history of its own collection and demonstrate the nature of the biases that may be inherent in the collection catalog. When the skeletons are from the historic period, all attempts to archive the appropriate historical documentation should be made. This will be the source material for future claims by descendant groups and will help in sorting out the legal and moral ownership morass.

Most descendant communities want to know as much as possible about their ancestors; therefore, this is a zone of accommodation that can be visited. Certainly from the scientific side, reburial without study is as wrong as the exhumation of skeletons without consultation with living relatives.

REFERENCES

Buikstra, Jane E., and Douglas Ubelaker, editors
 1994 *Standards for Data Collection from Human Skeletal Remains.* Arkansas Archaeological Survey Research Series, 44. Arkansas Archaeological Survey, Fayetteville.

Davies, Caitlin
 2003 *The Return of El Negro.* Viking, London.

Eco, Umberto
 1983 *The Name of the Rose.* Harcourt Brace, New York.

Eriksson, Gunnar
 1983 Linnaeus the Botanist. In *Linnaeus: The Man and His Work*, edited by Tore Frangsmyr, pp. 63–109. University of California Press, Berkeley.

Fawcett, Cicely D., and Alice Lee
 1902 A Second Study of the Variation and Correlation of the Human Skull, with Special Reference to the Naqada Cranium. *Biometrica* 1:409–467.

Gould, Stephen J.
 1978 Morton's Ranking of Races by Cranial Capacity. *Science* 200:503–509.
 1981 *The Mismeasure of Man.* Norton, New York.

Howells, William W.
 1973 *Cranial Variation in Man.* Papers of the Peabody Museum of Archaeology and Ethnology, Vol. 67. Harvard University Press, Cambridge, Massachusetts.
 1989 *Skull Shapes and the Map.* Papers of the Peabody Museum of Archaeology and Ethnology, Vol. 79. Harvard University Press, Cambridge, Massachusetts.

Hultkrantz, Åke
 1980 Anthropological Traditions: Comparative Aspects. In *Anthropology: Ancestors and Heirs*, edited by Stanley Diamond, pp. 89–105. Mouton, The Hague.

Knussmann, Rainer, editor
 1988 *Anthropologie: Handbuch der Vergleichenden Biologie des Menschen.* Volume I. Gustav Fischer, Stuttgart.

Krogman, Wilton M., and M. Yasar İşcan
 1986 *The Human Skeleton in Forensic Medicine.* Springfield: Charles C. Thomas.

Lindroth, Sten
    1983 The Two Faces of Linnaeus. In *Linnaeus: The Man and His Work,* edited by Tore Frangsmyr, pp. 1–62. University of California Press, Berkeley.

Maat, George, Jr., Raphae G. A. M. Panhuysen, and Rob W. Mastwijk
    2002 *Manual for the Physical Anthropology Report.* Barge's Anthropologica No. 6. Leiden University, Leiden.

Magner, Lois N.
    1979 *A History of the Life Sciences.* Dekker, New York.

Martin, Rudolf, and Karl Saller
    1957 *Lehrbuch der Anthropologie.* Gustav Fischer, Stuttgart.

Mbeki, Thabo
    2002 Speech at the Funeral of Sarah Bartmann, 9 August 2002. Department of Foreign Affairs, Republic of South Africa. Electronic document, http://www.dfa.gov.za/docs/speeches/2002/mbek0809.htm.

Morant, G. M.
    1923 A First Study of the Tibetan Skull. *Biometrica* 14:193–260.

Morris, Alan G.
    1992 *A Master Catalogue: Holocene Human Skeletons from South Africa.* Witwatersrand University Press, Johannesburg.
    1997 The Griqua and the Khoikhoi: Biology, Ethnicity and the Construction of Identity. *Kronos* 24:106–118.
    2003 Using Racial Terms in Anatomical Research. *Plexus: Newsletter of the International Federation of Associations of Anatomists* 2 (May 2003). Electronic document, http://www.ifaa.net/Plexus2.pdf, accessed May 23, 2006.

Morris, Alan G., and Phillip V. Tobias
    1997 South Africa. In *The Encyclopedia of the History of Physical Anthropology,* edited by Frank Spencer, pp. 968–976. Garland, New York.

Sealy, Judith
    2003 Managing Collections of Human Remains in South African Museums and Universities: Ethical Policy-Making and Scientific Value. *South African Journal of Science* 99:238–239.

Stepan, Nancy
    1982 *The Idea of Race in Science: Great Britain, 1800–1960.* Macmillan, London.

Tobias, Phillip V.
    1985 History of Physical Anthropology in Southern Africa. *Yearbook of Physical Anthropology* 28:1–52.
    2002 Saartje Baartman: Her Life, Her Remains, and the Negotiations for Their Repatriation from France to South Africa. *South African Journal of Science* 98(3/4):107–108.

Working Group on Human Remains
    2004 *Care of Historic Human Remains.* United Kingdom Department for Culture, Media, and Sport, London.

Workshop of European Anthropologists
    1980 Recommendations for Age and Sex Diagnoses of Skeletons. *Journal of Human Evolution* 9:517–549.

CHAPTER 11

Associated Records:
The Kennewick Project

TERESA M. MILITELLO, CHRISTOPHER B. PULLIAM,
AND NATALIE DREW

> Information is a source of learning.
> But unless it is organized, processed, and available
> to the right people in a format for decision making,
> it is a burden, not a benefit.
>
> —William Pollard, *The Soul of the Firm*

AN ENORMOUS AMOUNT OF ASSOCIATED DOCUMENTATION IS GENERATED THROUGH THE PRACTICE OF anthropology. Records that are traditionally associated with various activities may include documentary research, excavation notes and field forms, journals, field notes, interviews, laboratory analysis, observation notes, artifact inventories, photographs, maps, reports, and conservation surveys. Today, data generated in a variety of electronic forms are also an important and often overlooked part of the associated documentation of anthropological and particularly archaeological collections. Continuing technological advancements and changing scientific paradigms demand that all forms of documents associated with a collection are coalesced and available for future studies. Within archaeology, human skeletal remains have the capability to produce the most varied and voluminous documentation. Human remains are commonly segregated from general collections. As a result, they can become regarded as a single separate collection, and documentation generated from ongoing studies is not often coalesced with the data from their original context.

The management of associated documentation is frequently neglected or poorly understood since a great deal is generated, and it is not always clear what future researchers will actually want to use within the material. Archaeological projects and repositories do not usually have professionally educated archivists on staff. As a result, the methodology for processing associated documents may differ from that of archives and may be more like the curation of an artifact collection. Also, this deviation is due to the close relationship of the records and documents to specific remains, items, or artifacts in the collection.

Using the archaeological set of remains popularly known as Kennewick Man, one of the most thoroughly documented prehistoric individuals in the Untied States, we review the background that built the collection, outline its organization, and identify preservation needs of amassed associated documentation. This list includes radiographs, various computerized axial tomography (CAT) and magnetic resonance imaging (MRI) media, radiographs, photographs, negatives, videotapes, audiotapes, disks, sample residue from analysis, and impression casts, as well as a long paper trail.

PROJECT BACKGROUND

The Kennewick remains were discovered in July 1996 eroding from the banks of the Columbia River on land administered by the U.S. Army Corps of Engineers (USACE), Walla Walla District. Law enforcement and the local coroner were contacted, and they determined that the remains were not contemporary in nature. The coroner called in a local archaeological contractor to recover the remains. Scattered skeletal material and a small number of artifacts were gathered and removed to his office. The archaeologist, assisted by a university student, photographed and made a cursory examination of the skeleton. His initial conclusion was that the remains were historically associated.

Further study revealed incongruities. The cranium had features that were more typical of a Caucasoid classification, although a stone spear point was found embedded in the right ilium. A private archaeological contracting firm from Pullman, Washington, assisted in identifying that the specimen appeared to be an Early Archaic period projectile point. The archaeologist also began to revise his opinion of the age of the skeletal remains in light of these findings. He made plaster casts of the skull and the pelvis, and his daughter made a drawing of the skull. A local dentist was asked to radiograph and examine the teeth. Radiographs and CAT scans of the bones were made by technicians at the Kennewick Hospital. The remains were then sent to a private firm in Ellensburg, Washington, for analysis; one month later, they were examined at the archaeological contractor's office by a physical anthropologist from Washington State University. A bone sample was sent to the University of California, Riverside, for radiocarbon analysis, and another sample was sent to the University of California, Davis, for DNA analysis. The radiocarbon test yielded an approximate date of 9000 B.P. However, the DNA analysis had not been completed when the USACE, Walla Walla District, requested that the remains be returned to them. The remains were in the possession of the archaeological contractor until they were turned over to the Kennewick Sheriff's Department in September 1996. They were then transferred to the Pacific Northwest National Laboratory (PNNL) in Richland, Washington, for storage under agreement with the USACE.

In September 1996, the USACE, Walla Walla District, attempted to repatriate the remains to a consortium of Native American tribal groups under the Native American Graves Protection and Repatriation Act (NAGPRA). This action was halted by a legal suit filed by several prominent scientists in October 1996, who petitioned the constitutionality of NAGPRA and questioned the care of the remains. In 1997, USACE's Mandatory Center of Expertise for the Curation and Management of Archaeological Collections (MCX) was directed to establish an appropriate curatorial management plan for the remains and to organize all associated records. In 1998, the government was directed by federal court to transfer the Kennewick remains from PNNL to the Burke Museum of Natural History in Seattle, Washington, for curation until their final disposition was determined. An extensive process of inventory, documentation, and preparation of custom specialized storage housings was undertaken for the human remains collection. Finally, beginning in 1999, numerous extensive studies were conducted on the remains by the federal government in order to determine cultural affiliation.

THE ASSOCIATED RECORDS OF THE KENNEWICK MAN

During each one of the major events/activities just described, a large and diverse number of associated records were generated. This includes the documentation records that were transferred to the USACE for curation and those that were generated by the government. These materials include the following groups based on media type (summarized in table 11.1).

Table 11.1. Summary of Kennewick Remains Associated Records

Activity	Record Format	Description of Records
Discovery	Paper	Police reports
		Log of call to police
	Electronic	Electronic messages
Archaeological fieldwork	Paper	Contract w/coroner
		ARPA permit
		Excavation forms and notes
		Field catalog
		Report
		Correspondence (telephone, letters)
		Maps
	Photographs	Negatives and prints
	Electronic	Electronic messages
Archaeological analysis	Paper	Washington State site form
		Analysis records
		Notes on reconstruction
		Correspondence (telephone, letters)
		Transfer forms
		Chain of custody forms
		Drawings
		Reports
	Photographs	Negatives and prints
	Radiographs	X-rays of teeth and select bone fragments
	Electronic	Electronic messages
Transfer to Battelle	Paper	Correspondence with sheriff
		Chain of custody forms
		Transfer/evidence inventory
		Transfer forms
		Physical inventory with notes
		Correspondence (telephone, letters)
		Agreement
		Security access logs (building and room)
		Report of findings
	Electronic	Electronic messages
MCX involvement	Paper	Building evaluation for curation
		General report of findings
		Inventory and rehousing
		Memorandums for record (MFRs) and trip reports
		Catalog
		Correspondence (telephone, letters)
		Curation assessments at San Diego Museum of Man and Burke Museum
		Affidavits
	Electronic	Electronic messages
	Photographs	Building evaluation of Battelle for curation
		Curation assessments at San Diego Museum of Man and Burke Museum
Exit inventory	Paper	Notes—written and recorded
		Datalogger readings
		Conservation assessment forms
		Log-in/log-out sheets—security
		Catalog inventory
		Temperature and relative humidity readings
		Transfer forms
		Move plan
		Affidavits
		MFR/trip report

(continued)

Table 11.1. *(continued)*

Activity	Record Format	Description of Records
Burke inventory	Electronic	Electronic messages
	Photographs	Polaroids
	Paper	Entrance inventory
		Memorandum of agreement
		Condition assessment
		Catalog inventory
		Statements at press conference
		Datalogger readings
		Transfer, registration, and curatorial records
		Security logs
		Kennewick access logs
		MFR/trip report
		Affidavits
Rehousing	Electronic	Electronic messages
	Paper	MFR/trip report
		Catalog inventory
		Kennewick access logs
		Condition assessment report
		Datalogger readings
		Conservator's database
		List of materials used
		Affidavits
	Photographs	Negatives and prints
Initial analysis	Electronic	Electronic messages
	Paper	MFR/trip report
		Catalog inventory
		Kennewick access logs
		Condition assessment report
		Datalogger readings
		Conservator's database
		NPS notes
		Researchers' notes
		Security logs
		Transfer forms
		Researcher forms
		Request for access for research
		Reports
Carbon 14 dating analysis	Electronic	Electronic messages, CT scans
	Photographs	Negatives and prints
	Radiographs	CAT scans, X-rays, MRIs
	Impressions	Teeth
	Paper	MFR/trip report
		Catalog inventory
		Kennewick access logs
		Condition assessment report
		Datalogger readings
		Conservator's database
		NPS notes
		Researchers' notes
		Security logs
		Transfer forms
		Researcher forms
		Request for access for research
		Report
DNA analysis	Electronic	Electronic messages
	Photographs	Negatives and prints, Polaroids
	Paper	MFR/trip report
		Catalog inventory

Table 11.1. (*continued*)

Activity	Record Format	Description of Records
Biannual condition assessments	Electronic Photographs Paper	Kennewick access logs Condition assessment report Datalogger readings Conservator's database NPS notes Researchers' notes Security logs Transfer forms Researcher forms Request for access for research Reports Electronic messages Negatives and prints, Polaroids MFR/trip report Catalog inventory Kennewick access logs Condition assessment report Datalogger readings Conservator's database
	Photographs Electronic	Negatives and prints, Polaroids Electronic messages Digital images

Paper records have been generated during every activity associated with the Kennewick remains, from the initial discovery, to the archaeological fieldwork and analysis, to the transfer to PNNL then to the Burke Museum, and through all the sessions of analyses. As a result, there is more physical volume of paper records associated with these remains than any other format. The paper records include background records, administrative records, excavation records, analysis records, report records, museum records, and curatorial records.

Like the paper records, electronic records have been created during every activity. However, not all of these records have been made available to the government for curation, and not all of the electronic records that have been received were considered associated documentation to the Kennewick Man project. The MCX staff is mindful that the electronic records be regularly migrated to new technology so that they can continue to be read as technology changes. A decision made due to the ongoing litigation was that all electronic messages that were determined to be associated records would be printed on acid-free paper and curated with the other paper records.

Photographic records also were created during nearly every activity associated with the Kennewick remains. Most of the photographic records are 35mm negatives and color prints. However, permission was granted for the use of Polaroid images during three activities: the exit inventory at PNNL, the carbon 14 (C14), and DNA activities at the Burke Museum.

Images were generated from radiography, CAT scans, and MRIs during the government-sponsored analysis of the Kennewick remains. Some CAT scans and MRI images were printed on large-format sheet film, but the actual individual CAT scans and MRIs are electronic in nature. This electronic data is stored on digital audiotapes (DATs). These are in a cartridge format (slightly larger than a credit card) that is often used for storage of this type of information. Radiographs were captured electronically and printed on large-format film sheets, but medical protocol required that the electronic files be retained by the University of Washington, School of Medicine. Finally, a small number of impressions of the teeth and small areas of bone for taphonomic study were created during the physical analysis of the remains by the government. Because they contain information about the skeleton, the impressions are being treated as associated records.

ARRANGEMENT OF THE RECORD COLLECTION

Curation is the process of creating descriptive tools that make collections easier to use, establishing an authority for the holdings, and satisfying administrative needs. An associated record collection can be considered documentation because it provides documentary evidence concerning people, events, activities, objects, and ideas associated with the project.

After consulting with a variety of professionals regarding the current and future use of the Kennewick remains, it was determined that a modified archival approach would adequately unite and organize all of the associated records. Most discrete archival collections are static, while records associated with human remains can be quite dynamic (i.e., they can be added to as analysis and research are conducted over the years). Moreover, the archival approach was thought to offer the most efficient method for accessing these materials.

The primary arrangement of the Kennewick associated records is chronological. However, within a given series, subseries (groups), and folders (units), the arrangements may be chronological or alphabetical by topic. In a few cases, the original order of the items was maintained, for example the plan for the transfer of the collection from PNNL to the Burke Museum. The associated records follow a relatively simple archival hierarchical structure based upon the following elements presented in broadest to narrowest delineation.

Record Group
Series
Subseries
Folder

Record Group
The Record Group is the broadest delineation used in the arrangement scheme. The Kennewick associated records contain two Record Groups. Record Group I holds items that have been included in the Kennewick associated records for reference purposes only. These are documents generated prior to the involvement of the USACE-MCX personnel. These records were provided to USACE-MCX personnel for organization, when they were first directed to assume responsibility for the curation of the collection in October 1997. Record Group II consists of items that document the USACE-MCX-directed activities since their involvement in October 1997. Fifteen series are in this group.

Series
The series are the second level of categorization used in the arrangement scheme. A series consists of a group of materials related to a specific subject, function, material type, or activity and represents how the material naturally falls into categories. Two types of series, unique event series and redundant activities series, were identified during the processing of the collection. The majority of the Kennewick associated records is arranged into unique event series, usually based upon events or activities directed by the court. For example, all documents generated or related to the DNA sampling activities are contained within a single series, 15, entitled DNA Sample Activities. Redundant activities items are those generated by USACE-MCX personnel during

routine curation activities such as monitoring the humidity and temperature of the Delta Design storage cabinet or conducting the biannual conservation assessment of the remains and their storage environment.

Subseries

The third tier in the hierarchical arrangement is the subseries, which represents another assemblage of items based upon a common theme within an individual series. For instance, in series 5 (Transfer of the Collection to the Burke Museum), all standardized forms completed during the inventory process are arranged in their own subseries. For example:

> Series 5: Transfer of the Collection to the Burke Museum
> > Subseries 1: Standardized Forms
> > Subseries 2: Pretransfer Activities
> > Subseries 3: Transfer Activities
> > > Folder 1: Transfer Activities at PNNL
> > > Folder 2: Transfer Activities at the Burke Museum
> > Subseries 4: Posttransfer Activities

Folder

The finest level of categorization of records found within the Kennewick associated records is the folder. The folder represents a final array of items based upon a common theme within an individual group. The use of the folder designation is employed occasionally in most document collections; in the Kennewick Collection, only two groups have been arranged to this level of detail.

Item Listing

Every collection determines its own degree of processing, and some may need to be processed to a very detailed level. Due to the ongoing litigation, the Kennewick associated records have been processed with an evidentiary mind-set that imposes restraints that are not found in typical collections. It has been processed and described to the item level primarily because the entire collection may be required in the proceeding of *Bonnichsen et al. v. United States* (969 F. Supp of Appeals. 628 [D. Or. 1997], Ninth Circuit Court).

   This approach means that each document has been described individually and has been assigned a unique identifying number. Each item description includes the following available information: (1) document title, (2) authors or creators and affiliation, (3) recipients and affiliations, (4) subject or topic, (5) date of creation, and (6) format (e.g., original, facsimile, photocopy). If no document title or subject existed, the archivist created as full a description of the item as possible based on available information. Each item description is presented in a consistent format to facilitate retrieval of information. For example, all items that fall under the category of correspondence are presented in the following format:

> Author (affiliation)
> Recipient (affiliation)
> Subject
> Date
> Format
> Additional information

NUMBERING SCHEME

The numbering scheme adopted for the Kennewick associated records is based on a trinomial system that assigns a unique identifying number to each document. Each part (and its position in the trinomial) describes specific information. The first portion of the trinomial refers to the series designation. The second portion of the trinomial refers to the folder number within a series. Finally, the third part refers to the specific item number within that folder. Therefore, item number 15-3-6 is the sixth item in folder 3 of series 15. The identifying number has been recorded in the upper right hand corner of every page of every document.

As processing progressed, a decision was made to include and number items that were not present during initial numbering. Two ways to accommodate additional documents are through the use of addendums or through altering the numbering scheme. Because the overall arrangement of the Kennewick associated records is chronological, the use of addendums had the potential for confusion. Therefore, additional items are integrated in their proper chronological place and assigned a slightly altered version of the trinomial. Whenever this situation occurs and the proper number already has been assigned, the new item is assigned a number with an added letter designation to the folder number, the item number, or both (e.g., 15-3-6a). In this way, the Kennewick associated records can continue to expand logically to an indefinite size.

Nonpaper associated records, including photographic prints and negatives, Polaroid images, CAT scans, radiographs, casts, impressions, and electronic records, have been numbered in the following fashion. Photographic prints and negatives (35mm) have been assigned a series number, a roll number, and an image number. Polaroid images have been assigned a series number and a sequential number preceded by a "P" designation (e.g., series 5, P-1; series 10, P-1). Photograph logs have been prepared for all photographic materials. Radiographic prints of X-rays, CAT scans, and MRIs have been assigned a sheet number. Most sheets have multiple images on them. The sheet number is based upon the date the image was printed, the individual skeletal element depicted (e.g., cranium), and the original format (i.e., X-ray, CAT scan, or MRI). The format for the sheet numbers is date/format/skeletal element designation. Thus, the first sheet of CAT scans was assigned the number 2/26/99CT(1).

LABELING AND HOUSING

The physical arrangement of a collection involves not only putting the collection in order but also taking actions to slow physical deterioration. Preservation of a collection may involve unfolding documents for storage, removing damaging fasteners, identifying items in need of conservation treatment (e.g., cleaning of X-ray negatives), and placing the materials in archival folders, binders, and boxes.

All items of associated documentation in the Kennewick collection have been labeled. The file folders and paper-based items, over two linear feet total, are labeled in #4 (or HH lead) pencil. All paper documents (acidic or acid-free) are stored in buffered file folders. Furthermore, if a paper document is a photocopy rather than an original document, it is on acid-free paper. Additionally, due to the unique circumstances of the Kennewick associated records, all paper documents have been duplicated on acid-free paper and are stored in a secure, off-site location.

The labeling and storage of photographic materials differ from those of paper documents due to the different nature of the medium. The Polaroid images are housed within individual, unbuffered paper envelopes with archival foil-back adhesive labels in one twelve-inch, acid-free box. The record series designation and the individual Polaroid image number have been recorded on archival foil-back adhesive labels on each picture using a laser printer or archival indelible ink. All positive 35mm photographic images are labeled directly in archival indelible ink or laser-printed on archival foil-back adhesive labels with the following information: (1) series number, (2) roll number, and (3) image number. All prints, negatives, and contact sheets have been packaged in nine archival polyethylene sleeve pages and placed in archival photograph albums with slipcovers. Each sleeve page has the series number and roll designation recorded on it using either archival labels or indelible ink. Each photograph volume contains a table of contents page as well as copies of photograph logs for the rolls contained within a given volume. The contents of each album have been recorded on acid-free paper that has been placed in a polyethylene zip-lock bag and has been affixed to the spine of each volume with archival double-sided tape. Finally, each of the individual radiographs from the CAT scans, MRIs, or X-rays has been labeled directly in archival indelible ink with the sheet number and placed in two acid-free boxes.

The impressions made from individual skeletal elements are housed in polyethylene zip-lock bags, labeled in indelible ink, and placed in one food-grade polypropylene container. This container is labeled on the exterior with a laser-printed archival label using the catalog number of the skeletal element.

In summary, all containers used to house the Kennewick associated records collection are constructed of archival board or conservation board. Box labels have been generated on a laser printer using either acid-free paper or archival foil-back adhesive labels. The paper box labels have been inserted into polyethylene zip-lock bags that have been adhered to the boxes using archival double-sided tape. Finally, container listings have been placed appropriately within each relevant box. Table 11.2 provides a summary of preservation recommendations for housing the associated records.

THE FINDING AID

The term *finding aid* can refer to something broad or something specific. It may refer to a guide, index, inventory, or database that describes a collection. Used more specifically, a finding aid has a cover sheet that includes the collection title, where it is housed, and any restrictions on its use, the size, who processed it, the provenance, and any special notes. A finding aid was designed for the Kennewick associate records collection for the purpose of assisting users in retrieving documents and data. It serves to facilitate use of a collection and to minimize actual handling of the documentation. The finding aid includes the following sections:

- *Description*—a general description of the documents contained in the associated records collection
- *Historical note*—a brief history of the collection, including data such as its original disposition, discovery, and recovery of the remains
- *Scope and content note*—an explanation for the general approach taken while processing the collection. Additionally, any special or unusual actions taken to preserve or conserve parts of the collection would be described here.
- *Series notes*—notes about collection size, including title, brief description, dates, size, arrangement, subseries, and folder descriptions of the documents contained therein
- *Box list*—the contents list detailing all materials stored within each storage unit, be it a box, folder, or other type of container
- *Folder list*—a quick view of the finding aid by listing each folder number, title, and the inclusive dates contained in each file
- *Item list*—the individual documents contained within the collection
- *Individuals list*—all people involved with the collection and their affiliations

Table 11.2. Summary of Labeling and Storage Requirements for Associated Records

Record Format	Storage Requirement	Special Needs
Paper	Acid-free and alkaline-buffered folders	"Reformat" by photocopying to preservation standards on acid-free paper
	Acid-free and paper alkaline-buffered boxes	Monitor
Photographs		
Polaroids	Unbuffered envelopes	Digitize and save electronically
	Acid-free boxes	(cold storage desirable)
35mm prints	Polyethylene or polypropylene page sleeves	
	Archival binders	
Negatives	Polyethylene or polypropylene page sleeves	
	Acid-free, non-off-gassing binders	
Digital	Acid-free boxes	Print reference copies on manufacturer's recommended permanent paper
		Store raw image (tif format preferred) with metadata on CDs (three copies stored separately) or on active but redundant hard drives
		Migrate and refresh regularly
Radiographs	Acid-free tissue	Monitor
CAT scans, X-rays, MRIs	Acid-free boxes	
	Mylar sleeves if handled	
Electronic	Acid-free folders	Print reference copies on acid-free, buffered paper; black laser printing or preservation photocopying preferred
	Acid-free boxes	Migrate and refresh files regularly
Data audiotapes (DATs)	Acid-free boxes	Migrate and refresh regularly
Impression molds	Polyethylene bags	
	Acid-free boxes	

Note: If papers and photographic prints/negatives are stored in vertical boxes, they should be fully supported by padding out boxes that may not be completely filled.

CONCLUSION

The associated records for a collection of or one containing human remains may be minimal for an older collection with lost contexts, or they may be large and complicated. It is necessary to be mindful of the range of traditional and nontraditional records that exist and the variety of individuals that may use a collection. Also, it must be recognized that associated collection records are not static and should be regarded as important as the remains they document. The organization, agency, or responsible party that is administratively responsible for the collection must work with the curatorial repository in establishing and implementing an organization for the records that is consistent and useful. The involvement of physical anthropologists in the discussion as contributors and users of a collection is also helpful when determining the type and level of organization.

Archival procedures can provide useful organization, but not all institutions with collections of human remains have access to archivists. For example, in many academic collections, the physical anthropologist must manage the associated documents. Recommendations for archival enclosures that include papers and photographs have been developed by the American National Standards Institute (ANSI), the Society of American Archivists (SAA), and the American Institute for Conservation (AIC).

FURTHER READING

Fox, Michael J., and Peter L. Wilkerson

    1998 *Introduction to Archival Organization and Description: Access to Cultural Heritage.* Getty Information Institute, Los Angeles. Has an introduction to the principles of organization and description used in archives.

Pollard, C. William

    1996 *The Soul of the Firm.* Harper Business, Zondervan, Grand Rapids, Michigan.

Wythe, Deborah, editor

    2004 *Museum Archives: An Introduction.* 2nd ed. Society of American Archivists, Chicago. This book offers a comprehensive overview of archival work in a museum setting, including NAGPRA issues.

CHAPTER 12

Multidisciplinary Research Teams

Michael Trimble, Christopher B. Pulliam,
Nancy Odegaard, and Vicki Cassman

All but Death, can be Adjusted—
 Dynasties repaired—
Systems—settled in their Sockets—
 Citadels—dissolved—
Wastes of Lives—resown with Colors
 By Succeeding Springs—
Death—unto itself—Exception—
 Is exempt from Change—

—Emily Dickinson

In the current social climate, the study of human remains is less likely to be undertaken by a single individual than by a group of experts. This is especially true of important finds that have made headlines, such as the Ice Man, Kennewick Man, and Ramses I. It is also true of the legal and humanitarian missions that undertake the recovery and study of individuals recovered in mass graves in, for instance, Rwanda, Kosovo, and Iraq.

Group or team studies are more common now due to the growing public and scholarly interests in human remains. But how does group study actually function? Do experts come in individually to examine the remains? Or do experts work together at the same time, crowding around an individual and debating on the spot? This conjures up the paintings and images of the nineteenth-century autopsies where students sat in gallery seating watching the expert surgeons of the day open a cadaver. What about observers—who are they, and what rights and responsibilities do they have? What are the responsibilities of the coordinator? Many questions and even conflicts can arise, due to the social dynamics involved in coordinating any group effort, with professional egos, emotional descendants, sampling, or large numbers of people interacting in a small space, among a number of potential problems.

Historically, the study of human remains has been an individual effort or at most a small-group effort. However, early in the twentieth century, Julio Tello wrote about the need for a team effort for documenting Paracas mummies in Peru. He suggested teams, consisting minimally of archaeologist, photographer, and professional illustrator (Tello and Mejía 1979). His emphasis was on the need to document the opening of a mummy bundle, layer by layer, recording in detail the clothing and items and personal adornment associated with the individual. He realized how much information and context were lost by not recording the stratigraphy of the mummy bundle at the moment it is opened. Unfortunately, context is exactly what has been lost for most mummy bundles and especially for Paracas mummies (see chapter 9), as researchers must piece together what they can of the original bundles that are left.

Now a century later, we are writing about the same issues but taking Tello's ideas further as there are now even more interested parties, a greater number of techniques and analyses available, and wider sociopolitical implications involved in the study of human remains (Pye 2001). Human remains studies now need to involve a host of experts, any interested descendants, curatorial experts, and, in some cases, legal experts and the press. In one example presented here, the human remains known as Kennewick Man demonstrate the scale and changes that have taken place to illustrate the considerations that were needed for the coordinated study of this individual. A second example in this chapter considers the coordination of team study as part of the Iraqi Regime Crime Mission. The organizational structure described in this chapter is informed in part by the work of noted forensic scholar Clyde Snow, who popularized the use of forensic anthropology in 1984 when he traveled to Argentina to serve as a consultant in identifying victims of the Argentinean "dirty" war of 1974–1983. Snow's managerial or organizational skills, in conjunction with the Equipo Argentino de Antropolgiá Forense (EAAF), established a trend that utilizes forensic specialists for the recovery and documentation of physical evidence from human remains. Today, they and other similar organizations are involved in missions around the globe to reveal evidence of summary executions and torture. Though the forensic investigations are broadly envisioned as investigations of mass murder or war crimes, the focus is on the act and the criminal agency of the act as seen through the investigation of one body at a time (Laqueur 2002). Both examples of the study of human remains that are discussed here have been coordinated by the Mandatory Center of Expertise for the Curation and Management of Archaeological Collections (MCX-CMAC) of the U.S. Army Corps of Engineers.

THE COORDINATOR

Defining Stakeholders
To manage any team project involving human remains, a coordinator is needed. The coordinator is required to direct the larger program, research project, field effort, or other organized mission. An effective coordinator needs to have a solid background and education in anthropology, with a strong working knowledge of allied fields and subfields such as physical anthropology, archaeology, museology, conservation, and project management. The role of the coordinator is most important in the preplanning and planning phases of a project when the critical aspects of a project or study are being developed, organized, planned, and scheduled. Additionally, the coordinator should be more involved at a project's completion. For the rest of the project an effective coordinator is less visible, allowing the team members to perform the duties they have been assigned.

At the start of a project or mission, the coordinator assesses the stakeholders—any individual or group that can affect or is affected by the particular study, project, or mission. Stakeholders can impact nearly all aspects of a project including time frame, logistics, and the level of documentation produced. They may ask to be present for all or parts the study; they may wish to include specific techniques, procedures, or documentation in the process; or they may impact the members of the team. Some of the more common stakeholders involved in human remains projects are the following:

- Institutional or museum staff and officials
- Descendants (claimants or others)
- Religious groups
- Property owners where the human remains were found (including private or governmental agencies)

- Law enforcement agents
- Legal experts
- Scholars and subject matter experts
- Press agents representing the institution or the general public

Assembling Team Members

The next step for the coordinator is to delineate the specialists that will be required to complete the project or mission and to assemble the team. By allowing team members to focus on their particular specialties, they are able to bring full attention to their specific duties and responsibilities. The coordinator, on the other hand, maintains a holistic view of the project, focusing on the overall project goals, maintaining team morale and cohesion, providing for the general needs of the team members and stakeholders, mediating conflicts, and resolving professional differences. The following specialists may be needed for projects involving human skeletal remains.

- Medical pathologists (if a cause of death certificate is needed)
- Osteologists or experts that may be involved with osteological material
- Physical anthropologists
  - Paleopathologists
  - Dental experts
  - Taphanomic experts
  - Evidence technicians
- Archaeologists (potentially including specialists such as the following):
  - Geoarchaeologists or soil scientists
  - Mapping and geographic information system (GIS) specialists
  - Environmental specialists for the period/area represented
  - Material specialists if artifacts were associated with the remains
  - Taphonomy experts
- Conservators and collection managers
  - Curatorial experts
  - Storage experts
  - Policy experts
  - Archivists
  - Photographers
  - Database specialists
  - Preservation experts

Determining Techniques and Tools

After delineating and assembling the team, the coordinator interviews the team members in order to understand the specific techniques that will be used by the researchers conducting analysis on human remains collections. This enables the coordinator to anticipate any special needs—logistical, electrical, transportation related—that may be required to accomplish the individual studies/duties of the team members. Some of the techniques of analysis for osteological material include the following.

- Measurements of skeletal remains
- Photography (standard, detail, micro, UV, IR)
- X-ray imaging
- CT scan imaging
- MRI imaging
- Laser scan imaging

- Taphonomic peels
- Dental peels/casts
- Reassembly and reconstruction of osteological fragments
- Consolidation of bone
- Casting of cranium or other parts for reproductions
- Sampling for carbon 14 or AMS dating of the remains or calcium carbonate concretions
- Sampling of bone for DNA analyses of collagen
- Sampling of bone for stable isotope analyses for dietary reconstructions
- Sampling of bone for amino acid composition

Project Logistics

During the next step, the coordinator ensures that all logistical arrangements are planned, scheduled, and implemented. This could include providing the team members appropriate space, equipment, and tools to do their jobs and transporting the team or remains to or from remote locations. The type of equipment that may be used and stored for the analysis, physical care, and preparation of collections is diverse.

An efficient assembly, use, inventory, disassembly, and storage of items such as the following should be anticipated:

- Labeling supplies (ink, pens, adhesive/consolidant, scissors, tweezers, brushes)
- Boxing or housing materials (cardboard, bags, scissors, blades, sealer, cutting board, straight edge ruler, adhesive, foam padding—open- and close-cell, acid-free cards, Tyvek, PTFE film, Parafilm)
- Workstations
- Cabinetry or shelving for organizing the remains
- Personal protective equipment (PPE) (N-95 respirator, gloves, apron, goggles, organic vapor respirator)
- Surface padding (polyethylene foam, Tyvek, polyethylene plastic sheet) and beanbags
- Probes and other small tools (bamboo skewers, fine tweezers, fine artist's brushes)
- Sampling instruments and containers (scalpel handles and blades, jeweler's fine saw and blades, tweezers, filter paper, glass vials)
- Measuring devices (calipers, osteological measurement boards, cloth tapes)
- Lighting (general, directed lamps, flash lights, UV and magnification lamps)
- Written documentation supplies (pens, pencils, paper, paper clips)
- Photographic equipment (cameras, camera stands/tripods, lights, meters, backdrops, props and supports, labeling, color scales, power sources)
- Transport padding, containers, carts, and vehicles
- Security devices (locks, passwords)
- Magnification devices (loupes, lenses, Optivisors, microscopes)
- Recording devices, video, digital camera, or audio/tape recorders
- Disposal and break-down equipment (bins, bags, shredders)
- Document recording or archiving system

CASE STUDY 1: KENNEWICK MAN

In early 1999, the first of several formal multidisciplinary teams was formed to gather information to answer specific court-mandated questions regarding the applicability of NAGPRA to the remains popularly known as Kennewick Man. These remains, found on property administered by the U.S. Army Corps of Engineers' Walla Walla District, had become involved in a court case challenging NAGPRA. The National Park Service (NPS), who administer the NAGPRA legislation, wrote in a December 23, 1997, letter to the corps that "a Federal agency or museum has an obligation under NAGPRA to make reasonable efforts to determine whether human remains it possesses are Native American within the meaning of NAGPRA if there is a reason to consider this may be the case." In March 1998, by means of an interagency agreement, the Department of the Interior agreed to assist the corps in determining through scientific study if the human remains found near Kennewick, Washington, were Native American within the meaning of NAGPRA. By November 1998, a study plan drafted by the NPS was under peer review.

Under the coordination of the director of the corps' Mandatory Center of Expertise for Curation and Management of Archaeological Collections (MCX-CMAC), located in the St. Louis District, this two-day study and subsequent analysis and reporting were successfully completed. One of the major aspects of this coordination was the establishment of guidance for all participants (i.e., team members and stakeholders). This guidance was vital throughout the first study and all activities to date.

Since MCX-CMAC has been responsible for overseeing the curation of the Kennewick Man, there have been six major activities involving multidisciplinary teams, the largest of which occurred in April 2000. This group of twenty-five people was assembled for three days in April 2000 (1) to undertake a physical examination of the Kennewick remains, (2) to conduct sampling for the analysis of organic content of bone, and (3) to conduct sampling for ancient DNA analysis. This team included three MCX-CMAC anthropologists; an archaeologist, a public relations specialist, and an attorney from the Department of Interior; two attorneys from the Department of Justice; a curator and a collections manager from the Burke Museum; two conservators; three physical anthropologists; two DNA experts; tribal observers; and observers for the plaintiffs.

The physical anthropologists were selected because of their knowledge and reputation regarding the study of bone surface characterizations such as coloration, staining, weathering, fracture patterns, rodent or carnivore gnawing, and what might be learned about the original burial orientation of the skeleton by patterns of sediment deposition on the remains. The specialists responsible for microsampling and chemical analysis were selected because of their knowledge and reputation regarding the determination of feasibility to microsample bone for uncontaminated collagen protein for DNA and radiocarbon analysis. The conservators were selected because of their knowledge of archaeological conservation and familiarity with the Kennewick remains.

Before each research expert arrived, they were interviewed to know what they were planning, what they were bringing, and what they would require on the job. At the beginning of each session, the tasks or goals were explained by the MCX-CMAC director and, when applicable, by the Department of Interior team leader. Initially the invited experts would let the group know what their intentions were and how they physically planned to conduct the analyses. The team would go over these plans and ask for specifics or a test run on fragments of animal bone in the case of sampling, for instance. To the extent possible, all techniques that were suggested needed to be safe for the remains, efficient for the experts, and contribute to research goals. If an established method could be improved, then new methods would be implemented. One simple example was the conservator's replacement of metal dental tools with less damaging wooden probes for testing soils or bone hardness. In the case of sampling for DNA and collagen, the expert brought an electrical surgical saw that he used on paleontology specimens. After asking him to practice on a deer bone using a handheld jeweler's saw frame with fine-toothed blade, the team determined that the slower, more precise saw was far less wasteful and resulted in much less vibration and damage to the bone.

Based on the prestudy interviews, the experts were provided with the space and equipment they needed to accomplish their individual tasks. Conservators and collection managers were available to assist with locating, handling, and manipulating the bone fragments in order to prevent damage and maintain efficiency. The many observers were accommodated but were asked to take turns in the available chairs adjacent to the work area. The initial planning efforts of the coordinator enabled these intense undertakings to proceed smoothly to their conclusion, and the needs of all the stakeholders and the team members were appropriately addressed throughout the study. Advance preparations by the Burke Museum staff prevented logistic problems. The anticipation of questions and issues by the conservators and collection managers prevented a compromise of work efficiency. The role of the coordinator and the experienced team members enabled a complicated study session to be successful.

CASE STUDY 2: IRAQI REGIME CRIME MISSION

In the spring of 2004, the Department of Justice's Regime Crimes Liaison Office (RCLO) sought assistance in gathering data for the prosecution of the top fifty individuals in the Saddam Hussein regime in Iraq. Under this regime, it is believed that government leaders, police, and military personnel executed citizens, communities, and villages. Some estimates suggest that approximately three hundred thousand people were killed during a twenty-four-year period. But evidence was required if Iraq was to criminally prosecute these individuals for crimes against humanity.

Laqueur (2002) points out there are tensions between investigations of truth as remembering or communal therapy, and medicojuridical truth for legal or political action. Priorities must be made between political justice and communal healing. In this case, the team's purpose is to first assist in bringing governments and military members to trial for past crimes and second to return identified relatives to their families. In both humanitarian and judicial investigations, the political climate of a region greatly affects the success of a mission.

Legal prosecution requires evidence gathered using formal protocols. The scale of work is extensive because there are mass graves to excavate, whole communities to consider, and enormous emotional burdens. In a humanitarian case, the evidence may be based solely on verbal testimony from witnesses and scientific study of the remains may not be necessary. In a criminal trial, the scientific evidence must be well researched and documented under accepted national or international protocols. Both situations seek to determine the truth about the past, clarify what happened, and identify to whom it happened. The process for the Iraq Regime Crime Mission includes the following steps:

1. Finding the graves
2. Disinterment of the bodies
3. Identification of the individuals (sex, age, name)
4. Analysis of the remains for evidence of trauma
5. Stated cause of death and pathologist's report
6. Analysis of the associated grave goods for identification and evidence
7. Interviewing witnesses, reviewing documentary information
8. Establishing an archive for the evidence and study documents and reports
9. Producing a formal forensic report
10. Processing assembly of evidence for trial
11. Presentation of evidence at trial
12. Returning remains to surviving family members

From September 2004 through August 2006, a series of mass graves were excavated by a multidisciplinary team under the coordination of the RCLO and the MCX-CMAC director, to determine the cause of death for thousands of Kurdish, Shia, and Marsh Arab men, women, and children. The MCX-CMAC concluded, through a series of forensic excavations of numerous sites, that these locations had been used on a number of occasions for systematic executions. Since the first excavation, the Iraqi Regime Crime Mission has proposed to excavate an additional ten geographically distinct mass graves, which represent additional executions of individuals from the three affected culture groups in Iraq; the Kurds, the Marsh Arabs, and the Shias.

Once the trials for Saddam Hussein and officials from his regime began, the genocide cases were referred from the investigative court to trial court. Assembly of the most compelling cases was possible because the uniform quality and quantity of the statistical data produced through a legal/judicially oriented study.

Scientific study of human remains and mass grave forensic research seeks to direct the analysis of human remains and apply the findings or results to resolving scientific and legal issues. The experts and mode of organization are different from those in studies focused on humanitarian identifications. These differences always affect the types of personnel required for the team; the period of time the remains are studied, held, and returned; the types of evidentiary documentation and level of analysis; and the type of temporary storage or infrastructure that is required.

CONCLUSION

No matter what the focus, strong project guidance is required to assemble the group of technical experts, complete the project on time, and provide accurate and efficient documentation that could be used in scientific papers or court proceedings. Efficiency requires that everyone concentrate on their specific job. The coordinator must delineate the key positions that will provide leadership for the larger team as well as define all logistical issues. Recognizing and respecting the special skills, knowledge, experience, and abilities of each of the team members ensures that a project will be completed successfully with little to no conflict. In addition to the experts listed previously, it is not uncommon to include lawyers, engineers, political scientists, translators, law enforcement/security personnel, geneticists, archivists, conservators, and cultural anthropologists in the team as required.

The clear advantage of directed teamwork is that decisions are made on the spot by experienced people who are dealing directly with their subject specialty. The result is greater than the individual parts because the group shares information, solves problems, raises important issues, and thinks about the results of the work, all the while driven in their work by the needs of the mission and not one individual's personal agenda. This directed teamwork has provided a model for research that has fundamentally changed the organizational culture of how we study human remains.

REFERENCES

Laqueur, Thomas W.
2002 The Dead Body and Human Rights. In *The Body*, edited by Sean T. Sweeney and Ian Hodder, pp. 75–93. The Darwin College Lectures. Cambridge University Press, London.

Pye, Elizabeth
2001 Caring for Human Remains—A Developing Concern? In *Past Practice—Future Prospects*, edited by Andrew Oddy and Sandra Smith, pp. 171–175. The British Museum Occasional Paper #145. British Museum, London.

Tello, Julio C., and Toribio Mejía Xesspe
1979 *Paracas: Segunda Parte.* Universidad Nacional Mayor de San Marcos e Institute of Andean Research, Lima.

CHAPTER 13

Fieldwork

HEIDI ROBERTS AND JULIE EKLUND

> The greatest contribution archaeology has ever provided to society is the simple fact that everybody is destined to become a feature.
>
> —Anonymous

OSTEOLOGISTS AND FORENSIC ANTHROPOLOGISTS BECOME INVOLVED IN THE RECOVERY AND STUDY OF human remains under many different circumstances. What is considered appropriate in terms of handling and studying human remains varies considerably based on where the remains are found (e.g., which country and type of site) and the likely cultural affiliation of the individuals buried. In Egypt, for example, ancient remains from pharaonic or Greco-Roman times are regularly the subject of excavation and research; however, Muslim remains would not be considered appropriate for study.

Osteologists may be hired to excavate and analyze human remains because known burials cannot be avoided by planned development projects. In urban settings burials, and even whole cemeteries, may need to be relocated because highways, utilities, or other modern developments will disturb them, as in the case of the African Burial Ground in New York City or the Spitalfields Church in central London. Like archaeological excavations, these projects typically do not begin until a detailed plan of work and, in some cases, the research design are completed. Such plans may need to take into account the wishes of descendants or other parties now responsible for the remains, such as the current church parish (as is often the case in Europe when known burial grounds are disturbed). When multiple jurisdictions are involved, this process is often legalized in an agreement signed by all participants.

PERMISSION AND PERMITS

When osteologists excavate and analyze human remains recovered from an archaeological site, they typically are not involved in the process of obtaining a permit for the excavation and study of human remains. However, osteologists should verify that permission has been obtained and the permits are in order before beginning excavation and analysis. Laws and traditions regarding the excavation, handling, study, and storage of human remains vary considerably around the world. When working abroad, archaeologists and osteologists should be aware that in addition to obtaining permission to excavate from the host country's department of antiquities, usually several months in advance, occasionally special entry visas for foreigners must be obtained in advance as well. In most cases, sampling of human remains will require special permission separate from the excavation permit.

Most countries and local governments have laws regulating the treatment and disposition of inadvertently discovered human remains. The permits and procedures required may vary depending on whether the recovery of human remains during the course of excavation is intentional or accidental. Generally, permits will be required in advance of intentional excavation of burials, and additional policies will have to be followed if human remains are inadvertently discovered, which may result in the temporary or permanent suspension of excavation while consultation takes place with landowners, legal bodies, and descendant populations or any other parties with a claim to either the land or remains.

In the United States, legal jurisdiction is dependent on landownership. On federal and tribal lands, archaeologists must obtain an Archaeological Resources Protection Act (ARPA) permit for archaeological work, and any Native American remains would be subject to the conditions set out by the Native American Graves Protection and Repatriation Act (NAGPRA) and the agreements made during consultation with descendant tribal officials. In most cases, NAGPRA matters are decided prior to commencement of the project, and the agreed-on procedures are included in the excavation or treatment plan. When an archaeological site is on state, county, city, or private land an excavation permit is generally obtained from the state (see chapter 15 on law).

If remains are exposed by floods, earthquakes, erosion, or accidentally during excavation or modern development works, most state governments have laws that require immediate notification of law enforcement authorities, regardless of the age, affiliation, or jurisdiction of the human remains. If a determination of recent burial (i.e., potential crime scene) is made, the remains will be taken into custody by the appropriate law enforcement officials. If the burial is deemed not to be under the jurisdiction of law officials, depending on the context of the burial, a number of outcomes may be possible. If descendants can be identified, then they should be consulted prior to further handling or study. The burial may become part of an archaeological investigation if descendant issues are not in effect; for example, early Euro-American graves may be identified by associated items, but previous landownership may not be determined, thereby making it impossible to notify descendants, and such remains are regularly the subject of further research.

In other countries, other agencies and procedures are in place. In England, legal procedure is dictated by whether the land, where a burial is found, is consecrated. On unconsecrated land, the Home Office (the British equivalent to the U.S. State Department) must be contacted to obtain a license, either in advance of or upon accidental discovery of human remains, and conditions regarding excavation may be attached to the license on a case-by-case basis. However, if remains to be excavated are on consecrated ground, they fall under the jurisdiction of the Church of England. In such cases, the diocesan consistory court must grant permission for excavation, called a *faculty* (however, activities beyond transferring remains from one burial to another within consecrated ground may require additional licensing from the Home Office). Study may or may not be allowed, depending on the wishes of the church, and such remains are often reburied following excavation. Further requirements, such as advertising the intention to disturb human remains both in the newspaper and at the site, may be conditions of the legal permit issued, and there are several special cases or circumstances where other legal provisions would also apply. Typically, human remains recovered in England are either reburied or transferred to a local archaeological trust or other academic institution for study.

In other countries such as Egypt and Greece, all newly discovered material of antiquity, including human remains, is the property of the national government. Government departments responsible for cultural matters make decisions regarding their handling. Greece, for example, has thirty-nine regional ephorates (i.e., regional divisions of the Ministry of Culture) of prehis-

TELL HESI BIBLICAL SITE

Jeffrey Schwartz

Jeffrey Schwartz describes the beginnings of bioarchaeology and faunal analyses at biblical sites in an excerpt from his book *What the Bones Tell Us*:

When I wore the hat of human osteologist [at the site of Tell Hesi], I became involved in what eventually turned out to be the first systematic excavation of the Bedouin burials that typically compose the uppermost layers of any tell. These burials are densely packed and centuries old. It's easy to understand why certain groups would choose to inter their dead on the tops of tells. In this part of the world, a tell is the highest elevation and thus is closer to heaven. Petrie and all tell archaeologists knew about these burials. But, because they were considered too recent to be of importance, they were seen as nuisances and stood between the excavator and the important stuff. As such, they always ended up in the heap of discarded backdirt.

It took a bit of doing to convince the veterans to change their ways and excavate and save all bone with the same care they applied to walls and pots. I don't know how many burials were tossed over the side of the tell during the first week of excavations, but an urgent meeting with the directors of the dig eventually put an end to (most of) that. When the staff of Tell Hesi visited the excavations at Tell Gezer late in the 1970 field season, the director of that site chided us for taking time over these burials. He had taken care of the problem by bringing in the bulldozers. Nevertheless, in future seasons of digging at Tell Hesi, excavation of these burials—aimed at exposing and preserving them carefully for future study—became a priority.

. . . Osteological analysis, both human and faunal, quickly became during the 1970 archaeological field season an "in" thing to do on biblical sites . . . but even though interest in human and faunal osteological analyses grew, there was still resistance to them. For instance, I would be told, the Bedouin burials had nothing to do with the important activities recorded in the layers of a tell, and who cared anyway, what animals past societies had been hunting, herding and eating?

Source: From *What the Bones Tell Us* (New York: Holt, 1993) by Jeffrey Schwartz, pp. 9–10.

---

toric and classical antiquities. Any archaeological material of that age inadvertently discovered during building works would come under the jurisdiction of the local ephorate. Arrangements for their excavation, removal, and study would be made by the archaeologist in charge of the area. In many cases, formalized procedures for excavating human remains are a recent phenomenon, as documented by the case study by Jeffrey Schwartz.

ROLE OF THE OSTEOLOGIST

Osteologists are regularly members of excavation teams when the recovery of human remains is anticipated or part of a research plan. In cases where remains are accidentally discovered, it is not always possible to get an osteologist on site at short notice, but one may be called on postexcavation to undertake various degrees of identification and analysis, depending on the nature of the project. Although it is not always possible to include an osteologist on every excavation, if human remains are encountered, it is a good idea to arrange a site visit by an osteologist to provide advice regarding recovery and recording. Excavations of multiple burials or comingled burials will invariably benefit from the services of someone trained to deal with such complex material.

Prior to the implementation of NAGPRA in the United States in 1990, most of the available osteology manuals (Bass 1987; Steele and Bramblett 1988) ignored the process of consultation with descendants. Excavation, transportation, cleaning, and restoration were treated as a static must-do menu. With increased communication between descendants and osteologists, this process is often modified according to the descendants' wishes. Osteologists should be flexible in their approach and be prepared to modify or eliminate steps.

The role of the osteologist varies considerably based on the wishes and expectations of whoever is responsible for the remains. Whether human remains are excavated, whether any study is allowed, and whether the remains are to be reburied or placed in a museum for future study are all decisions that must be made rather than assumed, and the osteologist may or may not be involved in the process of making them. However, osteologists should make themselves available for consultation when appropriate and should be able to present the options available for any group of burials or remains encountered. Human remains are very sensitive material and may invoke strong reactions from those responsible for them (i.e., government representatives, descendants, or the local public); therefore, consultation is essential in designing a course of action when human remains are discovered. Expectations regarding the handling of remains must be made clear and understood among all parties involved in any given project to avoid disappointment or disagreements.

For example, in the early 1990s, one of the authors, Roberts, was hired by a coal mining company to relocate burials on leased Native American reservation lands. Earlier an ethnographer had worked closely to identify all burials and to devise a plan to remove and rebury them. Family members provided a checklist of wishes for each of the burials. The relatives of the deceased determined the treatment accorded each burial. Some burials were fully evaluated for age, sex, stature, pathological conditions, and the like; others required a simple inventory of the skeletal elements and grave goods. In all cases, lab work and destructive study were not allowed.

Because the objective of the work at this mine was the relocation of the burials, the osteologist was more of an applied osteologist than a researcher. Analysis was only done to verify the burial's identity and to document the removal and reburial process. If any research on these burials had been done, it would have been done against the wishes of the descendents. Explicit permission to conduct research would have been needed from family members to study the burials for information that was not requested by them.

Knowing whether one is required to perform applied or research osteology prior to going into the field is important. Although the distinction between the two functions may at times be blurred, it is essential to know whether one is merely to identify the skeletal elements retrieved and maintain individuals' integrity, whether basic osteological data may be collected, or whether a larger research agenda is called for. This will impact on many aspects of how fieldwork may be carried out. Often the techniques and methods employed will vary from burial to burial. For example, many Native Americans do not approve of the removal of human remains to a laboratory setting. Some southwestern tribes prefer that any analysis be conducted in the field. Because the allowed methods and procedures can vary, the first step in the fieldwork process is to familiarize oneself with the mortuary customs of the descendants' culture and to establish the methods and preferences of the next of kin.

Understanding the cultural beliefs associated with death is a prerequisite to interactions in the field. For example, the mine relocation project took place on the Navajo Nation. Navajo people believe that sickness can result from contact with the dead. Had the senior author not been aware of this belief, the behavior of the tribal monitors, who were often monitoring from hundreds of meters away, would have seemed unusual. Knowing that discussions about the work would have made the monitors uncomfortable was valuable knowledge in the field.

Many options may be considered in the course of planning arrangements for discovered burials. Whether remains may be excavated, by whom, and under what conditions, or whether they are to be preserved in situ are some of the first decisions to be made in the planning process. Whether any study will be allowed, under what terms and what time frame, whether destructive testing of any kind will be considered, or whether only visual study will be allowed must also be discussed. Decisions regarding the degree of cleaning that might be required for some study or what may be appropriate for sampling from both a scientific and cultural point of view will also need consideration. Finally, if material is to be placed in the care of a museum, any restrictions to access or study, in addition to preferred storage conditions and materials, should be made clear. Decisions may be based on financial, time, legal, or cultural grounds. What may be assumed or obvious to a trained osteologist may not be intuitive to anyone else, and a careful and considered approach is required from the outset, particularly when descendant populations are involved.

When osteologists begin working in the field with descendants, it is helpful to remember that, like a funeral director's work, the osteologists' work plan must take into account the wishes of the family, descendents, or affiliated group. Research is not generally the objective of the excavation and analysis, and some cultures find a focus on research disrespectful.

GETTING READY FOR THE FIELD

Understanding the Scope of Work
To prepare for fieldwork osteologists should learn as much as possible about the skeletal remains to be excavated. Some of the issues an osteologist should consider are the kind(s) of burial(s) to be excavated, the condition the remains might be in, the site location and ease of access, the weather conditions, the work environment, and any security issues. Each of these factors will affect the excavation and recovery efforts. For example, in 1990, Native American remains in a small rock shelter were reported by a local rancher. Roberts was asked to excavate and evaluate a "couple" of burials in a remote location of southern Utah by a U.S. Department of Interior archaeologist, who feared that the remains, which were not buried, were in danger of being vandalized and destroyed.

Preparations were made by Roberts and a fellow osteology student, Heather Hecht, to record and assist in the removal of the two to three inhumations. The fieldwork phase of the project was planned to take two days, possibly three days at most. The burials were located in a remote area, and to save travel time, the team planned to camp near the rock shelter. Imagine the surprise on the first day when entering the rock shelter and discovering that instead of two to three individuals, the site was an ossuary containing at least sixteen comingled individuals. Somehow plans were revised, and additional excavation help and supplies were quickly obtained so that the length of the expedition could be extended. After four harried ten- to twelve-hour days of excavation, the provenience of the remains were documented, and the remains were packaged for transport to a lab.

As this anecdote indicates, nonspecialists frequently do not understand the scope and complexity of fieldwork, and extra steps are sometimes needed to verify the number and type of burials, and the condition of the remains. This incident demonstrates that it is best to request pictures of the human remains to be recovered.

Before workers head out into the field, a contract should be negotiated and signed with the responsible party who will cover the costs of fieldwork and analysis. If an osteologist is hired on a time and materials basis, the labor rates and expenses should be negotiated and documented, preferably with a formal contract, before fieldwork begins. Cost estimates may include the osteologist's labor, equipment (i.e., special reburial boxes or caskets, dental cast for research questions related to epigenetic traits, portable tables, chairs, shade, or weatherproofing), expendable supplies (i.e., film, packaging materials, water, ice, forms, notebooks), accommodations, transportation costs, copying, and mailing. Estimating how long it will take to excavate human remains is difficult even after years of experience. For example, a burial covered with thousands of small shell beads or hundreds of artifacts will take considerably more time than one without associated artifacts. Ask archaeologists their expectations for grave goods, and factor that into the cost estimate. The final cost estimate should include all costs associated with the preparation, excavation, transportation, analysis, and report preparation.

When costs are difficult to estimate because little is known in advance or the burial excavation is unusual in scope or complexity, it is helpful to include assumptions in the cost estimate. In other words, prepare a narrative that describes what assumptions have been made to derive the budget. In the consulting industry, this is called a *scope of work*. For example, when a "couple of burials" turns into sixteen, additional funding can be requested if the original scope of work stipulated that the cost estimate was based on the fieldwork and analysis of two to three mostly excavated individuals with minimal grave goods. A scope of work that includes the location of the remains, the types of burials, anticipated grave goods, the condition of the burials, and the number of individuals allows for renegotiation of funding should the project change into something that was not originally in the budget.

Some other important matters to consider and stipulate in the contract are who pays for monitors or guides, what accommodations are, whether extra equipment is needed, and whether burials are accessible to two-wheel-drive vehicles. In some cases, the budget will need to consider the cost of storage facilities, security guards, mobile restrooms, and special insurance. Private companies or developers frequently require contractors to hold professional, general, and vehicle insurance, and evidence of insurance must be provided prior to fieldwork.

Safety is another important issue that should be considered before fieldwork begins. For example, you or your employees could be asked to examine human skeletons in the bottom of a six-foot-deep backhoe trench. A trench this deep probably would not comply with U.S. Occupational Safety and Health Administration (OSHA) regulations. You or your employees may not only face dangerous working conditions but may also be partially liable if the infraction results in a fine. To ensure safe working conditions and limit your liability, it may be a good idea to consult with local safety agencies and develop a plan that complies with any relevant regulations.

TYPES OF BURIALS

Deceased individuals may be laid to rest in a variety of ways. Individuals may be placed in tombs or catacombs, in bodies of water, in hollows of trees and rock crevices, or included in garbage deposits. However, most archaeological human remains are encountered as burials (either primary or secondary) and cremations. Human remains may be skeletonized, desiccated, or mummified, fragmented or reduced to ash. A good reference for burial type definitions is Roderick Sprague's (2005) guide to burial terminology. The type of mortuary practice and the condition of the skeletal remains affects the cost estimates, equipment preparation, and excavation methods.

Primary inhumations or burials, where individuals are laid to rest in the ground, are perhaps the most commonly encountered human remains and can take many forms. Individuals may be buried singly, in a pit, earth mound, or cist either as an isolated burial or as part of a formal cemetery. Individuals may also be buried within floors or structures within residential constructs. Secondary burials take place in a wide range of cultural contexts; these are when an individual's remains are buried following either a period of initial interment or some other mortuary practice such as defleshing or exposure to the elements. Secondary burials may take place at a specified interval after death (i.e., one year after an individual's death, or a community may exhume all the deceased every ten years) or when another individual requires a burial space.

Although individual primary burials may be straightforward in terms of excavation planning, many situations may arise where several individuals are interred together, either at the same time or over a sustained period. Mass graves as the result of catastrophic events, such as the plague, may consist of hundreds of individuals buried at effectively the same time without coffins or other individual demarcations. Cave sites that were regularly used as cemeteries by a group may contain a number of comingled burials. Formal cemeteries used over long periods of time may experience more recent burials cross-cutting older burials. Some cemeteries in Europe have been used for hundreds of years, and if built on the location of a pre-Christian sacred site, they may contain prehistoric, Roman, medieval, and more recent remains. The ability to separate individuals from each other depends on the amount of disturbance of the remains, the use of funerary furniture such as coffins, and the excavation technique. Detailed planning, numbering elements in situ, and careful bagging or boxing of individuals may assist in maintaining individuals separately. Low scaffolding over an excavation may be required to enable access to large areas of mixed burials. It is important to have some idea of the scope of such sites if excavations are required to adequately estimate the time, funding, personnel, and potential postexcavation preparation, housing, and study needed.

In the case of cemeteries where relatively recent remains may be encountered, additional health and safety considerations may be required. Although the threat of contracting a viral infection is slight, surgical gloves and other protective clothing such as masks and possibly respirators may be appropriate precautions, particularly if soft tissue is encountered. Arsenic is known to have been used for embalming historically. Lead coffins promote soft tissue preservation, and special arrangements may be required to deal with both the coffin and any remains (Kneller 1998). For a more detailed discussion of health and safety issues, see the next chapter on health concerns.

Conditions and Access
Prior to entering the field, in addition to knowing the scope of the site, getting a general idea of the site conditions, access, and any security issues can assist in the planning process. Such issues can determine how many archaeologists are required, what time of year might be best to excavate, how many hours a day one can work, whether any special supplies may be required, and other logistical details.

One of the most important factors to determine prior to commencing excavation is whether a site is typically wet or dry. Waterlogged materials will require different methods for recovery, storage, and handling in general, which is outside the scope of this book. Skeletal material within range of water table fluctuations may be considerably weakened by the action of water washing through the bone, and the assistance of a conservator may be particularly useful in such cases. Even typically dry sites during times of extremely wet weather may temporarily flood, and sump pumps may be required to enable excavation.

Access to a site is another important factor to consider. If the public would otherwise have access to the area under excavation, a secured perimeter around the area may be necessary. It is often considered inappropriate to have excavations of human remains visible to the public, both for the sake of sparing the sensibilities of unsuspecting members of the public and for site security. At church sites, it may be useful to know of any scheduled festivals or religious holidays,

RESCUING MUMMIES FROM URBAN CENTERS IN THE ATACAMA DESERT

Bernardo Arriaza

Mummies are preserved bodies where decomposition has been halted due to natural or human interventions. Mummies come in all sizes, shapes, types, and degrees of preservation. Experienced researchers know how much variation likely exists in their area, and they should be prepared to rescue or excavate the different types of mummies. In many places, such as in Chile, Peru, or Egypt, mummies can become frequent findings that intermingle with the living. Mummies suddenly pop to the surface when modern construction unveils ancient cemeteries or winds sweep away sand.

Unfortunately, at times mummies are also revealed as a consequence of treasure hunters destroying ancient sites to find artifacts. The looters take what they want but leave behind a ghostly landscape of broken garments and body parts that are collected and brought to a repository or museum. In places such as Arica, northern Chile, a small desert oasis in the Atacama where ten thousand years of humans have lived and died in a small area, a mummy rescue team always must be prepared to go to do fieldwork at a moment's notice. It is often a race between scientists and developers and looters. If you arrive late, many parts of the puzzle will be lost forever.

Along with a crew, emergency archaeological equipment is necessary. At the Paleoanthropology Lab at the Museo Arqueológico San Miguel de Azapa in Arica, a large toolbox with the basic equipment is always resting near the door of the lab. The emergency kit contains compass, lines, brushes, markers, tape, camera, bags, documentation materials, and other supplies. Large boxes and wooden stretchers of various sizes are on hand to bring the bioarchaeological remains to the museum. We also have a supply of archival bags, cardboard, and labeling materials to bring as well.

At the site, the basic protocol is to introduce yourself and the team, and ask who is in charge in order to coordinate a working strategy. This would include a quick verbal and visual survey to discover the extent of the find, including how many individuals have been discovered, and whether other finds or special features nearby are likely to be impacted that will also need excavation. At the site, often human remains are reburied by workers before the rescue crew arrives. It is important here to interact with the workers to get the needed information, but it is important to set limits and not allow the crew to begin to reexcavate the site. The site must be corded off, and if possible, the excavation area should be marked and delimited. Often curiosity is more powerful than management, and workers will likely find a way to continually stop by to see the digging and ask the same questions over and over. "What did you find? Where is the gold? How old is the find?" This is a golden opportunity to entice them to protect their past and to explain cultural changes and the vast amount of information that can be gathered with proper excavation and later laboratory techniques that can help not only to reconstruct the profile of the mummy as an individual but also to tell us about the paleoclimate, diet, lifestyle, and history of the area. We often reply that the gold is in the knowledge (this region of northern Chile has yielded few gold artifacts, so thankfully treasure hunting has not been as fierce as in other Andean coastal areas). People love to learn about popular science. This is teaching at its best.

It is also the proper time to tell the crowd about the local laws that protect their cultural patrimony and penalties involved in acts of desecration and looting. Unfortunately, the sad truth is that seldom are these laws in Chile and many other countries actually enforced, but that is another story. We explain to them that the mummy is not going to be on display so they do not come to the museum hoping to see "their mummy." We tell the crowd there is a mummy laboratory and special storage area and that this mummy(s) will contribute to knowledge of how people lived and died in the past. And it is this knowledge or the secrets that this individual will reveal that will be interpreted in the museum.

Often some people will stay for hours watching the rescue excavation and ask many questions. Sometimes we ask these inquisitive minds to answer the questions raised by newcomers, questions

RESCUING MUMMIES FROM URBAN CENTERS
IN THE ATACAMA DESERT (*continued*)

that we have already answered many times. This usually delights the senior viewers, because they feel empowered and useful.

After the mummy has been completely and methodologically excavated and recorded, the evidence must be lifted. This is often the uneasy part for us because we prefer to lift the mummy as a unit, and we will attempt this first. The worst-case scenario is when the body parts connecting the mummy are extremely desiccated and deteriorated and break easily. After many hours of hard work exposing, preparing, and recording the mummy in situ, it can be summarized as a groaning "Ohhhh" by the audience when the initial attempted lift is not successful. The faces of the crowd mirror the researcher's disappointment that the mummy cannot be taken as a unit. In such a case, it becomes better to abort the complete body lift that will continue to fall apart and recover the mummy by anatomical elements. Ideally, a flat stretcher covered with either a layer of acid-free cardboard or corrugated polyethylene is used. This is covered with a layer of sand, often that which the individual has been buried in, to accommodate and cushion fragile mummies or remains. Any separate grave good(s)—which has already been meticulously documented in terms of its context or relationship to the individual and other features using written description, drawings, and photos—is bagged, labeled, and placed in a separate padded and labeled box. In locations like Arica, Chile, where ancient mummies literally burst into modern life on a weekly basis, the wooden stretchers become the mummy's resting place for decades.

When available, the acid-free layer between the stretcher and the individual allows for less traumatic transfers of the mummy to a different future storage system should the opportunity arise. However, acid-free materials are not easily acquired, and sources for materials must be located well in advance and ordered to have on hand when needed. This often creates a budgetary dilemma in small regional museums where funds and proper materials are scarce. Therefore, if you are a visiting researcher, gifts of archival cardboard are a most welcome gift to small museums around the globe. Museums with little or no operating budgets usually place their limited resources into the public areas, and proper conservation and storage facilities and supplies are unfortunately often seen as a luxury that are upgraded only when special funds are acquired by a dedicated resourceful staff and other outside interested parties.

Once the transfer to the stretcher has been accomplished, the individual needs to be supported for movement from the site. This can be accomplished with more sand (though this adds considerably to the weight) or acid-free tissue if available or, for temporary use, a soft foam (polyurethane foam is not a long-term padding material since it degrades very quickly, leaving harmful and annoying residues behind). Transportation from the site to the museum or repository requires adequate padding underneath the stretchers, but not too much, because the stretchers should not bounce on bumpy roads. Estimating the weight of the mummy stretcher and proper amounts of padding comes with time and experience. Additionally, polyethylene sheet covers and blankets will be needed to prevent damage by sun, wind, and rapid loss of moisture.

After the excavation is finished, the site must be back filled and the local authorities thanked. In general, with the proper public relationships and courtesy, we have found that local companies are very cooperative, and they often like the added publicity of being seen in local papers as the Good Samaritan. Finally, mummy recovery is definitely a team effort; it is not a task for the lone archaeologist.

CREMATIONS

Marcia H. Regan

Cremation is the process of incinerating a body. It is usually intentional, as part of a mortuary rit-ual, but it can be accidental, as when a person is caught in a burning building. Cremation as part of a mortuary ritual is a phenomenon that is found worldwide, both in antiquity and in modern times. Because cremation can be part of the rituals of death, deposits of cremated human bone are cor-rectly called *cremation burials*, and the areas in which they are deposited are graves. Cremation burials should be afforded the same respect and care that are given to inhumation burials. In the United States, cremations fall under the purview of NAGPRA and similar laws.

Cremations are investigated archaeologically for the same reasons as inhumations—they pro-vide glimpses into the past. Cremations represent a nexus of cultural and physical information. Os-teologists attempt to determine age, sex, health status, and biological relationships; DNA fragments have been recovered and trace elements (for dietary and health reconstructions) have been assayed. Patterns of bone breakage and color provide clues to the physical properties of the crematory fire and the treatment of the body before and during burning. Mortuary analysts look at the patterns of cremations (who was cremated, how it was done, where were they buried) to gain insights into questions of social status and cultural organization. Changes over time and differences between contemporaneous cultures also provide insights into past cultural properties.

What should one expect when excavating cremation burials? First, we must recognize that cre-mation is a highly destructive process. Consequently, the body requires much less physical space for burial, and most mortuary offerings are destroyed. Movement of the body both during burning (a result of intentional stirring, reactions of the body's tissues to heat, or unintentional shifting of the pyre) and after burning (gleaning of the bones for burial elsewhere) means that the remains are almost never in normal anatomical position as they are in inhumations. In addition, cremated bone looks different than bone from an inhumation because burning induces changes in the color and physical properties of bone. Finally, excavators and analysts need to be aware that the final appear-ance of the cremated remains is affected by both cultural and physical variations.

Cultural variations are introduced before, during, and after the body is cremated. Variations *be-fore* involve how soon after death the body is cremated and how much "processing" of the body oc-curs before burning (i.e., was the body intact, or had it been dismembered or even defleshed?). Variations *during* result from differences in how the crematory pyre was constructed, the temper-ature of the fire and total time of burning, and how much stirring of the crematory fire ("tending") took place. Heated bone is very brittle while hot, and stirring of the fire results in more breakage of the bones. Variations *after* involve the location of final deposition. A body that is left in the same location as it was burned is called a *primary cremation*. Excavation of a primary cremation will show human bone in somewhat anatomical position. Frequently, though, the remains are gathered up (gleaned) after they have cooled and are buried elsewhere. Such a deposit is called a *secondary cre-mation*. Secondary cremations are sometimes, though not always, contained in a vessel. They are almost always completely disarticulated and are missing significant portions of the skeleton due to incomplete gleaning, destruction of the bone during burning, and even deliberate removal of bones for separate burial. For example, in the American Southwest, cremation burials from the Hohokam period rarely contain anywhere near a complete skeleton (judged by weight of the cremated re-mains). It has been thought that the Hohokam practiced partition or serial burial in which the re-mains of an individual are buried in more than one location.

Variations in the appearance of cremated bone are also introduced by the physical properties of the crematory pyre. The intensity and duration of the fire, coupled with the amount of soft tissue around the bones and the location of bones relative to the crematory fire, will result in differing completeness of burning. As the soft tissue burns away, exposure of the underlying skeleton leads to combustion of the organic component of bone (the collagen). As the collagen burns, character-

CREMATIONS (*continued*)

istic color changes occur: the bone is first blackened, then becomes blue gray, progressing to light tan and finally white. The mineral matrix of bone (the calcium and phosphate) does not burn, but it is changed. High temperatures cause fusion of the mineral crystals and result in changes in skeletal morphology: shrinkage, warping, cracking, and fissuring. As a result, cremation burials almost never contain unbroken larger skeletal elements.

Researchers have studied and documented what happens to bone as it is burned. The results are applicable not only to archaeological specimens but also to forensic cases. Discovery of burned human remains outside a known cemetery leads to questions regarding how the bones came to be there. Forensic anthropologists can use the knowledge about how bone in its various states responds to burning to answer questions about the state of a body (or body parts) before they were burned.

Inhumations from archaeological contexts in North America have been studied scientifically for over 150 years, but cremations were routinely ignored until relatively recently. Their fragmentary and incomplete nature led archaeologists to think that no information could be gained from their study. In the years after World War II, however, researchers have realized that cremations hold not only biological information (e.g., age, sex, nutritional and health status) but also cultural information relating to mortuary rituals and social organization.

As with inhumations, the treatment of cremated remains during and after excavation has changed in the past two decades with the advent of NAGPRA and input from native peoples. In my experience, the greatest changes have been seen in two areas. First, efforts are now made to keep the human remains and all associated mortuary artifacts together during excavation, laboratory analysis, and repatriation. Second, the soil matrix that is almost always excavated with cremated bone is also saved and repatriated. Previously, the dirt that surrounded the cremated bone was thrown away, because it contained no usable information, it took up space, and it was heavy. However, the dirt almost always contained minute flecks of bone. Respect for the people being studied dictates that all the bone is kept together, regardless of its size.

when working on site may not be appropriate. Rural sites may be more difficult to access generally, so more specific information about a site is essential to planning. Important considerations include the following:

- Is the site near a town, or will archaeologists have to camp out?
- Is there a nearby source of any food and water supplies?
- Is the site generally accessible, or will ladders/scaffolding or rappelling equipment be required?
- Have there been problems with looters on site previously?
- Does the site pose any unusual health risks (i.e., malaria, snakes or other dangerous wildlife, etc.)?
- Are emergency systems available that can be called upon (i.e., radios, air ambulances, etc.)?

Ensuring site security can be difficult depending on the situation. Some rural sites may require simply covering the excavation pit overnight or when not actively working on it to prevent accidental damage by falling soil or rain. Urban sites may be easier to secure if a perimeter fence of adequate height and durability has been constructed that can simply be locked or even have a security system installed. Some sites in the Middle East also employ armed guards for the security of both the site and the archaeologists.

Supplies and Materials

The supplies and materials required to excavate human remains are not very different from those used for archaeological excavations generally. The number of burials; whether the individuals were adults, juveniles, or infants; bone preservation; the depth of burial; and other site conditions will determine what materials should be brought into the field and in what quantities. Overburden can be removed with shovels and hand picks, but the remains themselves should be excavated with smaller hand tools. Trowel blades can be ground down, which can make them more useful for excavating around the rather intricate structures of skeletons. Wooden tools, such as skewers or sculpting tools, are particularly useful because they are less likely to scratch bone. Aluminum foil can be used for a little extra support when pressed around a bone just prior to lifting. Sieves of different mesh sizes (down to two square millimeters for head, abdominal, hand, and foot areas; particularly delicate remains and infants) should also be used to ensure that recovery is as complete as possible.

Basic Excavation Toolkit
- Shovels
- Small hand picks
- Trowels
- Measuring spoons or various sizes of scoops (i.e., teaspoon, tablespoon, ice cream scoop)
- Plasterer's leaf
- Dental scaler and other dental tools
- Bamboo skewers/wooden tools
- Paintbrushes
- Puffer
- Small hand sweeper and dustpan
- Sieves of different mesh sizes
- Aluminum foil
- Pencils and waterproof marker
- Recording forms and clipboard

Mapping Tools
- Spirit level
- Measuring tapes/ruler
- Plumb-bob
- Compass
- Graph paper/transparencies
- Drawing board
- Scales and labels
- Meter mapping grid

Photography Supplies
- Camera and tripod
- Film/memory card
- Labels, scales, and directional indicators
- Reflectors or artificial light sources

Recording Tools
- Calipers (spreading and sliding)
- Osteometric board
- Reference material (manuals, casts, etc.)

Packing Materials
- Polyethylene or paper bags
- Acid-free boxes
- Acid-free tissue
- Waterproof, moldproof labels

Other special equipment may be required for unusual sites or unusual situations encountered on site. Pin flags may be essential when surveying or identifying scattered remains or partially exposed burial grounds. Canopies or other small shelters may be required for rain cover or for shade in desert environments. As mentioned, sump pumps may be necessary in wet sites, and scaffolding or platforms of some kind may be useful when dealing with mass burials. Consolidants or materials for block lifting may also be useful.

Also, consider any specific sampling procedures or materials for analytical testing. Bone might be used for radiocarbon, stable isotope, or DNA testing, or soil from the surrounding grave cut fill may be useful for pollen research or to characterize the soil conditions (pH and water content). Such samples should be recorded and stored where they can be easily associated with the burial from which they came. Specific laboratories may request that sampling be undertaken in certain ways, and this should be planned for prior to excavation.

When fragile remains are anticipated, specialist materials may be required to facilitate lifting and handling. Very weakened skeletal material may be better preserved with the use of consolidants. Consolidants are typically polymer solutions that are either water or organic solvent based and applied to porous materials for increased strength and durability. They may be most appropriate in cases where remains will be studied and kept in a collection for research purposes, and the material could not withstand handling if untreated. The choice of consolidant is dependent on several variables, but particularly on the dryness of the bone in situ and the storage conditions the bone will be subjected to afterward. Consolidants are often best selected and applied with the aid of a conservator, as thorough application and cleaning of adhered soil is important, which may require the use of special techniques or materials for best results. The application of such artificial materials to indigenous remains may be objectionable, so such procedures would need to be discussed in advance. It is also important to remember that the addition of organic materials such as consolidants may complicate or prevent the use of certain analytical tests, such as radiocarbon dating.

If complex assemblages or very fragile remains are encountered that are not easily excavated on site, it may be an option to undertake a block lift. In a block lift, workers excavate widely around the assemblage, leaving the material to be recovered encased in soil, forming a pedestal, which is then protected with an impermeable layer and encased with a rigid cover to enable its removal as a block to an environment where it can be more easily dealt with. Block lifts will require additional supplies such as cling film, tissue paper, plaster or expanding foam, box-making materials for the outer container and possibly a winch if the block is too large to be lifted manually. Such undertakings should be planned carefully, as other considerations such as having adequate space to remove the block to, maintaining the block's context and orientation, ensuring its timely excavation, and addressing any special preservation problems must be considered, and such activities may best be done with the assistance of a conservator.

Adequate documentation supplies must also be assembled prior to entering the field. It is generally considered best practice to both photograph and produce scaled drawings of individual burial contexts. A skeleton recording sheet (see Buikstra and Ubelaker 1994) is regularly used when excavating a burial. A diagram of an adult skeleton where elements can be filled in when present or a series of tickboxes where the elements recovered can be marked will provide a basic inventory of each burial. It is a good idea to keep copies of this page with each skeleton box during transport and storage to facilitate later inventories, in addition to keeping the original with the fieldwork documents. If skeletal remains are in extremely poor condition and cannot be lifted without sustaining damage, or if they are to be analyzed as they are excavated, an osteologist should also have calipers (spreading and sliding), tape measures, an osteometric board, and any other required reference books or other material, such as casts for dental traits and pubic symphysis assessment.

Packing materials to transport excavated remains to their eventual deposition destination should also be arranged prior to undertaking excavation. Ideally materials used should be of preservation quality, such as acid-free boxes and tissue. When this is not possible, at least clean new materials should be used. Newspaper is not an ideal packing material, due to its acidity and the potential to transfer ink to bones, but if nothing else is available, it may be used for short-term storage in transit, provided all bones are placed in bags first. Cotton balls or straw should never be used in direct contact with bone, as fibers may become snagged on the bone structures or rough surfaces, causing damage. Boxes must be of sturdy construction (i.e., heavy corrugated cardboard or better) and adequate size to contain the remains of a single individual (at least sixty centimeters in one horizontal direction to accommodate an adult femur, the largest skeletal element).

Recently, there has been much discussion about the use of separate cranium boxes. Although smaller boxes to house individual crania add to the protection of delicate features, there is an added risk of their being stored or misplaced away from the rest of the skeleton. This is not an ideal situation. In order to keep individuals in one location and to protect crania, it may be best to use slightly larger skeleton boxes that can accommodate both the postcranial elements and a cranium box (see chapter 8). Only in cases where descendants have stipulated that artificial materials may not come into contact with remains can paper bags be used. In all other cases, polyethylene bags are recommended because they are acid-free, their contents are easily visible, they are less likely to rip or tear, they do not degrade with exposure to moisture, and the self-sealing varieties help prevent comingling. Polyethylene bags should always have small holes poked through them (large enough for air to pass through freely, but small enough that bone fragments will not be lost) to avoid condensation within the bag, which can result in mold formation. Even what appears to be "dry" bone may contain a high enough moisture content to be problematic if air transfer cannot occur. Also, bagged bone should not be allowed to bake in direct sunlight. Related to that, labels should be water- and moldproof (Tyvek labels provide both of these qualities), and ink should be indelible.

IN THE FIELD

Due to its complexity and the amount of information that can be obtained from well-preserved and well-excavated skeletal material when research is allowed, several special considerations above and beyond those standard to archaeological excavations deserve mentioning. Both the excavation and the documentation of human remains may require additional steps or thought beyond those basic to archaeology.

It is important to strive for the most complete and careful recovery possible to maintain the integrity of each individual. Basic archaeological excavation techniques are covered elsewhere (see Barker 1993; Drewett 1999; Collis 2001; Roskams 2001), but a number of points relevant to osteologists who have not been on an archaeological excavation before or for archaeologists who have not excavated burials before should be made here.

- *Take particular care around the ends of bones when excavating.* Due to their structure, the ends of bones are often very fragile and vulnerable. Their breakage not only is indicative of poor excavation technique but also can hinder osteometric analyses and assessment of age.
- *Lifting bones requires as much thought as clearing bones.* Much time is spent exposing bones, but lifting bones improperly can be as damaging as careless excavation. The complete clearing of the ends of bones and loosening the soil beneath bones prior to and during lifting, in addition to properly supporting bones along their length, is essential to prevent unnecessary breakage.
- *Try to fully excavate, record, and lift a skeleton in one working day.* Uncover as much of a skeleton as possible, and photograph and draw it before removing any bones. Account for each skeletal element first as they are exposed and again as they are lifted. If possible, shield bone from direct sunlight, which can quickly dry out a skeleton partially exposed in the ground for long periods of time. Nevertheless, very fragile or complex burials may take more than one day to excavate, but they should always be covered if left in situ overnight, to reduce the risk of damage, vandalism, or theft.
- *Keep the left and right sides bagged separately from the moment they are lifted.* Articulated skeletons can be better managed and packed if the right and left hands, feet, ribs, and upper and lower limbs are kept separately from the outset. Packing a skeleton in small units is best to prevent damage during transport. This also makes it easier to account for complete individuals. Remember to label each bag.
- *Remove as much soil as possible from the surface of bones during excavation, but be careful not to overclean.* If bone does not need to be cleaned, because it will be immediately reburied or it is already relatively clean, do not clean it further. Surface soil is often easiest to remove without damaging the surface of the bone immediately upon excavation. If such preliminary cleaning takes place, often later cleaning is minimal. Dry cleaning is always preferred to wet cleaning if it is possible to gently brush or pick soil off bone without damaging the surface; cleaning should stop if the surface of bone is being removed or visibly damaged. Soil left attached to bone can be damaging during transport, scouring the surface of bone with any movement.
- *Do not soak bones in water and always allow bone to dry slowly.* If wet cleaning is required, cold water should be used, and only to dampen the surface enough to remove any adhering soil. Bone should never be soaked, as this may cause it to weaken or disintegrate and will lengthen its drying time. Never scrub bone with stiff brushes (soft paintbrushes will often suffice). Avoid direct sunlight and heat sources when drying bone, because rapid drying can cause warping and cracking, and ensure that bone is completely dry prior to packing.
- *Remove soil from the cranial cavity.* Again, if immediate reburial is intended for remains, cleaning the cranium is not important and, in fact, should be avoided. However, soil left in crania hardens and can be very damaging during handling and transport. Care must be taken not to damage the fragile facial bones in the process of removing soil from the cranial cavity. If damage occurs, cleaning should stop.
- *Take particular care when packing crania.* Crania are very fragile and should always be packed to avoid bumping against other bones, particularly during transport. Do not store mandibles in articulation with crania, as teeth may become chipped or broken.
- *Do not overexcavate or overclean teeth.* Tooth sockets are often very fragile and cannot withstand strenuous cleaning. Very soft, natural bristle brushes and a little water may be used to clean teeth, using extreme care not to cause any abrasion. A toothbrush should never be used to clean teeth. Furthermore, calculus or other dental deposits may be dislodged with even gentle cleaning, which is particularly problematic for some research objectives, such as scanning electron microscope microwear studies.
- *Always pack lighter skeletal elements on top of heavier, denser elements and pad out fragile bones.* Delicate bones, such as ribs and cranial bones, can be unnecessarily broken or damaged by packing them inadequately. Heavy long bones should be placed at the bottom of boxes. Fragile bones, such as crania, should be padded with acid-free tissue paper. Bones should not shift around

within boxes when moved, so additional padding should be used at the top and bottom of boxes, at a minimum, with extra padding to fill any voids.

- *Be consistent when recording.* It is very important to be as consistent as possible when measuring, describing, or otherwise documenting human remains. Any measurements taken or terms to describe features should be clearly defined and illustrated when possible. A number of standardized systems for recording have been published, and following such a set of standards can minimize mistakes in recording and enable other researchers to better understand or make comparisons with other material.
- *Record everything.* Documenting burials requires most of the same basic information as any other archaeological feature, such as the location, depth, excavator, date, weather conditions, and other information relevant to the excavation. However, a number of other observations may also need recording. Where there is a visible grave cut, its shape and depth should be recorded. The orientation (north-south) and position of body (supine or flexed, face up or down, or to the side) and limb orientation should also be recorded. The general condition of bone should also be noted (see chapter 4). As burials are often regarded as a single context, the relationship between any grave goods and the skeleton should also be recorded. Whether any samples have been treated or stored differently from the rest of the skeleton must be noted. Some in situ measurements, particularly of long bones, may be useful, particularly if the bone cannot be recovered without breakage, and it should be noted that such measurements were made in situ.

SETTING UP A FIELD LAB

Setting up a field laboratory is particularly important on large projects and for research projects. Field laboratories may function as spaces to clean, document, properly pack, and temporarily store skeletal remains. Field labs may also serve as photography studios, conservation facilities, and space to work on unusual finds or block lifted materials. The facilities provided will depend on the functions to take place in a field laboratory and the scope of the project in general.

If a field lab is to serve as a research space, adequate table or desk areas must be made available. Good lighting is also important. Calipers, osteometric boards, and any comparative material required for analysis must be made available.

One of the most likely functions of a field laboratory is for cleaning skeletal remains. Although dry cleaning is always preferred over wet cleaning, if wet cleaning is required, a clean water source, basins or sinks with screened drains, and mesh racking for drying should be available if wet cleaning is necessary.

If a field lab is to be used for storage, adequate shelving is necessary. Decisions should be made in advance as to how associated objects will be stored, whether separately or together with the skeletal remains. This is often a logistical decision, dependent on the size and materials of the objects recovered. If associated objects are simply too large to fit in the skeleton box or of a material that will be best preserved in a different environment, it could be argued they should be stored separately. However, there is an increasing tendency to think individual burials should be maintained as single contexts postexcavation (see chapter 7), and this approach raises interesting storage and conservation issues that are only beginning to be dealt with (see chapter 9).

CASE STUDY: THE GIBBONS SPRINGS PROJECT

Osteologists are often asked to supervise the excavation of human burials during archaeological field projects. Human burials provide archaeologists with important data that can be used to reconstruct lifeways or to infer behavior. Variability observed in skeletal remains (artificial cranial modification, body preparation, and pathological conditions), grave furnishings (quantity, quality, variety, source), mortuary facilities (receptacle type, shape, dimensions, materials), and grave location (cemetery, midden, platform mound) are used by archaeologists to identify intrasite mortuary variability and to study sociocultural complexity.

This case study is about the prehistoric Native American skeletal remains recovered and studied from the Gibbons Springs Hohokam Village in Tucson, Arizona (Slaughter and Roberts 1996). One of the goals of the Gibbons Springs site data recovery project was to evaluate the excavation data, including the mortuary data, for evidence of social and economic differentiation between the residents of the walled compound and those who lived outside the compound (Roberts 1996).

Permits

In the mid-1990s, the construction of a housing and golf course development in Tucson, Arizona, threatened to destroy a large (400 by 500 meters) Hohokam Classic period (1200–1300) village. The site contained a walled habitation compound, surrounding four habitation structures, and a series of outlying agricultural and habitation structures. Although the property was privately owned, Pima County has a grading ordinance that requires all developers to obtain an archaeological clearance. The landowner also needed to obtain a flood control permit (404 Jurisdictional Waters) from the U.S. Army Corps of Engineers. The archaeological survey of the proposed development area determined that the Gibbons Springs site was significant and eligible for listing on the National Register of Historic Places. Because the site was considered significant no grading permits or flood control permits would be issued to the developer until an archaeological clearance was submitted to the State Historic Preservation Office and all relevant agencies.

To obtain a clearance letter, the developer would need to pay for archaeological data recovery of the site. The first step in the process was the preparation of a research design and data recovery plan. The data recovery plan included a two-step process, a testing phase and a complete excavation phase. The extent of the excavation would be determined, in part, by the research questions asked. The research design and the data recovery plan were submitted with an Archaeological Resources Protection Act permit application to the county and the Army Corp of Engineers. The land developer hired SWCA, Inc., Environmental Consultants, to prepare the permits and conduct the investigations at the site.

The data recovery plan and research design outlined the responsibilities related to the Native American consultation process, the osteological methods, and specific research questions relevant to the recovery of human remains. Since human remains were anticipated approval of the plan was needed from the state of Arizona, the Army Corps of Engineers, and the U.S. Advisory Council on Historic Preservation. Taking into account the wishes of the descendents, SWCA designed the excavation and analysis process to provide optimum information on mortuary variability.

Native American tribes in Arizona had developed a standard programmatic agreement, which outlined the methods and treatment of Native American human remains. This agreement, between the affiliated tribes, the Arizona State Museum, the archaeologists, and the property owners, was completed and filed with the Arizona State Museum whenever impacts to Native American sites were planned. Once the appropriate permits were obtained and the burial agreement was signed, the excavation could begin.

Discovery

The project was divided into two phases. The first phase, subsurface testing, would enable the archaeologist to discover what components of the site were buried and what the costs of excavating them would be. The second phase, data recovery, would entail the complete excavation of all archaeological features that were relevant to the research questions. During the data recovery phase, the features and aspects of the site that were relevant to the research questions would be the focus of excavation. Because the site was large, and some of it was completely buried, the testing phase included trenching with a backhoe and excavation with trowel and shovel.

Testing included surface collection of artifacts, excavation of 69 backhoe trenches across portions of the site, and excavation of units with trowel and shovel in the compound area. Three cremation features and one inhumation, representing a minimum of five individuals, were encountered in the backhoe trenches during testing. These features were excavated immediately, evaluated in the field, and stored until excavation of the village was completed. All bone scattered by the backhoe during the discovery of the remains was collected from the backdirt by screening in the vicinity of the burial. Standardized forms were completed on the burial practices and on the skeletal remains for each of the burial features and individuals represented.

Excavation

Complete excavation of the compound and outlying features resulted in the recovery of a small skeletal series that included a minimum of fifteen individuals (four adult males, two adult females, four adults of indeterminate sex, one juvenile, one possible juvenile, one infant, and two neonates/late fetal). All but two of the individuals were recovered from two small cremation cemeteries. The larger cemetery, containing a minimum of seven individuals, was located in the compound, and the second cemetery, located twenty meters north of the compound, contained the cremated remains of at least four individuals. Two other mortuary features, representing an adult inhumation and an urn cremation, were found outside the village core. All of the cremations consisted of osseous remains in uncovered urns or pits. The burials recovered from the cemeteries were in-the-flesh cremations that had been placed in ceramic vessels.

Once mortuary features were encountered during testing and excavation all work in the immediate vicinity was stopped until one of us verified that they were human. The remains were then collected (if scattered in the backhoe spoil piles) and placed in a bag covered with soil in the backhoe trench until the tribal representative was notified. Then excavation of the remains could begin.

The first step in the excavation process was to establish a datum near the mortuary feature. If the feature was located near the provenience grid, the horizontal and vertical grid coordinates were extended around the burial. When the features were located away from the main excavations, a subdatum was established and later surveyed in. The next step varied depending on the type of burial.

The single adult human inhumation was discovered during testing in the backhoe trenches. The bone fragments visible in the trench walls enabled us to estimate the body position. Once the extent and orientation of the skeleton were determined, the overburden was removed with a shovel until an outline of a burial pit was visible. Since a pit was visible, we excavated within the burial pit in ten-centimeter arbitrary levels until we estimated that we were fifteen centimeters above the skeleton. At this point we used a trowel to prevent damaging the bones. Once bone was encountered digging continued with wooden tools that included an array of homemade scoops and pointed sticks. All soil covering the skeleton was screened with one-eighth-inch screening. The analysis was performed when the skeletal remains were completely excavated and during the removal process. Portions of the vertebrae were fragmentary and heavily weathered, and when we removed them, they crumbled. Before the skeletal elements and grave associations were removed, the burial was drawn and photographed. Notes were taken on the body position, the skeletal elements present, the grave associations, and the location of the grave goods.

Cremations were excavated in a similar fashion. Cremations could be analyzed only if they were not contained in an intact burial urn, which in this case was a ceramic vessel. One juvenile cremation was in such a vessel and was left intact. Some of the bones visible at the surface of the vessel allow for a determination of juvenile. Care was taken to save the soil matrix, as well as the bone that was recovered from broken urns. Every effort was made to identify a pit outline and origination point so that the relationship between cremations within each cemetery could be determined. Mortuary data on the associated artifacts were recorded and the artifacts were kept with the human remains.

Setting Up the Field Lab

At the request of Native American representatives, the skeletal material remained on-site. A temporary lab was established in a large walk-in sized storage container that served as storage for the remains and the equipment. The storage container lacked electricity and windows. Because the weather in Tucson was sunny, warm, and calm, the examination of the remains was done outdoors with natural light on a portable table. Field laboratory equipment included one-eighth- and one-sixteenth-inch geological screens to remove the sediment from the cremated remains, a scale for weighing the remains, three graduated screens (1.9 centimeters, 9.52 millimeters, and 4.75 millimeters) for size sorting, lab equipment for measuring (sliding and spreading calipers, osteometric board, metric tape measure), dental casts for standardized descriptions of nonmetric traits, photographic equipment (35mm camera, digital camera, film, tripod, black velvet, scale), binocular microscope with battery light source or hand lens, various textbooks with good photographs and specialized references for pathological conditions and nonmetric traits, and recording forms for the mortuary practices and skeletal remains. Some of the forms were modified to accommodate specific research questions.

Since the grave goods would be kept in the field with the human remains, plans were made to have the analysts (ground stone, ceramics, flaked stone, etc.) visit the field lab to record the grave goods in greater detail.

Summary

Clear evidence of status differentiation was not found in any of the burials recovered from the Gibbons Springs site. The mortuary practices at Gibbons Springs closely conform to those reported at other Classic period sites in the region. While clear evidence for status burials was not found, one pattern associated with status burials at other Tucson Basin Classic period sites was observed. At Gibbons Springs, the burials with the greatest number of grave associations were not located in the cemeteries but were buried away from the other individuals outside the site core.

FURTHER READING

Baby, Raymond S.
    1954 Hopewell Cremation Practices. *Ohio Historical Society Papers in Archaeology* 1:1–7.

Binford, Lewis R.
    1963 An Analysis of Cremations from Three Michigan Sites. *Wisconsin Archaeologists* 44(2):98–110.

Brown, Keri A., Kerry O'Donoghue, and Terrance A. Brown
    1995 DNA in Cremated Bones from an Early Bronze Age Cemetery Cairn. *International Journal of Osteoarchaeology* 5:181–187.

Buckley, Laureen, Eileen Murphy, and Barra O'Donnachain

2004 *The Treatment of Human Remains: Technical Paper for Archeologists.* Human Osteoarchaeology Subcommittee of IAPA. Electronic document, http://www.instituteofarchaeologistsofireland.ie/Publications_Files/TreatmentofHumanRemains.doc, accessed May 23, 2006.

Buikstra, Jane E., and Mark Swegle

1989 Bone Modification Due to Burning: Experimental Evidence. In *Bone Modification,* edited by Robson Bonnichsen and Marcella H. Sorg, pp. 247–258. Institute for Quaternary Studies, University of Maine, Orono.

Fink, Thomas Michael

1996 Current Issues in Cremation Analysis: A Perspective from the American Southwest. Master's thesis, Arizona State University, Tempe.

Shipman, Pat, Giraud Foster, and Margaret Schoeninger

1984 Burnt Bones and Teeth: An Experimental Study of Color, Morphology, Crystal Structure, and Shrinkage. *Journal of Archaeological Science* 11:307–325.

REFERENCES

Barker, Philip

1993 *Techniques of Archaeological Excavation.* Third edition. Betsford, London.

Bass, William M.

1987 *Human Osteology: A Laboratory and Field Manual of the Human Skeleton.* 3rd ed. Missouri Archaeological Society, Columbia.

Buikstra, Jane E., and Douglas H. Ubelaker, editors

1994 *Standards for Data Collection from Human Skeletal Remains.* Arkansas Archaeological Survey Research Series No. 44. Arkansas Archaeological Survey, Fayetteville.

Collis, John

2001 *Digging Up the Past: An Introduction to Archaeological Excavation.* Sutton Publishing, Stroud.

Drewett, Peter L.

1999 *Archaeology: An Introduction.* Routledge, London.

Fink, T. Michael

1989 The Human Skeletal Remains from the Grand Canal Ruins, AZ T:12:14 (ASU) and T:12:16 (ASU). In *Archaeological Investigations at the Grand Canal Ruins: A Classic Period Site in Phoenix, Arizona.* Vol. 2, No. 12, edited by Douglas R. Mitchell, pp. 619–704. Soil Systems Publications in Archaeology, Phoenix.

Fink, T. Michael, and Charles F. Merbs

1991 Paleonutrition and Paleopathology of the Salt River Hohokam: A Search for Correlates. *Kiva* 56:293–318.

Kneller, Paul

1998 Health and Safety in Church and Funerary Archaeology. In *Grave Concerns: Death and Burial in Post-medieval England 1700 to 1850,* edited by M. J. Cox, pp. 181–189. CBA, York.

Morris, Donald H., and Dan Brooks

1987 Cremations at the Marana Sites. In *Studies in the Hohokam Community of Marana,* edited by Glen E. Rice, pp. 223–233. Anthropological Field Studies No. 15. Office of Cultural Resource Management, Arizona State University, Tempe.

Roberts, Heidi

1992 Pathological Conditions in Human Remains from Two Hohokam Sites in the Tucson Basin. Paper presented at the 66th Pecos Conference, Springerville, Arizona.

1996 Human Remains from the Gibbons Springs Site and Other Classic-Period Sites in the Tucson Basin. In *Excavation of the Gibbons Springs Site: A Classic Period Village in the Northeastern Tucson Basin*, edited by Mark C. Slaughter and Heidi Roberts, pp. 413–448. SWCA Archaeological Report No. 94-87. SWCA, Inc., Environmental Consultants, Tucson.

Roskams, Steve
2001 *Excavation*. Cambridge Manuals in Archaeology. Cambridge University Press, Cambridge.

Slaughter, Mark C., and Heidi Roberts
1996 *Excavations of the Gibbons Springs Site: A Classic Period Village in the Northeastern Tucson Basin*. SWCA Archaeological Report No. 94-87. SWCA, Inc., Environmental Consultants, Tucson.

Sprague, Roderick
2005 *Burial Terminology: A Guide for Researchers*. AltaMira, Lanham, Maryland.

Steele, D. Gentry, and Claude A. Bramblett
1988 *The Anatomy and Biology of the Human Skeleton*. Texas A&M University Press, College Station.

Stodder, Anne W.
1989 Background of the Bioarchaeological Resources Survey. In *Human Adaptations and Cultural Change in the Greater Southwest*, edited by Alan H. Simmons, Ann Lucy Wiener Stodder, Douglas Dykeman, and Patricia A. Hicks, pp. 167–190. Research Series No. 32. Arkansas Archaeological Survey, Wrightsville.

Thiel, J. Homer
1993 Human Remains from a Cremation Cemetery in El Reposo Park. In *Pueblo Viejo Archaeological Investigations at a Classic Period Cemetery in El Reposo Park, Phoenix, Arizona*, edited by Mark Zyniecki, pp. 39–68. SWCA Archaeological Report No. 92-75. SWCA, Inc., Environmental Consultants, Flagstaff.

White, Tim D.
1991 *Human Osteology*. Academic Press, New York.

CHAPTER 14

Working with the Dead
Health Concerns

Bernardo Arriaza and Luz-Andrea Pfister

Cursed be he that moves my bones.

—Epitaph on William Shakespeare's gravestone

Museums and other types of repositories represent unusual workplaces. They can bring together dangers from remote areas spanning thousands of years. Students and scholars involved in handling human remains commonly question the likelihood of contracting diseases while handling the dead. Viruses constitute the predominant concern and the worries are not unreasonable when bearing in mind a large proportion of the institutionalized human remains originate from people who succumbed to epidemics of smallpox, measles, and other viral infections. Add to this the "mummy curse," popularized by Carter's 1922 discovery of King Tut and the sudden and unexplained death of his crew members. In the Andes, even the *huaqueros*, or grave robbers, often have a small ceremony and pray to the spirits to protect them against evil forces before desecrating an ancient cemetery. But, is there anything to actually worry about when robbing, digging, or studying ancient mummies, skeletons, or artifacts? The simple answer is yes.

In this chapter, using our experience and a general survey of the paleopathological and clinical literature, we discuss the professional risks when handling the dead in archaeological or osteoforensic settings. We will underscore the most common threats to those involved in excavation, care, and research concerning human remains from archaeological and osteoforensic contexts. We will also provide suggestions for precautions that should be taken.

The hidden risks present in archaeological collections can be subdivided into biological and chemical hazards. In addition, we are emphasizing hazards that are inherent to the remains or artifacts, that is, poisonous materials used to make objects or process the remains; hazards inherent to the preservation, such as pesticides used in the past; and risks encountered during fieldwork.

BIOHAZARDS INHERENT TO HUMAN REMAINS

Are ancient viruses and bacteria a potential risk? The short answer is most likely no. Human pathogens—defined as microorganisms that cause disease in humans—do not live long enough in a corpse to present serious threats to researchers in archaeological or conservation contexts. Pathologists and forensic pathologists who deal with fresh corpses face, in contrast, a very different situation and have to take special precautions to avoid the potential transmission of infectious diseases.

Electron microscopy has revealed that some viruses, such as smallpox, have been well preserved in mummified tissues for as long as four hundred years, as in the case of skin lesions of a sixteenth-century Naples infant mummy (Marennikova et al. 1990). Despite the good structural preservation of the virus, its viability was shown to have been lost (Marennikova et al. 1990); in other words, the virus has become unable to cause disease or to reproduce in the laboratory. Of particular concern could be more recent human remains such as those of nineteenth-century smallpox victims mummified in the permafrost in the Artic. In spite of the fact that cold and dryness render permafrost as an ideal environment for tissue preservation, researchers have so far failed to recover live smallpox virus, and none of the investigators handling these infected individuals have become infected (Stone 2002).

A few reports state that ancient bacteria were found alive in the guts of mammoths from as far back as 11,600 years ago (Rung et al. 1997). While it is quite possible that the bacteria were found alive, it is highly unlikely that they were that old. So far no living ancient bacteria have been reported in the paleopathological literature. Thus, most living organisms found in dead corpses are probably recent contaminations or the result of the microorganisms living and reproducing in situ. It is also known that different agents (animals and microorganisms) that invade corpses and aid in their decomposition, including rodents, birds, bacteria, beetles, and flies, come in waves (Smith 1987).

Until proven otherwise, we will work under the assumption that living organisms found in the mummies are the product of relatively recent environmental developments. For example, after a body is exhumed, it is exposed to a new environment and thus new contaminant microorganisms may appear (fungi, bacteria, etc.). For the present, we have no evidence for the preservation of infective pathogenic bacteria or viruses in archaeological or osteoforensic contexts. The recently completed genome project for the 1918 Spanish influenza pandemic virus (Taubenberger et al. 2005) and subsequent characterization of the reconstructed virus (Tumpey et al. 2005) were possible in part through the recovery of genomic viral RNA from lung tissue of an Alaskan influenza victim buried in permafrost in November 1918. Frozen mummies are among the best preserved, and still no infective virus could be recovered. The fragmentary state of the RNA is one of the reasons the project required nearly a decade to complete. All living organisms, including pathogens, rely on nucleic acids (DNA and RNA) for their genetic code, and these nucleic acids are subject to damage and fragmentation over time, preventing the preservation of infective pathogens in mummified or skeletal remains. There should be no concern about the possibility of contracting smallpox from objects that were used by individuals afflicted with smallpox and are presently stored in museum collections.

What about Prions?
Discovered by Stanley Prusiner (1982), *prions* are proteinaceous infectious particles that lack nucleic acid and are remarkable for causing spongiform neurodegenerative diseases such as the Creutzfeldt-Jakob disease, bovine spongiform encephalopathy (mad cow disease), kuru, and scrapie (Prusiner 1998). The high resistance of this protein to physical and chemical inactivation (Rutala and Weber 2001) makes it a candidate for long-term preservation in human remains.

No research addressing the detection of prions in forensic or archaeological remains has been reported so far. However, Steadman and Merbs (1982) have argued in the anthropological literature that digging up old bones sometimes can affect a complete village. These scholars postulated that the Fore people of New Guinea suffered from a neurological disorder called *kuru* as a consequence of their mortuary practices. Caused by a prion, kuru is a transmissible chronic disease with a long incubation time and causes tremors, wasting, and dementia eventually followed by death. The Fore dug up the remains of their beloved one, cleaned the rotten flesh, and kept the bones in a shrine. The infection affected those doing the cleaning of the dead and probably was transmitted by these morticians, women, to their children. Thus, researchers excavating forensic cases or in ethnohistoric cemeteries particularly in this region of the world should be aware of this potential hazard and use protective personal equipment (PPE).

Molds

Museums with leaky roofs or basement storage areas with high humidity may become a haven for the development of mold and are a nightmare for conservators. Curators must prevent outbreaks of mold on human remains and artifacts for optimal preservation, but also because they may represent a threat to their own health. Susceptible individuals are at risk of developing mold-induced hypersensitivity pneumonitis (HP), also known as extrinsic allergic alveolitis, which is the result of an immunologically induced inflammation of the lung parenchyma in response to inhalation exposure to a large variety of antigens, including mold. Despite the large number of individuals exposed to potential HP-causing antigens, the prevalence and incidence are low, probably due to environmental or genetic cofactors necessary to trigger the development of the disease (Fink et al. 2005). Kolmodin-Hedman et al. (1986) describe a case of a museum worker affected by an allergic reaction to fungal spores. This worker reported ten episodes of fever, chills, nausea, and coughing during a one-year period. Symptoms appeared at the end of the working day and disappeared after resting a few days at home. Museum workers should therefore be aware of potential risks and prevent inhalation of spores when working with moldy artifacts.

CHEMICAL HAZARDS—PESTICIDES AND HEAVY METAL POISONING

One may encounter a variety of potential hazards in museum collections related to the past use of pesticides as well as those inherent to the objects or remains themselves. Here we will focus on arsenic, lead, and DDT, since case studies associated with funerary contexts have already been described in the anthropology and museum world.

Arsenic Poisoning

From the 1800s through the 1970s, arsenic powder was widely used as a museum pesticide (Seifert et al. 2000) and in taxidermy (National Institute for Occupational Safety and Health [NIOSH] 1979). Major pathways for exposure are inhalation, ingestion, and skin contact. Arsenic may be present in many traditional remedies and artifacts, and toxicity comes from drinking contaminated water or exposure to arsenic dust residues from excavations or pesticides. Millions of people worldwide are affected by arsenic toxicity (Ratnaike 2003). Water contamination with arsenic is the consequence of natural arsenic leaking into aquifers but also during mining and other industrial processes. Arsenic pesticides have already been implicated in occupational skin cancers among farmers (Spiewak 2001).

Both acute and chronic exposures to arsenic are highly toxic. Arsenic inactivates up to two hundred enzymes in the human body (Ratnaike 2003) and has a variety of multisystemic toxic effects (Abernathy et al. 1999; Graeme and Pollack 1998). Acute intoxication symptoms include dysphagia (difficulty in swallowing), nausea, vomiting, abdominal pain, diarrhea, intense thirst, muscle cramps, encephalopathy (brain disorder), and peripheral neuropathy, while chronic poisoning manifestations include skin rash, hyperkeratosis (thickening of the skin) in the palms and soles, skin pigmentation, and conjunctivitis (pinkeye). In addition, chronic toxicity or arseniasis has been reported to produce cancer of the bladder, kidney, liver, and uterus. Arseniasis is a worldwide phenomenon but occurs particularly in developing countries.

Are museum specialists and researchers at risk? It is a possibility, particularly if they are studying ancient objects infused with arsenic powder. Smith and Coulehan (2002) reported one case of a museum specialist who suffered from sensory neuropathy and signs of exposure to heavy metals.

In 1986, while working in northern Chile analyzing an Andean mummy, one of us was not using protective clothing and was told at the time that there was nothing to worry about. The mummy was beautifully dressed and had on its head a highly decorated turban and a pretty yellow powdery bag pinned to the headdress. His upper torso was covered in the same yellow pigment. A pigment sample was sent with Vicki Cassman to the Winterthur Museum Analytical Laboratory in Delaware. The bright yellow pigment was pure arsenic. In this region arsenic is regularly found in the soil and water. Thus, the fear of handling the dead or their artifacts especially in this part of the world may not be unfounded at all. The hidden risks are real, not just in the form of spirits of the dead but as lethal toxins.

Mild arsenic absorption may occur from casual skin contact and inhalation. Thus museologists, researchers, and archaeologists should be aware if they are working with toxic artifacts or if they are excavating in areas with high levels of arsenic in the soil. If they develop nausea and rashes, arsenic may be to blame. Today NAGPRA (Native American Graves Protection and Repatriation Act) repatriation has spotlighted new analyses of ancient artifacts (Odegaard and Sadongei 2005; Osorio 2001). Unfortunately for American Indian tribes and museum workers, it has been discovered that many artifacts are indeed contaminated with multiple toxic elements (Odegaard 2001; Odegaard and Sadongei 2005). Past museologists used arsenic and other metals in good faith to preserve objects for future generations. Each of these artifacts could be a potential health hazard to those that come in intimate contact. As Seifert et al. (2000) have stated, the moral of the story is that all artifacts undergoing repatriation, either to Native Americans or museums abroad, must be tested for toxic contaminants.

Lead Poisoning
Our understanding of the toxic effects of lead has changed dramatically in the past three decades. In recent years, the focus has shifted away from occupational high-dose exposure to the consequences of lower-dose exposures that cause no clinical symptoms. In both children and adults, lead toxicity is associated with multisystemic manifestations (Bellinger 2004). It was suggested that, in children, lead interferes with several stages of synaptic neurotransmission and during the early postnatal period may have permanent effects (Johnston and Goldstein 1998). While exposed children have deficits in IQ scores as well as attention and language disorders, in adults elevated lead levels appear to adversely affect cognitive functions as well (Needleman 2004; Schwartz et al. 2000). This might be an issue in museums that, for instance, have replicas with metal-based paint and hands-on experiences. It was suggested that while in adults symptoms might be reversible after the lead exposure stops (Yokoyama et al. 1988), in children they might not be (White et al. 1993).

An interesting case reported by the *New Yorker* involved a forty-three-year-old art conservator in New York who suffered from severe occupational lead poisoning in 1979 (Roueché 1986). The case illustrates very well how, when working with unknown pigments, we may expose ourselves to health hazards. The art conservator in question worked for three months restoring an ancient Peruvian funerary textile that her deceased husband, an art dealer, had purchased several years before his death. The cloth was produced in the Chancay period, dating between 1000 and 1500.

On a routine medical examination shortly after she had started working on the Peruvian tapestry, she was told she had a low hemoglobin level without apparent cause. Three months later she was suffering from stomach and burning pains that came and went. Additionally, she complained about being tired all the time and having muscle aches and occasional dizzy spells. Everything seemed to irritate her, especially her children.

Exams revealed an enlarged spleen, and laboratory tests confirmed the low hemoglobin levels. The blood smear revealed that 40 percent of the red blood cells were spotted with blue marks (basophilic stippling), which suggested toxicity. Her lead blood level was seventy-two micrograms per deciliter (the normal value is about ten), confirming the diagnosis of lead poisoning. As an art conservator, she was exposed to lead-based paint!

Inspection of her home-based studio revealed that the textile had a painted abstract design that she was sewing onto a mount and retouching using a red pigment that had also been found in the same Chancay tomb. She had applied the paint solution with a brush, and when dry, she brushed it to an even texture and then blew off any residue. With time, her conditions worsened. However, after diagnosis and almost a year of treatments, her condition returned to normal with average levels of hemoglobin and lead.

The red pigment used by the art conservator was sent to a mineralogist for analysis, who determined that it was indeed cinnabar or mercuric sulfide, an inorganic mercury salt, which does have some bioavailability, and chronic exposure could result in some effects, yet in this case study there was no evidence for mercury poisoning. Additional testing with electrothermal atomic absorption confirmed the presence of lead at 8.9 parts per thousand (close to 1 percent). The fabric had a lead concentration of 380 parts per million—a high concentration—which accounted for the severity of the poisoning. She contaminated herself in three ways. She smoked during her work, increasing the chances of contaminating herself by bringing her fingers often to her mouth. She wetted the repair sewing thread with her lips when it slipped out of the eye of the needle. She also inhaled loose pigment. The art conservator thought the pigment she used to prepare the paint was cinnabar. Cinnabar is mercuric sulfide, which is largely insoluble in tissue fluids, and whether inhaled or ingested, it can pass more or less harmlessly through the body. The odd thing is that the Chancay people did not use lead pigments to paint their textiles. Thus, most likely an unscrupulous dealer added red lead to the cinnabar to make it go further and add to profits.

DDT

Another highly toxic chemical used in museums until 1972 is the organic pesticide DDT (dichlorodiphenyl trichloroethane). Today many artifacts have survived the depredation by microorganisms, fungi, and insects likely thanks to its use. Yet, this forgotten substance has been brought into the spotlight once again with the analysis of artifacts associated with repatriation. Unprotected handling and cleaning of the artifacts may create potential risk to museum workers. DDT causes dizziness, nausea, abdominal pain, vomiting, and irritation of the skin and eyes, and recently it has been linked to the risk for developing several cancers (Jaga and Brosius 1999). Therefore, top museums are implementing safety norms that range from wearing protective gear, washing hands after working with museum objects, and improving ventilation systems to prevent contaminated dust particles from being inhaled. In North America, artifacts are beginning to be tested for the presence of DDT and other organic pesticides and heavy metals such as mercury and arsenic (Odegaard 2005; Palmer et al. 2003).

HAZARDS DURING FIELDWORK

Valley Fever

A particularly common hazard for American archaeologists is coccidioidomycosis, or cocci for short, a fungal infection also known as valley fever. Since the 1960s, several reports in the literature document the occurrence of multiple valley fever outbreaks in archaeological excavations in the southwestern United States (Breternitz 1972; Werner et al. 1972; Perera and Stone 2002;

Petersen et al. 2004). Cocci is a systemic infection caused by the inhalation of *Coccidioides immitis* airborne spores. The fungus grows during a saprophytic phase in the upper twenty centimeters of soil in the southwestern United States, as well as in parts of Mexico, Central, and South America. When the soil is disturbed by workers or natural events such as high winds or earthquakes, the fungal arthroconidia (spore) become aerosolized (airborne) and may be inhaled. Millions of spores are found in a cubic inch of dust, yet in laboratory studies as few as ten arthroconidia were shown to be sufficient to cause infection in dogs and monkeys, and severe infections are related to inhaling aerosols containing high doses of arthroconidia.

Only 40 percent of the infected individuals will have a manifest infection that ranges from an influenza-like illness to severe pneumonia, and in rare occasions it may cause extrapulmonary disseminated disease. The primary infection is limited to the lungs, with the first symptoms appearing between seven and twenty-one days after exposure. These may include fever, chills, night sweats, chest pain, cough, appetite loss, weight loss, muscle and joint aches, and malaise (Galgiani 2000). Thus, archaeologists should be cautious when these symptoms appear after digging.

In patients with healthy immune systems, most infections are self-limiting (Blair et al. 2005) and resolve within a few weeks, without antifungal therapy. Some people are more susceptible than others and may develop severe lung disease or disseminated chronic illness, including soft tissue and bone destruction. The susceptibility is higher in immune-compromised individuals, pregnant women (third trimester), and individuals of African and Asian descent including Native Americans (Louie et al. 1999).

Cocci affected ancient people as much as it affects modern populations. It has been reported in ancient north Amerindians and even prehistoric dogs (Harrison et al. 1991). Besides fieldworkers, it also has affected staff of repositories and museums during cataloging and processing of archaeological materials. An increased incidence in recent years is the consequence of the drastic demographic expansion in endemic areas with the migration of Americans to the Sunbelt states. In Nevada, newspaper headlines have read "New Epidemic in the Valley" due to high winds and massive earth movement for new home construction.

Infections with *C. immitis* have a seasonal pattern, and this fact may be important in deciding when to dig. Infection rates usually spike during the first few weeks of hot, dry weather that follow an extended period of rain. There is a correlation between above-average rainfall during winter and spring and high infection rates the following summer. The increased moisture provides favorable growth conditions for *C. immitis* and consequently a greater production of arthroconidia. In brief, to avoid dust and respiratory infections during excavations, dust control and masks are highly recommended. Limiting ground disturbing activities is another primary weapon against infection. The seasonal character of infections should be considered when planning fieldwork in endemic areas, favoring activities during the winter, when infection rates are lowest.

Histoplasmosis

Histoplasmosis is another mycosis (disease caused by a fungus) caused by the fungus *Histoplasma capsulatum*. It represents an occupational risk for people working in environments where bird or bat excrements accumulate over years, such as buildings and caves inhabited by them or in wooded areas where birds congregate habitually. Histoplasmosis is found worldwide and is an endemic mycosis in the United States (Kurowski and Ostapchuk 2002). Disruption of dry and dusty soils from these places releases fungal spores into the air, where they can be inhaled. Cases have been reported from all over the world except Antarctica, and the most endemic regions are the river valleys of the Ohio, Mississippi, and St. Lawrence.

In histoplasmosis, unlike coccidioidomycosis, there are no known differences in susceptibility or resistance to infection among ethnic groups. After an incubation period of five to eighteen days in most individuals, histoplasmosis is asymptomatic and only incidentally discovered (Wheat 2003) or manifests as a mild flulike condition with fever, cough, chest pain, and fatigue. The symptoms may last for several weeks. If the exposure is intense or the individual has an impaired immune system, the disease may have a course similar to tuberculosis. If untreated, it may cause disseminated histoplasmosis in which the infection spreads beyond the lungs to affect other organs and is potentially fatal (Wheat 1996).

A disposable face mask will not provide sufficient protection (no proper face seal, no adequate level of filtering). Therefore, respirators with NIOSH-approved high-efficiency particulate air (HEPA) filters are indicated. Additional protective gear is needed to avoid contamination from secondary dust inhalation. This means that you need disposable hooded overalls, shoe covers, and rubber gloves that are discarded after use (placed in secure containers, such as double-thickness heavy-duty plastic bags, and taken to a hazardous waste facility) (Ferguson 2001).

Hantavirus

Contact with rodents, rodent nests, and droppings are a common occupational exposure for archaeologists, forensic anthropologists, and museum personnel when examining artifacts and materials exposed to rodents. Among rodent-borne viruses, hantaviruses are a major concern. In humans, they are associated with two major diseases, hemorrhagic fever and hantavirus pulmonary syndrome (Maes et al. 2004; Schmaljohn and Hjelle 1997). Hantavirus pulmonary infection is a severe and often fatal respiratory illness; nevertheless, the potential risk of acquiring it has only been recognized since the summer of 1993, when an outbreak of hantavirus pulmonary syndrome (HPS) inundated the southwestern United States.

Hantaviruses are enveloped negative-sense RNA (Schmaljohn 1996) viruses that naturally cause persistent asymptomatic infections in rodents, who shed virus in feces, saliva, and urine. During the summer of 1993, the rodent population was tenfold higher than in previous years, which was attributed to an abnormally large amount of rodent food brought on by increased rainfall, resulting in an abnormally frequent human-rodent contact, which in turn was the ecological opportunity for the resident hantavirus to infect humans as a novel host species (DeFilippis and Villarreal 2001; Morse 1994).

Hantaviruses belong to the family Bunyaviridae. A characteristic shared by four of the five genera included in this family is that they are primarily maintained in nature by replication in arthropod hosts (mosquitoes, phlebotomine sandflies, culicoid flies, ticks, and thrips) with alternating amplification cycles in vertebrate species. In contrast, members of the *Hantavirus* genus are found in specific rodent reservoir species. The first member of this genus, isolated in 1976 (Lee et al. 1978), was named *Hantaan virus* after the Hantaan River close to the location of some of the initial Korean cases, and it became the prototype of its genus.

In November 1993, Sin Nombre virus (SNV) was identified as the causative agent of HPS in the southwestern United States, and the deer mouse, *Peromyscus maniculatus*, was shown to be the rodent reservoir. The deer mouse is common and widespread in rural areas throughout much of the United States; on average, approximately 10 percent of them show evidence of infection with SNV (Engelthaler et al. 1998; Abbot et al.1999). Within the next several years, HPS was demonstrated to occur throughout the Americas from Canada to Patagonia and was found to be caused by at least ten different hantavirus species, each associated with a different rodent species, all members of the subfamily Sigmodontinae (distributed only in the New World).

Hantavirus infections are associated with domestic, occupational, or recreational activities that bring humans into contact with infected rodents, usually in rural settings. For humans, hantavirus infections occur primarily in adults in the United States and occur throughout the year, but higher numbers are reported during the spring and summer. Unfortunately, this is the time when archaeologists do most of their fieldwork. Person-to-person transmission has not been associated with HPS cases in the United States. However, person-to-person transmission, including nosocomial transmission (acquired at hospitals) of Andes virus, was well documented for a single outbreak in southern Argentina and suspected to have occurred much less extensively in another outbreak in Chile associated with the same virus (Wells et al. 1997).

The antiquity of HPS in the Americas is unknown, but

in Navajo medical traditions, mice are considered to be the bearers of an ancient illness that even predates the bubonic plague in the Navajo region. Healers say that when mice enter the home, they put people at risk of infection, as people come into contact with mice droppings and urine. The illness enters through the mouth, the nose or the eyes, and it usually attacks the strongest and healthiest of the Navajo people. Therefore, traditional medicine prescribes avoiding mice, keeping them out of the hogans (homes), and isolating food supplies. Some of the Navajo elders had predicted the 1993 HPS outbreak. In addition, their oral tradition says that in 1918 and 1933–34, there were similar outbreaks, after increases in rainfall produced increases in the piñon crop and the number of mice. (Centers for Disease Control and Prevention 2004)

Old and New World hantaviruses are believed to be transmitted by the same mechanisms. Human infection occurs most commonly through the inhalation of infectious, aerosolized saliva, or excreta. Transmission can occur when dried materials contaminated by rodent excreta are (1) disturbed and inhaled, (2) directly introduced into broken skin or conjunctivae, or (3) ingested in contaminated food or water. Transmission has also been documented after rodent bite.

After infection with SNV, there is an incubation period of two to three weeks, followed by the rapid onset of an influenza-like illness. Four to ten days after the initial phase of illness, the late symptoms of HPS appear. These include coughing and shortness of breath, and the lungs fill with fluid. The most prominent features of this phase are hypotension and shock, with a mortality rate of 37 percent. The recovery of those that survive is quick, with rapid resolution of shock and lung lesions within three to six days.

Hantaviruses have lipid envelopes that make them susceptible to desiccation and to most disinfectants. Depending on environmental conditions, these viruses probably survive less than one week in indoor environments and much shorter periods (perhaps hours) when exposed to sunlight outdoors. The greatest risk of exposure is associated with the removal of rodent carcasses, nests, and feces, because this could potentially lead to the inhalation of airborne contaminated particles.

Fink (2001) describes detailed recommendations to prevent hantavirus infection. These include rodent control procedures and rodent excreta and nest disposal procedures. Regard all rodents as potential hantavirus sources, and do not attempt to identify the rodent, which may lead to hantavirus exposure. Fink (2001) provides useful charts that outline the steps that may be taken to control rodents, birds, and their excreta. The services of a licensed pest control officer (PCO) are recommended.

Plague

Plague caused by *Yersinia pestis* is one the most devastating acute infectious diseases experienced by mankind, estimated to have killed one-fourth of the European population in the Middle

Ages. It has a venerable antiquity and has persisted to modern times (Perry 1997). In the United States, around ten cases occur each year, predominantly in the Southwest (New Mexico, Arizona, Colorado, Utah, and California) (Enscore et al. 2002). The present pandemic of plague probably began in the 1860s in China, spreading to Hong Kong in 1894 and subsequently spread by rats along major trade routes, transported in ships to California and port cities of South America, Africa, and Asia. The infection was transferred to sylvatic rodents, which represent the main source of infection in the United States today. It is established currently in mammal populations on all continents except Australia and Antarctica (Girard et al. 2004).

The *Y. pestis* bacterium predominantly affects rodents. Humans acquire the bacteria through bites of fleas infected from domestic rats, mostly in densely populated cities of countries with low hygienic standards, or sporadically in the open country from infected wild rodents. There are three major forms of the disease: bubonic, septicemic, and pneumonic plague, the most common being bubonic plague. During an incubation period of two to six days after the bite of an infected flea (Putzker et al. 2001), *Y. pestis* proliferates in the regional lymph nodes, causing a painful swelling, called *bubo*, in one anatomic region, typically found in the armpit, neck, groin, or upper thigh area, depending on the location of the flea bite. Accompanying symptoms include sudden onset of fever, chills, headaches, and weakness. Plague is unique for the sudden onset of symptoms and the fulminated clinical course that can cause death as quickly as two to four days after the onset of symptoms. At least 50 percent of the affected individuals will die from infection if untreated. Septicemic plague is a more severe form of the disease characterized by early bacteremia (bacteria in the bloodstream) and absence of bubo. Patients with bubonic or septicemic plague may develop a secondary pneumonia, which is highly contagious by airborne transmission. Untreated pneumonic plague is invariably fatal.

Plague is today a treatable disease, requiring immediate antibiotic therapy and hospitalization. Any person exhibiting plague symptoms should immediately seek medical attention. Major risk factors for humans contracting plague include contact with diseased wild mammals and/or their infected fleas, and exposure to infected fleas carried by mammalian pets (principally dogs and cats) (Mann et al. 1979). During fieldwork in endemic areas, spray insecticide on rodent carcasses and rodent nests to avoid flea bites.

Digging Problems and Clouds of Dust

A typical problem at all excavations is the inhalation of dust. Occupational exposure to dust doubles the risk of developing chronic obstructive pulmonary disease (COPD), and archaeologists as well as physical and forensic anthropologists active in fieldwork are often exposed to huge clouds of dust (figure 14.1). Unfortunately, it is not uncommon to see documentaries showing archaeologists surrounded by a dust cloud when screening excavated soils, while not wearing a respirator. It may not look cool being protected, but wearing a particle-filtering disposable N-95 respirator (dust-filtering mask) is the only way to prevent COPD due to chronic dust exposure. Some researchers have suggested that genetic factors are associated with susceptibility to COPD (Ugenskienė et al. 2005; Hegab et al. 2004). Unfortunately, no test is available to determine individual susceptibility to COPD, and therefore prevention is the way to go.

COPD is an umbrella term for two respiratory diseases, chronic bronchitis and emphysema (ATS Statement 1995). Chronic bronchitis is an inflammation of the respiratory airways, associated with irritation that causes excessive mucus production and bronchial wall swelling causing coughing and breathing difficulties. Emphysema is a disorder characterized by damage to the alveoli, which in turn causes lungs to become noncompliant. Normal lung tissue can expand and snap back, just like an elastic band. This stretch allows us to exhale air from the lungs after

Figure 14.1.   Archaeologists at work in the field in a cloud of dust. Photo courtesy of Luz-Andrea Pfister.

inhalation. Emphysema causes air to become trapped in the lungs, making it hard to catch a breath and causing fatigue.

COPD affects both men and women from an age as early as thirty. While smoking accounts for the vast majority (about 80 percent) of the COPD cases, clearly other factors such as dust are also involved (Pauwels and Rabe 2004), and occupational environments have been linked to its development (Hendrick 1996). Field archaeologists who smoke and have exposure to dust are at an even higher risk of developing COPD. The most common complaint is gradual and progressive shortness of breath while exerting oneself. This becomes pronounced with any sort of chest infection. In many individuals, a chronic cough is the first sign of the illness. In late stages of the disease, chest X-rays show the lungs to be hyperinflated. Some people develop heart failure as a result of COPD. Dust from excavations also may harbor other risks depending on the geographic area—for instance, valley fever and histoplasmosis. Therefore, wearing a dust-filtering mask should be a regular practice for archaeologists in the field.

Summary
Pathogenic bacteria and viruses that were once the cause of death of individuals excavated in archaeological or osteoforensic contexts do not represent a health risk to archaeologists and museum personnel. In contrast, organic pesticides and heavy metals represent a real threat. Moreover chronic dust exposure during fieldwork constitutes a risk factor for chronic obstructive lung disease. Hantavirus and valley fever are potentially dangerous conditions that could afflict fieldworkers in endemic areas. Prevention is the key.

RECOMMENDATIONS FOR PREVENTION

For the Lab

1. Use dust-filtering respirator mask and disposable gloves while working in the lab, particularly when working with soil samples.
2. Avoid bringing the hands to your nose, eyes, and mouth while working with bones and artifacts.
3. Avoid smelling artifacts or unknown powder.
4. Wear a lab coat, and wash it separately from other clothes.
5. Have suspicious substances tested.
6. Be aware that collections and artifacts may contain powerful toxic substances.

For the Field

1. Learn about the common threats in your excavation area before doing fieldwork.
2. Use dust-filtering respirator masks when digging, particular on windy days.
3. Avoid working against the wind.
4. Wear protective gear to excavate packrat middens.
5. Shower after excavation; if this is not possible, nose and face cleaning is recommended.
6. Have coccidioidomycosis and hantavirus tests done if you are feeling sick after fieldwork in endemic areas.

Figure 14.2.   A dust-filtering repiratory mask. Illustration by Teresa Moreno.

Figure 14.3.   Lab coat. Illustration by Teresa Moreno.

Figure 14.4.   Removal of disposable gloves. Illustration by Teresa Moreno.

PERSONAL PROTECTIVE EQUIPMENT GUIDELINES

Nancy Odegaard

Editors' note: These guidelines are aimed at museum workers and cultural representatives who may be required to handle artifacts that have been contaminated with pesticide residues.

Personal protective equipment is used to prevent inhalation, ingestion, skin absorption, or transporting contaminants out of the work area.

Air-Purifying Respirators

An air-purifying respirator is a protective device used to protect the wearer from inhaling harmful contaminants. It removes contaminants from the air using a filter (for particles) or absorbent cartridges (for specific organic vapors, acid gases, and mercury vapor). Before using a respirator, the user should be medically certified, fully trained, and fitted, as required by the U.S. Occupational Safety and Health Administration (OSHA). Facial hair, even stubble, will prevent a good fit.

Air-purifying respirators are available in both disposable and reusable styles. Disposable N-95 respirators are lightweight masks covering the nose and mouth. They are useful for low-level exposures to oil-free dusts, powders, and mists. Examples include residues of pesticides and metals, clay, silica, wood dust, plant fibers, and mold. N-95 respirators should be discarded when soiled or when breathing resistance increases. Respirators labeled N-95 OV remove both particles and nuisance levels of organic vapors.

Note that products labeled "dust masks" or "surgical masks" do not protect the user from residual pesticides or other toxic particles.

Reusable cartridge respirators are needed where airborne contaminant levels may exceed OSHA levels. The user is protected only if using the correct cartridge for the specific contaminant. Cartridges are color coded for the contaminant removed.

For example, magenta P-100 cartridges remove toxic particles, and yellow cartridges remove organic vapors and acid gases. Additional information is available from OSHA, respirator manufacturers, and safety catalogs.

Do not crumple masks or respirators before or during use. Discard them by placing them into a polyethylene bag before disposal.

Protective Apparel: Lab Coats, Smocks, and Aprons

A properly designed garment made of suitable protective material should be worn over exposed areas of the body. Cotton or alternative materials such as Tyvek or Kleenguard provide practical and economical ways to protect clothing from dirt, dusts, and most particulates.

To be effective, protective garments should cover the front of the body and the arms. They also must be maintained, cleaned, and inspected regularly for damage.

Protective Gloves

The hands are the part of the body most likely to come into contact with pesticide residues during the handling of artifacts. Some pesticide chemicals can go through the skin and can cause illness in other parts of the body. Wearing gloves helps protect people from skin irritation and other effects of chemical exposures.

Protective gloves are available in a variety of materials and designs. The selection of gloves should be based on the potential and severity of possible chemical exposure as well as their suitability for the operation performed. Chemical, puncture, tear and abrasion resistance, and degree of dexterity required all must be considered in glove selection (technical representatives of major glove manufacturers are good resources to consult). Gloves made of materials such as nitrile rubber, neoprene, polyvinyl chloride (PVC), and butyl rubber offer good protection to a range of

PERSONAL PROTECTIVE EQUIPMENT GUIDELINES (*continued*)

pesticide products and are particularly appropriate for those containing organic solvents. Disposable, powder-free nitrile gloves offer puncture resistance, comfort, and dexterity and are a suitable choice for handling potentially contaminated specimens.

Gloves should be selected that fit the hands comfortably and that are flexible enough to grip artifacts. To determine your proper hand size, use a tape measure to find the circumference of your hand around the palm. This measurement, in inches, is the closest to glove size. Most gloves are sized according to a man's hand:

Glove size:	XS	S	M	L	XL
Hand size:	6–7	7–8	8–9	9–10	10–11

Gloves should be examined carefully before use for any signs of wear or tear, particularly in the areas between the fingers. If there is any doubt about their protectiveness, they should be replaced. Use of damaged or worn gloves or the wrong type can actually increase the hazards because skin absorption is enhanced through the confined skin contact within the glove.

The face or any other exposed parts of the body should not be touched when wearing the gloves.

Follow these steps to remove gloves that have been used for handling artifacts contaminated by pesticides:

1. Using the fingers of one gloved hand, pinch the other glove at the base of the palm, and peel off the glove.
2. Continue to hold the glove and with the ungloved hand reach about an inch under the other glove on the palm side of the wrist; then pinch and peel off the other glove.
3. Once both gloves have been removed without skin contact and the contaminated sides of the gloves are facing in, they should be disposed of and should not be used again.

REFERENCES

Abbott Ken D., Thomas G. Ksiazek, and James N. Mills
1999 Long-Term Hantavirus Persistence in Rodent Populations in Central Arizona. *Emerging Infectious Diseases* 5(1):102–112.

Abernathy, Charles O., Yung-Pin Liu, David Longfellow, H. Vasken Aposhian, Barbara Beck, Bruce Fowler, Robert Goyer, Robert Menzer, Toby Rossman, Claudia Thompson, and Michael Waalkes
1999 Arsenic: Health Effects, Mechanisms of Actions, and Research Issues. *Environmental Health Perspectives* 107:593–597.

ATS Statement
1995 Standards for the Diagnosis and Care of Patients with Chronic Obstructive Pulmonary Disease. *American Journal of Respiratory and Critical Care Medicine* 152:S78–S119.

Bellinger, David C.
2004 Lead. *Pediatrics* 113(4):1016–1022.

Blair, Janis E., Jerry D. Smilack, and Sean M. Caples
2005 Coccidioidomycosis in Patients with Hematologic Malignancies. *Archives of Internal Medicine* 165(1):113–117.

Breternitz, David A.
1972 Comments on Lung Fungus and Archaeology in Colorado. *All Points Bulletin* 9:6. Newsletter of the Denver Chapter, Colorado Historical Society.

Centers for Disease Control and Prevention
2004 Navajo Medical Traditions and HPS. In *All about Hantaviruses*. Electronic document, http://www.cdc.gov/ncidod/diseases/hanta/hps/noframes/navajo.htm, accessed May 23, 2006.

DeFilippis, Victor R., and Luis Villarreal
2001 Viral Evolution. In *Fields Virology*, 4th ed., edited by David M. Knipe and Peter M. Howley. Lippincott Williams and Wilkins, Philadelphia.

Engelthaler, David, Craig Levy, Michael Fink, Dale Tanda, and Ted Davis
1998 Short Report: Decrease in Seroprevalence of Antibodies to Hantavirus in Rodents from 1993–1994: Hantavirus Pulmonary Syndrome Case Sites. *American Journal of Tropical Medicine and Hygiene* 58(6):737–738.

Enscore, Russell, Brad Biggerstaff, Ted Brown, Ralph Fulgham, Pamela Reynolds, David Engelthaler, Craig Levy, Robert Parmenter, John Montenieri, James Cheek, Richie Grinnel, Paul Ettestal, and Kenneth Gage
2002 Modeling Relationships between Climate and Frequency of Human Plague Cases in the Southwestern United States, 1960–1997. *American Journal of Tropical Medicine and Hygiene* 66:186–196.

Ferguson, Rob
2001 Histoplasmosis: The Poop on Occupational Mycoses in Archaeological Contexts. In *Dangerous Places: Health, Safety, and Archaeology*, edited by David A. Poirier and Kenneth L. Feder. Bergin & Garvey, Westport, Connecticut.

Fink, Jordan N., Hector G. Ortega, Herbert Y. Reynolds, Yvon F. Cormier, Leland L. Fan, Teri J. Franks, Kathleen Kreiss, Steven Kunkel, David Lynch, Santiago Quirce, Cecile Rose, Robert P. Schleimer, Mark R. Schuyler, Moises Selman, Douglas Trout, and Yasuyuki Yoshizawa
2005 Needs and Opportunities for Research in Hypersensitivity Pneumonitis. *American Journal of Respiratory and Critical Care Medicine* 171(7):792–198.

Fink, Michael
2001 Of Mice and Man: What Archaeologists Should Know about Hantavirus and Plague in North America. In *Dangerous Places: Health, Safety, and Archaeology*, edited by David A. Poirier and Kenneth L. Feder. Bergin & Garvey, Westport, Connecticut.

Galgiani, John
2000 *Coccidioides immitis*. In *Principles and Practices of Infectious Diseases*, 5th ed., edited by G. L. Mandell, J. E. Bennett, and R. Dolin, pp. 2746–2757. Churchill Livingstone, Philadelphia.

Girard, Jessica M., David M. Wagner, Amy J. Vogler, Christine Keys, Christopher J. Allender, Lee C. Drickamer, and Paul Keim
2004 Differential Plague-Transmission Dynamics Determine *Yersinia pestis* Population Genetic Structure on Local, Regional, and Global Scales. *Proceedings of the National Academy of Science USA* 101(22):8408–8413.

Graeme, Kimberlie A., and Charles V. Pollack Jr.
1998 Heavy Metal Toxicity, Part I: Arsenic and Mercury. *Journal of Emergency Medicine* 16(1):45–56.

Harrison, William R., Charles F. Merbs, and Chester R. Leathers
1991 Evidence of Coccidioidomycosis in the Skeleton of an Ancient Arizona Indian. *Journal of Infectious Diseases* 164(2):436–437.

Hegab, Ahmed E., Tohru Sakamoto, Wataru Saitoh, Hosam Massoud, Hosny Massoud, Khalid Hassanein, and Kiyohisa Sekizawa
2004 Polymorphisms of IL4, IL13, and ADRB2 Genes in COPD. *Chest* 126(6):1832–1839.

Hendrick, David J.
1996 Occupation and Chronic Obstructive Pulmonary Disease. *Thorax* 51:947–955.

Jaga, Kushik, and Denton Brosius
    1999 Pesticide Exposure: Human Cancers on the Horizon. *Reviews on Environmental Health* 14(1):39–50

Johnston, Michael V., and Gary W. Goldstein
    1998 Selective Vulnerability of the Developing Brain to Lead. *Current Opinion in Neurology* 11:689–693.

Kolmodin-Hedman, Brigitta, Göran Blomquist, and Eva Sikstrom
    1986 Mould Exposure in Museum Personnel. *International Archives of Occupational and Environmental Health* 57:321–323.

Kurowski, Rene, and Michael Ostapchuk
    2002 Overview of Histoplasmosis. *American Family Physician* 66(12):2247–2252.

Lee, Ho W., Pyung W. Lee, and Karl M. Johnson
    1978 Isolation of the Etiologic Agent of Korean Hemorrhagic Fever. *Journal of Infectious Diseases* 137:289–308.

Louie, Leslie, Susanna Ng, Rana Hajjeh, Royce Johnson, Duc Vugia, S. Benson Werner, Ronald Talbot, and William Klitz
    1999 Influence of Host Genetics on the Severity of Coccidioidomycosis. *Emerging Infectious Diseases* 5(5):672–680.

Maes, Piet, Jan Clement, Irina Gavrilovskaya, and Marc Van Ranst
    2004 Hantaviruses: Immunology, Treatment, and Prevention. *Viral Immunology* 17(4):481–497.

Mann, Jessica M., William J. Martone, John M. Boyce, Arnold F. Kaufmann, Allan M. Barnes, and Neil S. Weber
    1979 Endemic Human Plague in New Mexico: Risk Factors Associated with Infection. *Journal of Infectious Diseases* 140:397–401.

Marennikova, Svetlana S., E. M. Shelukhina, O. A. Zhukova, N. N. Yanova, and V. N. Loparev
    1990 Smallpox Diagnosed 400 Years Later: Results of Skin Lesions Examination of 16th Century Italian Mummy. *Journal of Hygiene, Epidemiology, Microbiology, and Immunology* 34(2):227–231.

Morse, Stephen S.
    1994 Hantaviruses and the Hantavirus Outbreak in the United States: A Case Study in Disease Emergence. *Annals of the New York Academy of Sciences* 740:199–207.

National Institute for Occupational Safety and Health
    1979 *Health Hazard Evaluation Report.* No. HHE 78-095-596. National Institute for Occupational Safety and Health, Cincinnati, Ohio.

Needleman, Herbert
    2004 Lead Poisoning. *Annual Review of Medicine* 55:209–222.

Odegaard, Nancy
    2001 Methods to Mitigate Risks from Use of Contaminated Objects, Including Methods to Decontaminate Affected Objects. *Collection Forum* 17(1–2):117–121.

Odegaard, Nancy, and Alyce Sadongei
    2005 *Old Poisons, New Problems: A Museum Resource for Managing Contaminated Cultural Materials.* AltaMira, Walnut Creek, California.

Osorio, Ana Maria
    2001 Tribal Repatriation of Sacred Objects: Public Health Issues. *Collection Forum* 17(1-2):82–92.

Palmer Peter T., M. Martin, G. Wentworth, N. Caldararo, L. Davis, S. Kane, and D. Hostler.
  2003 Analysis of pesticide residues on museum objects repatriated to the Hupa tribe of California. *Environmental Science & Technology* 15 37(6):1083–8.

Pauwels, Romain A., and Klaus F. Rabe
  2004 Burden and Clinical Features of Chronic Obstructive Pulmonary Disease (COPD). *Lancet* 364(9434):613–620.

Perera, Phillip, and Susan Stone
  2002 Coccidioidomycosis in Workers at an Archeologic Site—Dinosaur National Monument, Utah, June–July 2001. *Annals of Emergency Medicine* 39(5):566–569.

Perry, Robert D., and Jacqueline D. Fetherston
  1997 *Yersinia pestis*—Etiologic Agent of Plague. *Clinical Microbiology Review* 10:35–66.

Petersen, Lyle R., Stacie L. Marshall, Christine Barton-Dickson, Rana A. Hajjeh, Mark D. Lindsley, David W. Warnock, Anil A. Panackal, Joseph B. Shaffer, Maryam B. Haddad, Frederick S. Fisher, David T. Dennis, and Juliette Morgan
  2004 Coccidioidomycosis among Workers at an Archeological Site, Northeastern Utah. *Emerging Infectious Diseases* 10(4):637–642.

Prusiner, Stanley B.
  1982 Novel Proteinaceous Infectious Particles Cause Scrapie. *Science* 216(4542):136–144.
  1998 Prions. *Proceedings of the National Academy of Science USA* 95(23):13363–13383.

Putzker, Michael, Henner Sauer, and Dirck Sobe
  2001 Plague and Other Human Infections Caused by *Yersinia* Species. *Clinical Laboratory* 47(9–10): 453–466.

Rang, Camilla U., Riitta Mikkola, Sören Molin, and Patricia L. Conway
  1997 Ribosomal Efficiency and Growth Rates of Freshly Isolated *Escherichia coli* Strains Originating from the Gastrointestinal Tract. *FEBS Letters* 418(1–2):27–29.

Ratnaike, Ranjit N.
  2003 Acute and Chronic Arsenic Toxicity. *Postgraduate Medical Journal* 79(933):391–396.

Roueché, Berton
  1986 Annals of Medicine. Cinnabar. *New Yorker*, December 8, 94–102.

Rutala William A., and David J. Weber
  2001 Creutzfeldt-Jakob Disease: Recommendations for Disinfection and Sterilization. *Clinical Infectious Diseases* 32(9):1348–1356.

Schmaljohn, Connie M.
  1996 *Molecular Biology of Hantaviruses.* Plenum Press, New York.

Schmaljohn, Connie, and Brian Hjelle
  1997 Hantaviruses: A Global Disease Problem. *Emerging Infectious Diseases* 3(2):95–104.

Schwartz, B. S., W. F. Stewart, K. I. Bolla, D. Simon, K. Bandeen-Roche, B. Gordon, J. M. Links, and A. C. Todd
  2000 Past Adult Lead Exposure Is Associated with Longitudinal Decline in Cognitive Function. *Neurology* 55:1144–1150.

Smith, Kenneth G. V.
  1987 *A Manual of Forensic Entomology.* Cornell University Press, Ithaca, New York.

Smith, Barbara, and Bill Coulehan

    2002   Potential Exposure to Arsenic and Other Highly Toxic Chemicals When Handling Museum Artifacts. *Applied Occupational and Environmental Hygiene* 17(11):741–743.

Spiewak, Radoslaw

    2001   Pesticides as a Cause of Occupational Skin Diseases in Farmers. *Annals of Agricultural and Environmental Medicine* 8(1):1–5.

Steadman, Lyle B., and Charles F. Merbs

    1982   Kuru and Cannibalism? *American Anthropologist* 84:611–627.

Stone, Richard

    2002   Public Health: Is Live Smallpox Lurking in the Arctic? *Science* 295(5562):2002.

Taubenberger, J. K., A. H. Reid, R. M. Lourens, R. Wang, G. Jin, and T. G. Fanning

    2005   Characterization of the 1918 Influenza Virus Polymerase Genes. *Nature* 437(7060):889–893.

Tumpey, Terrence M., Christopher F. Basler, Patricia V. Aguilar, Hui Zeng, Alicia Solórzano, David E. Swayne, Nancy J. Cox, Jacqueline M. Katz, Jeffery K. Taubenberger, Peter Palese, and Adolfo García-Sastre

    2005   Characterization of the Reconstructed 1918 Spanish Influenza Pandemic Virus. *Science* 310(5745):77–80.

Ugenskienė, Rasa, Marek Sanak, Raimundas Sakalauskas, and Andrew Szczeklik

    2005   Genetic Polymorphisms in Chronic Obstructive Pulmonary Disease. *Medicina (Kaunas, Lithuania)* 41(1):17–22.

Wells, Rachel M., Sergio Sosa Estani, Zaida E. Yadon, Delia Enria, Paula Padula, Noemi Pini, James N. Mills, Clarence J. Peters, Elsa L. Segura, and the Hantavirus Pulmonary Syndrome Study Group for Patagonia

    1997   An Unusual Hantavirus Outbreak in Southern Argentina: Person-to-Person Transmission? *Emerging Infectious Diseases* 3(2):171–174.

Werner, S. Benson, Demosthenes Pappagianis, Irena Heindl, and Arthur Mickel

    1972   An Epidemic of Coccidioidomycosis among Archeology Students in Northern California. *New England Journal of Medicine* 286:507–512.

Wheat, L. Joseph

    1996   Histoplasmosis in the Acquired Immunodeficiency Syndrome. *Current Topics in Medical Mycology* 7:7–18.

    2003   Current Diagnosis of Histoplasmosis. *Trends in Microbiology* 11(10):488–494.

White, Roberta F., Robert Diamond, Susan Proctor, C. Morey, and Howard Hu

    1993   Residual Cognitive Deficits 50 Years after Lead Poisoning during Childhood. *British Journal of Industrial Medicine* 50:613–622.

Yokoyama, K., S. Araki, and H. Aono

    1988   Reversibility of Psychological Performance in Subclinical Lead Absorption. *Neurotoxicology* 9:405–410.

CHAPTER 15

The Law of Human Remains and Burials

SHERRY HUTT AND JENNIFER RIDDLE

The day is not far distant when the students of the law, the teachers of the law, and the examiners in the law will be dissatisfied with an equipment of knowledge which attempts only the dogmatic side, and neglects the universal, and even the specific historical background of legal institutions.

—John H. Wigmore, 1915 (the father of anthropology of the law upon his study of 5,000 years of legal tradition including treatment of human remains)

WHEN ENCOUNTERING HUMAN REMAINS IN COLLECTIONS OR ARCHAEOLOGICAL SITES IN GENERAL, there are layers of state, federal, and international laws that build on the common law to be considered. Issues of legality and ethics come together to create an intricate dance that can often leave the archaeologist confused and wondering if he or she is working within the confines of good science and the law. This chapter, while by no means a "how-to guide," will attempt to aid researchers in their quest to act responsibly by discussing the universal common law as well as international laws and United States state and federal laws governing archaeological resources and investigations.

Given the many-layered laws pertinent to human remains that have evolved over time, this treatment of the topic is itself archaeology of the law. This discussion will begin at the bottom stratum—that is, the foundation of law still in effect, the common law of the dead and burials. This level is that of the law of organized communities, families, cultures, and social groups. The next level ascending is the law of political entities, the laws of nations. It is not possible in this one chapter to be all inclusive as a survey of nations. Instead, the laws of nations will be referred to as they have given the subject particular attention, because of extrinsic pressure, looting, or intrinsic recognition of human rights of indigenous minority groups. The next stratum of this archaeological/legal inquiry will address state and local laws, including zoning, health and safety codes, and the protection measures since 1989, when *National Geographic* shed light on rampant looting and called on the United States to examine its humanity. The top stratum is composed of the court-made law, cases in the United States and other countries, which impact the curation of human remains.

Given the complexity and plethora of existing laws, the caveat of this chapter must be stated explicitly and early on: this chapter is *not* an official guide to laws. With old laws constantly being amended and new laws promulgated, it is impossible to make this chapter a step-by-step guide to the legalities of dealing with human remains anywhere in the United States or the world. Instead, the intent is to give the reader a familiarity with the most important laws, present the issues that someone working in the field will encounter, and recommend further resources for those who need specific information for a particular area.

THE COMMON LAW

The common law is the root form of all law in present day civil society. It is also a body of living law that functions to set parameters on conduct, in tandem with statutory authority or, in the absence of specific legislative guidance, as sole authority by default. Civil courts will rely on common law and statutes in rendering decisions. Common law is most aptly described as the unwritten, generally understood mores regulating the interaction of inhabitants of a region.[1]

The common law of human remains and burials in the United States, for example, is derived from the common laws of England, Spain, and France. While each of these contributing sources has some differences, most notably in the succession of real estate upon death or dissolution of marriage, they are united in the regard for human remains and burials. While landowners typically have rights to all that is embedded in their land, all of the common law sources regard human remains as "quasi-property"[2]—that is, not subject to such ownership. The descendents retain rights of control and access and obligations for care in their deceased ancestors, regardless of where they are buried.

Oliver Wendell Holmes, the well-known jurist, and John Wigmore, the law professor best known for his writings on the rules of evidence, attribute the similarity to the common derivation from Roman law.[3] In Roman law, human remains were regarded as the eternal responsibility of the eldest son to care for in the tomb of ancestors. Human remains and burials were not thought of as property but as *res religiosae*—that is, sacred property that is *res omnium commercium*, not transferable in the marketplace. In Roman law, so sacrosanct was the burial place that even those individuals held as slaves during their lifetime were released from servitude at death to allow the family the ability to care for the remains and burial site in perpetuity. This rule was followed in the United States in the slavery period, when slaves were released on death to their families, so that the families would have the ability to attend to the disposition of the remains.[4] Retention or dismemberment of the bodies of former slaves only occurred as punishment for errant behavior or to protect against rebellion by the living.[5] Grave robbing was one of the earliest identified crimes.

In modern times, the quasi-property theory of human remains and burials has persisted, regardless of age, location of the burial, or ownership of the land. Wrongful exhumation of bodies gives rise to criminal sanctions of theft, civil sanctions of trespass, and tort claims for damages by the aggrieved descendents who become distraught at the damage or exhumation of burials.[6] The legal remedy is to enjoin the possessor from continuing to hold the remains in hostile possession to the rights of the descendants, who have the obligations of care and in whom custody should be enforced. Thus, one does not return human remains in the common law, so much as they cease to be possessed wrongfully. Damages arise from entry into the grave without permission from the descendents and from the denial of their access to a grave, human remains, and grave goods, which under the common law are all considered grave desecration. The tort of grave desecration arises from interference with the customary obligations of the descendent causing anguish.

INTERNATIONAL CONVENTIONS AND THE LAWS OF NATIONS

International Conventions

The international community often comes together in a series of conventions to discuss various issues affecting countries around the world. At these conventions, provided people can agree with each other, accords are passed that form the basis of international law. The word *law* can be somewhat misleading, however, given that there is no international enforcement agency that supersedes state sovereignty. Nonetheless, if the powers that be in a given country agree with the accord, the country will sign the accord and, in nations such as the United States, pass a law through Congress stating that it is bound to the provisions of the accord. Once countries have signed the accords they become binding agreements. These are important distinctions because they illustrate that while there are international agreements detailing how cultural resources around the world should be handled, it is up to the individual country to actually enforce these international "laws."

Most of the international agreements with regard to cultural property were contained within peace accords resulting from international armed conflict. Examples of early treaties that formed the basis of international law of cultural property are as follows:

- *Treaty on Friendship and General Relations* between the United States and the Kingdom of Spain, 1902. This accord pertained to the retention of national ownership of sunken vessels once located.[7] It was invoked one hundred years later to assert the rights of Spain over those of treasure salvers off the coast of Virginia.
- *Hague Convention*, 1907,[8] which protected personal property, artwork, and cultural items from being carried off as spoils of war. Forty countries ratified the agreement, including the United States, Britain, France, Germany, and Russia.
- *Treaty of Versailles*, 1919, which gave the Allies the ability to return stolen items and obtain reparations for items that were destroyed
- *Roerich Pact*, 1935,[9] which accorded neutral status in times of war to artistic and scientific institutions

Hague Convention

UNESCO (described in the next section) was founded in 1945, and one of the first cultural property conventions to come forth was the Hague Convention, or the 1954 Convention for the Protection of Cultural Property in the Event of Armed Conflict.[10] As its name implies, the participant countries were worried about damage to "cultural property" (which included architecture, art, and archaeological materials among other things) through warfare—not surprising given the state of the world at the time. The agreement is an interesting one in that it spells out the signatories' responsibility for building sites for their cultural property that can withstand basic warfare and then states the responsibilities of invading armies and occupying forces toward the artifacts. Though unrealistic to think invading forces would stop the tank for a Picasso, when it is hard enough to stop bulldozers working in the name of progress from disturbing human remains, it is nonetheless the newly formed international community's first step in recognizing the importance of cultural heritage and the need to protect it.

UNESCO

The first major convention that was not war related came in 1956 in the form of the General Conference of the United Nations Educational, Scientific and Cultural Organization (UNESCO), meeting in New Delhi. This accord speaks to the importance of cultural resources as a whole and proclaims that the entire global community is richer for the preservation of all cultural items regardless of where they are found. The accord outlines the responsibilities of participant countries in regulating archaeological investigations, setting up permit protocols, and the need for reporting all finds, stating that any unreported finds are subject to confiscation by the country in which the work is taking place. The agreement states that foreign archaeologists should have equal access to sites provided they are qualified workers. Member states are directed to set up museums to facilitate cross-cultural comparisons and international research as well as preserve cultural materials. Excavators must publish their findings and public education is made a priority.

The accord then addresses the illicit antiquities trade and encourages member states to adopt laws regulating trade and discouraging smuggling and "clandestine" excavations. Return of artifacts to the countries of origin is requested if the excavations were clandestine. The accord concludes by stating that excavations should not be undertaken in occupied territories and in the case of unexpected finds, artifacts should be returned to the country of origin after the occupation has ended.

The major international regulation in effect today came in 1970, the UNESCO Convention on the Means of Prohibiting and Preventing the Illicit Import, Export and Transfer of Ownership of Cultural Property.[11] *Cultural property* in this accord is defined as follows:

For the purposes of this Convention, the term "cultural property" means property which, on religious or secular grounds, is specifically designated by each State as being of importance for archaeology, prehistory, history, literature, art or science and which belongs to the following categories:

(a) Rare collections and specimens of fauna, flora, minerals and anatomy, and fossils;
(b) property relating to history, including the history of science and technology and military and social history, to the life of national leaders, thinkers, scientists and artists and to events of national importance;
(c) products of archaeological excavations or of archaeological discoveries;
(d) elements of artistic or historical monuments or archaeological sites which have been dismembered;
(e) antiquities more than one hundred years old, such as inscriptions, coins and engraved seals;
(f) objects of ethnological interest;
(g) property of artistic interest, such as:

(i) *pictures, paintings and drawings produced entirely by hand;*
(ii) *original works of statuary art and sculpture in any material;*
(iii) *original engravings, prints and lithographs;*
(iv) *original artistic assemblages and montages in any material;*

(h) rare manuscripts and incunabula, old books, singly or in collections;
(i) postage, revenue and similar stamps, singly or in collections;
(j) archives, including sound, photographic and cinematographic archives;
(k) articles of furniture more than one hundred years old and old musical instruments.

Human remains, though not specifically mentioned, fall under the category of cultural property in articles a–c and f. As the title implies, this accord is concerned with the import and export of cultural materials and defines the rights and responsibilities of member states in retaining their "cultural property" and making the export of artifacts without permission of the country of origin illegal. The accord states that member countries should create offices in charge of regulating artifact movement and archaeological investigations. Article 5 states:

To ensure the protection of their cultural property against illicit import, export and transfer of ownership, the States Parties to this Convention undertake, as appropriate for each country, to set up within their territories one or more national services, where such services do not already exist, for the protection of the cultural heritage, with a qualified staff sufficient in number for the effective carrying out of the following functions:

(a) Contributing to the formation of draft laws and regulations designed to secure the protection of the cultural heritage and particularly prevention of the illicit import, export and transfer of ownership of important cultural property;
(b) establishing and keeping up to date, on the basis of a national inventory of protected property, a list of important public and private cultural property whose export would constitute an appreciable impoverishment of the national cultural heritage;

(c) promoting the development or the establishment of scientific and technical institutions (museums, libraries, archives, laboratories, workshops . . .) required to ensure the preservation and presentation of cultural property;

(d) organizing the supervision of archaeological excavations, ensuring the preservation "in situ" of certain cultural property, and protecting certain areas reserved for future archaeological research;

(e) establishing, for the benefit of those concerned (curators, collectors, antique dealers, etc.) rules in conformity with the ethical principles set forth in this Convention; and taking steps to ensure the observance of those rules;

(f) taking educational measures to stimulate and develop respect for the cultural heritage of all States, and spreading knowledge of the provisions of this Convention;

(g) seeing that appropriate publicity is given to the disappearance of any items of cultural property.

The 1970 UNESCO, though not without problems, is a concerted attempt to regulate and protect cultural heritage. As of June 2003, one hundred countries had ratified the agreement, by adding the United States, making it a truly global law.[12] Critics of the 1970 UNESCO Convention believe that it focuses too much on cultural patrimony and is overly nationalistic, depending upon a nation to identify and seek to preserve sites. It does not recognize a "good faith" purchaser as most European countries do; that is, if an object was illegally exported from a country and purchased by an unsuspecting buyer in another country, under UNESCO, it would be returned to the country of origin, leaving the buyer without the object and without compensation. To rectify this situation, the 1995 UNIDROIT, United Nations International Institute for the Unification of Private Law, Convention on Stolen or Illegally Exported Cultural Objects was born.[13]

UNIDROIT
UNIDROIT requests that the possessor of stolen items return them, but it allows for compensation at a reasonable amount to be paid by the country requesting return from an otherwise good faith purchaser. The UNIDROIT Convention also states that artifacts recovered from an unreported archaeological site are considered stolen and must be returned to the country of origin. The convention provides for compensation to "owners" of disputed cultural property that is returned to another country if they can prove that they exercised due diligence in investigating the origins of the artifact before purchase. While some may find the idea of countries having to "buy back their cultural heritage" offensive, the provision encourages private collectors to return pieces to the public domain. Finally, the convention is not retroactive; therefore, museum collections in existence prior to 1995 are unaffected.[14]

In addition to global agreements, there are also regional agreements that are worth briefly mentioning. For example, the European community has passed the European Union Directive on the Return of Cultural Objects and the European Union Regulation on the Export of Cultural Goods. The agreements, involving all members of the European Union, regulate the return of cultural objects and set up uniform rules and check points at countries' borders when exporting objects.[15]

Cultural Property Implementation Act and National Stolen Property Act (NSPA)
Two U.S. laws are tied to international agreements: the Cultural Property Implementation Act (CPIA)[16] and the National Stolen Property Act (NSPA).[17] The CPIA emanates from the UNESCO Convention and allows the United States to place import restrictions on archaeological items brought into the United States, having been looted from a source country. The restrictions are put into place at the request of a member country to the Cultural Property Advisory Committee,

which makes recommendations to the president for the listing of specific items. The United States customs agents will then seize the item upon entry and hold it for the claimant nation. Such was the case in *United States v. Antique Platter of Gold*,[18] in which the purchaser of the fourth-century gold platter saw the item seized and returned to Italy. The customs forms indicated that the item was from Switzerland, in an effort to frustrate the act. The purchaser claimed that he was an innocent owner and that the forfeiture was an excessive fine. The courts held that the theories of innocent owner and fines do not apply to the civil seizure of the CPIA.

In contrast, the NSPA is a criminal law that makes it a felony to knowingly sell, transport, receive, or conceal goods valued in excess of $5,000, in interstate or foreign commerce. Protected items include those removed from a museum or a site of national patrimony identified by the source country. This law is the statutory form of the McClain doctrine, which upholds the patrimony laws of other nations and enforces them in the United States. When a defendant conspired to import stolen Egyptian antiquities by disguising them as cheap souvenirs, he received a thirty-three-month prison sentence.[19]

OTHER NATIONS

Laws pertaining to cultural property generally and human remains and burials specifically vary greatly from country to country. In some nations the laws have been formed as part of treaties and acknowledgments of indigenous cultures, while in others the laws have developed in response to rampant looting of archaeological sites. The following is merely a sample of such laws.

Australia

Australia has a history of cultural property protection laws that span the century and follow the model of national ownership, which has evolved to acknowledge ownership in indigenous groups of their cultural items and human remains. In 1906, an ethnological committee was formed to study export controls of aboriginal items. Customs controls were put into place in 1913. The Aboriginal and Torres Strait Islander Heritage Protection Act of 1984 protects sites of significance to Aboriginals from looting and desecration, although the minister of the commonwealth must determine whether a site merits protection. The Protection of Movable Cultural Heritage Act of 1986 makes it illegal to export, without a permit, the "moveable culture of Australia."

The Australian laws controlling illicit excavation and export are item specific and are not based on aboriginal custom and property rights, but rather, upon the assertion of ownership and control by the nation. However, in the 1992 landmark court decision of *Mabo v. Queensland*,[20] the High Court of Australia deferred to the common law of property ownership in the country and applied that common law to aboriginal people. The end effect was to afford Aboriginals property rights to communal property. The Native Title Act of 1993 put the court decision into legislative form as to land title, but the rule of law having been acknowledged as applying generally to aboriginal people, claims to movable cultural property have also been established. As a result of this turn of events, human remains have been repatriated to the aboriginal community, and they have been given management authority over Uluru National Park, an area of cultural importance to aboriginal people.

New Zealand

Under the 1840 Treaty of Waitangi, New Zealand ceded all rights of sovereignty to the English Crown, while reserving to the Maori, "properties which they may collectively or individually possess." While the treaty speaks of land, fisheries, and estates, it has been interpreted to include cultural items as they are inseparable from use of the land in Maori life and custom. The treaty was not an effective tool for repatriation until it was reinforced in 1975 by the Antiquities Act. This law requires that any artifact found in New Zealand is to be reported to the designated government official, who then places the matter of ownership before the Maori Land Court. The government of New Zealand has interceded on behalf of the Maori people to retrieve a tattooed head from a London action house, which was repatriated to the Maoris for disposition under Maori custom.

Canada

Canada has a Historic Sites and Monuments Act, laws for the issuance of a permit for archaeological excavation and protection legislation. "Historic sites and monuments" are defined as follows:

> "historic place" means a site, building or other place of national historic interest or significance, and includes buildings or structures that are of national interest by reason of age or architectural design.

The Historic Sites and Monuments Board makes recommendations to the Cultural Minister who may

(a) by means of plaques or other signs or in any other suitable manner mark or otherwise commemorate historic places;

(b) make agreements with any persons for marking or commemorating historic places pursuant to this Act and for the care and preservation of any places so marked or commemorated;

(c) with the approval of the Governor in Council, establish historic museums;

(d) with the approval of the Treasury Board, acquire on behalf of Her Majesty in right of Canada any historic places, or lands for historic museums, or any interest therein, by purchase, lease or otherwise; and

(e) provide for the administration, preservation and maintenance of any historic places acquired or historic museums established pursuant to this Act.

Permit regulations incorporate the following definitions:

> "Archaeological artifact" means any tangible evidence of human activity that is more than 50 years old, in respect of which an unbroken chain of possession cannot be demonstrated. (*artefact archéologique*)
>
> "Archaeological site" means a site where an archaeological artifact is found. (*lieu archéologique*)
>
> "Class 1 permit" means a permit that entitles the permittee to survey and document the characteristics of an archaeological site in a manner that does not alter or otherwise disturb the archaeological site. (*permis de classe 1*)
>
> "Class 2 permit" means a permit that entitles the permittee to survey and document the characteristics of an archaeological site, to excavate an archaeological site, to remove archaeological artifacts from an archaeological site, or, to otherwise alter or disturb an archaeological site. (*permis de classe 2*)

An application for a class 1 permit must include

• the name and qualifications of the applicant and of all persons who will be working on the proposed project;

• a description of the project, including a map and geographic coordinates of the project area; and

• the objectives of the project.

In addition, an application for a class 2 permit must include

- plans for conservation of archaeological artifacts proposed to be collected under the permit, including arrangements with the Prince of Wales Northern Heritage Centre to accept those artifacts;
- a copy of the project budget, including funds allocated for the preservation of archaeological artifacts, and a confirmation of the project funding;
- a description of the manner in which the archaeological site will be restored;
- a showing that the applicant has demonstrated the expertise in archaeology necessary to conduct the project;
- a showing that the scientific and cultural benefits of the project outweigh the adverse impact of the project on the archaeological site; and
- that the applicant has complied with all conditions precedent to obtaining such a permit set out in any applicable land claims agreement.

A person who excavates an archaeological site shall, on completion of the excavation, restore the site, as much as is practicable, to its original state. A report of work done under a class 2 permit must note the name of the permittee, the date of the report, and the permit number. It should also include, for each archaeological site visited, a description of the work undertaken, including a description of the site; a map of the site, drawn to scale, showing all archaeological features and excavation units, representative photographs of the site, measurements of the depths at which all archaeological artifacts were found and their horizontal provenience, and a catalog of all archaeological artifacts and faunal remains collected, on paper and in electronic form; a description of the methods used in data acquisition, recording, and analysis, including those used in field, archival, and laboratory investigations; a description of any archaeological artifact conservation treatments and the name of the conservator; and an interpretation of the significance of the site based on a summary examination of the findings resulting from the work.

No person shall possess or sell an archaeological artifact that was removed from an archaeological site on or after June 15, 2001, unless they hold a class 2 permit, during the term of the permit and for three months after the expiration of the permit. No person shall search for archaeological sites or archaeological artifacts, or survey an archaeological site, without a class 1 or 2 permit. The prohibition on possession does not apply to the Prince of Wales Northern Heritage Centre.

Japan
In Japan, laws have been passed to preserve and respect the modern vestiges of the Ainu culture, through allowance of practices, preservation of language, and the acknowledgment of claims to group property. Previous laws with regard to property of aboriginal people, the Hokkaido Ex-Aborigines Protection Act (#27/1899) and the Asahikawa Ex-Aborigines Protection Land Disposition Act (#9/1934), have been abolished and replaced with general laws respecting the culture of Ainu people generally. Human remains or burial items not claimed by living descendents are no longer subject to protection.

Taiwan
Taiwan provides a good representative example of what nations are beginning to assert as preservation and protection of historic and archaeological assets of a nation. As such, a detailed description follows:

- *Antiquities*—means objects having historic or artistic value that are suitable for appreciation, research, development, or promotion, or any objects being designated as such by the Ministry of Education
- *Historic sites*—means ancient buildings, traditional gathering habitations, ancient markets and streets, archaeological sites, and other historic or cultural vestiges that are designated and publicly declared as such in accordance with this act
- *Ethnic arts*—means the distinctive arts of a nation or a location
- *Folk customs and related cultural artifacts*—means the cultural artifacts in relation to food, clothing, habitation, travels, ancestor worship, beliefs, festivals, entertainment activities, and other customs or habits of the citizenry
- *Vistas of natural culture*—means the designated natural areas, animals, plants, or ores having value in being preserved for their historic culture or for the purposes of preserving nature
- *Historic buildings*—means the ancient buildings, traditional gathering habitations, ancient markets and streets, and other historic cultural vestiges that have not been designated as historic sites but have historic or cultural value

Historic sites, whether they are buried underground, submerged underwater, or exposed on the surface of the land, are considered owned by the nation. Anyone who discovers a historic site must report the discovery directly to the local government or to a local police station, which shall in turn inform the local government. The local government will then notify the Ministry of the Interior, who handles such matters.

Laws provide for the protection of historic sites at the national and city level. Both buildings and "vistas of natural culture" are protected. Antiquities not privately owned are to be recorded in the Ministry of Education. The Ministry of Education may designate antiquities that are rare and valuable as "significant antiquities" and significant antiquities that have higher cultural value as "national treasures." Private owners of antiquities may apply to the Ministry of Education for appraisal and registration of privately owned antiquities. Significant antiquities may not be transferred to a person who is not a national of the Republic of China.

The government encourages the public exhibition of privately owned antiquities by public preservation institutions. The government may purchase privately owned antiquities and encourages voluntary donations. The government also encourages private individuals and institutions to purchase and import rare and valuable antiquities of Chinese culture that are scattered in foreign countries.

Any public or private construction must immediately end if any antiquity is found during such construction and shall then be handled in accordance with the law. Permits may be given to excavate antiquities in the path of construction and the private enterprise may be compensated for the damages or losses suffered by the delay of construction.

As to permits for excavation: The excavation of antiquities shall be conducted by public preservation institutions as designated by, or scientific research institutions as approved by, the Ministry of Education, under the supervision of the Ministry of Education if they have obtained an excavation license from, and are supervised by the Ministry of Education. Should it be necessary to invite foreign experts to participate in an excavation conducted in accordance with the preceding article, an application for approval of such invitation shall be submitted to the Ministry of Education in advance.

The government promotes the development of public museums to which material confiscated or purchased by the government will be given. Historic preservation of buildings is also promoted with a 50 percent tax reduction for those listed by the ministry as historic. Owners of such buildings have an obligation to provide for their protection with fire and burglar alarms.

Ethnic arts and folk customs are also protected and may receive government assistance to ensure their continuity.

There is also a criminal sanction for those who impact cultural sites.

Any person who commits any of the following offenses shall be punished with imprisonment for not more than five years, detention, and/or a fine of not more than NT$30,000:

1. destroying or damaging public-owned antiquities;
2. destroying or damaging historic sites;
3. transferring ownership of antiquities in violation of government authority;
4. shipping national treasures or significant antiquities out of the country without applying for permission in advance, or not shipping back such national treasures or significant antiquities within the period prescribed in a permit;
5. moving or demolishing a first-class historic site without permission of the competent authority of such historic site; or
6. altering or damaging a vista of natural culture.

Such antiquities, national treasures, and significant antiquities as described in items 3 and 4 shall be confiscated. For those items that cannot be confiscated, any benefit obtained therefrom shall be collected and retained by the government.

Any person who commits any of the following offenses shall be punished with imprisonment for not more than three years, detention, and/or a fine of not more than NT$20,000:

1. excavating the antiquities without a permit; or
2. catching and hunting, netting and fishing, picking and plucking, chopping and felling, or damaging designated valuable and rare animals and plants.

Any person who commits any of the following offenses shall be punished with a fine of not more than NT$50,000:

1. transferring ownership of national treasures or significant antiquities without a prior approval from the Ministry of Education;
2. re-reproducing public-owned antiquities without the permission from, or supervision of, the original preservation institutions;
3. not immediately reporting to the competent authority, or not ceasing construction work in accordance with regulations after discovering antiquities, historic sites or cultural remains having the value of historic site, during construction, or not handling the matter in accordance with applicable provisions hereof;
4. inviting foreign nationals to excavate antiquities without approval;
5. repairing historic sites without permission;
6. not adopting necessary measures to maintain a historic site in accordance with the notification from the competent authority;
7. not repairing a historic site in accordance with its original appearance; or
8. destroying the integrity of, covering the appearance of, or obstructing the observation passage to a historic site.

UNITED STATES FEDERAL LAWS

U.S. federal law started much like international law in that there was a first attempt at regulating activity regarding cultural objects that became more refined with time. There are two types of laws: compliance and enforcement.[21] For example, the National Historic Preservation Act is a compliance law, one that requires that a federal agency require planning activities in conjunction with federally funded undertakings. The Archaeological Resources Protection Act is both an enforcement and compliance law—that is, enforcement when there is looting of cultural resources and compliance when a permit is requested.

Antiquities Act

The first major federal law designed to protect archaeological resources came in the form of 16 USC 431-433, or the American Antiquities Act of 1906.[22] This law was enacted to address the looting of sites in the west as the railroads made their way to the Pacific. It is site oriented rather than focused upon movable property. Human remains and burials would be protected in situ, and excavation of sites for the first time would be regulated by the government agency with the specific land management oversight in the form of permits issued for scientific data recovery. Section 1 of the act made it illegal to "excavate, injure, or destroy any historic or prehistoric ruin or monument, or any object of antiquity" (16 USC 431-433) located on government land without the permission of the secretary in charge of the land. If the law was broken, a fine of no more than $500 was issued with the possibility of jail time not to exceed ninety days.

Section 2 gave the president the right to designate structures or areas as national monuments—the first of which was Casa Grande Ruins in Arizona. President Theodore Roosevelt proclaimed seventeen such sites between 1906 and 1909.

Section 3 required archaeologists to obtain a permit, which initially could be issued by the secretaries of the interior, agriculture, or war, before conducting any archaeological investigations on government land (16 USC 431-433). In 1916, the National Park Service was created to manage and conserve federal lands, and some of the permitting responsibilities were transferred to it.

The permitting section of the act has been superseded by ARPA, and the criminal section has been largely superseded by ARPA and the fact that the Antiquities Act was ruled unconstitutional in the Ninth Circuit. This appellate court, which embodies the western states comprising the area of most pristine sites, found the phrase "object of antiquity" too vague to place criminal defendants on notice of the parameters of the offense.[23] The ability of the president to use the law to proclaim national monuments remains.

National Historic Preservation Act

From such humble beginnings came the much larger and far more comprehensive National Historic Preservation Act (NHPA) of 1966,[24] a very important piece of legislation that, among other things, created the National Register of Historic Places, gives grants and administers tax benefits to preserve historic areas, and establishes state and tribal historic preservation officers (SHPOs and THPOs), who oversee the administration of the law on their respective state and tribal lands. The purpose of the NHPA is in part to

- preserve a living part of our community life and development in order to give a sense of orientation to the American people;
- preserve significant historic properties from loss and substantial alteration;
- preserve irreplaceable heritage in the national interest and for future generations of Americans;
- increase knowledge of historic resources, establish better means of identifying and administering them, and improve planning and execution of federally assisted projects;
- assist state, local, and tribal governments in undertaking preservation and supporting preservation by private means, and supporting the preservation efforts of the National Trust for Historic Preservation.

Four criteria determine whether a property, district, landscape, or traditional cultural property can be deemed significant and thus entitled to the provisions of the NHPA and be eligible for listing on the National Register. The secretary of the interior's standards for assessing site significance are as follows:

A. By association with events that have made a significant contribution to the broad patterns of our history
B. Properties that have an association with the lives of persons significant in the nation's past
C. Buildings that embody distinctive characteristics, the work of a master, possess high artistic value or technology
D. Sites that have yielded or may be likely to yield information important in history or prehistory

Section 106 of NHPA requires that any project conducted on federal land or receiving federal funding must assess its potential impact on cultural resources that are, or are eligible for, listing on the National Register before it can proceed. In short, any planned construction or earth-moving activities that may impact archaeological sites, criterion D, must be preceded by an archaeological impact survey as part of the planning process. If the surveys indicate that irreplaceable resources will be lost due to construction, a treatment modality must be determined, which may include data retrieval, avoidance, or some other form of mitigating the harm to the site and the loss of knowledge that will occur. In this manner, section 106 does not stop the progress of infrastructure development; it merely asks what is the impact and what can and should be done, before the action is undertaken.

Section 110 applies section 106 to federal agency action. Each agency must set up a preservation program "for the identification, evaluation, and nomination to the National Register of Historic Places, and protection of historic properties." The agencies are responsible for issuing ARPA permits to excavate on their lands when appropriate.

The NHPA is a planning compliance law and does not have enforcement provisions. Items exhumed as part of an undertaking and mitigation activities remain the property of the landowner authority, federal, state, local, tribal, and, in some cases, private. Items that come into federal possession are subject to the Curation Regulations provided for in ARPA, as discussed later. Human remains and burials are not automatically protected by the NHPA, although there are significant sites, such as battlefields, that do contain burials of human remains.

National Historic Landmarks, whether designated by the president or Congress, are automatically considered significant and receive a higher level of protection than National Register–listed or –eligible properties. In the case of *In re the Exhumation of Meriwether Lewis*,[25] the court held that even though a law professor and media corporation had secured permission from a descendant of Lewis for an exhumation, and even though the state was ready to give permission to open the gravesite within the landmark, the National Park Service controlled the site and had authority over the National Historic Landmark in which the family had previously allowed the deceased to be permanently entombed. The state did not have authority to permit opening the grave.

Archaeological Resources Protection Act
In 1979, Congress was again moved to act for fear that looting of archaeological sites on the public land would result in the catastrophic loss of information. The Archaeological Resources Protection Act (ARPA),[26] was passed:

The purpose of this chapter is to secure, for the present and future benefit of the American people, the protection of archaeological resources and sites which are on public lands and Indian lands, and to foster increased cooperation and exchange of information between governmental authorities, the professional archaeological community, and private individuals having collections of archaeological resources and data which were obtained before October 31, 1979.

ARPA sets forth a specific permitting criteria for those who desire to excavate on federal and Indian lands, in order to ensure that the excavation, undertaken to yield information in the national interest, has the controls in place to ensure that the information will be obtained by those trained in the proper area of archeology, that the reports will be completed which give value to the enterprise and that the items will remain government property, to be curated under regulations to be established. The act also states that the permit can be revoked at any time; no permit is required for Native peoples collecting on Native lands; and in addition to a federal permit, if a non-Native person wants to excavate in Native lands, he or she must also have permission from the tribe. The issuing entity has the responsibility to monitor the permit and its conclusion, setting time limits for completion.

After regulating who can excavate when and where, the act defines the penalties for illegal collecting or destruction of archaeological resources. The penalties are much stiffer than the ones defined in the American Antiquities Act of 1906 and include both criminal and civil sanctions. The criminal penalties are for a first offense, a fine of no more than $100,000 and/or prison time of no more than a year (misdemeanor). However, if the archaeological or commercial value of the objects stolen plus the cost to repair the damage to the site is more than $500, then the offender can be fined up to $250,000 and/or spend up to two years in prison. For all subsequent violations, the offender can be fined up to $500,000 and/or get a prison sentence of up to five years. In November 2002, the United States Sentencing Commission established guidance for federal judges for all cultural resource offenses that would in many cases suggest a higher level of punishment than the statutory maximum. It is now up to Congress to amend the law to allow the guidelines full effect. In addition to fines and incarceration, the offender may be required to pay for the cost of reburial of human remains by the tribe.

Civil penalties are imposed by the land manager, who issues a notice of violation to the responsible party. The amount of the penalty assessment has no cap, as do criminal fines, and is based on the damage assessment, which details the damage to the resource and the cost of restoration and repair. To calculate the fine, the agency determines the archaeological or commercial value of the object stolen and/or the area impacted and the cost to repair the site from which the object came. If a large site is corrupted to the point that a complete excavation is the only option, the price tag could be well in the tens of thousands of dollars. For a second offense, the fine is doubled. If the land manager and the responsible party do not agree on an amount to be paid they proceed to an Administrative Law Judge court of the Department of the Interior. The first such case was brought by the U.S. Department of Agriculture, Forest Service.

In addition to, or in place of, civil penalties or criminal prosecution, the agency can seize and forfeit to the agency any vehicles or tools used in the commission of the offense. If the violation occurs on Indian country, the seized items go to the tribe. The items taken from federal or Indian land will also be subject to forfeiture.

Curation Regulations
The Curation Regulations, promulgated in 1989,[27] were authorized in ARPA and set the standard for the care and treatment of federal collections, from ARPA permits, NHPA undertakings, and general federal collections. The regulations apply to human remains and burial items while they are in federal custody.

These regulations require the following:

- The federal agency is responsible for procuring long term care.
- Repositories contracted to retain collections must have all of the conditions of care specified in the contract and the federal agency does not relinquish responsibility.
- The facility must employ professional archival practices and maintain the field notes, records, photos, and records of loans with the items. The facility must control access, security, rodents, insects, mold, breakage, temperature, and moisture changes.
- Guidance must be in place for long term loan, use, and access.

Native American Graves Protection and Repatriation Act

Perhaps the most specific of all federal human remains and burial protection legislation is the Native American Graves Protection and Repatriation Act (NAGPRA).[28] The concerns of Congress to be addressed by the law were stated by one of the sponsors, Congressman Morris Udall: "For decades, the skeletal remains of American Indians were removed from their burial sites, studied, catalogued, and relegated to the bins of museums and science. This legislation is about respecting the rights of the dead, the right to an undisturbed resting place."[29]

In 1990, after compromises reached by the archaeological, museum, and tribal communities, a bill reached the floor of Congress that the Senate passed unanimously and the House by acclamation.[30] NAGPRA provides a means for the common law of cultural property to apply to Native American and Native Hawaiian human remains, funerary objects, sacred objects, and objects of cultural patrimony. Funerary objects are placed with or intended for burials, sacred items are those used by traditional religious leaders in ceremony, and cultural patrimony is the inalienable items that help to define the culture.

Federal agencies and museums that receive federal funds must summarize their Native American and Native Hawaiian collections and enter into consultations with tribes to determine whether federally recognized tribes and Native Hawaiian organizations (NHOs) wish to make claims for repatriation of items. As to human remains and associated funerary objects, the consultation is intended to aid the museums and federal agencies in compiling an itemized inventory, such that lineal descendents and culturally affiliated tribes can make claims for repatriation. NAGPRA then builds on this consultation by providing a process for repatriation and for making decisions on competing claims.

NAGPRA is Indian law. It is located in the Indian law section of the United States Code for a reason. NAGPRA acknowledges the government to government relationship of the United States to federally recognized tribes that supersedes obligations to consult with the public as a whole on matters involving the cultural property of tribes and individual Native Americans making claims as lineal descendents.[31]

NAGPRA is divided into two distinct parts. Section 7 details the process of repatriation of NAGPRA-protected items in collections, and Section 3 addresses the disposition and immediate determination of ownership for NAGPRA-protected items prospectively excavated or discovered on federal and Indian lands.

In the repatriation process, inventories of human remains and associated funerary objects, which are item-by-item lists, are the result of consultation with tribes and summaries of the remainder of the collection are sent widely to tribes as they form the basis of information given to tribes that prompts the consultation. Inventories are sent to the National Park Service (NPS), National NAGPRA Program, as are summaries. In the inventory, the museum or federal agency makes a decision as to cultural affiliation, or the inability to determine cultural affiliation, for each individual. The law specifies the repatriation process for affiliated and "culturally unidentifiable" Native American human remains. Notices of affiliations made in inventories are published in the *Federal Register*, and a tribe may claim the remains, taking control no sooner than the thirty-first day after publication. Culturally unidentifiable human remains are subject to disposition with permission of the secretary of the interior on a case-by-case basis until future regulations establish a process. Dispositions of culturally unidentifiable human remains are also published in the *Federal Register*. The unidentifiable human remains are subject to consultation to determine whether identification can be reasonably made, until disposition occurs. When tribes or NHOs come to repatriation agreements with museums or federal agencies on cultural items—that is, unassociated funerary items, sacred items, and items of cultural patrimony—the museum or agency prepares a notice of intent to repatriate that is sent to NPS for publication in the *Federal Register*. If there are no competing claims in thirty days, on the thirty-first day repatriation can occur. As a practical matter, the tribe and the museum or federal agency begin consultation on the manner of transfer of possession once they have come to an agreement on transfer of control.

NAGPRA requires consultation with tribes and NHOs prior to the removal of human remains or funerary objects from tribal, NHO, or federal land. Where there is an agreement in place prior to the discovery of a NAGPRA-protected item, the event is called an "intentional excavation." The disposition of such items follows the agreement. When no agreement is in place, the event is called an "inadvertent discovery," and all work must cease for thirty days while consultation occurs to reach an agreement on disposition. The law assumes that advance planning is better than stopping a project to do remedial planning.

NAGPRA is property law and follows the common law of property as discussed earlier. Items in collections, perhaps long separated from the land, follow the common law of human remains and funerary items. Lineal descendents, those who can show an unbroken chain of descendency, regardless of tribal membership, can claim human remains, associated funerary objects, and, in some cases, the sacred items of their ancestor. Where there are no lineal descendents, or none making a claim, the culturally affiliated federally recognized tribe has standing to make a claim for repatriation. When there are new finds on the land, lineal descendents still have priority. Next in line are tribes for all items located on their tribal lands. Thereafter, the disposition is to the culturally affiliated tribe or NHO; and failing that, the tribe that was the aboriginal occupant of the area of the find, unless some other group with standing to make a claim can show stronger association. Those remains in collections not culturally identified are listed as "culturally unidentifiable" and those on the land not claimed remain as "unclaimed." Future regulations will guide the disposition process for unidentifiable and unclaimed human remains and funerary items.

Disputes over repatriation, section 7 determinations, are referred to the Review Committee for an advisory opinion. This is not a predicate to court action, but provides a means to have the facts examined by an expert neutral panel. Disputes can arise when more than one tribe or NHO make competing claims and the decision of the land manager or museum is questioned, or a dispute can arise between a tribe and a museum or federal agency if the claimant disagrees with a decision on cultural affiliation or lack thereof, or a dispute may question whether the item falls within NAGPRA. A tribe or NHO making an initial claim must show that they have standing to make a claim under the law, that the item is a NAGPRA-protected item, and that they have cultural affiliation. A museum may overcome the claim of a tribe, once established, if they can prove that they have the right of possession; that is, under the common law of property, they hold title that falls in a chain that began with the initial separation from the group in a manner that was with permission of the initial owner.

NAGPRA does not require that science be undertaken to make a cultural affiliation determination. It does not prohibit science, which is typically undertaken in consultation with the consulting tribes. It does allow a museum or federal agency with NAGPRA-protected items in the collection to receive permission from the secretary of the interior to retain the item until the end of the study that is of major benefit to the United States.

NAGPRA prohibits illegal trafficking of Native American human remains and cultural items.[32] As to human remains, it is illegal to sell, purchase, use for profit, or transport for sale or profit the human remains of a Native American, taken from any location, of any age, unless the actor has the right of possession, which under the common law would mean the descendent with authority to put the remains into the marketplace. One who undertakes the same activity with Native American cultural items in violation of the act also commits a crime. Violation of NAGPRA can be committed by either removing the item from federal or Indian lands, including the lands of a Native Hawaiian organization, such as an ARPA violation, or by trafficking in items from museum or federal agency collections that are subject to the repatriation provisions. For instance, a museum that retains an item for sale at an auction, when that item is a NAGPRA-protected item, has committed an act of trafficking. The first offense is a misdemeanor; the second offense is a felony. The new sentencing guidelines heighten the penalties, but require a value calculation to determine the severity of the penalty.

THE LAWS OF STATES, LOCAL GOVERNMENTS, AND TRIBES IN THE UNITED STATES

State, local, and tribal laws all impact the regulation and treatment of human remains, burials, and other cultural items. State law will include regulatory sections, such as health and safety laws for treatment of human remains and licensing for funeral homes and cemeteries, as well as a criminal code for desecration of burials and theft of cultural items from state and private land. Local governments, towns, and cities will have zoning laws which regulate the use of land, public or private. Tribal code will regulate activities on tribal lands and have a minor crimes code that applies to tribal members for actions on tribal land. The Supreme Court has determined that prosecution for major crimes in Indian country is punishable by federal law.

State Law

Most states have burial regulatory laws that place responsibility for issuing permits in a state agency and give state law enforcement authority to investigate burial desecration as a state offense. Most states protect sites on state and private land, in marked and unmarked burials. A compilation of state repatriation, reburial, and grave protection laws was prepared by the Natural Resources Conservation Service in 1997, and it remains a good overview of state law.[33] A few representative examples follow.

- *Arizona*—When human remains will be or have been found on state or private land, the Arizona State Museum must be contacted. The museum becomes the repository for repatriation not accomplished by immediate agreement. Sale of human remains or grave goods is a crime.
- *Arkansas*—The Arkansas Archaeological Survey is the permit authorizing entity. State law prohibits activity without a permit affecting human remains and burials in marked or unmarked, unregistered, or otherwise abandoned sites on public or private land.
- *California*—requires that activity cease when burials are located on state or private land. The state repatriation law affords standing to make claims to tribes that may not also be federally recognized.

- *Colorado*—In similar fashion to many states, upon the discovery of a burial the coroner and/or police are called to the scene to determine that the burial is not recent. Impact to Native American graves requires the input of the Commission on Indian Affairs.
- *Florida*—The medical examiner must first determine whether the burial is recent (i.e., seventy-five years or fewer); if older, the state archaeologist steps in to determine the familial or ethnic group associated with the burial to be contacted for disposition.
- *Hawaii*—It prefers that burials remain in situ, but when development is certain the Island Burial Council directs the reburial of human remains. For burials that are not Native Hawaiian, the Department of Natural Resources makes a determination whether to preserve or rebury the remains.
- *Ohio*—It protects burial markers and historic structures, but human remains not cognizable as individuals do not have protection.
- *Oregon*—It requires permission from Indian tribes in the vicinity of the excavation before a permit will be issued. All items retrieved in an archaeological excavation will be reinterred at the expense of the archaeologist under the supervision of the tribe.
- *Pennsylvania*—Oil and gas development is restricted in areas of archaeological sites. A treatment plan for human remains is required prior to excavation.
- *Texas*—Protections include aboriginal campsites, dwellings, and habitation sites. The Texas Historical Commission is responsible for issuing permits and site protection.
- *Washington*—It recognizes Indian burial grounds as irreplaceable and nonrenewable resources subject to protection on public and private lands. Inadvertently exposed burials are to be reinterred, paid for by the state. A tribe may bring a civil action against any person who violates the act.

Local Regulation

The power to zone land for particular uses stems from the police power of government to set limits on private property use in order that communities may be planned for use in a harmonious manner. Uses that endanger others, such as health issues emanating from burials or harm to descendents from the disrespectful treatment of burials, rise to the level of public nuisance. Even in a free society that exalts private land use, one may not use their land in such a way that it creates a nuisance for others, nor may anyone be involved in private pursuits at the expense of the rights of others.

Limitations on government power are embodied in the Fifth Amendment to the U.S. Constitution, which requires that individuals be compensated for a taking of their property by government action. There are numerous court cases in the historic preservation and burial law arena dealing with claims of Fifth Amendment takings for impositions on private action on private land by preservation codes. Courts typically uphold the regulations. The following examples may help explain how this occurs.

In an Iowa case, the court determined that the inability to develop a home site over a burial ground was not a Fifth Amendment taking when the builder was denied a construction permit for the desired spot on the lot.[34] The court found that the burial preexisted the private ownership of the land and there is no right to disrupt a burial and thus no obligation of the state to issue the permit. The lot was still usable for its intended purpose as a home site, just not within the building envelope that included the burial area.

In Minnesota, a couple was denied a permit to sell dirt from an ancient Indian mound on their farm for road construction fill.[35] The court found that there was no Fifth Amendment right to devastate an archaeological site and the use of the land as a farm was unimpeded. Farming was the expected economic use of the land.

In Indiana, when a couple purchased land and then chose to use it to mine for archaeological sites, they were denied a permit to do so.[36] The court found no Fifth Amendment taking to occur as excavation permits are not issued as a matter of right.

Tribal Code

In 1992, the Historic Preservation Act was amended to create Tribal Historic Preservation Officers (THPOs), who function on tribal land in the place of State Historic Preservation Officers for the state in which the tribal lands are located. THPOs provide a means for contractors to have a contact officer for activities which may impact sites of historic or cultural interest of the tribe and they serve to administer the NHPA and tribal code on tribal lands. Fifty-seven tribes now have THPOs.[37]

Tribal preservation codes and preservation offices predated 1992 and even the 1966 passage of the NHPA. The Coeur D'Alene tribe had a grave desecration law enacted in 1962 and the Yakima Nation graves protection law dates to 1953. The Navajo Nation had a permitting provision for archaeological excavations nine years before ARPA was enacted in 1979, and the Zuni had a similar code in 1972.

CASE LAW OF HUMAN REMAINS AND BURIALS

The United States has a long history of court decisions which pertain to human remains and burials. In the 1829 case of *Beatty v. Kurtz*,[38] the United States Supreme Court resolved an issue regarding privatization of church property including the cemetery. The Court held that, although the group was not incorporated and although none of the congregation who brought the suit was a trustee, they all had standing to sue over use of their common church property, under the theory that they were all voluntary members of a society of common interest. In 1896, the Supreme Court held that preserving battlefields is in the national interest.[39]

Burials as Treasure Trove

The common law of finds that may apply to treasure trove does not apply to burials in the United States. Burials are considered intentional placements and not abandoned property. In the state court case of *Charrier v. Bell*, the individual digging on private property without permission of the private landowner, and eventually the state, when the plantation became a state park, could not claim that Indian gravesites were treasure trove and thus available for him to find.[40]

Permits

Permits are required for archaeological excavation and there is no constitutional right to a permit. This was the holding in *United States v. Austin*, which upheld a criminal conviction for digging in a cave on BLM land without a permit.[41] However, the trial court in *Bonnichsen v. United States*[42] distinguished Austin, saying that had Austin wished to conduct scientific study instead of merely sell the human remains he may have been justified in his actions. The plaintiffs in this civil action requested possession of human remains and an "access to study." The *Bonnichsen* court determined that ARPA did apply, and the court would issue an ARPA permit, although it later reviewed the ARPA permit provisions and determined that being restrictive the parties could meet instead and devise a scope of work by court order. By not following the requirements of ARPA, the court created a standard in the Ninth Circuit that established a means to circumvent the act.

Native American Human Remains

The *Bonnichsen* court also determined that before NAGPRA can apply to very old human remains, it must be determined that there is a significant relationship between the remains and a specific Indian tribe.[43] The court did not accept the argument of the Society for American Archaeology that Native American, which is defined as "indigenous," applies to those inhabitants of North America prior to first European contact, 1492.

In a separate case, in the state of Washington, the court upheld an action brought by a tribe against an archaeological consulting firm for mistreatment of human remains.[44] The court reasoned that the tribe was a third party beneficiary of the contract between the city and the firm.

In a claim by non-Indians for the remains of Geronimo, the court held that non-Indians did not have standing to come into court and claim the remains of an Indian, unless they were descendants with family authority to make a claim.[45]

CONCLUSION

Understanding the laws pertaining to human remains and burials is not difficult when one realizes that the laws are based on just a few consistent rules emanating from the common law. At the heart of these rules is the concept of respect for the dignity of human beings, regardless of the country or culture involved. Cultural dignity and the undertakings of science are not hostile concepts, as long as those desiring to undertake science obtain permission from those who hold the property right to the human remains and other cultural items. The advancement of knowledge is made all the more profound when the culture contributing the objects of inquiry is involved in furthering the venture.

NOTES

1. For further discussion of the common law, see Sir William Blackstone, *Commentaries on the Laws of England* (Philadelphia: William Young Birch, and Abraham Small, 1803); Roscoe Pound, *The Spirit of the Common Law* (Buffalo, N.Y.: Hein, 1968); W. S. Holdsworth, *A History of English Law*, Vol. 111 (London: Methuen, 1923); Frederick Pollock, *An Essay on Possession in the Common Law* (Oxford: Clarendon, 1888); Oliver Wendell Holmes Jr., *The Common Law* (London: Macmillan, 1881).

2. Margaret Bowman, "The Reburial of Native American Skeletal Remains: Approaches to Resolution of a Conflict," *Harvard Environmental Law Review* 13 (1989):167–208.

3. Albert Kocourek and John H. Wigmore, *Sources of Ancient and Primitive Law* (Boston: Little, Brown, 1915). Wigmore went further to trace the derivations of the common law principles to ancient Egypt.

4. Charlton McIlwain, *Death in Black and White: Death, Ritual, and Family Ecology* (Cresskill, N.J.: Hampton, 2003).

5. Douglas R. Egerton, "A Peculiar Mark of Infamy: Dismemberment, Burial and Rebelliousness in Slave Societies," in *Mortal Remains*, ed. N. Isenberg and A. Burstein (Philadelphia: University of Pennsylvania Press, 2003). But see also *Bones in the Basement: Postmortem Racism in Nineteenth-Century Medical Training*, ed. R. L. Blakely and J. Harrington (Washington, D.C.: Smithsonian Institution Press, 1997), discussing that while African Americans were not treated as humans in life, their bodies were used without permission of their families for medical research, a fact revealed in 1989 at the Medical College of Georgia, Augusta.

6. Bowman, "The Reburial," 167.

7. 33 Stat. §22105, July 3, 1902.

8. 36 Stat. §2277, Oct. 18, 1907.

9. 168 U.N.T.S. 289, April 15, 1935.

10. 249 U.N.T.S. 240, May 14, 1954.

11. 823 U.N.T.S. 231, 1972.

12. See www.unescosources.org.

13. 86 Stat. 1297, 19 U.S.C. §§2091–2095.

14. For more information on international conventions, recommendations, and charters regarding historic preservation, see www.international.ICOMOS.org/e_charte.htm.

15. See, generally, State Department, www.exchanges.stte.gov/education/culprop.

16. 18 U.S.C. §§542–545, 19 U.S.C. §1593.

17. 18 U.S.C. §§2314–2315.

18. 991 F. Supp. 222 (S.D.N.Y. 1997), aff'd 184 F.3d 131 (2nd Cir. 1999).

19. *United States v. Schultz,* 333 F.3d 393 (2nd Cir. 2003).

20. No. 2 175 C.L.R. 1.

21. For further explanation of the law, see Sherry Hutt, Caroline M. Blanco, and Ole Varmer, *Heritage Resources Law: Protecting the Archeological and Cultural Environment* (New York: Wiley, 1999).

22. For a thorough discussion of the Antiquities Act, see Mark Squillace, "The Monumental Legacy of the Antiquities Act of 1906," *Georgia Law Review* 37 (2003):473; and Ron Lee, *The Antiquities Act of 1906, 1970,* due to be released in 2006 by the NPS upon the centennial of the act.

23. *United States v. Diaz,* 499 F.2d 113 (9th Cir. 1974).

24. 16 U.S.C. §470a–x.

25. 999 F. Supp. 1066 (M.D.Tenn. 1998).

26. 16 U.S.C. §470aa–mm.

27. 36 CFR Part 79, September 1989.

28. 25 U.S.C. §§3001–3013, November 16, 1990.

29. Morris Udall, 136 Cong. Rec. E3484 (1990).

30. For detailed treatment of the legislative process and events of the first twelve years of the law, see T. Mckeown and S. Hutt, "In the Smaller Scope of Conscience: The Native American Graves Protection and Repatriation Act, Twelve Years After," *UCLA Journal of Environmental Law and Policy* 21 (2002–2003):153–212.

31. 25 U.S.C. §3010.

32. 18 U.S.C. §1170.

33. Order number 40-3A75-7-102.

34. *Hunziker v. State,* 519 N.W.2d 367 (Iowa 1994).

35. *Thompson v. City of Redwing,* 455 N.W.2d 512 (Minn. App. 1990).

36. *Whitacre v. Indiana,* 619 N.E.2d 605 (Indiana App., 5th Dis. 1993).

37. For information on THPOs, see www.NATHPO.org.

38. 27 U.S. 566 (1829).

39. *United States v. Gettysburg Electric Railway,* 160 U.S. 668, 1896.

40. 496 F.2d 601 (La. App., 1st Cir. 1986).

41. 902 F.2d 743 (9th Cir. 1990).

42. 9969 F. Supp. 628 (D. Or. 1997).

43. F.3d (9th Cir. 2004).

44. *Lummi Nation v. Golder Associates, Inc.,* 236 F. Supp.2d 1183 (W.D. Wash. 2002).

45. *Idrogo v. United States,* 18 F. Supp.2d 25 (D.D.C. 1998).

FURTHER READING

Craib, Donald Forsyth
   2000   *Topics in Cultural Property Law.* Society for American Archaeology, Washington, D.C.

Cunningham, Richard B.
   1999   *Archaeology, Relics, and the Law.* Carolina Academic Press, Durham, North Carolina.

Gerstenblith, Patty
   1995   Identity and Cultural Property: The Protection of Cultural Property in the United States. *Boston University Law Review* 75:559–688.

Hutt, Sherry, Caroline Blanco, Walter Stern, and Stan Harris
    2004 *Cultural Property Law: A Practitioner's Guide to the Management, Protection, and Preservation of Heritage Resources.* American Bar Association, Chicago.

Jackson, Percival E.
    1950 *The Law of Cadavers and of Burial and Burial Places.* Prentice Hall, Upper Saddle River, New Jersey.

King, Thomas F.
    1998 *Cultural Resources Laws and Practice.* AltaMira Press, Lanham, Maryland.

Phelan, Marilyn
    1998 *The Law of Cultural Property and Natural Heritage: Protection, Transfer and Access.* Kalos Kapp Press, Evanston, Illinois.

Price III, Marcus
    1991 *Disputing the Dead: U.S. Law on Aboriginal Remains and Grave Goods.* University of Missouri Press, Columbia.

Richman, Jennifer, and Marion Forsyth
    2003 *Legal Perspectives on Cultural Resources.* AltaMira Press, Lanham, Maryland.

CHAPTER 16

Respect for the Dead, Respect for the Living

LYNN S. TEAGUE

> Justice is the first virtue of social institutions, as truth is of systems of thought, . . . Each person possesses an inviolability founded on justice that even the welfare of society as a whole cannot override.
>
> —John Rawls, *A Theory of Justice*

RESPECT FOR THE DEAD, AND FOR THEIR LIVING BIOLOGICAL AND CULTURAL RELATIVES, IS ESSENTIAL IN dealing with the treatment and disposition of human remains. Few would argue with this statement, yet interpretations differ. What does it mean to act with respect in this context? It is more than avoiding obvious forms of burial desecration. It should be more than compliance with the letter of repatriation laws. It is not found in attempts to mimic indigenous customs (especially the spurious "pan-Indian" practices that are offensive to many traditional people). It cannot be a matter of simply agreeing with whatever we are asked to do. It surely is more than some special form of politeness. It is often an area in which we find substantial tension between traditions and science. How do we go about communicating and acting with respect in this difficult setting? What does it really entail? The issues related to the treatment of human remains will be examined here in the context of the idea of justice as fairness and how respect fits into this picture.

THE IDEAS OF JUSTICE, FAIRNESS, AND RESPECT

The tension between tradition and science is often framed as a contest that can have only one winner. What set of values will win? Will it be the deeply embedded concerns of a small group within society, or the search for some scientific truth that is of value to the society as a whole? These arguments are rooted not just in different specific priorities, but in different ways of understanding how priorities are determined justly.

In his important study in moral philosophy, *A Theory of Justice*, John Rawls (1999) identifies justice as fairness. He rejects utilitarian values that posit that society should override the interests of an individual or a group in pursuit of the greatest benefit to society as a whole. Rawls argues that to respect persons is to recognize that they possess an inviolability founded on justice that even the welfare of society as a whole cannot override. It is to affirm that the loss of freedom for some is not made right by a greater welfare enjoyed by others (513).

Thus, the argument that contributions to science might yield some result beneficial to society as a whole does not justify ignoring the dignity of the deceased and their relatives, as defined in their own terms. NAGPRA and many state laws give biologically and culturally related groups a substantial role in decision making, rather than automatically favoring an overall good of society. Thus, the U.S. government is coming down on the side of justice as fairness rather than utilitarianism. The introduction of repatriation law is the government's attempt to prohibit the perceived interests of society at large in scientific research from automatically triumphing over the traditional concerns of indigenous people.

However, even within the confines of federal law, decision making regarding the treatment of human remains is not a cut-and-dried matter. In cases such as Kennewick Man, the U.S. courts have demonstrated that no one set of interests will always prevail. Sometimes scientific interests will be given precedence, and in other cases indigenous interests will take precedence, depending on the circumstances of the case at issue. In the ensuing potentially complex decision-making process, it is certain that those who proceed with real respect, grounded in concern for fairness and justice, will encounter fewer problems than those clinging to an adversarial position.

The ways in which societies have defined respectful treatment of the dead are enormously diverse, and the ways in which those remains have been treated in practice are even more varied. Phillipe Ariés (1981), in *The Hour of Our Death*, discusses the many ways in which Europeans have treated the dead, through centuries of shifting belief and practice. Similarly, indigenous groups have had very different ideas about respectful ways of treating the dead, and there is abundant evidence that those ways have changed through time (Pearson 1999).

Today it is widely believed that scientific study of the remains of the dead can be both beneficial to society and respectful. A recent survey shows that many representatives of tribes and indigenous communities share this belief (Hall and Wolfley 2003). Almost half of respondents in a survey of tribal and community representatives believed that some specific kind of scientific study of human remains produced useful information. Those same respondents were likely to regard at least one form of scientific study as appropriate and respectful.

Thus, the central problem has not been failure to adhere to a single set of specific, universally acceptable practices in treatment of the dead. It is meaningless to speak of "respectful treatment" as if there were practices that, if adopted, would place the museum curator or the agency official beyond reproach. So, if there is no one set of acceptable practices, what can we do to ensure that our decision making is firmly grounded in respect?

The real problem has been that the relatives of the dead too often have been excluded from decision making. Developers, agency officials, archaeologists, and museum curators have made decisions considering only the values and priorities of their own communities of like-minded people. Repatriation laws at both federal and state levels now provide the biological and cultural relatives of the dead with specific rights that begin to correct this basic imbalance in decision making. Where can we go from there to ensure that we carry out our treatment of human remains and our repatriation activities with respect?

We cannot be certain that our decision making is firmly grounded in respect until we establish what appropriate respect entails. This brings us closer to the essence of the issue—the importance of the concepts of fairness and justice. Whose values matter, and how are they weighed in decision making? Respect requires fairness and justice, yet what do these terms really mean? The answers aren't necessarily self-evident. The kind of respect that matters in this context is rooted in our most basic concepts and beliefs and is expressed in our every action.

LEGAL COMPLIANCE

Before the passage of NAGPRA and similar state laws affecting the treatment and disposition of burials, some American Indian groups made their concerns known to museums and other institutions. For example, the Intertribal Council of Arizona's 1983 document "Guidelines for Treatment of Remains of Indian People in Archaeological Sites" was an attempt to establish

GUIDELINES FOR TREATMENT OF REMAINS OF INDIAN PEOPLE IN ARCHAEOLOGICAL SITES

ITCA Cultural Resources Working Group, 1983

Indian peoples in Arizona, like most peoples of the world, feel strongly that the remains of the deceased should not be disturbed once they are finally laid to rest. These feelings are part of the religious and cultural heritages of Indian peoples and extend to the remains of prehistoric people as well as to deceased to whom actual kin ties can be traced.

As a consequence, Indian peoples' experiences:

- Reading about or observing archaeologists digging burials
- Viewing displays of human remains in museums and exhibits have led to much distrust of archaeology as a discipline. As few Indian people are involved in the range of archaeological activity and research, these experiences come to represent archaeology. They stand out in Indian peoples' perception of what archaeologists do and what archaeology is about, symbolizing an apparent lack of respect for the dead and an insensitivity towards the feelings of the living. These perceptions are a major stumbling block to better cooperation and communication between Indian people and archaeologists.

However, tribes recognize that archaeological excavations will continue due to federal laws based on concerns for scientific recovery of data about life in the past. These excavations will often involve inhumations or cremations. Tribes are also aware that federal laws regarding cultural resources expressly recognize Indian concerns. The Archaeological Resources Protection Act requires that a tribe be given notice prior to the issuance of an excavation permit for a site which is considered to be of religious or cultural importance. The American Indian Religious Freedom Act also requires consultation with tribes regarding projects that would impact religious sites.

The following are a set of Guidelines that tribal representatives have drawn up with the Inter Tribal Council of Arizona for treatment of Indian remains in archaeological sites.

Avoidance

1. If at all possible, remains of Indian people should be avoided. They should not be disturbed.

As archaeologists cannot usually predict the location of burials, the corollary of this guideline is that excavation of any kind should be avoided unless it is <u>certain</u> that there will be land modification activities that will disturb sites.

Reinterment

2. After all options proposed by a tribe or an agency are considered and if disturbance cannot be avoided because of a project, then the remains of Indian people—inhumations or cremations—should be re-interred after scientific data have been recorded. Data collected from the analysis of human remains of Indian people must be provided to the tribe(s) and permission to report or publish sensitive data should be obtained from the tribe(s). *(Revised September 2005)*

Reinterment after scientific analysis should be as close to the original location as possible without the risk of additional disturbance by project activities, or at a site agreed to by concerned tribes.

Indian people realize that all potentially useful data from human remains cannot be predicted at any point in time and acknowledge that certain remains may be of unique scientific value requiring extensive research. Indian people also know that many skeletal and cremated remains have limited research value and sit on shelves for years, or worse, are destroyed, lost or thrown out.

If archaeologists in their professional judgment, after direct consultation with concerned tribes, and consideration of these guidelines, decide that certain remains need to be available for the future research, these should be carefully stored, catalogued, and protected.

(continued)

standards for respectful treatment of remains. In the 1970s and 1980s, museum practices began to change in response to this and similar documents, although institutional compliance was voluntary.

Now that explicit laws exist, compliance with NAGPRA (PL101-601) and with similar state laws regarding the treatment and disposition of human remains is a minimum standard for respectful treatment of human remains and their living cultural and biological relatives (see chapter 15). Numerous publications address NAGPRA compliance, and it is not necessary to review this topic in detail here. *Keepers of Culture* by Roger Echo-Hawk (2002) is especially recommended as a clear and thoughtful guide to NAGPRA.

WHOSE REMAINS?

NAGPRA is only concerned with protecting the remains of Native Americans. However, some state laws (e.g., ARS §41-844 and 41-865 in Arizona) include remains of persons of any ethnic or racial origin within their scope. With or without legal requirements, those who are responsible for human remains should extend the principles of consultation and respect to the biological and cultural relatives of all whose remains are in their care. It is not only indigenous people who have been historically disadvantaged in the power equations of our society. African Americans have seen their cemeteries go under developers' blades for lack of the political leverage to preserve them. Hispanics have seen their pioneer cemeteries become parking lots. The descendants of farming families have been unable to protect their family cemeteries once property leaves their ownership. Remains of a wide variety of ethnic and racial backgrounds can be found in museums and other institutions.

Responsible people, whether they are businessmen, agency officials, archaeologists, or museum curators, are committed to respectful and dignified treatment of the remains of the dead, regardless of the ethnic or racial origin of those remains. The cornerstone of any effort to achieve this goal must be consultation with all of the affected parties, in search of a fair and just outcome.

WHO TO CONSULT? RESPECT AND CULTURAL AFFILIATION

Deciding who is biologically or culturally related can be an extremely complex matter, especially when remains are of great age. Some of the most difficult cases to date in repatriation have focused on these issues. In addition, many remains are affected by state laws or by no laws at all, and still require establishment of cultural or biological affiliation.

The Kennewick district court decision (Jelderks 2002) has implications for how decisions regarding cultural affiliation are made when remains are subject to NAGPRA. That decision did not accept the traditional evidence submitted in that case as adequate grounds for a determination of cultural affiliation. However, Kennewick was an extreme example. The remains were older than most human remains that will be encountered in the field or in an institution. The oral traditions presented in evidence in the Kennewick case were simple assertions of residence in the region since the time of creation, without supporting detail. The Kennewick decision therefore is in no sense a wholesale rejection of oral tradition as evidence. NAGPRA itself prohibits such wholesale dismissal, and fairness also argues for the consideration of traditional histories.

Representatives of traditional communities have found wholesale dismissal of their oral traditions and histories offensive to their cultures, and a significant obstacle to their having a fair and just role in deciding the treatment and disposition of remains. At the same time, NAGPRA and many state laws, as well as sound scholarly practice, demand consideration of a wide range of forms of evidence in assessing affiliation. Works by Teague (1993, 2002, 2003) and Whiteley (2002) offer thoughts on ways to integrate oral tradition into broader considerations of group history and identity. As Whiteley (2002:408) succinctly observes:

> Both [indigenous and archaeological] claims to authority involve a politics of those who get to define what is truth in a particular social system, and such truth underwrites claims to power (cf. Foucault 1980). But some of these privileged claims must be suspended if we are to gain useful common ground. While according full epistemological respect to differently constituted histories, we need to assess the exact terms of difference, the grounds of similarity, what may be proposed as a conjoint perspective, and what must remain as difference.

This suspension of claims to power would not be satisfactory to extremists who demand unquestioning acceptance of either archaeological or traditional histories. However, this approach reflects fair and respectful consideration of those histories, which can lead to productive dialogue and reasoned and fair decision making.

This suspension of claims to power should not be confused with what Echo-Hawk (2002:78–83) describes as "negotiated cultural affiliation," which "ignores matters of evidence and shifts the focus away from research and assessment." This approach is often popular with the tribe with which an institution chooses to negotiate and is expedient for those unwilling or unable to devote resources to research, but it opens the door to many problems. Echo-Hawk goes on to accurately observe that "by including cultural affiliation as a condition for repatriation, NAGPRA requires museums and federal agencies to respect and honor the status of culturally affiliated tribes by denying claims made by tribes with no affiliation." In this as in so many other ways, real respect lies in willingness to seek the difficult but appropriate solution in preference to the easy way out. The appropriate solution may entail giving up claims of power, but it does not permit giving up concern for truth.

CONSULTATION

When we encounter the remains of the dead, we confront deep layers of meaning for ourselves and for others. Opportunities for misunderstanding are many. Nevertheless, it is consultation that lies at the heart of any respectful approach to the treatment of human remains. Because there is no one simple answer to how human remains should be treated, legally or ethically, consultation with biologically and culturally affiliated groups and with other interested parties is the cornerstone of any reasonable treatment plan, whether at the point of discovery, curation, or repatriation. The object of consultation is development of a plan for the treatment and disposition of human remains and funerary objects.

Clarifying the Process

Many misunderstandings can be avoided by simply discussing process early in a consultation. What are the expectations of the various parties regarding the topics on the table and how and when they will be addressed? Some of this may be dictated in very general terms by statute and rule, but laws are intentionally very broad in their requirements, leaving room to adjust the consultation process for the needs of the parties and the situation.

Some of the process-oriented questions are very basic; some are more complex. What laws apply, and how do they impact the process? Who has the authority and responsibility for communicating on behalf of the various parties? Who is responsible for creating a record of consultation and related activities? Who pays the expenses for meeting travel? Who makes the basic arrangements for lodging and meals? Do scheduling demands arising outside the process have an impact on the various stages of consultation? Is it necessary to develop individual or joint proposals for funding, and, if so, what impact does this have on scheduling? Once these and other questions of process are answered, it is important to record them and ensure that everyone has the same understandings.

Who Speaks for the Group?

In the past, institutions and agencies often have consulted groups by simply directing questions to someone they knew within the tribe or community. This is inappropriate. When NAGPRA or many state laws are at issue, there are government-to-government relationships that must be recognized. However, even outside this constraint, the right of a tribe or community to designate its own representatives must be respected. At the same time, groups must acknowledge that they have a responsibility to respect the process by making clear who speaks for them. It may be desirable to have a range of community members express their thoughts to institutional or agency staff, but in the end authority must be clearly designated.

The Medium and the Message

The goal of consultation is the development of a plan for the treatment and disposition of remains that both meets legal requirements and is characterized by respect and dignity. Consultation can be conducted through various media to achieve these ends. Letters and telephone calls are sometimes adequate when the matters to be resolved are routine and the parties are already familiar with one another's concerns. However, meetings are often essential to effective consultation.

The people involved in consultation on behalf of tribes, of institutions, and of other parties are usually very busy people. Scheduling meetings therefore is often one of the hardest tasks. Nevertheless, it is essential that the interested parties be represented by individuals who have a meaningful role in the decision-making process. It is often true that no one present at a meeting can make final commitments on behalf of their group. Museums have governing boards, tribes have councils and legislatures, and everyone has an administrative hierarchy. Any or all of the participants may also have advisory groups who must be informed and consulted before final decisions are made. However, since respectful decision making has the goal of establishing plans for treatment and disposition that all can live with, meetings must have the participation of people having a significant role in their own group's decision making, people who can raise and respond to the questions necessary to move consultation forward. A decision to be represented only by lower-level personnel is basically a power play, an attempt to obtain information while revealing nothing. No matter who does it, it is fundamentally disrespectful to both the process and to the other parties present.

Once appropriate people are gathered for a meeting, it is inevitable that the parties will have different values and interests. In an ideal meeting, all participants can express their own points of view, argue for what they value, and be heard by the whole group respectfully. This scenario is sometimes difficult. People on all sides of any question can regard an expression of values different from their own as a personal affront. Participants can help to diffuse these situations by directing attention back toward substantive issues and mutual respect. It is even better, however, to minimize these problems by planning the meeting in ways that encourage a cooperative and productive atmosphere.

Meeting Basics

Consultation advice to museums has sometimes included encouragement to emulate the traditional practices of the tribes or communities that will be present. This approach is almost certain to be awkward, it can easily go over the edge into parody, and it is not particularly useful. Instead, it is helpful to think in terms of the principle underlying basic courtesy: consideration for others.

Representatives of tribes and communities come from a wide range of backgrounds. It is not uncommon for a group to be represented by administrators and politicians, by attorneys, and also by traditional representatives who may have little experience of academic or agency bureaucracy. Traditional representatives also may have less familiarity with the English language than others, and in many cases they include elders who tire easily, require assistance for mobility, or have other physical restrictions.

Planning to address these issues must begin long before a meeting. Inquiring about the needs of those who will attend is an important first step. If the representatives include the elderly, then meeting at locations that entail extreme elevations or high temperatures can be dangerous for those with heart conditions. Arrange meetings at places that aren't inherently dangerous and that have adequate access for those who use wheelchairs or walkers. It is often helpful to vary meeting locations, so that everyone does not have to travel for every meeting. This can also permit wider participation in meetings by both community members and institutional staff.

It isn't necessary to arrange a traditional feast for visiting representatives. However it is courteous to provide food for those attending a lengthy meeting. Coffee, water, and sodas with a few snacks are often appreciated. On-site lunches can be both efficient and helpful, to avoid forcing participants to travel considerable distances to eat and to ensure that dietary restrictions can be accommodated.

Many traditional groups prefer to begin or close meetings with prayer. Inquire ahead of time about preferences in this regard. However, everyone should bear in mind that requiring that all who are present participate in prayer is both illegal and disrespectful of the beliefs of those who prefer not to do so.

Consultation on New Discoveries

Special problems occur when there are new discoveries of human remains. If a discovery is associated with ongoing construction there is invariably great time pressure on all parties, to avoid costly delays of work. Discoveries during nonarchaeological ground-disturbing activities (e.g., on private lands) can also suffer from lack of archaeological information bearing on important questions of cultural affiliation. There are also concerns associated with the treatment of human remains in the field.

The best approach is the development of specific plans before the time of need. This has become common practice under Arizona repatriation statutes. Long-term agreements have been developed through extensive consultation, outlining procedures acceptable to the various groups likely to be culturally affiliated with remains in specific geographic areas. Criteria have been embedded in the agreements to distinguish between remains culturally affiliated with the different groups (in southern Arizona, e.g., O'odham, Hopi, Yaqui, Apache, and Hispanic). Those criteria reflect evidence drawn from traditional knowledge, archaeology, history, and other sources to allow reasonable determinations to be made on grounds that the various potential claimants have contributed to and agreed on, along with the Arizona State Museum, which administers the Arizona statutes. The agreements allow acquisition of information not immediately available, from archaeology or other sources, to assist in making determinations of cultural affiliation. Provision is also made in the agreement for identifying remains that are not culturally affiliated with any of the groups involved in developing the agreement, in which case a new consultation must be sought with appropriate culturally or biologically affiliated organizations or individuals.

The agreements go on to describe the recording and recovery procedures requested by the respective groups, and the appropriate procedures based upon the cultural affiliation determination. Those discovering the remains, whether archaeologists or developers, can choose to accept the terms of this blanket agreement and sign on as a party to the agreement. In that case, they can quickly proceed with recording and removing remains and proceeding with their other activities. They can also choose to reject those terms and request a separate consultation. This option is more time-consuming but is an important alternative for those who believe they have special needs or wishes that would affect implementing an agreement.

An interesting point in all this is that Arizona law does not require that evidence of cultural affiliation be presented unless there is a dispute between claimants. Otherwise, the law requires only an assertion of cultural affiliation by a recognized group. In practice, all of the participants have found that evaluation of evidence of cultural affiliation is to their own advantage.

Consultation on Existing Collections

Major repatriations can involve many consultation meetings and many participants. In May 2001, the Arizona State Museum repatriated under NAGPRA human remains and more than twenty-six thousand funerary objects to a group of claimants led by the Gila River Indian Community. The claimants included the Gila River Indian Community, the Salt River Pima-Maricopa Indian Community, the Tohono O'odham Nation, the Ak-Chin Indian Community, Zuni Pueblo, and the Hopi Tribe. Eight official consultation meetings were held over fifteen months, in addition to numerous less formal meetings and conversations. The participation of representatives of the Bureau of Indian Affairs, as the controlling federal agency, was essential.

The participants in each meeting varied depending on the issues on the agenda. All of the claimants, with the exception of Zuni Pueblo, chose to be represented at one or more meetings, especially when issues like cultural affiliation and the overall scope of the repatriation were on the agenda. However, meetings with narrower focus were attended by smaller numbers of representatives. Some meetings were held in Tucson at the Arizona State Museum, where it was possible to show representatives both collections and records. Other meetings were held at the Gila River Indian Community, where a wider range of community members could attend.

PROVIDING INFORMATION AND ACCESS TO CLAIMANTS

The process of fair and respectful consultation thrives on accurate and thorough communication. Sometimes this isn't pleasant, because sometimes the past isn't pretty. Having to tell someone that the postcranial elements of a burial have been discarded is difficult. It is more difficult when one is pressed for an explanation, and the truthful one is that a previous curator discarded human remains that he found "uninteresting." In the past, those who obtained materials from indigenous people seldom supposed that they would ever be accountable to the relatives of the deceased for their practices in acquiring and curating either human remains or objects. Many collectors assumed that all was fair in love, war, and collecting for museums. For an excellent example of this kind, see Carl Lumholtz's (1990:92–98) own explanation of how he acquired Tohono O'odham *Wi'ikita* paraphernalia.

It is also sometimes feared that full disclosure of available information will make it more likely that the relatives of the dead will seek repatriation of remains and objects. Failure to disclose information for this reason is unworthy of any respectable agency or institution. In the case of remains and objects subject to NAGPRA, it is also illegal.

Sometimes representatives of traditional groups are not familiar with the common practices of museums and agencies or with the specific practices of a particular institution. As a consequence, they may not know the right questions to ask in order to obtain the information that they need. The fair thing is to provide all available information.

ANALYSIS AND RECORDING

A great deal of debate has centered on the issues surrounding analysis and recording of remains and funerary objects. Some of these issues are being addressed in detail elsewhere in this volume, but they are so central to the concerns of indigenous people and of scientists that they require some attention here.

Traditional perspectives on scientific study vary greatly. Virtually no indigenous groups have approved of destructive analysis, such as that required for DNA study. Many groups do not object to noninvasive and nondestructive analysis. On the other extreme are those groups opposed to any study or recording.

Two kinds of concern about study of remains can be identified. The first is rooted in the issues of fairness and justice that were discussed earlier. When relatives of the deceased have had no voice in decision making, then study may be objectionable regardless of whether a particular kind of recording or analysis is intrinsically offensive to cultural traditions. The second kind of concern arises when a form of study is specifically offensive to cultural traditions. It can be hoped that respectful dialogue will end problems of the first sort, and lead to greater clarity in identifying and addressing problems of the second sort.

This point is especially important because accurate inventories are not optional for responsible institutions or agencies, while the recording and study necessary to produce accurate inventories can seem undesirable to representatives of traditional tribes and communities. A relevant case was brought by Hui Malama I Na Kupuna O Hawai'i Nei (Hui Malama) in United States District Court in Hawaii in 1995. In this case (*Na Iwi O Na Kupuna O Mokapu versus John Dalton* (894 F.Supp. 1397 [D. Hawaii]) Hui Malama alleged that the U.S. Navy, through the Bishop Museum, conducted additional scientific research on the remains in spite of an agreement between the parties. Hui Malama demanded that the Bishop Museum return the remains to them promptly, delete the alleged additional tests from the inventory, and place under seal the additional research and release the information only with Hui Malama's permission.

The court found that the Bishop Museum was within its rights, and its responsibilities, to conduct tests and analyses needed for completion of accurate descriptions for purposes of inventory. It also found that no explicit agreement regarding tests or analysis existed, and further that had there been an agreement it would not have been valid. A valid agreement on the treatment and disposition of remains can only follow an official finding of cultural affiliation. The court also ruled that NAGPRA is not a withholding statute under the Freedom of Information Act, and that the results of analyses could properly be disseminated by the museum.

This tells us something of the legal position. A less adversarial example can be found in the Arizona State Museum repatriation of remains and objects from the Gila River Indian Community in 2001. Museum staff and students spent more than two years recording remains and objects involved in that repatriation. Although the materials had been studied earlier, catalog information was not sufficiently complete and accurate for a final inventory. However, in deference to the wishes of the claimants, no destructive or invasive procedures were carried out. Equally important, at every stage claimant representatives were informed of what was being done. Members of the claimant communities were employed by the museum during the recording process, so that there was always firsthand knowledge of procedures and progress. All information obtained during the effort was made available to the claimants. Restrictions on use of photographs and other records were negotiated with the claimants during the frequent consultation meetings. The result, a smooth repatriation process working from an accurate inventory, was a benefit to all the participants.

CEREMONIES

Special issues can arise when representatives wish to conduct ceremonies for the dead. The issues that can arise include appropriateness of the ritual and the individuals conducting it, requests for privacy, deposition of organic materials in collection storage areas, and issues associated with smoke from burning sage or tobacco.

The first important concern is cultural affiliation. Once cultural affiliation is established, tribal and community representatives should have reasonable private access to human remains and funerary objects for purposes of their ceremonies. However, there is a potential for great offense if indiscriminate access is granted to religious practitioners from groups without established affiliation. In many cases, moving remains and objects to a separate area for ceremonial purposes is desirable, so that only culturally affiliated remains and objects are present during religious activities.

The second important rule for access to collections for traditional ceremonies is that the participants should have authorization for their requested activities from the decision-making body of their own tribe or community. Passing judgment on who is and who is not an acceptable traditional religious practitioner is not a responsibility that an institution or agency should take on. Even within a tribe or community, not everyone is qualified to do everything, and it is that community that must decide this issue.

Now and then, groups have followed an opposite course, asking museum staff to carry out activities that are basically religious in nature—for example "feeding" religious objects with appropriate substances. Complying with such requests presents two potentially serious problems. First, the institution becomes responsible for the appropriate conduct of traditional religious practices, which is not within the scope of reasonable institutional responsibilities. Second, it is disrespectful of the beliefs of staff members to ask that they carry out religious activities that they themselves do not believe in and that may even conflict with their own religious beliefs. Usually some staff members do not find the activity objectionable, but the situation can create unfair pressure to appear to find the activity acceptable. In some cases, a member of the traditional group is on the institutional staff. That individual can carry out the activities, so long as the arrangement is understood as access provided to a community member, not staff access to fulfill an institutional responsibility.

Most institutions allow visitors to handle collections only when a staff member is present. These policies can conflict with the need for privacy for traditional ceremonies and prayers. Again, cultural affiliation and the status of any existing or future repatriation claim matter. In general, private access makes the best sense only after an official repatriation proceeding has reached the point that it is legally clear to whom the remains and objects in question might be repatriated. In granting private access, the institution gives up a degree of control over what is done to and with the materials, and should only do this when it has effectively discharged its responsibilities to other potential legitimate claimants.

An extreme case occurs when a group requests loan of materials that are subject to repatriation, prior to official decisions regarding cultural affiliation or without the consent of all groups determined culturally affiliated. Such a case has already occurred. A representative of Hui Malama obtained materials from the Bishop Museum, ostensibly on loan, and promptly buried them (National Park Service 2003). Other potential claimant groups argued that the Bishop Museum was at fault for having ignored their legal rights in the matter, effectively repatriating the materials prior to completion of the appropriate NAGPRA processes, and the NAGPRA Review Panel agreed. The same principles would apply in the seemingly less problematic instance of private access within the physical confines of the institution. Again, respect must be given to all of the potentially culturally or biologically affiliated groups, not just one or more that are favored by an institution.

Other ceremonial concerns focus on practical matters of institutional security and conservation. Instances of groups asking to have organic materials deposited with remains and funerary objects are a common example. Normally this would not be regarded as good museum practice, but this is another instance in which it is appropriate to give up some claims to power in favor of dialogue and compromise. For example, in some cases material might be left in place for a time, and then removed. The Arizona State Museum has had successful arrangements of this kind, in which corn pollen is deposited during prayers by group representatives, and then swept up and disposed of respectfully after a mutually acceptable period of time. Each case must be considered on its own merits.

Ceremonies involving smoke are very common, and can raise several issues. It is best if such ceremonies are conducted in a private area away from the collection as a whole. A further complication in this case is very practical. Smoke sets off smoke detectors, and that brings fire trucks. Therefore, smoke detectors should be disabled before a ceremony. However, it is important to keep disabled smoke detectors limited to a restricted area and to the time period of the ceremony itself. This will avoid endangering staff and other collections.

With these reasonable precautions, it is possible to respect the wishes of culturally related groups to carry out their traditional religious activities, while maintaining adequate care for collections and staff.

A LAST IMPORTANT POINT

Anyone who has worked with issues of human remains for a few years has heard many accusations that focus on motives. Some are perennial favorites. Tribal and community representatives accuse academics of working for their own personal or institutional advancement rather than scientific knowledge and truth. Archaeologists and museum personnel accuse tribal representatives of political rather than religious or traditional motives. These accusations usually are intended to suggest that there is no reason to take the people involved seriously.

These accusations are unproductive, even when they contain a substantial element of truth. In the end, all groups should receive respect for their concerns and issues. The real question is

SPIRIT CAVE MAN: A BODY OF CONTENTION

Cheryl A. Gregory

Spirit Cave Man was unearthed at Spirit Cave, Nevada, in 1940, by the husband-and-wife team of archaeologists S. M. and Georgia N. Wheeler, who considered him to be "a young adult male" that was "approximately 1500 to 2000 years old" (Barker et al. 2000b:1). However, it was R. Erv Taylor of the University of California, Riverside, Radiocarbon Laboratory who determined the actual age of Spirit Cave Man—a revelation most unexpected and a major scientific discovery (Tuohy and Dansie 2002).

Spirit Cave Man, also referred to as "Burial #2," was living in the Grimes Point/Stillwater area, Churchill County, Nevada, in 9419 B.P., plus or minus twenty-five years (Barker et al. 2000b:1). Although he is partially mummified, he is still the oldest mummy in North America. He was only 5'2" tall, and various estimates place his age between forty and fifty-five years old at the time of his death. He was found "wrapped in two tule mats" with an additional "twisted skin robe also wrapped around the mummy" (Whaley 2000; Tuohy and Dansie 2002). The textiles are distinctive with a "sophisticated warp-face-plain-weave (diamond plaited)" pattern that "disappeared around 8800 years B.P." (Barker et al. 2000b:6). The moccasins on his feet are well preserved, made from three different animal skins, and are "different from any known pair in the great Basin" (Tuohy and Dansie 2002). Analysis has shown that Spirit Cave Man's hair and dental morphology are biologically related to northern Asians and Native Americans; however, his cranial morphological measurements, when statistically compared to a sample of contemporary populations worldwide, are not within the range of variation represented in that sample (Barker et al. 2000b:1).

University of California, Davis, physical anthropologists requested a "collaborative investigation of early human remains from western Nevada" in 1996 (Barker et al. 2000b:1; see also Whaley 2000). Since most of the forty-one sets of human remains targeted for this study came from Bureau of Land Management (BLM) lands, including those of Spirit Cave Man, the Nevada State Museum requested authorization from the BLM for consumptive testing, DNA analysis, or radiocarbon dating; and the BLM proceeded to notify the Northern Paiute tribal governments to obtain their response to this request (Barker et al. 2000b:1).

The response of the Northern Paiute tribes was immediate and firmly against any consumptive testing; it also included their assertion of cultural affiliation with Spirit Cave Man. The Fallon Paiute–Shoshone Tribe, representing all Northern Paiute tribal governments, officially asserted its cultural affiliation with Spirit Cave Man via the provisions of NAGPRA, reiterated its opposition to consumptive testing, and requested immediate repatriation of his remains along with all funerary objects associated therewith (Barker et al. 2000b:2). The chair of the Fallon Paiute–Shoshone Tribe submitted evidence and arguments for affiliation in December 1999. As a result of the Fallon Paiute–Shoshone Tribe's strong opposition to consumptive testing because of its destructive nature, Nevada State Museum officials withdrew their request for such testing in April 2000 (Whaley 2000).

NAGPRA makes a clear distinction between human remains discovered prior to its inception on November 16, 1990, and those found thereafter. Human remains located after November 16, 1990, "on aboriginal lands as defined by the ICC (Indian Claims Commission), in lieu of other contrary evidence, is sufficient to determine affiliation [36 CFR 10.6 (a)]." Those human remains discovered or removed prior to NAGPRA undergo evaluation of the circumstances and evidence supporting a claim of affiliation; and, there must be a preponderance of "geographical, kinship, biological, archaeological, anthropological, linguistic, folklore, oral tradition, historical, or other relevant information or expert opinion" that establishes the claimed affiliation (Barker et al. 2000a:46–47).

The expert testimony provided by tribal elders in the Determination of Cultural Affiliation of Ancient Human Remains from Spirit Cave, Nevada, was that the Northern Paiute have been in the Spirit Cave area from "time immemorial," which means they have "a relationship of shared group identity between the Northern Paiute and the people who interred the remains from Spirit Cave"

SPIRIT CAVE MAN: A BODY OF CONTENTION (*continued*)

(Barker et al. 2000a:61). Strong archaeological evidence supports the Fallon Paiute–Shoshone Tribe's contention of a continuous cultural sequence for at least four thousand years. However, thirty-three ethnographic informants' accounts "[point] unmistakably to core elements in the legend as demonstrating the presence of another group living in the area either before or at the same time as the ancestors of the Northern Paiute" (Barker et al. 2000a:59–60). The BLM determined the evidence linking the Northern Paiute to the early Holocene period, when Spirit Cave Man lived, does not support an argument for Northern Paiute affiliation to Spirit Cave Man.

Based on the criteria mentioned here, the BLM made a preliminary Determination of Cultural Affiliation of Ancient Human Remains from Spirit Cave, Nevada, July 26, 2000, and issued a press release August 15, 2000, stating that the ancient human remains from Spirit Cave were Native American but were not culturally affiliated with the Fallon Paiute–Shoshone Tribe or any other known contemporary group; additionally, the federal government would retain ownership of these remains. Any disputants to the preliminary determination had until October 2, 2000, to provide written statements and evidence to the state director, Bureau of Land Management (BLM 2000-79). In 2002, the Fallon Paiute–Shoshone Tribe appealed their case to the secretary of the interior based on a recommendation they had received from the National Park Service, NAGPRA Review Committee. Six of the seven review committee members agreed that the Nevada State Office of the BLM had not been objective in its assessment of the information provided, the preponderance of the evidence supported the Fallon Paiute–Shoshone Tribal claim of affiliation, and the Spirit Cave human remains and funerary objects should be repatriated (NAGPRA Dispute Findings Federal Register 2002:[67]69:17463; Nevada State Museum 2004).

In uncontested cases of affiliation, the BLM negotiates the place and manner of repatriation. However, the law allows for the BLM to defer repatriation of remains and/or objects if they are "indispensable for the completion of a specific scientific study, the outcome of which would be of major benefit to the United States." When affiliation has not been determined, control and ownership of the remains reside with the government until enough evidence is found for affiliation, at which time the remains are repatriated (Barker et al. 2000b:3).

Two of the biggest questions that have gone unanswered are, What should be done with ancient human remains where evidence for affiliation is difficult to find? and How should institutions and anthropologists handle Native American remains without clear or hard evidence for descendants? The NAGPRA Review Committee's Nineteenth Meeting minutes in Juneau, Alaska, April 2–4, 2000, regarding the "Discussion of Draft Principles of Agreement for the Disposition of Culturally Unidentified Human Remains," reveal the positions taken by Native Americans and the scientific community:

> Ms. Dale Ann Frye Sherman of the National Congress of the American Indian (NCAI) suggested that a "speedy repatriation of human remains should occur regardless of educational, historical or scientific value"; Native American perspective should determine disposition of all clearly Native American human remains.
>
> Mr. Harry, representative of the Pyramid Lake Paiute Tribe, stated, "It cannot and will not support granting standing to the scientific communities or museums for making decisions regarding their deceased relatives."
>
> Mr. Moyle, Fallon Paiute–Shoshone Tribe, asserted that Native American beliefs and tribal ways cannot be compromised regarding the outcome of human remains, artifacts, or funerary objects. "NAGPRA is human rights legislation, and language must be drafted that supports immediate repatriation of Native American ancestors without catering to the interests of the scientific community."

(continued)

whether a legitimate and coherent case is being made, not whether the motives of the group representative making the case are as pure as the driven snow. All of us live in complicated worlds. If we can respect that in one another, we can move forward with the fairness and justice that are the essence of real respect.

REFERENCES

Ariés, Philippe
   1981 *The Hour of Our Death*. Knopf, New York.

Barker, Pat, Cynthia Ellis, and Stephanie Damadio
   2000a *Determination of Cultural Affiliation of Ancient Human Remains from Spirit Cave, Nevada*. Bureau of Land Management, Nevada State Office, Las Vegas. Electronic document, http://www.nv.blm.gov/cultural/spirit_cave_man/spirit_cave_man2.htm, accessed May 23, 2006.
   2000b *Summary of the Determination of Cultural Affiliation of Ancient Human Remains from Spirit Cave, Nevada*. Bureau of Land Management, Nevada State Office, Las Vegas. Electronic document, http://www.nv.blm.gov/cultural/spirit_cave_man/spirit_cave_man2.htm, accessed April 23, 2006.

Echo-Hawk, Roger
   2002 *Keepers of Culture: Repatriating Cultural Items under the Native American Graves Protection and Repatriation Act*. Denver Art Museum, Denver.

Ezra, David A.
   1995 Na Iwi O Na Kupuna O Mokapu, Heleloa, Ulupa'U A Me Kuwa'A'Ohe, by and through their guardians, Hui Malama I Na Kupuna O Hawai'i Nei, a Hawai'i nonprofit corporation, Plaintiffs, v. John Dalton, in his capacity as the Secretary of the Department of the Navy and Bernice Pauahi Bishop Museum, a Hawai'i Corporation, Defendants. Civ. No. 94-00445 DAE. pp. 1402. P. vol. 894 F. Supp. 1397. United States District Court, D. Hawai'i.

Hall, Teri R., and Jeanette Wolfley
   2003 A Survey of Tribal Perspectives on NAGPRA: Repatriation and Study of Human Remains. *Archaeological Record* 3(2):27–34.

Jelderks, John
  2002 Opinion and Order for *Robson Bonnischen et al. v. United States of America et al.* Civil No. 96-1481-JE.

Lumholtz, Carl
  1990 *New Trails in Mexico: An Account of One Year's Exploration in North-western Sonora, Mexico, and South-western Arizona 1909–1910.* University of Arizona Press, Tucson.

National Park Service
  2003 Native American Graves Protection and Repatriation Review Committee Findings and Recommendations and Minority Opinion Regarding a Dispute between the Royal Hawaiian Academy of Traditional Arts and the Bernice Pauahi Bishop Museum. *Federal Register* 68(161):50179–50180.

Native American Graves Protection and Repatriation Review Committee
  2000 Meeting Minutes, Nineteenth Meeting, April 2–4, 2000, Juneau, Alaska, National Park Service, United States Department of the Interior. Electronic document, http://www.cr.nps.gov/nagpra/REVIEW/meetings/RCMIN019.HTM, accessed April 23, 2006.
  2002 Dispute Findings, April 10, 2002, National Park Service, United States Department of the Interior. *Federal Register* (67)69:17463. Electronic document, http://www.cr.nps.gov/nagpra/REVIEW/RCNOTICES/RCF5.htm, accessed April 23, 2006.

Nevada Bureau of Land Management
  2000 BLM Makes Spirit Cave Man Determination. Release Number 2000-79, August 15. Electronic document, http://www.nv.blm.gov/cultural/spirit_cave_man/SC_final_July26.pdf, accessed April 23, 2006.

Nevada State Museum
  2004 Spirit Cave Man Update. June. Nevada Division of Museums and History, Las Vegas. Electronic document, http://dmla.clan.lib.nv.us/docs/museums/cc/update.htm, accessed April 23, 2006.

Pearson, Michael Parker
  1999 *The Archaeology of Death and Burial.* Texas A&M University Press, College Station.

Rawls, John
  1999 *A Theory of Justice.* Revised ed. Belknap Press, Cambridge, Massachusetts.

Teague, Lynn S.
  1993 Prehistory and the Traditions of the O'odham and Hopi. *Kiva* 58(4):435–454.
  2002 O'odham Identity in Oral Tradition and in the Archaeological Record. Paper presented at the Society for American Archaeology, Denver.
  2003 Cultural Identity in the Textiles, Traditions, and History of the O'odham and Their Neighbors. Paper presented at the Society for American Archaeology, Denver.

Tuohy, Donald R., and Amy Dansie
  2002 *An Ancient Human Mummy from Nevada.* September 5. Nevada Division of Museums and History. Electronic document, http://dmla.clan.lib.nv.us/docs/museums/cc/mummy.htm, accessed April 23, 2006.

Whaley, Sean
  2000 Tribe's Claim to Remains Suffers Blow. *Las Vegas Review-Journal*, August 16. Electronic document, http://www.reviewjournal.com/lvrj_home/2000/Aug-16-Wed-2000/news/14180036.html, accessed April 23, 2006.

Whiteley, Peter M.
  2002 Archaeology and Oral Tradition: The Scientific Importance of Dialogue. *American Antiquity* 67(3):405–416.

CHAPTER 17

The Body in the Museum

MARY M. BROOKS AND CLAIRE RUMSEY

How do modern westerners turn their dead into family, community or national ancestors? Individuals do this through sensing their presence and through talking to the dead (both surprisingly common activities), and through "linking objects"—symbolic places and things that represent the dead, whether it be the grave, or a place s/he frequented, a piece of clothing, or photograph.

—Tony Walter

WHEN WE LOOK AT A DEAD BODY FROM WHATEVER PERIOD OR CULTURE, WE ARE ALL LOOKING, IN SOME sense, at ourselves and our own end. Beyond this, our fascination may be motivated by intellectual, scientific, forensic, religious, or emotional curiosity. Both religious relics and bodies in museums are recontextualized human remains, removed from the graveyard or tomb, sites often associated with both literal and metaphorical pollution, into another sacred context where they are preserved for a different function. Reliquaries literally turn bones into objects, encased in precious metals and ornamented with precious stones, whereas museums objectify the bones conceptually for research and display. Whether the motivation is theological or analytical, macabre or morbid, the display of dead bodies is an increasingly contested issue. Displaying bodies can serve as connection of the past with the present, and the dead with the living, offering succor, solace, inspiration, or information, but it also renders them ambivalent: both "persons and things" (Geary 1986:169).

Museums have to respond to and reconcile increasingly complex and conflicting agendas. Factors to be considered include religion (Cox 1996; Richardson 2000), reburial (Chamberlain 1994; Parker Pearson 1999), validation for retaining human remains (Boddington et al. 1987; Chamberlain 1994; Parker Pearson 1999), the premise for display (Kirshenblatt-Gimblett 1998; Swain 1998; Vaswani 2001), and consent or nonconsent (Fuller 1998:50–58; O'Rorke 2001). These issues are often interrelated and there is a fine line between socially acceptable and unacceptable treatment of human remains (O'Rorke 2001; Vaswani 2001). This chapter aims to explore these issues as a means for developing a framework for more informed and explicit decision making while acknowledging that attitudes—and hence practice—will inevitably evolve.

At the turn of the twenty-first century, several exhibitions in London displayed dead human bodies; they were hugely popular. *London Bodies: The Changing Shape of Londoners from Prehistoric Times to the Present Day* at the Museum of London (October 27, 1998–February 21, 1999) attracted 15,600 visitors, with the highest average daily figures for any of the museum's special exhibitions since 1992 (Swain 1999). *Body Worlds: The Anatomical Exhibition of Real Human Bodies* in the Atlantis Gallery, London, a nontraditional gallery space, invited visitors to gaze on the plastinated bodies, making an object out of that which we experience daily as living beings. Fourteen million people are said to have visited *Body Worlds* international touring exhibitions between the mid-1990s and 2004 (Walter 2004:604). The London exhibition (March 23, 2002–February 9, 2003) had an average of 3,200 visitors daily. While lines were forming in London's East End to see the plastinated bodies, "Ginger," a Late Predynastic Egyptian man, "Pete Marsh," a recovered bog body, and wrapped Egyptian mummies were all on long-term display at the British Museum. These were not the only bodies on display. The Museum of London experienced a dramatic increase in visitors once the coffin containing the body known as "The Roman Lady" was opened in 1999. Jenny Hall, the museum's Roman curator, reported a 70.8 percent increase in visitors compared with the previous year (personal communication, March 13, 2001); visitors "waited for up to two hours to view the sarcophagus" (Barham and Lang 2001:50).

BODY OR OBJECT?

Western culture increasingly commoditizes the body itself. Bodies and body parts have long been "used" for religious veneration or political purposes. Relics were—and remain—an important element in Christian practice, inspiring piety and awe. Defined in Catholic canon law as "the remains of honourable objects, or of saints, or beatified persons . . . such as their body, head, arm, forearm, heart, tongue or leg" (Martiz 1983:844, cited in Beck 2001:17), such relics have religious value but also a commercial role in attracting pilgrims and hence generating income for churches and monasteries. Some treasured relics had checkered histories. They were moved, or even stolen, so communities could benefit from the religious and secular status generated by their possession and display. The fate of St Oswald's body is one example. A cult sprang up venerating Oswald's body after he was killed fighting pagans in 642. It was finally preserved in sections in different religious communities (Ford 2000). Powdered "mummy," supposedly derived from actual Egyptian mummies, was traded for medicine, and whole bodies were sold for anatomization until legislation such as the UK's Anatomy Act outlawed this (Richardson 2000; Crowhurst 2000).

Politics may also influence the afterlife of bodies and act to objectify them. The display of Lenin's embalmed body, nicknamed "the smoked fish," is intimately linked with Russian political developments (Chamberlain and Pearson 2001:35–37). Eva Peron's embalmed corpse functioned both as a political and saintly relic. Her embalmed body was transported to Italy, exhumed, taken to Spain, and finally returned to Argentina for display before reburial in a glass-topped coffin in an alarmed vault (Chamberlain and Pearson 2001:40–41). Similar concerns about the political status and financial benefit derived from the possession and display of bodies influence museums. Some of the controversy over the final resting place of the body of Otzi, the Iceman, found in a glacier on the border between Austria and South Tyrol, was fueled by concerns for local political status and financial benefits (Fowler 2000:162–163).

Not everyone finds treating a once-living body as an object problematic. Jeremy Bentham (1748–1832), the utilitarian philosopher and jurist, positively welcomed it (University College London 1993; Fuller 1998). Bentham viewed religion as a hindrance to the advancement of medical research and hoped to show that the human corpse was a beautiful and useful thing. He proposed that bodies should be treated to create sculptures, which he described as "auto-icons" (Richardson and Hurwitz 1987). In accordance with his principles, Bentham willed his body to his friend Dr Thomas Southwood Smith, author of *The Use of the Dead to the Living* (1824), which promoted the benefits of research into dead bodies to advance the medical treatment of the living (Marmoy 1958). Bentham's body was publicly dissected in the presence of many leading radical and political thinkers, a year before the passing of the 1832 Anatomy Act, for which he had campaigned. This act made it legal for bodies other than those of executed criminals to be used for medical dissection (Richardson 2000:16; Fuller 1998). Bentham did become his own "auto-icon." His cleaned skeleton was padded, dressed in his own clothes, and has been on display in University College London since 1850 (Fuller 1998; Marmoy 1958) (figure 17.1). Until von Hagens developed his "plastination" technique, Bentham's free-will decision to have his body displayed in a secular context was probably unique in the UK.

Figure 17.1.   As consent is a key part of the debate on the display of human bodies, it should be noted that Jeremy Bentham requested that his body should be publicly displayed after his death. Reproduced with permission of Special Collections, University College London.

WHO OWNS A BODY?

Such commoditization may elevate human remains into the realm of the holy, make them an object of trade, allow them to function as political symbols, or render them functional in medical or scientific terms. Ultimately, it is this process that enables Western museums to display human remains as museum objects, although the museum context also intensified some questions. Is a body on display a human being or an object? Who "owns" a human body, and who controls what happens to it after death?

Responsibility for the recently deceased usually lies with surviving relatives but ancient remains may become public property, often becoming central to religious beliefs, national identity, or scientific research. U.S. property law "upholds individual ownership provided the body parts are not separated from the body," while indigenous groups tend to favor group "ownership" (Lock 2001:86). Tristram Besterman, then director of the Manchester Museum (2003), notes that United Kingdom law appears to enshrine a curious ambiguity. It is not possible to "own" parts of a body, although it is possible to "possess" them.

Manchester (1987:167) has argued that archaeologists have a responsibility to the person whose bones they are excavating and studying:

> Although in most instances, those remains are solely osseous, they do represent a person with emotions, sensations and physical and psychological reactions very similar to our own. The skeletal remains should not, therefore, be viewed by the osteoarchaeologist as mere bones. Some attempt should be made to add flesh and blood to the bones, to bring back to life these past peoples and to understand the suffering and psyche of our ancestors.

Note that the bones are said to "represent" the person rather than "being" the person. This linguistic shift has the effect of distancing the bones from the individual even though Manchester is arguing for a closer connection between the excavation and the remains. There is no attempt to explore the ethical consequences of considering "mere bones" as a person. In a similar elision, Manchester Museum sells a postcard showing an unwrapped mummified body and elaborate painted coffin lid, dating from about 2650 B.P., with the following description: "Wooden coffin and remains belonging to Asru, chantress of Amun." Even though Asru's name is known, the language here appears to depersonalize her, favoring her coffin above her individual identity.

SACRED BODIES?

Social and religious attitudes to bodies of the long dead and the recently dead clearly differ in different cultures. Appropriate approaches to human remains in Western culture are often contradictory. The general secularization of Western culture enables the view that the value of some human remains lies in their potential contributions to paleoarchaeology or medical research. However, people still care desperately about the whereabouts of the bodies of their loved ones, as part of the mourning process, and wish to ensure that these are "properly" treated (Hallam and Hockey 2001; Russell 2001:23–24).

What Constitutes a Body?

Medical research is raising difficult issues regarding the legal rights to genetic material and is refining ideas about the possibility of patenting increasingly small elements of the human body, changing ideas about the boundaries and definitions of the body. Perception of what is considered a "body part" varies. How do these legal frameworks affect attitudes to bodies and body parts in museums? *The Medicine Man* exhibition (British Museum, June–November 2003;

Arnold and Olsen 2003) presented part of Henry Wellcome's (1853–1936) vast collection of medically related material. The display included some pieces of tattooed skin. These have been divorced from the person, possibly a French sailor, who originally decided to ornament his skin, acquired first by Henry Wellcome and then passed finally to the Science Museum (SM A680). During this transition from living body to museum display, their meaning and value has shifted. No longer a personal decoration, presumably with some symbolic or aesthetic significance, the skin fragments have become an artifact, exhibited without any recognition that they were once part of a living human being. Should fragmentary remains be considered as much as "human remains" as the preserved flesh and bones of complete bodies, such as those of the famous bog people? Hair is an extension of the human body, albeit dead, that can function as both physical memorial and as a commodity. Should such locks, or hair made into memorial jewelry, be subject to the same concerns that apply to a whole body? The form in which human remains survive does seem to influence how they are categorized and whether they are exhibited. Do archaeologists, curators, and the viewing public perceive the so-called cremation slag in a funerary urn as requiring the same respect in handling and display as a whole body (Henderson et al. 1987:81–100)?

Material discontinuity of the body has been a Western theological and social concern for centuries and is still very much part of contemporary concerns although Christian teachings on the need to preserve the whole body as a prerequisite for eternal salvation have varied (Brandes 2001).

Last Resting Places?

Attitudes to bodies in nonmuseum contexts color attitudes to bodies within museums. In many ways, a recent debate over medical needs, ethics, and organ donation programs parallels the issues faced by the museum community but without, however, the tradition of displaying bodies alongside artifacts and the complex problems that this brings. There seems to be a conflict in defining an appropriate cutoff point at which human remains become considered as acceptable for excavation, except in cases of contemporary criminal and medical investigations in which case relatives give consent (Magee 2001:8). Interestingly, this debate is taking place at a time when British medical schools are moving away from using donated bodies to lifelike plastic models for teaching anatomy (Feinmann 2002:87). Despite the nearly universal human instinct to treat the dead with respect and to develop complex ceremonial rituals, legislation for intervention in human burial sites is complex and varies greatly in different countries.

Interpretation of "respectful" treatment of human remains is variable within countries, reflecting the range of religious beliefs and opinions found in a society. The debate becomes even more complex when different cultures and countries are involved. Remains of indigenous people now in Western museum collections were often acquired at the time of colonialism and hence represent not just a spiritual and social abuse but also political injustice. For Native Americans and Australian aboriginal peoples, letting the dead remain in their resting place is of central importance to the dead and the living. For some groups, removal may be irreligious and could endanger the welfare of the current community. Unless sensitively approached, there may be potential for conflict between the community and academics, researchers, archaeologists, or physical anthropologists. McGowan and Laroche (1996:109–121) trace clashes between these different physical and metaphysical attitudes to human remains. First Nation peoples are increasingly taking a proactive stance regarding the return of their ancestors' bodies. The Foundation of Aboriginal and Islander Research Action (FAIRA) has been working with UK museums to undertake research to enable repatriation of returns. The Manchester Museum, in cooperation with FAIRA, has returned four aboriginal skulls collected in the nineteenth century. The transfer ceremony included an antidote for any curses possibly incurred by the museum (Heywood 2003:7; Ward 2003).

Bodies without clear descendant communities seem to be excluded from these changed approaches. Parker Pearson (1999:191) asks, "What about the remains of ancestors so ancient that they are likely to have passed on genes to everyone on the planet? Do they belong to any one ethnicity or nation?" UK guidelines for bodies from pagan burials, excavated outside Christian burial grounds, are not clear. Such excavated bodies could remain in storage indefinitely. Since these groups are marginal in contemporary Western society, they may not be able to exert any formal requirement by the law or the church to rebury such human remains. These distinctions between differing religions seem contradictory and unjust. Why should the remains of humans thought to have practiced an ancient or less influential religion have different institutional treatment and rights of reburial than those in a currently practiced religion? Ratan Vaswani, the UK Museums Association's ethical adviser, argues that the views of predominant contemporary religions influence ideas of what constitutes suitable approaches to human remains by defining "respectful" treatment of all human remains in terms derived from practices associated with their own faith (personal communication, August 20, 2001). As an example, he cites the hypothetical case of a New Age group who claim to follow an ancient Egyptian faith. Such a group might object to the display of Egyptian mummies in museums since this would be taboo according to their religious practice. This seems to result in the paradox that Maori heads are, properly, withdrawn from display but Egyptian mummies remain on display (Vaswani 2001). This continues to be an unresolved issue.

What Frameworks Exist to Aid Decision Making?
Legal and ethical frameworks would seem to provide a structure for those working with human remains. Despite the considerable amount of legislation as well as international and national ethical guidelines in existence, their interpretation may sometimes be unclear.

In the United Kingdom, the legal framework for acquiring, storing, or displaying human remains can sometimes be surprisingly unclear. For example, there was some doubt as to the legality of the London *Body Worlds* exhibition under legislation governing the use of bodies and body parts. The Department of Health finally decided that it could proceed (Jury 2002:14). Guidance in ethical codes tends to focus on general principles rather than specific practice. The International Council of Museums (ICOM) *Code of Ethics and Standards for Museum Practice* recommends museums should have clearly defined policies for responding to "requests for removal from public display of human remains," and these should be handled with "respect and sensitivity." A specific section discusses the need to "house" human remains and other "material of sacred significance . . . securely and respectfully" (ICOM 2002:19). Such material should be available to appropriate researchers but not to "the morbidly curious" (ICOM 2002:19). Barbian and Berndt (2001:259) take issue with this limitation, arguing that "morbid" curiosity is as valid as any other form of curiosity. The UK Museums Association *Code of Ethics* requires museums to "respect the interests of originating communities" (2002:17), which clearly has significance for appropriate approaches to human remains.

McGowan and Laroche (1996:119) highlight the potential for conflict between cultural and scientific approaches, while stressing the importance of viewing "human remains as a discreet material requiring unique considerations that are separate and apart from any other materials." The common strand in all these ethical codes is their stress on the importance of respecting the needs of the originating peoples. These guidelines give museum professionals the responsibility of assessing the degree of sensitivity of the material to be displayed for the relevant community. Problems may arise in the different roles of such sensitive material in different collections, such as historical, anthropological, or medical museums, or mixed collections. Ratan Vaswani notes that British codes do not address such cross-disciplinary issues (personal communication, August 20, 2001). Codes also tend not to engage with the potentially conflicted role of museums in defining identities (or possibly undertaking advocacy on behalf of certain social/racial groups) or their function as gatekeepers (or oppressors) in establishing significance or controlling access. As noted elsewhere, this may result in contrasting approaches to human remains with surviving descendant communities, such as Maoris, and those from "lost" communities, such as pharaonic remains.

Ethical guidelines are clearly open to interpretation. Words such as *respect* and *tact* are repeatedly used. Herein lie several potential problems. How can *respect* be defined? Can *respect* be codified within such policies on the basis of the needs and opinions of specific local communities, or should there be national or international standards? What may cause offence varies between different ethnic and religious groups and may result in different perceptions of respectful practice in different museum contexts. In some cases, this concept of respect has been enshrined in law. The Arizona State statute ARS 41-844 states that "a repository charged with the care or custody of human remains, funerary objects, sacred ceremonial objects . . . shall maintain them with appropriate dignity and respect" (Beck and Teague 2001:9). Where there is no legislation, some museums may feel the need to draw up specific policies for their human remains collections.

Discussion of the display of human remains tends to stress the importance of appropriate approaches but gives little guidance as to what these may be. The ICOM *Code* requires that public display should be carried out, "with great tact and with respect for the feelings of human dignity held by all peoples" (ICOM 2002:19), implying that this also applies to "lost" peoples. Issues of "Storage, Display, Interpretation and Return of Human Remains" are addressed by the UK Museum Ethnographers Group's *Professional Guidelines* (1994), although Pye (2001:172) notes that "archaeological conservators may feel that these issues will not directly affect them." Commenting on the ICOM Code, Per Kåks, then a member of ICOM's Ethics Committee, discussed changing attitudes to human remains and material of ritual significance. He argues that *respect* may mean "not just a question of showing the objects in a solemn setting, but perhaps of not showing them at all, or not allowing them to be handled except by very few and relevant persons" (Kåks 1998:10). This view is echoed by the UK Museums Association (2002:17), which suggests that museums "consider restricting access to certain specified items, particularly those of ceremonial or religious importance, where unrestricted access may cause distress to actual or cultural descendants." Likewise, the Museum Ethnographers Group (1994:22) argues for restricted access to human remains, "where unrestricted access may cause offence or distress to actual or cultural descendants." These are radical positions. Museums are often attacked for not displaying more of their collections. Here are recommendations to elect voluntarily to restrict access.

Kåks (1998:10–11) cites two problematic examples that demonstrate the complexity of the interlinking of national identity and politics versus the public fascination for seeing human remains. In the first case, an African Khoisan man (formerly known as Bushmen) was removed from display at the Museu Darder, Banyoles, Spain. Objections were raised at the time of the Barcelona Olympics and the Senegalese ambassador, responding to requests from the Organisation of African States, raised the matter at UNESCO. Paradoxically, objections from the Dutch Museums Association and Arctic Peoples Alert resulted in increased publicity and interest in the display of the body of a Greenland hunter, temporarily loaned to the Kunsthal, Rotterdam, from Westfries Museum, Hoorn, The Netherlands.

The Human Tissue Bill (April 1, 2006) also stresses the concept of consent which will be applied to current and future collecting policies (Department for Culture, Media and Sport 2003). A licensing system is proposed for museums holding material less than one hundred years old (Fielder 2004:20). Some British museums are actively setting up policy groups to review their practice concentrating on repatriation issues. In general, although some museums are developing proactive policies, many are favoring caution (Fielder 2004:27).

What's in a Name?
Describing bodies in museums is often difficult. The use of a particular term—*body, corpse, human remains, human preparation, specimen preserved in fluid*—is highly indicative of underlying attitudes and assumptions. The *Human Bodies, Human Choices* report into the extensive holdings of human remains in British hospitals openly grapples with this problem, noting, "There was no agreement on the most suitable collective term for human organs and tissue" (Department of Health 2003:10). Suggestions included *human substance, human material, human tissue*, and *materials of human origin*. The Museum Ethnographers Group (1994:22) defines *human remains* "as including both prehistoric and historic biological specimens as well as artifacts (i.e., items made from human remains which have been altered by deliberate intent)." In contrast, the exhibition *Spectacular Bodies* (Kemp and Wallace 2000) conformed to the museological norm of naming artists in the catalog entries. Human remains are cited as being made by "Anon," surely an absurd, if not offensive, application of standard practice. In the case of a sprang cap preserved on a naturally mummified head in the Petrie Collection, University College London, a conscious decision was taken to describe the combined artifact/human body part by the neutral term *find* (Javér et al. 1999).

The frequency with which human remains displayed in museums are given nicknames is significant in several ways (see the box in this chapter). The body of a man from the Fiskerton site is known as "Fissured Fred" (Chamberlain and Pearson 2001: 71). A naturally mummified Late Predynastic (5350 B.P.) Egyptian man on display in the British Museum is widely known as "Ginger." The museum's website explains this nickname derives from the color of the mummy's skin (British Museum 2000). Another body recovered from a peat marsh displayed in the British Museum is formally described as Lindow II but has been nicknamed "Pete Marsh." As well as avoiding the problematic issue of whether the body being displayed is a corpse or an artifact, this practice renders the alien dead body familiar and safe and draws it within the circuit of the living by making it less of the "other." Kirk and Start (1999) note that archaeologists often give names to skeletons, possibly as a more memorable means of identification than a number. They argue that this also "recognizes [the skeleton's] individuality, again promoting the idea of a respectful approach" (201).

DISPLAYING THE BODY

There is a long tradition of displaying bodies and body parts in museums. After the Enlightenment, they could be presented as part of scientific, ethnographic, archaeological, or medical exhibitions. Research by Wiltschke-Schrotta (n.d.) into the cultural and curatorial concerns involving human remains in museums focused on two collections: the National Museum of Natural History, Washington, D.C., and the Natural History Museum, Vienna. She notes that the initial motivation for the acquisition of human remains was to create a systematic human biology collection; display was not the primary goal. However, anthropological and science mu-

CARING FOR AN EGYPTIAN MUMMY AND COFFIN

Laura S. Phillips and Linda Roundhill

During pharaonic times in Egypt, mummification, as well as funerary scenes decorated on coffins, served to protect the deceased during the perilous journey through the underworld on the way toward obtaining eternal life. This journey was frequently interrupted when tombs were robbed for valuables by local thieves and even government officials (Taylor 2001). Much later, in the late nineteenth and early twentieth centuries, European and American museums encouraged yet more raiding in response to the Western fascination with Egyptian civilization. The Washington State Museum, now the Burke Museum of Natural History and Culture in Seattle, Washington, got caught up in this fad when, in 1902, a University of Washington regent purchased for the museum a Ptolemaic Period (2250–1980 B.P.) mummy and a Twenty-first Dynasty (2909–2839 B.P.) coffin from the National Museum of Egyptian Antiquities. Nearly a century later, this mummy and coffin have become an important part of Seattle's history.

Finding a Home

More than one hundred years of research and exhibition have taken their toll, and the Burke Museum's mummy and coffin were identified in the late 1990s as badly in need of conservation and a stable, protective environment. By this time, the museum had redefined its mission to focus on the Pacific Rim, and it recognized that the Egyptian collection fell outside its scope. The expense required for proper care might be better spent finding them a more appropriate home. Other institutions with more extensive Egyptian holdings had contacted the museum in the past, and one museum in 1998 wanted to offer Pacific Rim collections in exchange.

Intensive internal museum discussions ensued. Not only were the mummy and coffin outside the museum's mission, but the display of human remains is now a significant concern for the community. Native American remains are not displayed; other human remains are rarely displayed, and then only after consultation with the affected community. It seemed obvious, therefore, that the best solution was to transfer the collection. However, the mummy and coffin had become closely linked to the history and identity of the Burke Museum. For decades, schoolchildren eagerly flocked to the museum to see Seattle's only Egyptian mummy and coffin (figure 17.2). Today, nostalgic requests to view the mummy and coffin occur frequently.

Constructing Storage: Multiple Considerations

The museum's ultimate decision to keep and properly care for the mummy and coffin derived from the outpouring of community care, support, and continued interest. More than $35,000 was contributed to conserve the collection, as well as to design and build an environmentally stable case. While the museum anticipated the conservation work to take more than a year, the exhibit case, based on a hermetically sealed case design by the Getty Conservation Institute (GCI), was expected to take little or no design time, and to be built quickly, easily, and locally (Maekawa 1998). Although the conservation work was completed within the estimated time frame by Linda Roundhill, Art and Antiquities Conservation, the case could not be built as planned.

The new case needed to be designed for both display and storage, and would need to address specific environmental conditions and contextual factors. For almost ninety years, the mummy and coffin were continually displayed one inside the other as if they belonged together. The possible continuation of this practice created many problems for a variety of reasons: interpretive, spiritual, curatorial, and matters pertaining to public accessibility.

(continued)

CARING FOR AN EGYPTIAN MUMMY AND COFFIN (*continued*)

Figure 17.2. The Burke Museum's Egyptian mummy and coffin on display at Denny Hall, University of Washington, in the 1940s. Photo courtesy of *Seattle Times*.

Interpretive

Displaying the mummy and coffin as one object, while visually dramatic, creates the impression that they belong to the same artistic and ritual traditions. While both are recognizably Egyptian examples of funerary sacraments, their provenances were separated in time by nearly one thousand years. Both artistic styles and burial customs had changed considerably in that time, and even though the label may be explicit, the visual impact would be misleading.

Spiritual

Although the deceased has been dead for more than two thousand years and has already suffered the indignity of being removed from her burial context, displayed, studied, and handled, would it be proper to continue this trend? Should this mummy be forced to rest in the coffin of another individual whose name is clearly painted in the inside? Are the prayers and incantations depicted all over the coffin the correct ones for this deceased? From the perspective of the deceased, whose spirit may well be still conscious of the present (most religious traditions imply this), are we honoring the dead by continuing to display the body in this way?

Curatorial

Both the coffin and the mummy are fragile, have suffered from overexposure, and require an environment free of ultraviolet light radiation. Yet, they require different stable, controlled environments to ensure survival. The coffin's gessoed and painted wood must be kept at constant temperature and normalized relative humidity to minimize movement of the wood relative to the

CARING FOR AN EGYPTIAN MUMMY AND COFFIN (*continued*)

brittle paint layers. The mummy, though it would benefit as well from such conditions, should furthermore have an oxygen-free atmosphere to control biological degradation of the remains and prevent further deterioration of the extremely degraded linen.

Public Accessibility

The coffin is a funerary device but also a work of art. The entire coffin (minus the foot end and the undersides) is painted with ceremonial art and depictions of the underworld journey. The art on the inside is by far the most interesting visually and from a scholarly viewpoint. The mummy, on the other hand, is not primarily an art object, but human remains, despite traditional treatments of mummies in museums that often imply otherwise. The mummy, however, has a beautiful gilded mask and painted cartonnage (plaster-soaked linen) panels that are artistically significant. The museum is not interested in parading the coffin and mummy for the benefit of those with morbid fascinations but as a fine example of Egyptian funerary art and as representative of the beliefs of a past civilization.

Addressing Multiple Considerations

The coffin and mummy continue to instruct and inspire awe. It was therefore essential for the museum to develop a method of display and storage that would speak to all four of the aspects mentioned. The mummy and coffin would need to be in proximity because they share the same acquisition source and broad cultural context, but they must be in separate spaces to prevent misinterpretation and to provide the best possible environments. Furthermore, the coffin needs to be viewed from all angles with adequate safe lighting within, while the mummy should be provided with a private space that can be accessed on occasion for viewing or study, but is respectful of the spirit of the deceased.

It was with all these requirements in mind that the museum staff consulted with several professionals in the fields of storage, display, manufacturing, and conservation and ultimately developed the display case assembly described here.

Initial Planning

Based on the storage criteria just described, the museum's initial plan included separate cases that could be stacked for more efficient storage. Each case would have unique environmental conditions based on the GCI's design specifications. GCI specifications were sent to two local museum case fabricators, and both said it was too technical for them. In addition, the extruded metal frame parts essential to the hermetically sealed system could not be fabricated locally and would be cost-prohibitive because new die had to be made. As an alternative, one case fabricator provided us an estimate for a fir-framed case; the other quoted the cost to design (not build) a medite MDF-framed case for $4,500. Out of frustration, GCI was contacted. Staff there were quite helpful and generously offered one of their extra cases, gratis. Unfortunately, the size of the case did not meet the museum's needs.

A Revised Plan

Based on further discussions with the conservator, the museum decided that neither the mummy nor the coffin required a hermetically sealed case as long as the environment could be controlled. The museum then hired Snow & Company, a small contracting firm with experience in metal fabrication, as well as home and boat construction. This company suggested a single case with separately sealed compartments. The frame would be constructed of stainless steel with interior anodized aluminum extrusions. Air exchange would be minimal due to gaskets, but the case would not be hermetically sealed.

(continued)

CARING FOR AN EGYPTIAN MUMMY AND COFFIN (*continued*)

Our concern about storing the coffin and mummy together was minimized by the new design (figure 17.3). The coffin is placed in an upper partition with one-quarter-inch UV-filtered laminated glass on four sides and on top to ensure adequate views from all angles for research and display purposes. The mummy is respectfully placed in a discrete, nearly flush drawer below. The drawer can be pulled out and locked in place for display. Visitors and researchers can view the mummy through a glass covering on the top of the drawer. When not on display, the drawer is kept closed and locked.

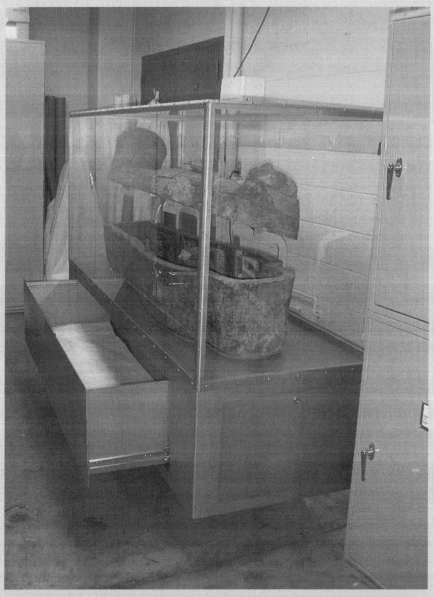

Figure 17.3.   The newly designed stainless steel case built by Snow & Company, Seattle, Washington, was the product of consultations with many experts. Photo courtesy of Burke Museum.

CARING FOR AN EGYPTIAN MUMMY AND COFFIN (*continued*)

The coffin, housed in the top portion of the case, is composed of a lid and base. The lid is mounted at an angle on Ethafoam-covered solid-anodized-aluminum frames with stainless steel sockets, and formed to the lid interior to ensure adequate weight distribution and minimal movement during earthquakes. The base rests on one-quarter-inch-thick Ethafoam to prevent direct contact with the steel base.

The stabilization of environmental conditions is particularly important for the coffin, given its sycamore wood construction and gesso and paint overlay. The frame of the case top was sealed with silicone gaskets, then four holes were drilled in the bottom of the top portion of the case. In one hole is a removable, gasketed screw fitted with an ACR SmartReader Plus 2 datalogger to measure temperature and relative humidity. One hole houses a fiber optic cable (discussed later). The other two holes are fitted with tubes, part of a passive system designed to regulate the relative humidity and air quality. CICU Air-Safe System (developed by NoUVIR Research in Seaford, Delaware) conditions and re-circulates the air in the top portion of the case. Air in the top portion of the case is expelled through one polypropylene tube into two cartridges fitted with microparticulate filters, a NIOSH/MSHA-certified acid gas/organic vapor filter, and a NIOSH/MSHA-certified formaldehyde/ammonia filter, and forty cubic inches of conditioned silica gel. The filtered air is then circulated back into the case through the second hose. The replaceable cartridges, enclosed in a 0.0005-inch-thick polyethylene bag, are accessible via a locked, separate side compartment in the lower portion of the case.

In order to adequately view the funerary texts and ritual scenes painted on the coffin, interior case lighting was essential. To prevent light and heat damage, a five-foot-long aluminum tube housing a three-hundred-strand capacity fiber optic cable was attached to the lid mount. Fiber optic light is emitted in a sixty-degree cone from fifty-eight holes arrayed linearly along the one-inch-square tube. The fiber optics provide an even light that illuminates the painted interior of the coffin. The light source, a 120-volt, 60-hertz illuminator with a 100-watt MR16 quartz halogen lamp and fan, is stored in a separate, vented compartment in the lower portion of the case, on the opposite end of the case from the compartment that houses the passive air quality system and provides access to the datalogger. A dimmer was added to the illuminator to provide variations in light as needed.

The mummy comprises the human remains as well as her accompanying cartonnage mask and body panels. An oxygen-free environment would help prevent further linen deterioration and insect damage. The cartonnage pieces are important for the mummy's journey to the afterlife and need to rest on top of her. The solution is a custom-made anoxic Keepsake bag. This nearly clear polyethylene bag houses the mummy as well as an oxygen scavenger and is heat sealed to provide a permanent oxygen-free environment. It can be opened and resealed as many as twelve times. A padded muslin cover fits over the entire case for storage. The case rests on lockable casters which are removable for display and storage.

The Journey Continues

Sadly, disassociated Egyptian mummies and coffins abound in museums around the world. In the future, respect for these burial objects and human remains may require returning them to proper entombment. However, many are in poor condition and cannot be returned to their original provenience due to the lack of adequate field collecting data. Museums can serve a positive role as respectful caretakers and educators. Successful attempts to rehouse these mummies and coffins require careful, considered thought along with expert and community involvement to preserve the dignity of the deceased and ensure their continued journey.

seums have often developed permanent displays, which tend to remain unchanged for many years. Native American human remains were on display in the National Museum of Natural History, Washington, for almost twenty-five years. These were removed from display in 1991 in response to the 1989 National Museum of the American Indian Act (NMAI) and the 1990 Native American Graves Protection and Repatriation Act (NAGPRA). The physical anthropology displays in the Natural History Museum, Vienna, were closed partly because of concerns over their link with Nazi racist ideology. However, Wiltschke-Schrotta's research in Europe and the United States makes clear that the public remain fascinated by displays of such material. Cordova and Bernal (2001) corroborate this public fascination for human mummies in Chile.

More than 130 British museums hold human remains, some in large quantities, such as the Natural History Museum, London (twenty thousand specimens), and the University of Cambridge (eighteen thousand specimens) (Connor 2000:12). The majority are in storage. The Hunterian Museum collection of human remains is an example of a collection that has always had a primary teaching function. John Hunter was a pioneering eighteenth-century surgeon who collected this material during his working life as teaching aids and to develop more effective and innovative surgical techniques. Parliament purchased the collection after Hunter's death in 1793 for the Royal College of Surgeons of England (RCSE 1993). It then comprised 13,687 specimens representing 500 species of animals and plants, including human remains. The original museum opened in 1813 and by 1941 the collections had increased to 65,000 specimens (RCSE 1993). It was originally used as a reference and educational collection for medical students and scientific researchers. During World War II, three-quarters of the original collection was destroyed by bombing. The surviving collection was divided between the Wellcome Museum of Anatomy and the Hunterian Museum; the latter containing mainly surviving material from the original collection. The new museum reopened in 1963 but was not open for public viewing until 1995. Until 2002, the present collection has been laid out as Hunter collated the material for his medical research. Human tissue and bone samples therefore sat alongside animal and plant specimens.

Human remains may also appear in unexpected contexts. Filey Museum, a small local museum on the Yorkshire coast, displays a skull recovered from a local Neolithic burial chamber, resting on a small shelf alongside social history objects. The label explains that this skull was used by a nineteenth-century parson to illustrate his lectures on Yorkshire archaeology. The focus here is entirely on the skull's later function as a teaching aid.

Using the human body as the central focus of temporary exhibitions is more unusual. *London Bodies* and *Body Worlds* offer contrasting approaches to the display of human remains and highlight the issues involved.

CASE STUDY 1: *LONDON BODIES*—THE CHANGING SHAPE OF LONDONERS FROM PREHISTORIC TIMES TO THE PRESENT DAY

London Bodies aimed to "explore how the physical appearance of London's inhabitants has changed from prehistory to the present day, based on archaeological and historical evidence" (Ganiaris and Calver 1999:24) by "unlock[ing] the secrets of skeletons excavated over the last twenty years" (Museum of London [1998]). This exhibition was presented as educational, using historic skeletal material and facial reconstructions to address social and medical issues affecting London populations. Publicity stressed the use of scientific analysis and technology to re-create Londoners' ancestors. Seven complete skeletons, from the prehistoric to the Georgian period, were selected from the museum's collection of 6,500 skeletons of past Londoners, together with other body parts (Ganiaris and Calver 1999; Museum of London [1998]). The skeletons were arranged in a broadly chronological progression, presented almost as if they were in transparent coffins, "laid out in marble dust on mortuary trolleys" under Perspex (Plexiglas) tops (Swain 1999). This was intended to evoke a "laboratory atmosphere" (Ganiaris 2001:268). Contemporaneous art and artifacts, particularly dress, underwear, and shoes, were displayed alongside the skeletons in order to present the physical bodies of Londoners and explore their state of health as well as how they sought to modify their appearance.

This exhibition seems to have been developed as a result of a new director's awareness of the potential of this part of the collection and formed part of the relaunch of the Museum of London. Simon Thurley "immediately identified the public interest there would be in this work [research into excavated skeletons]—London Bodies was born" (Swain 1999). The special nature of this material was recognized right from the start in order to "safeguard the interests of the other key part of the team, the human skeletons at the centre of the exhibition" (Swain 1999). Initially, it was not clear whether the exhibition would contravene the licenses granted for the excavation of the skeletons. Home Office advice suggested there was no clear legal framework, but it was felt that display would not be illegal. The museum developed two ethics papers to ensure that suitable respect was accorded to the human remains, one for internal use and one for the press and public. Drawing on established legal and ethical frameworks, this statement defined practice, including control of handling and press photography (Ganiaris 2001:268).

Despite this clear commitment to treating the remains with respect, the press launch seems to have stressed the sensational aspects. Journalists were invited to a themed breakfast of "long bone toast" and "bloody (strawberry) fruit juice" before being given flashlights and being briefed by white-coated specialists in a darkened basement illuminated with a single light (Swain 1999). Nevertheless, the museum made clear its legal and scientific responsibilities in caring for the human remains. Barham and Lang (2001:45) argue that the Museum of London gained valuable experience in balancing respect with access which was of benefit later when conducting the opening of the fourth-century Roman coffin from Spitalfields.

Before visitors entered the exhibition, three large signs made the contents very clear. Anyone with potential religious, ethical, or personal objections was made aware of the nature of the material displayed. Visitors were also asked to show appropriate respect. Unaccompanied children were not allowed into the exhibition, and, in recognition of the multicultural nature of London's schools, teachers organizing group visits were carefully briefed and parental permission was required (Ganiaris 2001:268). The exhibition was accompanied by a range of events aimed at adults, mainly lectures, or family groups, including hands-on workshops making face jugs, hand casts, "makeovers" in Tudor or Elizabethan styles, as well as storytelling sessions. Activities for children specified a suitable age range and seem to have been carefully designed not to focus on the skeletal remains presented in the exhibition. The exhibition flier enticed visitors with the prospect of seeing "our ancestors" and invited them "to see how you measure up to Londoners of the past," emphasizing how the skeletal record revealed people's health and appearance (Museum of London [1998]). The museum's website archive presents a summary with images. Interestingly, the exhibition flier does not show whole bodies. Similarly, a xeroradiograph of a skull, a strongly stylized image, is on the cover of the accompanying book, while the inside shows "dry" skull and bones (Werner 1998). The introduction by the then-director overtly justifies the museum's collection of skeletons: "The 6500 skeletons in the Museum's stores hold important information about the spread and development of a number of diseases of the bone such as rheumatoid arthritis. This historical enquiry therefore provides us with a lesson not only in social science but also in medical science" (Werner 1998). This argument is continued throughout the book, with a focus on the recovery of the skeletons, their analysis, and conservation. The clear and accessible discussion of technical details of the evidence that can be obtained from skeletal material is accompanied by lavish color illustrations of excavations, skeletons, grave goods, and facial reconstructions as well as contemporaneous art. This has the effect of connecting the dry bones with live people, particularly in the examination of the use of clothes and corsets to protect and modify the body form. Some more detailed case studies explore named individuals. The book ends with a brief photo essay showing contemporary Londoners, old and young, of different racial origin; there are no modern skeletons. The ethics of dealing with human remains are discussed in a brief paragraph of justification: "The disturbance of burials and the clearance of graveyards is usually a consequence of property development, and in fact the involvement of archaeologists is normally the best assurance that exposed skeletons will be treated with the maximum respect" (White and Ganiaris 1998:19).

Interestingly, in light of the number of skeletons both displayed in the exhibition and held by the Museum of London, White and Ganiaris (1998:19) go on to state that "it is relatively simple to perform a scientific study of the remains before they are reburied." Swain (1999) notes that, although the majority of the skeletons will be reburied, "this may be some time off" as scientific work will take time to complete. In the meantime, the skeletons are treated in a professional manner and kept in secure storage. It is worth noting that Jack Lohman (2003), current director of the Museum of London, has publicly stated that he would like the museum's entire human remains collection to be reburied. A more recent comment made by the museum's head of early London history, Hedley Swain, suggests that a major shift in attitudes to bodies in museums is taking place: "People making decisions should ask themselves whether they would feel comfortable about their bodies being dug up and stuck in a cardboard box" (Harris 2004:7).

CASE STUDY 2: *BODY WORLDS*—THE ANATOMICAL EXHIBITION OF REAL HUMAN BODIES

Body Worlds contrasts with the *London Bodies* exhibition in many ways. It is an international traveling exhibition, displayed in Japan, Germany, Switzerland, and Belgium, which was organized by the Institute of Plastination rather than by a formally established museum. The Institute was founded by Gunther von Hagens in 1993. Von Hagens, who has been visiting professor at the School of Medicine, Dalian, China, since 1996, developed the technique for the preservation of human tissue known as *plastination*. He presents himself as a scientist and an anatomical artist, saying, "There are obviously aesthetic elements to what I am doing but I am chiefly a scientist who wants to enlighten people by means of aesthetic shock rather than cruelty shock" (Jeffries 2002:2). The exhibition consisted of plastinated bodies, actual bodies preserved through a complex process involving injection with formaldehyde, dehydration using acetone, and impregnation under pressure with a liquid polymer solution before being posed for display. The plastination is carried out by the Institute's "factory" in China by "highly skilled dissectors" (Ashton 2003: 8). Walter (2004: 605) notes that not all of them have medical training. G. von Hagens himself sees his goals as both aesthetic and instructive, clearly aligning his work with the historical tradition of medical and anatomical art such as the anatomical waxworks made for medical education and now displayed at the La Specola Museum of Natural History, University of Florence. He claims he is seeking "the democratization of anatomy" (2002:21). Great stress is placed on the fact that all the plastinated bodies are donated for public display, although von Hagens has been accused of obtaining bodies illegitimately (Harris and Connolly 2002). Both the exhibition and the website (www.bodyworlds.com) invite visitors to donate their own bodies. The exhibition includes a shrine to the donors with a plastinated body holding its own heart surrounded by historical images, which also serves to justify von Hagens's own practice. One exhibit, incorporating a cross into a "Vanitas-plastinate," is intended as an appreciation of the positive role played by Christianity as a religion supportive of anatomical research.

The results are neither art nor purely science since the bodies are often positioned in dramatic poses, although von Hagens aims to display the dead human bodies as beautiful and educational items rather than morbid and gruesome (O'Rorke 2001). There is certainly a strong didactic element. Healthy and diseased samples were paired throughout the exhibition, as if promoting moral and healthy living. The plastinated smoker's lungs are highlighted on one of the exhibition's many posters. However, certain exhibits seemed to have been assembled to generate amusement, such as the goalkeeper catching his own intestines or "Mystical," a witch-type figure flying on her broomstick wearing comic spectacles with her facial skin pulled up to form her hat. This uneasy balance between education and entertainment typifies the general tone of the exhibition.

The main gallery was light and open and the display seemed to be aiming for a young and funky image, appealing to a wide range of visitors, rather than evoking the image of a stuffy, dark, old-fashioned medical museum. About twenty-five plastinated whole bodies, usually male, were displayed in dramatic postures, dissected to show various anatomical features but "animated" through "action" poses. A series of Perspex (Plexiglas) display cases contained at least 170 other body parts. These included sectioned or dissected body/skeletal parts intended to show the result of injuries and medical reasons for death, such as brain hemorrhage.

A special section, the climax of the display in the London exhibition, was devoted to gestation. A pregnant woman is shown reclining with her arm lifted behind her head, a classic female pose for sculpture or painting, but opened up to reveal her fetus still intact. Plastinated fetuses, complete with skin, were placed in boxes lined with black velvet as if these bodies were vulnerable and precious. This display method probably also offered some protection against damage or theft, although one fetus was actually stolen from the Body Worlds exhibition at the California Science Center (Jablon 2005). Some compared the development of healthy babies with diseased babies, such as with spina bifida or encephalitis, each labeled with an explanation of the defect. This raises issues about attitudes to healthy babies and deformed babies. The London exhibition lacked the notification included in the Brussels display that this section might be disturbing to visitors (Walter 2004:624).

The nature of the displays themselves raised issues of appropriateness and respect. The plinths for the central figures, which were supported or hung from slick modern metal structures, consisted of loose piles of bricks. This seemed very cheap and potentially unstable. The trees and plants which were placed as barriers and dividers all around the main hall in the exhibition seemed inappropriate, an effect reinforced by attendants happily walking about watering the plants while visitors were present. They were also ineffectual at preventing close contact with the plastinated bodies. The plastination treatment using resin would suggest that the bodies are fairly stable; they are said to "be expected to remain stable for at least four thousand years" (Walter 2004:606). However, the high light levels and lack of any immediate evidence of environmental control and monitoring raises issues about their long-term conservation. The exhibition was notable for the lack of any smell. Although a relief, this further distanced the experience of the exhibition from any understanding of the nature of human remains and death.

There was a clear contrast between the labeling of the complete posed plastinated bodies and that of the cased exhibits. Labels for the whole bodies tended not to be related to medical issues but focused more on artistic explanations of the pose and why a particular individual had been chosen—for example, on account of muscle tone. The surrounding museum style exhibits were accompanied by explanatory text which varied uncertainly between plainer "layman's" vocabulary and more technical medical terminology, while stressing health issues. Some exhibits were unlabeled, undermining the exhibition's educational claims.

Body Worlds' advertising literature is somewhat contradictory. Although it describes the exhibition as educational and scientific, "A Medical Dictionary in Three Dimensions" (Body Worlds 2002), the sensational images of whole bodies in dramatic postures and tasteless slogans such as "Skinless Wonders" tend to contradict this stance. The byline on one leaflet, "You've got one last shot to visit . . . Prof. Gunther von Hagens's *Body Worlds*" (2002), is accompanied by a photograph of "The Baseball Player," a plastinated body posed with a ball and photographed dramatically from above. This leaflet is crammed with information—a time line of anatomical history, a minibiography of von Hagens, and anatomical details illustrated with plastinated bodies. Both leaflets (2002 and ca. 2002) stress that the bodies are "authentic" and were donated by people, "specifically for the purpose of being plastinated for educational purposes." The institute offers a free information pack and waives the entrance fee for children under six years old.

The substantial and well-illustrated, multiauthored publication accompanying the exhibition combines the same themes of education, explanation, and promotion (Kunkel 2002). Wrapped around the central section on the human body are several defenses of the exhibition looking at reactions of visitors, displaying bodies, and legal issues. G. von Hagens's own contribution outlines the history of anatomical dissection and different techniques of body preservation, including the plastination technique, as well as his own life and experiences in developing this process. Ethical issues are addressed as well as theological questions regarding the nature of a plastinated body (Bauer 2002).

In some ways, this exhibition could be seen as the realization of Bentham's vision of using bodies of ancestors as sculpture. However, it is important to remember that this exhibition is not a museum display and so is outside the normal parameters of museum ethics. The institute functions as a business rather than a museum or charity. *Body Worlds* seems to be a cross between a medical, art, and freak show, using both educational and gratuitously sensationalist strategies to attract huge numbers of visitors.

London Bodies and *Body Worlds* both showcased the human body, in one instance displaying naturally preserved historic skeletons and, in the other, artificially preserved contemporary bodies. There are more parallels than may initially appear when comparing a museum exhibition with what appears to be the public outreach arm of a partly scientific and partly commercial organization. Both appealed to the public's ever-present curiosity about the human body, both raised unresolved issues about the legality of such displays, both used dramatic visualizations to enhance understanding, and both offered catalogs. However, there is a fundamental difference between the Museum of London's use of dry archaeological bones and *Body Worlds*' use of curiously lifelike plastinated flesh. The intellectual framework of the exhibitions is crucial. *London Bodies* "framed" the body within a popular but educational context. *Body Worlds* also has an educational goal but uses sensational display far more overtly to engage visitors' attention.

DOES CONSENT MAKE A DIFFERENCE?

Jeremy Bentham gave his full consent to the dissection and preservation of his dead body and asked for it to be placed on public display. Can there therefore be an argument against his "auto-icon" being displayed? Does the consent of a person, for their body to be used either for medical research or for museum display, eliminate ethical problems—or changes in public taste and susceptibility—in displaying human remains? This is particularly problematic where the display of the bodies of children and babies is involved: how can they give consent?

In contrast to Bentham, the Irish giant known as O'Brian, now displayed in the Hunterian Museum, made clear his wishes. He did not wish to be exhibited after his death. He had been involved in freak shows during his life but asked specifically to be buried at sea to avoid being dissected by surgeons. John Hunter managed to acquire his body by bribery and added the highly prized skeleton to his collection (Richardson 2000). The display text clearly states O'Brian's wishes. While this is an honest gesture on the part of the museum, it still seems contradictory. Consent in this case had been disregarded. However, the context is significant: at the time of O'Brian's death, body snatching was rife because medical researchers were desperate for bodies to dissect (Richardson 2000).

THE VISITOR AND THE BODY: ATTRACTION AND REVULSION

What do visitors think and feel about seeing bodies in museums? Do attitudes differ to seeing adults, children or embryos, healthy and unhealthy bodies, or historical and contemporary bodies? Richardson (2000) describes the act of watching the dead, which she dates back to the fourteenth century, a custom whereby the corpse was watched over nonstop by relatives in the home, during the period between death and burial. Such practices are no longer prevalent in modern Britain. The contemporary Western experiences of dead bodies are usually limited and usually take place in formalized medical surroundings. Viewing bodies outside the locale of death—the hospital, the hospice, the undertaker's chapel, the crematorium, or the graveyard—is usually anomalous. These are generally places to avoid unless personal loss takes us there or we are exploring graveyards for family history where the dead are usually at a safer distance.

Nevertheless, Western practices of burial and memorializing of the dead do change and practice alters, sometimes over relatively short periods of time (Hallam and Hockey 2001:4–5). These shifts can also be detected in the range of different attitudes visitors bring to viewing a dead human body in a museum. It could be argued that museums are playing an important role in introducing visitors, who may primarily experience death on cinema and television, to the reality of the dead human body. "We do not want to confront our mortality and, to that end, death is treated as a medical failure and is hidden from society at large. . . . Archaeology is the only medium by which many people will ever see or touch the remains of dead bodies" (Parker Pearson 1999:183). Similarly, Sledzik and Barbian (2001:227) have argued that displaying human remains can be beneficial as "the chance to see human specimens offers them [museum visitors] knowledge of themselves." Certainly, some visitors clearly feel connections across the barriers of time and death. One man "bought a flower to place on the lid of the case containing her [the Roman Lady's] coffin" (Barham and Lang 2001:53).

Different societies have evolved complex ways of dealing both with physical and emotional consequences of death. There are clearly differing levels of acceptability in relation to the excavation and display of human remains. Mary Douglas's (1984:2) analysis of the concepts of "rituals of purity and impurity" and the relationship of pollution beliefs to social life are useful here. A dead body is, in some senses, ultimate disorder. Displaying bodies in museums is an anomaly in Douglas's terms and hence needs a different way of thinking in order to render it possible. In Western museums, temporal or geographic distance enables this justification and objectification. Bodies become nonbodies and can be regarded as objects, divorced from spiritual or conceptual frameworks, whether artistic, historical, scientific, or medical. Human remains are displayed as clean bones or preserved specimens, frequently obscured by liquid in glass jars. Cases and bottles act as additional barriers and exclude any smells that might have connotations of death and decay. Complete skeletons or flesh and bones preserved artificially, as with the embalmed Egyptian mummies, or naturally, as in the case of bog bodies, seem unlike the living body. It is also the basis of the complex clashes of meaning and cultural need that underlie the repatriation debate.

Flesh was also a factor in the debate over whether Otzi, the Iceman, should be displayed and how this should be done. Hans Rotter, a theologian and priest from Innsbruck University, argued that "the fact that the Iceman from Haulabjoch is so well-preserved and his human features are so clearly visible does call for a certain piety" (Fowler 2000:163). Jeremy Hill, curator of the Iron Age Collections, Prehistory and Early Europe at the British Museum, notes that Lindow Man, whose flesh is also clearly preserved, is "probably the second most visited display in the British Museum, after 'Ginger' and the other Mummies" (personal communication, August 1, 2001). Wholley (2001:277) has explored the issue of "morbid" attraction with the abnormal and the corporeal, arguing that museums need to focus explicitly on issues involved with such material, particularly soft tissue collections, in their human remains policies. Ganiaris (2001: 271) notes that, of all the bodies displayed in the *London Bodies* exhibition, the skeletons of a child with rickets, a mother and fetus, and a skull with desiccated skin appeared to cause "some disquiet." These human remains clearly produced a greater emotional response possibly because of their various links with perceived deformity, gestation, and human flesh.

Rumsey (2001) undertook a small "snowball" survey exploring attitudes to the display of bodies in museums. Eighty-two percent of the respondents thought it was important to see skeletons or human remains in museums, while 17 percent were against this; one person was undecided. Those in favor thought such displays were important in enabling people to understand evolution and the lives of our ancestors. Some people made complex judgments relating to the origins of the human remains: "Since I have no religion, the 'feelings' of the person whose remains are on view are not important. However, if cultural feelings were involved, for instance, New Zealand Maoris, then I would object" (Rumsey 2001:63). Those who were against displays felt they were disrespectful, one person explaining that a TV program had influenced the formation of this view. Another respondent argued that a "skeleton should own some privacy" (Rumsey 2001:64). Others made a distinction between placing human remains on public display and using remains for medical research. One person argued that other display methods, such as digital techniques, enabled the educational points to be made without displaying actual human remains. The question "Which of the following types of human remains would you not like to see in a museum?" produced some revealing answers, with clear distinctions being made between displaying recent human remains as opposed to prehistoric remains, dry bones as opposed to flesh, and partial mature remains as opposed to complete babies. Fifty-five percent were against the excavation of twentieth-century British graveyards due to concerns about the impact of disturbing the recent dead on surviving family members. Nevertheless, people thought that medical research was important, and 71 percent would be willing to donate their bodies for this purpose. Despite this, an overwhelming 60 percent disliked the idea of displaying a preserved and complete human infant. In addition to the wet and dry issue highlighted by this experiment, it was clear that the group had issues relating to potential death and decay. The false teeth were received with equal repulsion, while the baby teeth were found to be less offensive. This is highly ironic since the false teeth were the only items used in the experiment that were not actual human or animal tissue. Could it be that the false teeth, intimate objects worn internally by living people, imply old age and the potential decay of human flesh, and this factor made people uncomfortable? In contrast, the "innocent" and "clean" children's teeth drop out naturally and could be perceived as sentimental keepsakes, especially as they were presented in a little decorative glass box.

The results of "The Use of Human Remains in Museum Exhibits" survey undertaken by the National Museum of Health and Medicine of the Armed Forces Institute of Pathology (Barbian and Berndt 2001:257) supports Rumsey's study. Both the staff and visitors surveyed felt that displaying human remains can have an educational benefit. Visitors responded positively to the display of real human remains and felt that these, when appropriately labeled, provided the opportunity for learning. However, there was some feeling that such an experience might not be suitable for younger children (Barbian and Berndt 2001:264–265).

CURATORIAL APPROACHES

Curatorial attitudes to the display of human remains seem to reflect this ambivalence as well as some conflict between professional and personal attitudes. "There is no doubt that skeletons are crowd-pullers" (Parker Pearson 1999:183). Salisbury and South Wiltshire Museum (SSWM), a small local museum, has no specific policy for displaying human remains and regards them as a good magnet to increase visitor numbers because they are so popular. SSWM displays one skull purely as "set dressing" within a general medical instrument display, suggesting the skull is seen as an artifact like any other object rather than as human remains (Rumsey 2001:10–11). One of the explicit motives behind the *London Bodies* exhibition was to "achieve a goal that is central to the Museum's current strategy: to reverse a slow but continual downward trend in visitor figures" (Swain 1998:14).

It is not just the display of the human remains that needs to be considered but also supporting text and interpretation. The popularity of "Ginger" in the British Museum has already been noted. He is displayed in an interpretative reconstruction, lying on a padded mount in what appears to be a burial position, surrounded by grave goods; these objects are not actually from his grave (Chamberlain and Pearson 2001:96). The British Museum website relates a slightly disconcerting anecdote about the apparent loss of part of one of his fingers. This seemed to disappear within a day of the body being placed on display in 1900, but, to quote the website, "almost disappointingly," it was found recently to be "clutched tightly in his fist" (British Museum 2000). The tone here is rather disturbing—why should the recovery of part of a human body in the museum's care be "disappointing"? Possibly this reflects a generalized discomfort with the notion of displaying such a "lifelike" body. A comparable ambivalence may be reflected in the punning title of the webpage discussing conservation issues: "A Sensitive Subject." Barbian and Berndt (2001:258) argue that carefully developed labeling using accessible language is important to make the display of human remains into an educational experience. They also acknowledge that more research is needed to understand the impact of such displays on young children (265).

Visitors' views on the *London Bodies* exhibition were collected through a market research survey and a comments box. Most were positive (110 positive to 62 negative), and only one visitor expressed concern over ethical issues of displaying human remains (Swain 1999). *Body Worlds'* marketing stresses the positive response of many visitors, highlighting endorsement by celebrities. However, the exhibition provoked strong reactions from religious bodies, the medical profession (Feinmann 2002:86; Jury 2002:14), and city authorities (*The Independent* 2003:15) as well as individuals. One visitor was even moved to attack the plastinated bodies physically in protest (Chrisafis 2002).

It is important for museums to remember that different social and cultural groups have different attitudes. English Heritage's small survey of visitors to its Avebury museum found that most people approved of keeping the Neolithic child skeleton on display. However, a "surprising number of those against its continued display were American tourists" (Chamberlain and

Pearson 2001:184). Jeremy Hill (personal communication, August 6, 2001) reports that the visitors who were troubled by the display of Lindow Man, even in a more conservation-friendly environment with lower light levels in the Roman Britain and Celtic Europe Galleries, tended to be those from first world nations who personally had concerns about the display of human remains in museums.

Some institutions traditionally control access to human remains collections to avoid inappropriate use. The RCSE's Wellcome Museum of Pathology, which contains bodies of the recently deceased donated for medical research, has a controlled access policy agreed to by Her Majesty's Inspector of Anatomy. According to RCSE curator Simon Chaplin, it is only open to medical students, professionals, and, under specific conditions, art students (personal communication, August 9, 2001). The Hunterian Museum at the Royal College of Surgeons reopened to the public in February 2005 following a major redevelopment. The new displays include fetal specimens and wet tissue preparations. However, post-1950 human specimens acquired under the 1988 Anatomy Act or the Human Tissues Act will not be on public display. Under the terms of the Anatomy Act, donated bodies are only kept for three years and will then be cremated or returned to their relatives for burial. An annual remembrance service is held for those who donated their bodies (Simon Chaplin, personal communication, February 24, 2004).

In contrast, Sledzik and Barbian (2001:229) report that, in their experience, visits by descendants of human specimens held at the National Museum of Health and Medicine can be constructive and "mutually supportive" and note that "families take great pride that their relative is part of this unique collection" (230). Nevertheless, there are clearly many ethical issues to be considered regarding the family or descendants of an individual whose remains are in a museum before analysis, experimentation, or display takes place.

CHANGING POLICIES AND PRACTICES

Attitudes clearly are changing. Excavation, analysis, documentation, handling, display, labeling, storage, and access, including publicity and press information, all need to be considered. Following the Alder Hey scandal, the establishment of the Retained Organs Commission, and the Human Tissues Act, UK institutions holding human remains, particularly those within hospitals and medical institutions, are changing their practices (Butler 2001). The Hunterian Museum has removed from display at least five fetal samples collected since the 1950s, although the museum has received no public complaints, and these are not covered by the act. The museum does exhibit the full skeletons of several criminals but has a policy of allowing descendants to request the return of these remains to the family for reburial. So far, only one such request has been made (Gooderham 2004).

Some museums are mediating the experience by involving visitors in the viewing decision by alerting them to the nature of the display before they enter the gallery. This was done at the *London Bodies* exhibition (Swain 1998). In the case of *Digging for Dreams,* a touring exhibition originally shown at Croydon Clocktower museum, shrouds were placed over exhibits of Egyptian human remains so that visitors could choose whether or not to raise them and to look. Visitor feedback, which was largely positive, was encouraged within the exhibition itself on a comments board. Accommodation can be reached to ensure that display of human remains can satisfy the requirements of both contemporary tribal groups and museums.

Wiltschke-Schrotta (n.d.) describes the successful approach adopted by the Museum of Man, San Diego. The 1998–1999 exhibition *The Mysteries of the Mummies* was ceremonially cleansed and blessed by the local Native American tribe. No complaints were received about this highly popular exhibition. Such engagement could extend to museum websites and advertising.

VIEWS ON DISPLAYING HUMAN REMAINS

Responses to the question "Which of the following types of human remains would you not like to see in a museum?" (Rumsey 2001):

- A baby's skeleton
- A medically preserved baby (flesh intact)
- A medically preserved adult body (flesh intact)
- A prehistoric skeleton
- A skeleton from the early twentieth century
- A skeleton from the late twentieth century
- Medically preserved human organs/body parts

Other responses included the following:

- None of the above
- Nothing ever offends
- Don't mind
- Only where relatives would object
- Fetuses of any kind
- The elderly

The fifty-one respondents ranged in age from below twenty to above sixty years old, with the majority between thirty and fifty years of age. Fifty-three percent were female, and all were British. Respondents included representatives of five religions (Church of England, Protestants, Catholic, Jewish, and Muslim), although the majority identified themselves as having no religion; the next largest group was members of the Church of England. Over 30 percent identified themselves as occasional museum visitors, 14 percent said they were regular visitors, and 13 percent said they never visited museums. Over 45 percent stated that they watched archaeological programs on television. For example, *Meet the Ancestors*, a British program that often undertakes skeletal reconstructions, was watched by 30 percent of the respondents (Rumsey 2001).

Although images on National Museums of Scotland Mummy Project website (n.d.) include wrapped and unwrapped mummies with xeroradiographs as well as computer reconstructions of some mummy heads, the complexity of the issue is openly acknowledged, "Our challenge is to understand them [the mummies] whilst respecting their human dignity."

The Mary Rose Trust is responsible for the bodies of ninety-two drowned sailors raised in 1982 with Henry VIII's flagship. The trust (2000) states that its staff "reject any attempt to use the material [human remains] in a public exhibition or allow it to feature in the popular press or television."

CONCLUSION

Human remains in museum collections are different, not least in the conflicting views surrounding them. The two case studies presented in this paper demonstrate both the popularity of displays of human remains while highlighting the many contradictions that underpin this, including sensationalism and commoditization. Cultural changes are resulting in new legal obligations. Open debate is vital to negotiate appropriate policies and procedures for human remains in different collections, balancing culturally sensitive approaches to preservation or repatriation with institutional goals of education, access, and meeting visitor expectations. Better communications between museum professionals and their varied source and user communities may enable these interlinked issues to be more effectively managed, resulting in practices which enshrine consensual custodianship and respect.

ACKNOWLEDGMENTS

We would like to thank Nell Hoare, OBE, director, Textile Conservation Centre, University of Southampton, for permission to publish. Thanks are also due to many colleagues, especially Dinah Eastop, senior lecturer, Textile Conservation Centre, University of Southampton; and the curators, conservators, and archaeologists who so generously shared information and ideas with us, particularly Bill White, Centre for Human Bioarchaeology, Museum of London.

REFERENCES

Arnold, Ken, and Danielle Olsen
    2003 *Medicine Man: The Forgotten Museums of Henry Wellcome.* British Museum Press, London.

Ashton, Robert
    2003 Life after Death: My Future as a Skinless Wonder. *The Independent on Sunday,* July 6, 8.

Barbian, Lenore, and Lisa Berndt
    2001 When Your Insides Are Out: Museum Visitor Perceptions of Displays of Human Anatomy. In *Human Remains: Conservation, Retrieval, and Analysis: Proceedings of a Conference Held in Williamsburg, VA, Nov 7–11th 1999,* edited by Emily Williams, pp. 257–266. BAR International Series 934. Archaeopress, Oxford.

Barham, Elizabeth, and Rebecca Lang
    2001 Hitting the Ground Running—Excavations and Conservation of a Roman Burial in the Media Spotlight. In *Human Remains: Conservation, Retrieval, and Analysis: Proceedings of a Conference Held in Williamsburg, VA, Nov 7–11th 1999,* edited by Emily Williams, pp. 45–54. BAR International Series 934. Archaeopress, Oxford.

Bauer, Alex W.
    2002 Plastinated Specimens and their Presentation in Museums—A Theoretical and Bioethical Retrospective on a Media Event. In *Prof. Gunther von Hagens's Body Worlds: The Anatomical Exhibition of Real Human Bodies,* edited by Albrecht Kunkel, pp. 216–228. Institut für Plastination, Heidelberg.

Beck, Elke
    2001 "Es Ist Alles Tot Ding"?!? Considerations in Dealing with Relics. In *Human Remains: Conservation, Retrieval, and Analysis: Proceedings of a Conference Held in Williamsburg, VA, Nov 7–11th 1999,* edited by Emily Williams, pp. 17–22. BAR International Series 934. Archaeopress, Oxford.

Beck, Lane, and Lynn Teague
    2001 Reburial Laws in Action: Case Studies from Arizona. In *Human Remains: Conservation, Retrieval, and Analysis: Proceedings of a Conference Held in Williamsburg, VA, Nov 7–11th 1999,* edited by Emily Williams, pp. 5–10. BAR International Series 934. Archaeopress, Oxford.

Besterman, Tristram
    2003 *Human Remains: Objects to Study or Ancestors to Bury.* Transcript of the Institute of Ideas Debates, May 2. Electronic document, http://www.instituteofideas.com/transcripts/human_remains.pdf, accessed May 23, 2006.

Boddington, A., Andrew N. Garland, and R. C. Janaway, editors
    1987 *Death, Decay and Reconstruction: Approaches to Archaeology and Forensic Science.* Manchester University Press, Manchester.

Body Worlds

2002 *You've Got One Last Shot to Visit Prof. Gunther von Hagens's Body Worlds.* Advertising leaflet. 8th ed. Body Worlds, London.

ca. 2002 *Discover the Mysteries under Your Skin.* Advertising leaflet. Body Worlds, London.

Brandes, Stanley

2001 The Cremated Catholic: The Ends of a Deceased Guatemalan. *Body & Society* 7(2–3):111–120.

British Museum

2000 *Conserving "Ginger," a Predynastic Egyptian: A Sensitive Subject.* Electronic document, http://www.british-museum.ac.uk/compass/, accessed September 3, 2003.

Butler, Toby

2001 Body of Evidence. *Museums Journal* 101(8): 24–27.

Chamberlain, Andrew

1994 *Human Remains.* British Museum Press, London.

Chamberlain, Andrew T., and Michael P. Pearson

2001 *Earthly Remains: The History and Science of Preserved Human Bodies.* British Museum Press, London.

Chrisafis, Angelique

2002 Lecturer's Body Blow Costs Exhibition £30,000. *The Guardian,* March 28. Electronic document, http://www.education.guardian.co.uk/higher/arts/story/0,,675371,00.html (accessed June 30, 2006).

Connor, Steve

2000 Alarm Raised over Return of Human Remains. *The Independent,* May 16, 12.

Cordova, Julia, and Jorge Bernal

2001 Fascinación por las Momias: Reforzamiento de la Vida. *Chungará* 33(1):91–93.

Cox, Margaret

1996 *Life and Death in Spitalfields 1700–1850.* Council for British Archaeology, York.

Crowhurst, Flora

2000 Ancient Egypt and English Museums: Attitudes Displayed toward Egyptian Antiquities in the 19th Century, with Specific Reference to the Cultural Biography of an Egyptian Mummy and Coffin. (Haslemere Museum). Master's thesis, Textile Conservation Centre, University of Southampton.

Department for Culture, Media and Sport (DCMS)

2003 Working Group in Human Remains Report. November. Electronic document, http://www.culture.gov.uk/global/publications/archive_2003/wgur_report2003.htm, accessed May 23, 2006.

Department of Health, Clinical Ethics and Human Tissue Branch

2003 *Human Bodies, Human Choices.* Summary of Responses to the Consultation Report. Department of Health, London. Electronic document, http://www.culture.gov.uk/global/publications/archive_2003/wgur_report2003.htm, accessed May 23, 2006.

Douglas, Mary

1984 *Purity and Danger: An Analysis of the Concepts of Pollution and Taboo.* Ark Paperbacks, London.

Feinmann, Jane

2002 Vein Glories. *OM* [*Observer Magazine*], October 13, 86–87.

Fielder, Laura

2004 The New Human Tissue Bill—Solving Some Problems by Creating Others? A Discussion of the Impact of the Human Tissue Bill. Master's thesis, University of Southampton, Southampton.

Ford, David Nash
2000 Shrines to St. Oswald, King of Northumbria. Electronic document, http://www.britannia.com/church/shrines/oswald.html, accessed May 23, 2006.

Fowler, Brenda
2000 *Iceman: Uncovering the Life and Times of a Prehistoric Man Found in an Alpine Glacier.* Macmillan, London.

Fuller, Catherine, editor
1998 *The Old Radical: Representations of Jeremy Bentham.* The Bentham Project. University College London, London.

Ganiarus, Helen
2001 *London Bodies*: An Exhibition at the Museum of London. In *Human Remains: Conservation, Retrieval, and Analysis: Proceedings of a Conference Held in Williamsburg, VA, Nov 7–11th 1999*, edited by Emily Williams, pp. 267–274. BAR International Series 934. Archaeopress, Oxford.

Ganiaris, Helen, and Andrew Calver
1999 London Bodies on Display. *Museum Practice* 4(2):24–28.

Geary, Patrick
1986 Sacred Commodities: The Circulation of Medieval Relics. In *The Social Life of Things*, edited by Arjun Appadurai, pp. 169–191. Cambridge University Press, Cambridge.

Gooderham, Dave
2004 Murderer Laid to Rest after 200 Years. *East Anglian Daily Times*, August 17. Electronic document, http://www.eadt.co.uk/content/news/story, accessed August 20, 2004.

Hallam, Elizabeth, and Jenny Hockey
2001 *Death, Memory and Material Culture.* Berg, Oxford.

Harris, Ed
2004 17,000 Skeletons in the Cupboard. *Evening Standard*, January 6, 7.

Harris, Paul, and Kate Connolly
2002 World Trade in Bodies Is Linked to Corpse Art Show. *The Observer*, March 17, 13.

Henderson, Janet, Robert C. Janaway, and Julian R. Richards
1987 Cremation Slag: A Substance Found in Funerary Urns. In *Death, Decay and Reconstruction: Approaches to Archaeology and Forensic Science*, edited by A. Boddington, A. N. Garland, and R. C. Janaway, pp. 81–100. Manchester University Press, Manchester.

Heywood, Felicity
2003 Human Remains Decisions Held Up by Delays from DCMS Working Group. *Museums Journal* 103(9):7.

The Independent
2003 Court Overturns Ban on Corpse Show. February 22, 15.

International Council of Museums
2002 *Code of Ethics for Museums.* ICOM, Paris.

Jablon, Robert
2005 "Body Worlds" fetus stolen from display. *Chicago Sun-Times* 31 March. Electronic document, http://www.findarticles.com/p/articles/mi_qn4155/is_20050331/ai_n1350683 8 (accessed July 12, 2006).

Javér, Anna, Dinah Eastop, and Rosalind Janssen
1999 A Sprang Cap Preserved on a Naturally Dried Egyptian Head, circa 300 AD. *Textile History* 30(2):135–154.

Jeffries, Stuart
  2002 The Naked and the Dead. *The Guardian*, March 19, 2.

Jury, Louise
  2002 Anatomy Exhibition for Human Consumption. *The Guardian*, March 21, 14.

Kåks, Per
  1998 Human Remains and Material of Ritual Significance. *ICOM News* (ICOM '98 Special Issue):10–11.

Kemp, Martin, and Marina Wallace
  2000 *Spectacular Bodies: The Art and Science of the Human Body from Leonardo to Now.* Hayward Gallery and University of California Press, Berkeley.

Kirk, L., and S. Start
  1999 Death at the Undertakers. In *The Loved Body's Corruption: Archaeological Contributions to the Study of Human Mortality*, edited by Jane Downes and Tony Pollard, pp. 200–208. Cruithne Press, Glasgow.

Kirshenblatt-Gimblett, Barbara
  1998 *Destination Culture: Tourism, Museums and Heritage.* University of California Press, Berkeley.

Kunkel, Albrecht, editor
  2002 *Prof. Gunther von Hagens's* Body Worlds: *The Anatomical Exhibition of Real Human Bodies.* Institut für Plastination, Heidelberg.

Lock, Margaret
  2001 The Alienation of Body Tissue and the Biopolitics of Immortalised Cell Lines. In *Commodifying Bodies*, edited by Nancy Scheper-Hughes and Loïc Wacquant, pp. 62–91. Sage, London.

Lohman, Jack
  2003 International Perspectives on Museums in South Africa and London. Lecture, International Council of Museums, UK AGM, London, October 16.

Maekawa, Shin
  1998 Design and Construction of the GCI's Hermetically Sealed Display and Storage Case. In *Oxygen Free Museum Cases*, edited by S. Maekawa, pp. 31–51. Research in Conservation Series. Getty Conservation Institute, Los Angeles.

Magee, A.
  2001 Boy's Grave May Bear Witness to Brutal Regime. *The Times*, April 20, 8.

Manchester, Keith
  1987 Skeletal Evidence for Health and Disease. In *Death, Decay and Reconstruction: Approaches to Archaeology and Forensic Science*, edited by A. Boddington, A. N. Garland, and R. C. Janaway, p. 167. Manchester University Press, Manchester.

Marmoy, Charles F. A.
  1958 The "Auto-Icon" of Jeremy Bentham at University College London. *Medical History* 2:77–86.

Mary Rose Trust
  2000 *Code of Practice.* Unpublished museum document. Mary Rose Trust, Portsmouth.

McGowan, Gary S., and Cheryl J. Laroche
  1996 The Ethical Dilemma Facing Conservation: Care and Treatment of Human Skeletal Remains and Mortuary Objects. *Journal of American Institute of Conservation* 35:109–121.

Museum Ethnographers Group
  1994 Professional Guidelines Concerning the Storage, Display, Interpretation and Return of Human Remains in Ethnographical Collections in United Kingdom Museums. *Journal of Museum Ethnography* 6:22–24.

Museum of London

[1998] *Exhibitions and Events October & November '98*. Museum leaflet. Electronic document, http://www.museum-london.org.uk/MOLsite/exhibits/bodies/bodies.htm.

Museum of Man, San Diego

n.d. Electronic document, http://www.museumofman.org/index.html.

Museums Association

2002 *Code of Ethics for Museums*. Museums Association, London.

National Museums of Scotland Mummy Project

n.d. The NMS Mummy Project. Electronic document, http://www.akhet.co.uk/nmsmummy.htm (accessed June 30, 2006).

O'Rorke, I.

2001 Skinless Wonders. *The Observer Review*, May 20, 5.

Parker Pearson, Mike

1995 Ethics and the Dead in British Archaeology. *The Field Archaeologist* 23:17–18.

1999 *The Archaeology of Death and Burial*. Sutton, Gloucester.

Pye, Elizabeth

2001 Caring for Human Remains—A Developing Concern? In *Past Practice—Future Prospects*, edited by Andrew Oddy and Sandra Smith, pp. 171–176. British Museum Occasional Paper 145. British Museum Press, London.

Richardson, Ruth

2000 *Death, Dissection and the Destitute*. 2nd ed. University of Chicago Press, Chicago.

Richardson, Ruth, and Brian Hurwitz

1987 Jeremy Bentham's Self Image: An Exemplary Bequest for Dissection. *British Medical Journal* 295:1995–1997.

Royal College of Surgeons of England (RCSE)

1993 *A Guide to the Hunterian Museum*. Bicentenary ed. RCSE, London.

Rumsey, Claire

2001 Human Remains: Are the Existing Ethical Guidelines for Excavation, Museum Storage, Research and Display Adequate? Master's thesis, University of Southampton, Southampton.

Russell, Scott

2001 Dealing with Human Remains. An Approach from the Northern Marianas. *Pacific Preservation*. *CRM* 24(1):23–24.

Sledzik, Paul, and Lenore Barbian

2001 From Privates to Presidents: Past and Present Memoirs from the Anatomical Collection of the National Museum of Health and Medicine. In *Human Remains: Conservation, Retrieval, and Analysis: Proceedings of a Conference Held in Williamsburg, VA, Nov 7–11th 1999*, edited by Emily Williams, pp. 227–235. BAR International Series 934, Archaeopress, Oxford.

Swain, Hedley

1998 Displaying the Ancestors. *The Archaeologist*, 33:14–15.

1999 Displaying the Ancestors. Unpublished paper.

Taylor, John H.

2001 *Death and the Afterlife in Ancient Egypt*. University of Chicago Press, Chicago.

University College London

1993 Jeremy Bentham. Bentham Project, University College London. Electronic document, http://www.ucl.ac.uk/Bentham-Project/info/jb.htm (accessed June 30, 2006).

Vaswani, Ratan

2001 Remains of the Day. *Museums Journal* 101(2):34–35.

von Hagens, Gunther

2002 My Week: Gunther von Hagens—The Professor Who Performed the First Public Autopsy in Britain for 170 Years. *The Independent*, November 23, 21.

Walter, Tony

2000 Bereavement, Biography and Commemoration. *Journal of the Social History Curators Group* 25:9–16.

2004 Plastination for Display: A New Way to Dispose of the Dead. *Journal of the Royal Anthropological Institute* 10(3):603–627.

Ward, David

2003 Return of Aboriginal Remains. *The Guardian*, July 30. Electronic document, http://www.guardian.co.uk/uk_news/story/0,,1008520,00.html, accessed May 23, 2006.

Werner, Alex

1998 *London Bodies: The Changing Shape of Londoners from Prehistoric Times to the Present Day*. Museum of London, London.

White, Bill, and Helen Ganiaris

1998 Excavating Bodies: Excavating and Analysing Human Skeletons. In *London Bodies: The Changing Shape of Londoners from Prehistoric Times to the Present Day*, edited by Alex Werner, pp. 14–21. Museum of London, London.

Wholley, Anna L.

2001 The Attraction of the Macabre: Issues Relating to Human Soft Tissue Collections in Museums. In *Human Remains: Conservation, Retrieval, and Analysis: Proceedings of a Conference Held in Williamsburg, VA, Nov 7–11th 1999*, edited by Emily Williams, pp. 275–281. BAR International Series 934. Archaeopress, Oxford.

Wiltschke-Schrotta, Karin

n.d. [ca. 2000] *Human Remains on Display—Curatorial and Cultural Concerns*. Final Report, Fellowships in Museum Practice. Electronic document, http://museumstudies.si.edu/Fellowships/FMPFinalReportSchrotta.htm, accessed May 23, 2006.

Afterword

I tell you, the more I think, the more I feel that there is nothing more truly artistic than to love people.

—Vincent Van Gogh

CHANGE HAS FORCED A REEVALUATION OF HOW WE CARE FOR AND MANAGE EXISTING HUMAN REMAINS collections. As the legacy of curatorial complacency is revealed and determined to be unacceptable, conservators and others have been asked to participate in new team efforts to improve preservation. This is a new and challenging role for conservators who traditionally work with artifacts, the objects made through human skill, not the remains of the humans themselves. Conservators normally examine, assess condition, investigate technology, and analyze composition of materials for the purpose of long-term preservation. Expanding this role to include human remains collections is a very recent evolution and relates to the use of conservation to preserve all types of collections held within museums, repositories, libraries, and academic institutions.

Caring for human remains as a collection mirrors the change in perspective within bioarchaeology, from individual cases to anthropological population studies. The care and management of entire collections is more complex but provides more effective preservation because it addresses storage environment, handling, labeling, support, packing, documentation, security, examination, and safety. Physical anthropologists often refer to human remains collections as analogous to a special collection in libraries where lending is not allowed and preservation is the main goal. Curation and conservation should be equal partners in research and should work together with descendants to care for the dead.

To preserve what is important necessitates respect and the cooperation of all concerned. The care and management of human remains collections is not the sole concern of any one profession. On one hand, some feel current curation concerns are a whim that we will look back on in years to come and say this was an unfortunate diversion taking us away from real science. On the other hand, NAGPRA legislation, if considered as the editors do—as chiefly civil rights legislation—reflects not a temporary swing but growth and maturity of a pluralistic society in terms of respect for others, both living and dead.

Discussions about what is cultural patrimony belonging to a community versus patrimony belonging to the global community were beyond the scope of the curation guidelines provided here. Though these higher-level philosophical issues were not specifically discussed in this volume, examples from a range of situations were presented in other contexts. Disputes of various types surround or have surrounded the following examples that were brought up by various contributors in this volume: the struggle in South Africa to repatriate Bushmen relatives from a century ago; the repatriation from the United States of Ramses I, an Egyptian pharaoh living a millennium ago; and Kennewick Man, who roamed North America almost ten thousand years ago.

Respect, not sentimentality, is a professional obligation. We cannot just give lip service to the issues of human remains collections. We hope this volume opens up minds and helps a new generation achieve the potential for more respectful curation for institutionalized human remains collections.

Beanbag Pattern for Skull

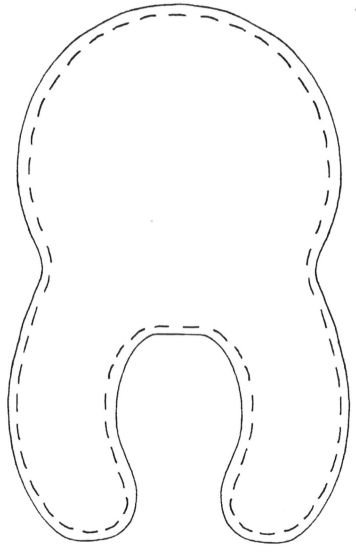

Beanbag pattern for a skull support. Photocopy and enlarge this image by 200% to obtain the correct pattern size. Illustration by Caroline Sakaguchi Kunioka and Jennifer Allen.

Index

AA. *See* cold vapor atomic absorption

AAM. *See* American Association of Museums

AAPA. *See* American Association of Physical Anthropologists

AAR. *See* amino acid racemization dating

Aboriginal and Torres Strait Islander Heritage Protection Act, 228

accelerator mass spectroscopy (AMS), 70

access: to collections, 109, 254; and condition assessments, 41, 43; to databases and records, 158, 168–69; to law enforcement collections, 35–36; policies for, 25–26; to sites under excavation, 189, 193

accessions, mission statements for, 23–24

Aconcagua, Cerro, 143–44

acrylics, 85

adhesives, 85; alternatives to, 88–92; in reconstruction and restoration, 86–87

African Americans, 248

AIC. *See* American Institute for Conservation

Ainu people, 230

airing, of cabinetry, 107

Ak-Chin Indian Community, 252

algae, 34

allergic reactions, 207

American Academy of Forensic Sciences, 14, 29

American Anthropological Association, 13

American Antiquities Act (1906), 233

American Association of Anthropology, 6

American Association of Museums (AAM), 12, 21, 22

American Association of Physical Anthropologists (AAPA), 9, 12, 258

American Board of Forensic Examiners, 14

American Institute for Conservation (AIC), 12, 104, 172

American National Standards Institute (ANSI), 172

amino acid racemization (AAR) dating, 70

AMS. *See* accelerator mass spectroscopy

analysis: of human remains and funerary objects, 253–54; instrumental, 69, 70–73

anatomy, displays of human, 276–78

Anatomy Act (United Kingdom), 262, 263

Andes societies, funerary practices in, 129–33

Angel, Larry, 157

animals, in Andean burials, 130–31, 139

ANSI. *See* American National Standards Institute

anthropology, 129, 163; biological, 8–12; ethics in, 5–7

Antiquities Act (New Zealand), 229

antiquities trade, 225–26

Archaeological Institute of America, 14

Archaeological Resources Protection Act (ARPA) (U.S.), 184, 199, 233, 234–35, 240

archaeology, xvii–xviii, 6; permits and permissions for, 183–85; salvage, 131, 134–36, 190–91; treatment of human remains in, 247–48; U.S. case law and, 240–41

Archaic period, in Chile, 130–33

Arctic Peoples Alert, 267–68

Argentina, 143–44, 176

Arica burials, 132, 133, 190–91

Arizona, treatment of burials in, 199, 238, 246–48, 252, 267

Arizona State Museum, 114, 199, 238, 255; destructive testing policy of, 74–75; documentation system in, 157–58; repatriation consultations by, 252, 254

Arkansas Archaeological Survey, 238

ARPA. *See* Archaeological Resources Protection Act

arsenic, as health hazard, 207–8
artifacts, 58, 100, 158, 230, 265; in Andean burials, 129–48; curation of, 142–43. *See also* funerary objects
Asahikawa Ex-Aborigines Protection Land Disposition Act, 230
Atacama Desert mummies, 190–91
Atlantis Gallery (London), human bodies displayed at, 261–62
Australia, 13, 153, 228
Australian Archaeological Association, 13
auto-icons, 262
Avebury, skeleton displayed at, 281–82
avoidance, 247
Azapa Valley, 131

Baartman, Sarah, 153
bacteria, 32, 206, 212–13
bags, 52, 109, 112, *113*, 196
beanbags, for support, 52, 53–54, *293*
Beatty v. Kurtz, 240
Bedouin burials, 185
belief systems, 151, 186–87
Bentham, Jeremy, 262–*63*, 278
biohazards, 205–7
Biometric school of measurements, 156
Bishop Museum, 253–54, 255
Blakely, Bob, 157
bleach, 82
BLM. *See* Bureau of Land Management
Blumenbach collection, 152
bodies: displaying, 261–63, 266–67, 268–78, 279–80, 281–83; social and religious attitudes toward, 264–68, 280–81
Body Worlds: The Anatomical Exhibition of Real Human Bodies, 261–62, 266, 276–78
bonding, 36, 86
bone, 264; cleaning of, 206–7; composition of, 29–31; deterioration of, 32–34; fossilized and subfossilized, 31–32; handling of, 52, *54*–58
Bones Version 1.0 software, 159, *295*–96
Bonnichsen v. United States, 240
borescopes, 62–63
Botswana, 153
boxes, 52, 110–*11*, 196
British Museum, 262, 264–65, 280, 281
bronchitis, chronic, 213
buildings, 104–5
Bureau of Indian Affairs, 158
Bureau of Land Management (BLM), 256, 257

burials, xvii, 185, 186, 224, 279; Chilean, 129–36, 190–91; excavating, 188–89, 193–98; Peruvian, 136–41; state laws on, 238–39, 248; U.S. case law on, 240–41
Burke Museum: Egyptian mummy in, 269–73; Kennewick Man and, 35, 120–21, 164, 179
Bushmen. *See* Khoisan peoples

Cabezas Largas sector, looting in, 136–37
cabinetry, 106–7
cadavers, 152
California, 238
calipers, 58–*60*
camelids, skin and fur from, 130–31
Camino Real Alto, 81
Canada, cultural properties laws in, 229–30
Carlos Museum. *See* Michael C. Carlos Museum
Casa Grande Ruins National Monument, 233
casts, casting, 50, 63, 164; considerations in, 64–67
catalog numbers, 108–9, 122
catalog system: collections, 108–9, 157–58; Kennewick collection, 169, 170; labeling procedures, 112–17
Catholic Church, 147–48, 262
CAT scans, of Kennewick man, 164, 167, 170
cave sites, 189
cellulose polymers, 86
cemeteries, 189; Paracas, 133, 136–37
ceremonies, human remains used in, 81, 129
Cerro El Plomo, 143
Cerro El Toro, 143
Chancay burials, 208–9
Charrier v. Bell, 240
Chatters, James, 35
chemicals, 83; hazards from, 207–9
children, Inka sacrifice of, 141, 143–46
Chile, burials in, 130–36, 143, 190–91, 208
Chinchorro burials, 130–31
Christianity, 262, 277
chronic obstructive pulmonary disease (COPD), 213–14
Church of England, 184
Chuscha, Cerro, 143
cleaning, 78, 187, 197; aqueous and mechanical, 79–80; and condition assessment, 43–44; ritual, 206–7; solvent, 81–82
Cleveland Museum of Natural History, 25, 27
clothing, 133; protective, 50, *215*, 216–17
coatings, 84
coccidioidomycosis (cocci), 209–10

and preservation of, 163–72; of mummy bundles, 145–46; tools used for, 58–63; of treatment, 78, 87
dust, inhalation of, 213–14
Dutch Museums Association, 267–68

EAAF. *See* Equipo Argentino de Antropología Forense
Echo-Hawk, Roger, 249; *Keepers of Culture,* 248
Egypt, 228; mummies from, 262, 268, 269–73; return of Ramses mummy to, 123–25
electronic records, 167
Emory University, 123
emphysema, 213–14
endoscopy, 61
England. *See* Great Britain
English Heritage, on skeletal displays, 281–82
environmental scanning electron microscope (ESEM), 72
Equipo Argentino de Antropología Forense (EAAF), 176
ESEM. *See* environmental scanning electron microscope
Ethafoam, 52
ethics, 97, 98, 100, 266–67; biological anthropology, 8–12; professionalism and, 5–7
ethnicity: determining, 159–60; human remains and, 152–56
European Union Directive on the Return of Cultural Objects, 227
European Union Regulation on the Export of Cultural Goods, 227
excavation, xvi, xvii, 32, 230, 231; permissions for, 183–84; supplies and materials for, 193–96; techniques of, 196–98; treatment of human remains during, 247–48
Exeter, religious votives from, 147–48
exhibits, of human bodies, 261–62, 274–78, 281, 282
In re the Exhumation of Meriwether Lewis, 234
extrinsic allergic alveolitis, 207
ex-votos, 147

facilities, appropriate, 104–5
FAIRA. *See* Foundation of Aboriginal and Islander Research Action
Fairfield Processing, 53
Fallon Paiute-Shoshone Tribe, 256–57
feathers, in Paracas burials, 139

Federal Bureau of Investigation, 35
field laboratories, 198, 201
fieldwork: health risks in, 209–14; by osteologists, 187–98, 200–201
Fifth Amendment (U.S. Constitution), 239
Filey Museum, 274
finding aids, 171
fire, 105
First Nations, 265
Fiskerton site, 268
"Fissured Fred," 268
Florida, 239
foodstuffs, in mummy bundles, 138, 142
Fore, 206–7
forensics, 29, 152, 180–81
fossils, fossilization, bone, 31–32
Foundation of Aboriginal and Islander Research Action (FAIRA), 265–66
Freedom of Information Act, 254
freeze drying, 145
freezing, as pest management, 118
funerary bundles. *See* mummy bundles
funerary objects, 100, 129, 252; Egyptian, 123–25, 269–73; inventory and analysis of, 253–54; religious votives as, 147–48
fungi, 34, 207; diseases from, 209–11

GCI. *See* Getty Conservation Institute
Georgia State University, 157
German school of measurements, 156
Geronimo, 241
Getty Conservation Institute (GCI), 269, 271
Gibbons Springs project, 198–99; burial excavation at, 200–101
Gila River Indian Community, 252, 254
"Ginger," 262, 268, 280, 281
glossary, of condition terminology, 37–41
gloves, 52, *215,* 216–17
grave robbing, 224
graves, desecration of, 224
Great Britain, 153, 156, 184; attitudes toward death in, 279–80; body display in, 261–63, 264–65, 266–67, 268, 274, 280–83
Greece, 184–85
Greenlanders, 268
Griqua, 153
guidelines, for treatment of human remains, 99–100, 246, 248, 265–67
"Guidelines for Treatment of Remains of Indian People in Archaeological Sites," 246, 248

Kurds, 180, 181
kuru, 206–7

labeling, 196; Kennewick Man records, 170–71, *172*; procedures for, 112–17
laboratories, field, 198
Lacey, Edmund, 147
Lambert, Patricia, 258
land, zoning, 239
landownership, 184. *See also* property
law, 223; international conventions, 224–27; of other nations, 228–32, 266; state, local, and tribal, 238–40, 267; U.S., 224, 227–28, 232–38
law enforcement cases, access and documentation in, 35–36
lead, exposure to, 208–9
Lenin, 262
light, deterioration from, 105, 117
lighting, photographic, 63, *68–69*
Lindow II, 268, 280, 282
Linnaean classification, 154
Linnaeus, Carl, 154
Lipe, William, "A Conservation Model for American Archaeology," xv–xvi
Llullaillaco, Cerro, 144
loans, of burial materials, 255
logistics, multidisciplinary research, 178
London, human body displays in, 261–62, 266, 274–76, 278, 281, 282
London Bodies: The Changing Shape of Londoners from Prehistoric Times to the Present Day, 261, 274–76, 278, 281, 282
long bones, handling of, 54, *57*
looting, 223; Paracas cemeteries, 136–37; and U.S. laws, 233, 234–35
Luz Canun, María de la, 81

MA. *See* UK Museums Association
Mabo v. Queensland, 228
Manchester Museum, 264, 265–66
Mandatory Center of Expertise for the Curation and Management of Archaeological Collections (MCX-CMAC), 164, 167, 176, 179, 180–81
Maoris, 228–29, 280
Marsh Arabs, 180, 181
Mary Rose Trust, 283
masks, 213, 214, *215*
mass graves, 180–81, 189
Maya, 81
Mbeki, Thabo, 153
McClain case, 23

McClain doctrine, 228
MCX-CMAC. *See* Mandatory Center of Expertise for the Curation and Management of Archaeological Collections
measurements, 156; tools used for, 58–63
mechanical stress, 32, *33*
medical specimens, 31, 152, 274, 280; display of, 276, 277–78, 282
medicine, bodies used in, 264–65
The Medicine Man, 264–65
meetings, consultation, 251, 252
MEG. *See* Museum Ethnographers Group
Mejía Xesspe, Toribio, 137
mending, 86
mercury, 70–71
metric markers, 62
Mexico, 23, 81
Michael C. Carlos Museum, Egyptian collection in, 123–25
microorganisms, 205–6
Microsoft Access, 158, 159
Minnesota, 239
mission statements, 22–24
mold, 32, 34, 207
molding, mold-making, 63; considerations in, 64–67
monitors, Native American, 186
Montagu, Ashley, 8
Morton collection, 152
mortuary rituals, 7, 81, 131
Moyle, Mr., 257
MRI images, 167, 170
multidisciplinary teams: organization of, 176–78; in Kennewick Man analysis, 179–80
mummies, 2, 256; Atacama Desert, 190–91; Egyptian, 262, 266, 268, 269–73; frozen, 145–46; preventive pest control and, 117–18; transportation of, 123–25; viruses in, 205–6
mummy bundles, 175, 217; artifact contexts, 142–43; Inka sacrificial, 141, 143–46; from northern Chile, 130–36; Paracas, 136–41
Museo Arqueológico San Miguel de Azapa, 190
Museu Darder, 267
Museum Ethnographers Group (MEG), 13, 268
Museum of London, 261
Museum of Man, 282
museums, 99, 231; codes of ethics, 266–67; human body display in, 261–62, 264, 267–68, 274, 279–83; skeletal collections, 151–56
Museums Australia, Inc., 13
The Mysteries of the Mummies, 282

NAA. *See* neutron activation analysis

NAGPRA. *See* Native American Graves Protection and Repatriation Act

Na Iwi O Na Kupuna O Mokapu vs. John Dalton, 253

National Archives of Australia, 106–7

National Congress of the American Indian (NCAI), 257

National Geographic, on looting, 223

National Historic Landmarks, 234

National Historic Preservation Act (NHPA) (U.S.), 232–34

National Museum (Peru), 133, 136–37

National Museum of the American Indian Act (NMAIA), 98, 274

National Museum of Health and Medicine, 25, 281, 282

National Museum of Natural History (Washington, D.C.), 268, 274

National Museum of Scotland Mummy Project, 283

National NAGPRA Program, 236–37

National Park Service (NPS), 25, 27, 178, 233, 236–37

National Register of Historic Places, 199

National Stolen Property Act (NSPA), 227, 228

National Trust for Historic Preservation, 233

National University of San Marcos, 141

Native American Graves Protection and Repatriation Act (NAGPRA), xviii, 1, 83, 98, 25, 157, 158, 184, 193, 208, 236–38, 240, 248, 252, 253–54, 255, 274; Kennewick Man and, 164, 178–79, 249; and Spirit Cave Man, 257–58; unaffiliated remains and, 155–56

Native Hawaiian organizations (NHOs), 236, 237, 238

Natural History Museum (Vienna), 268, 274

Natural History Museum (London), 27, 274

Navajo Nation, 186, 212, 240

Nazi Party, 8

NCAI. *See* National Congress of the American Indian

Neanderthals, 87

neglect, 105

El Negro, 153

Netherlands, 268

Neumann, Georg, 157

neutron activation analysis (NAA), 71–72

Nevada Division of Museums and History, 258

Nevada State Museum, 256

New Guinea, kuru in, 206–7

New Zealand, 228–29, 280

NHOs. *See* Native Hawaiian organizations

NHPA. *See* National Historic Preservation Act

Niagara Falls Museum and Dare Devil Hall of Fame, 123

nicknames, for displayed human bodies, 268

NMAIA. *See* National Museum of the American Indian Act

NMR. *See* nuclear magnetic resonance spectroscopy

Northern Paiute, and Spirit Cave Man, 256–57

notes, in collection archives, 49–50

NPS. *See* National Park Service

NSPA. *See* National Stolen Property Act

nuclear magnetic resonance spectroscopy (NMR), 71

numbering, 108–9, 122, 170. *See also* catalog system; labeling

O'Brian, display of, 279

offerings, 136. *See also* funerary objects

Ohio, 239

Optivisors, 50, *51*

oral tradition, 249

Oregon, 239

organic materials, 255

Organization of African States, 267

osteologists: fieldwork procedures by, 187–98; permitting process, 183–85; role of, 185–87

osteology collections, 26; assessing condition of, 29, 32–45; documentation systems for, 157–58

Oswald, St., 262

Otzi, 262, 280

ownership, of human remains, 184–85, 264

Pacific Northwest National Laboratory (PNNL), 35, 164

packing, 124, 196, 197–98

padding materials, *51*, 52

Paracas Necrópolis site, burials from, 133, 136–41, 175

Parafilm M, 88

pathogens, risks from, 205–7

PCE. *See* plasma chemical extraction

Peabody Museum of Archaeology and Ethnology, 157

peer evaluation, 10

Pennsylvania, 239

permissions and permits, 231, 240; Canadian archaeology, 229–30; for human remains excavation, 183–85, 199

About the Editors and Contributors

Vicki Cassman is a conservator and archaeologist and assistant professor of anthropology in the Department of Art Conservation at the University of Delaware. Her research interests include archaeological textiles, curation and management of anthropological collections, NAGPRA, and Andean archaeology.

Nancy Odegaard is a conservator for the Arizona State Museum and professor in the Departments of Anthropology and Materials Science and Engineering at the University of Arizona. Her research interests include archaeological and ethnographic material culture, conservation and management of collections, NAGPRA, and Southwest anthropology.

Joseph Powell is an associate professor of anthropology at the University of New Mexico. His research focuses on human craniodental micoevolution during and after the Pleistocene-Holocene transition. This research has been carried out in both North and South America and ancient Egypt, and it has resulted in twenty-seven refereed journal articles and one book (*First Americans: Race, Evolution, and the Origin of Native Americans*, 2005).

Marta P. Alfonso has worked on several archaeological and paleopathological projects in Chile, where she also collaborated on museum projects. She is currently pursuing a Ph.D. in bioanthropology at the State University of New York, Binghamton.

Bernardo T. Arriaza is a physical anthropologist at the Universidad de Tarapacá, Centro de Investigaciones del Hombre en el Desierto, Museo Arqueológico de San Miguel de Azapa, in Arica, Chile. His research interests include Chinchorro mummies, paleopathology, and biological-cultural interactions.

Lane Beck is an associate curator at the Arizona State Museum and associate professor in the Department of Anthropology at the University of Arizona. Her research specialties include bioarchaeology and mortuary analysis, and her curatorial work centers on museum database systems and repatriation.

Mary M. Brooks is a senior lecturer and convenor for graduate-level courses in "Museum Studies: Culture, Collections, and Communication" at the University of Southampton. An accredited conservator/restorer of United Kingdom Institute for Conservation, she has a special interest in the contribution that object-based research and conservation approaches can make to the wider interpretation and presentation of cultural artifacts.

Phillip Cash Cash (Cayuse/Nez Perce) is a doctoral candidate in the Joint Program in Anthropology and Linguistics at the University of Arizona, where he is writing his doctoral dissertation on Nez Perce and Sahaptin, two endangered languages from the southern Columbia Plateau of western North America. Prior to his doctoral candidacy, he worked in the Repatriation Office of the Department of Anthropology, National Museum of Natural History, Smithsonian Institution, in Washington, D.C.

Natalie Drew is a member of the Academy of Certified Archivists and has served as senior archivist for the MCX-CMAC for the last thirteen years.

Julie Eklund is currently a Ph.D. candidate in archaeological conservation at the Institute of Archaeology, University College London. Her research focuses on the history of conservation treatments and the effects of treatments on DNA.

Diane L. France is the director of the Human Identification Laboratory at Colorado State University, president-elect of the American Board of Forensic Anthropology, president of NecroSearch International, and owner of France Casting, a small business specializing in replicas of osteological materials.

M. Thomas P. Gilbert is a molecular biologist whose research is centered on the retrieval and subsequent use of nucleic acids from old, chemically treated, and degraded specimens.

Cheryl A. Gregory is a graduate student of anthropology at the University of Nevada at Las Vegas focusing on ethnoarchaeology.

Monica Gustafsson works as a senior conservator at Västsvensk Konservering, Studio of Western Sweden Conservators. She is the instructor for Collections Care and Management at International Museum Studies, Museion, University of Göteborg, and at the Department of Conservation.

Ronald S. Harvey worked as assistant and then senior conservator at the Milwaukee Public Museum. He relocated to Maine and opened Tuckerbrook Conservation, a private practice, in 1990. His interests include archaeological, ethnographic, and human remains as well as packing and exhibition collections.

Sherry Hutt is the program manager for the National NAGPRA program in the Department of the Interior. She retired from the Superior Court Bench in Arizona after seventeen years as a judge to form Cultural Property Consulting, Inc. to write, train, and offer dispute resolution in cultural property matters with tribes, museums, and government agencies.

Caroline Sakaguchi Kunioka is an objects conservator in private practice in Los Angeles.

Teresa M. Militello is a private consultant for museums, archaeological companies, and curation facilities.

Teresa Moreno is an assistant conservator for the Arizona State Museum at the University of Arizona. She specializes in the conservation of archaeological and ethnographic objects.

Alan G. Morris is an associate professor in the Department of Human Biology at the University of Cape Town. His research includes osteological variation of modern and fossil humans, origin of southern African populations, and history of biological anthropology.

Ann Peters researches social roles of textiles and meanings expressed in dress and material culture of the Andean region of South America. Her work considers ethnographic, historic, and archaeological contexts.

Luz-Andrea Pfister researched infectious diseases in Switzerland and at Harvard University before turning her focus to ancient disease. She is pursuing a Ph.D. in anthropology at Arizona State University.

Laura S. Phillips has been the Archaeology Collections Manager at the Burke Museum, University of Washington, since 1993. Her research has focused on shell middens along the northwest coast of the United States, as well as on issues of site stewardship and collections curation. She teaches in the University of Washington's Museum Studies Program and manages the internship program for its Museology Certificate Program.

Christopher B. Pulliam works in the U.S. Army Corps of Engineers' Mandatory Center of Expertise for the Curation and Management of Archaeological Collections.

Marcia H. Regan is a bioarchaeologist with extensive human osteology experience in the American Southwest. She lives in Minnesota, where she works in contract archaeology. She has also taught at Arizona State University, Tempe, and Hamline University, St. Paul, Minnesota.

Jennifer Riddle is a bioarchaeologist with the Harry Reid Center for Environmental Studies. Her research interests include U.S. and international laws relating to archaeology and human remains as well as more traditional topics such as paleopathology.

Heidi Roberts is the founder and president of HRA, Inc., Conservation Archaeology. Since 1979, she has worked as a contract archaeologist and human osteologist throughout the Great Basin and the southwestern United States.

Linda Roundhill has been working as a conservator of objects for twenty-two years and currently has a private studio, Arts and Antiquities Conservation, in the Seattle, Washington, area.

Claire Rumsey is learning and access officer at Beaulieu National Motor Museum in Hampshire, England.

Alyce Sadongei (Kiowa/Tohono O'odham) is the assistant curator for Native American Relations at the Arizona State Museum. She has worked at the National Museum of the American Indian, Smithsonian Institution, and with numerous tribal communities across the country in the areas of museum planning, repatriation, and cultural programming.

Jeffrey Schwartz is a professor of physical anthropology in the Department of Anthropology at the University of Pittsburg. His main research interests include evolutionary biology, human and faunal analyses, and dentofacial growth and development.

David Smith is an adjunct conservation scientist at the Arizona State Museum and a lecturer in analytical chemistry at the University of Arizona. He has over thirty years of experience in the analysis and characterization of materials.

Renée A. Stein is a conservator at the Michael C. Carlos Museum of Emory University.

Lynn S. Teague is an archaeologist specializing in indigenous traditions of the Sonoran Desert. She served as statewide coordinator for the Arizona repatriation statutes and also NAGPRA coordinator for the Arizona State Museum, Tucson, until her retirement as curator of archaeology at the museum in 2002.

Michael (Sonny) Trimble is the director of the U.S. Army Corps of Engineers' Mandatory Center of Expertise for the Curation and Management of Archaeological Collections.

Annick Vuissoz is a conservator of archaeological and ethnographic objects. She is currently an instructor at the University of Applied Sciences of Western Switzerland, Neuchâtel. Her interests include objects, the analysis of past treatments, and the impact of treatments on further analysis.

Lai (Alex) Yip is a Microsoft Certified Professional and currently works as a software developer. He also has taught courses in computer science at the University of Nevada, Las Vegas.

Bones Software

The Bones Version 1.0 software, for streamlining the skeletal inventory process, is available for download on the AltaMira Press website (www.altamirapress.com).